Welcome to Soviet America:

Special Edition

Michael T. Petro, Jr.

Dedication

This book is dedicated to the memory of my father and mother. It is further dedicated to all patriotic American citizens of this generation and all previous generations, who have risked their lives, limbs, livelihood, and liberty to challenge criminals at all levels, whether foreign or domestic, public or private. I salute those Sovereign American culture warriors who are now rising to meet the current threat to truth and freedom within the United States of America.

Table of Contents

Part One: Know Thy Enemy

Part Two: The Long March Toward Soviet America

Part One:

Know Thy Enemy

Mask-Wearing Predators
Are Seizing Power Over We The People!

Before we investigate America's well-planned, incremental deterioration into a Soviet-style nightmare, we will review the manner in which the founders of the old Soviet Union succeeded in imposing a godless Communist slave state upon the people of Russia. A brief examination of the goals and tactics of Vladimir Lenin, Joseph Stalin, and Nikita Khrushchev will provide the reader with valuable insights into the psyches of those who are building their Soviet America!

Embracing the wisdom of the brilliant Chinese military strategist Sun Tzu who said "Know thy enemy," a summary of the psychology and philosophy of Soviets, socialists, and other sociopaths will be provided. As a Sovereign American, you are being challenged by aggressive Soviet American cold warriors. They are ruthless predators who possess "a lust for power over others" - and they are rapidly accumulating Soviet-style governmental power over you and your loved ones! To achieve victory and restore traditional American-style liberty for yourself and your posterity, you must understand your political opponents - as well as yourself. Your devotion to truth and your love of liberty must exceed their dedication to deceit and their "lust for power" over you and your loved ones!

According to David Horowitz, a former leftist radical raised by Communist parents, "When you're a radical, what you are thinking of is power. It's about power. You adopt this position, you take that issue, but it's all about power...They want to know what they can get away with...You get power and you change everything." And what kind of change do they believe in? "These people want to destroy the system we live under... They are still seeking to overthrow the system and to create a socialist future." Ultimately, closet Communists such as feminist leader Betty Friedan have been working surreptitiously "to create a Soviet America."

Chapter One

Soviet Russia:
How It Got That Way & Who Done It!

The Demise Of The Romanov Dynasty:
From Bad, To Worse, To Near Hell On Earth!

"Pearson describes something of the nature of life in the Soviet Empire: like the fabled Narnia of CS Lewis, the Soviet Empire remained a joyless land where there was always winter, but never Christmas." - Gary Selikow[1]

From 1613 to 1917 Russia was ruled by a long chain of Czars (also spelled "Tsars") while under the Romanov Dynasty. In Russia a Czar was considered royalty with all the power and wealth of a king. Until 1861, 95 percent of the Russian people were serfs who worked under the thumb of the nobility. Under this system Russia was a stagnant nation with widespread poverty, and it lagged far behind Western Europe.

From 1894 to 1917 Russia was ruled by Czar Nicholas II, who was to become the last Romanov ruler. Czar Nicholas II was an incompetent, indecisive autocrat who ruled over the Russian people with a cold heart and a heavy hand. He suppressed religious freedom, brought military defeat in an unpopular war, and was insensitive to poverty, hunger, and other hardships among the peasants. In 1905 his Palace guards fired upon a peaceful group that had come to his Winter Palace to present their grievances. The guards killed more than 100 people and wounded about 300 others. This massacre was dubbed "Bloody Sunday" and sparked a revolution that placed the Czar's throne in jeopardy.

The people were fed up with the Romanov Dynasty, including Czar Nicholas II, and desperately longed for leadership more responsive to their needs. In February of 1917 the Russian people, backed by frustrated Russian troops, forced Czar Nicholas II to abdicate the throne; thus ending more than 300 years of Romanov rule. The Romanov Dynasty was replaced with the Provisional Government, led by Alexander Kerensky, a socialist who wanted to establish a democracy for the Russian people.

Vladimir Lenin: Communist & First Soviet Dictator

In 1898 followers of Communist theoretician Karl Marx formed the Russian Social Democratic Worker's Party. This party later split into two factions: the Bolsheviks (the "majority" in Russian), and the Mensheviks (the "minority" in Russian). As written by Robert V. Daniels[2] in *Red October: The Bolshevik Revolution of 1917*, the primary difference between Bolsheviks and Mensheviks "was more temperamental than doctrinal." Both Bolsheviks and Mensheviks were Marxists; however, the Bolsheviks, led by Vladimir Lenin, believed in the "dictatorship of the proletariat." So, under the inspiration and leadership of the Bolsheviks, the proletariat (the workers and peasant farmers) would rise up and forcefully overthrow the ruling bourgeoisie (middle class). In opposition, the Mensheviks, led by L. Martov, preferred a less aggressive approach, and believed revolution should begin within the bourgeoisie.

When the Czar was in power many who had threatened the Romanov Dynasty had been banished from Russia. However, once the Czar was dethroned, exiled Marxist revolutionaries such as Vladimir Lenin, Leon Trotsky, and Joseph Stalin, all returned to their Russian homeland. Upon their arrival in Russia, Lenin and Trotsky began to work feverishly to undermine the newly formed Provisional Government in the minds of the Russian people. Consequently, many groups called upon the Provisional Government to hold elections so the Russian people could freely choose their own Constituent Assembly. The Bolsheviks joined the chorus demanding an election. However, Russia was a large, impoverished, disorganized country, so the Provisional Government faced a myriad of problems in attempting to hold an election. After many postponements an election was scheduled for November 25, 1917. However, before the election could be held, the Bolsheviks seized power from the fledgling Provisional Government on the 7th of November.

Bolshevik Coup d'état, One More Time!

The people demanded the election be held as scheduled, regardless of the Bolshevik coup d'état. Because the Bolsheviks had also demanded an election before they seized power, the election was conducted, under Bolshevik rule, from November 25th through November 27th, 1917. The election was a stunning defeat for the Bolsheviks, who received a mere 25 percent of the vote. The newly elected Constituent Assembly scheduled their first session for January 18, 1918. Upon arrival they found themselves surrounded by armed soldiers and sailors. The newly elected Bolshevik minority was repeatedly disruptive during their first session, and made it impossible for the non-Bolshevik majority, or bourgeoisie, to speak. (This was clearly a foreshadowing of Bolshevik Democrat behavior in 21st century Soviet America.) When the bourgeoisie protested, they found themselves looking down the barrels of rifles and pistols pointed at them by Bolshevik-controlled soldiers and sailors.

In spite of this potentially deadly form of intimidation, the bourgeois members of the newly elected Constituent Assembly rejected the platform of the Bolsheviks, so the Bolsheviks walked out of the meeting. When the bourgeoisie arrived the following day for a second meeting, they were met once again by armed troops. But this time they also received notice of a decree issued by the Bolsheviks, a decree abolishing the freely elected Constituent Assembly. While 75 percent of the Russian people had rejected Communism, Lenin had thrust Communism upon them at gunpoint. It was the second Bolshevik coup d'état in just a few months.

Historians and fellow travelers could now clearly understand what Lenin meant when he said, "…one of the basic conditions for the victory of socialism is the arming of the workers and the disarming of the bourgeoisie." However, Lenin had not been in power long enough to disarm the bourgeoisie with various gun control schemes. Consequently, in the summer of 1918 the bourgeoisie, also known as the White Russians, rose up in open rebellion and a bloody civil war ensued against the Bolsheviks, who were also referred to as the Red Russians. But under the brilliant direction of Leon Trotsky, a large Red army was assembled and the White Russians - along with the freedom and self-determination they sought - were crushed in 1920.

Welcome To Soviet Russia!

In 1921 the Bolsheviks outlawed the existence of their pesky competition, the less aggressive Mensheviks. In 1922 they established the Soviet Union and formed the All Russian Communist Party to function as the sole, unchallengeable ruling party of the Union of Soviet Socialist Republics, or USSR. Under the ruthless leadership of Lenin, world Communism was on the march. Clearly, the much-celebrated "October Revolution," like everything else celebrated by Communists, was a blatant fraud. The Soviet Union was not formed by a revolution of the people; it was created by a revolution against the people. By demanding an election and casting their votes, the vast majority of Russians demonstrated they wanted a democracy created by the people, but instead they got Communism created by the Bolsheviks. Welcome to Soviet Russia! (Soviet Russia was a term used after the Bolshevik takeover and before the formation of the Soviet Union, and also when Russia operated as the controlling nation within the Soviet Union)

In his 1848 pamphlet, *The Communist Manifesto,* Karl Marx, with the assistance of Frederick Engels, outlined the principles of Communism. The *Manifesto* clearly contains a plan for those who possess "a lust for power over others" because it provides guiding principles for seizing and maintaining control of government. Once in control it further outlines the measures needed to ensnare the entire population and rob its residents of their money, property, freedom, and dignity. The principles outlined in the *Manifesto* were enthusiastically endorsed by some of the deadliest genocidal maniacs to have ever walked the Earth. The list includes Vladimir Lenin, Joseph Stalin, Nikita Khrushchev, Mao Zedong (also spelled "Mao Tse-tung"), Pol Pot, Fidel Castro, as well as others. When examining the impact of Marx's *Manifesto*, it is clear that the Devil himself could not have come up with a more diabolical scheme.

Guided by the principles of Karl Marx, Vladimir Lenin had overthrown the Russian Provisional Government, ousted the Russian Constituent Assembly, exterminated the opposition, established the Soviet Union, and became its first dictator. Thus, Lenin took the theories of Marx and successfully put them into action. Those who pursue Communism by combining the theories of Marx with the actions of Lenin, or the theories of Marx as applied by Lenin, are referred to, by some, as Marxist-Leninists.

So, in a very short period of time the dictatorship of the Czar was replaced with the dictatorship of Lenin. The beleaguered Russian people found that, in less than six months they had come full circle, fighting to dethrone one tyrant only to end up with another tyrant. Even more foreboding, the Czar's capacity to directly inflict pain and death upon others was limited - even in time of war - due to his ineffective leadership. But under the intelligent, methodical, fanatical leadership of Lenin, the pain and death suffered under the Czar was most likely viewed as "the good ole days."

Shortly after the Bolsheviks seized power, Czar Nicholas II, along with his entire family and his servants, were escorted into a single room where they were shot and butchered to death. Their bodies were burned and buried. Soon the Bolsheviks assembled a secret police, banned firearms, built slave labor camps, confiscated homes, farms, and businesses, took over banking and finance, confiscated food from peasants, closed churches, and shot "counter-revolutionaries."[3] This, of course, was Comrade Lenin's way of saying, "Welcome to Soviet Russia."

As a consequence of Marxist doctrine, Russians who had too much food in their homes, or who appeared too well dressed, and those who spoke in a manner that suggested a high level of education, soon found themselves standing in front of a firing squad.[4] Why? Under Bolshevik class warfare rules of engagement, such conspicuously modest prosperity was conclusive evidence that they were members of the bourgeoisie. And, as Karl Marx had written, the bourgeoisie, or middle class, were the exploiters of the proletariat, or working class. Under the dictatorship of the proletariat, social justice demanded punishment for membership in the exploiting class, and a frequent punishment in Soviet Russia was death.

From 1917 to 1920 the Bolsheviks had to end an unpopular war with Germany and another war with Poland. They also had to fight and win a civil war with the bourgeoisie White Russians. Under Lenin's leadership the Bolsheviks survived each of these challenges, but Russia was now worse off economically than under the Czar. Communism was not delivering the promises of Karl Marx. The government ran nearly everything, and everything the government ran was in shambles. (Sound familiar?)

Bolsheviks Need Something To Steal

To save his Marxist, anti-capitalist revolution, Lenin did what any desperate anti-capitalist would do: he resorted to capitalism. He believed Russia was far too underdeveloped for full-fledged socialism, and thus he needed capitalism as a steppingstone toward a workers' paradise. After all, how can government thieves confiscate and redistribute the wealth of others, if there is no wealth to confiscate and redistribute? So, in 1921 Lenin adopted the New Economic Policy, or NEP. Under this policy many confiscated, government-run businesses were transformed into privately operated businesses. Peasants were permitted to keep some of what they produced, and trade and commerce were restored so private business transactions could ensue. Government retained control of heavy industry, banks, and other financial institutions. To the dismay of other anti-capitalist Bolsheviks, agricultural and industrial productivity began to improve across the nation. Even under conditions of widespread blight, by reversing his "Bolshevik Big Brother" socialist policies, Lenin had unleashed the enterprising spirit of the Russian people and modest prosperity was achieved rather quickly. The future changed from bleak to bright. Indeed, fascist-style capitalism had rescued Communism.

By implementing his New Economic Policy, Lenin was admitting that neither government programs nor a socialist economy could generate sufficient wealth to rescue a nation from poverty. Through the NEP he acknowledged that government can either encourage wealth building among the people through the free enterprise system, or it can discourage wealth building among the people through the restrictions of socialism. From an economic standpoint, the only thing a socialist government does well is to confiscate the wealth of others. But any thief can do that!

Joseph Stalin: Communist & Second Soviet Dictator

Vladimir Lenin's vision of prosperity was short-lived. After suffering a series of strokes he died in 1924. (Some claim he died of syphilis.[5]) Following a power struggle among the Bolsheviks, Joseph Stalin became Lenin's successor. Through years of careful scheming, Stalin outfoxed the brilliant Russian strategist, Leon Trotsky, who was a close associate of Vladimir Lenin and a potential successor. For this reason Stalin saw Trotsky as a competitor and constant threat to his leadership, so Trotsky was exiled in 1929. Trotsky eventually settled in Mexico, where he was murdered in 1940 by Ramon Mercader, one of Stalin's assassins.

As a former exiled revolutionary, experienced bank robber, cold-blooded assassin, and religion-hating atheist, Joseph Stalin was well suited to embrace the theories of Karl Marx and the practices of Vladimir Lenin - both of whom were also godless atheists. Lenin had caused the starvation of five million people through his collectivization of farming,[6] and he exterminated countless other innocent victims for reasons that make no sense to people of conscience. But the mind-boggling body count racked up by Stalin would make both Lenin and Hitler look like clumsy amateurs. Starting with Czar Nicholas II, followed by Lenin, and then by Stalin, the political leadership of the Russian people went from bad, to worse, to near hell on Earth.

By 1928 Russian agricultural and industrial productivity had returned to pre-World War I levels. For this reason Joseph Stalin ended Lenin's New Economic Policy in 1929 and returned to a centrally planned, socialist economy. Stalin's alternative to the NEP was the five-year government plan. Thus, psychologically incapable of learning from profound life experiences, Soviet leaders would return to the devastation of full-blown socialism with renewed vigor.

If You Can Earn It, Communists Can Steal It!

Stalin sought to fill the Soviet treasury through the industrialization of cities, the collectivization of farms, and the conquest of neighboring countries. Yes, Communists often stuffed their coffers by looting conquered satellite nations. Although Soviet factories produced little to be exported, some revenue was generated through the exportation of grain produced on the collective farms. Also, billions were confiscated from American taxpayers and "redistributed" to Stalin in the form of supplies during World War II to help the Soviets defeat the Nazis. This benefited America's war effort, but it also helped create the illusion that the Soviet Union was a prosperous, socialist, "workers' paradise."

It should be noted that one of the reasons the Soviet Union collapsed from within was because it ran out of nations to conquer and loot - without risking nuclear annihilation. Socialism, which is based on continuing govern-ment confiscation of other people's money and property, eventually gener-ates insufficient funds as victims are progressively picked clean. Such chronic theft demoralizes workers and they become reluctant to constantly feed the unquenchable appetite of parasitic government. Thus, to survive, socialist nations must expand across the globe to find new victims. While weaker victim nations are forcefully overthrown and looted, stronger victim nations, such as the USA, are infiltrated and pilfered through foreign aid and other government "redistribution" scams, such as the 21st century UN "cap and trade" scam.

Many nations, such as Czechoslovakia, involuntarily surrendered their wealth to the Soviets after they were invaded and looted. As noted above, the U.S. Government had voluntarily turned over massive amounts of American taxpayer funded property to the Soviet Union during World War II. But President Ronald Reagan had a different foreign policy viewpoint. Instead of aiding the Soviets or simply trying to contain them, when standing near the Berlin Wall, which was part of the Iron Curtain built by the Soviets to keep people from escaping their "workers' paradise," President Reagan demanded, "Mr. Gorbachev, tear down this wall!" And as history has demonstrated, when socialist governments run out of both domestic and foreign victims (and domestic and foreign benefactors) they inevitably run out of money and collapse, as we saw with the USSR in 1991. Observing the slow, piecemeal collapse of the Soviet Union's socialist economy (and their own economic retardation), the Soviet Chinese modified their socialist economy and embraced fascist-style capitalism on such a wide scale that Soviet China has not only survived - but has prospered.

I'm From The Government, And I'm Here To Kill You!

The number of people starved, beaten, tortured, shot, stabbed, and worked to death by Stalin is the subject of much debate. Stalin committed mass murder by numerous means, but primarily through mass starvation, slave labor camps, and large-scale executions. He may have starved to death six million people in the Ukraine between 1932 and 1933.[7] Millions were worked to death in the Gulag, or system of slave labor camps. An estimated one million people were executed for fabricated crimes against the state. Much of this was done through a series of notorious purges where Communist Party members and others were subjected to "show trials" and then executed for "treason" or other crimes against the state. Through such executions Stalin eliminated anyone who would remotely pose a threat to his authority. Through mass starvation, slave labor camps, political executions, and deportations, Stalin created a climate of absolute terror in the Soviet Union that kept him in power until his death in 1953. Under the madness of Stalinism, the entire Soviet Union became a gigantic killing field, the magnitude of which only another Marxist could appreciate!

To fully grasp the extent of the homicidal and genocidal tendencies of Lenin, Stalin, and Khrushchev (discussed below), let us examine the work of R. J. Rummel,[8] a professor, researcher, and author of the classic book, *Death By Government.* Professor Rummel conducted exhaustive studies on genocide and estimates that 61,911,000 people were murdered by the Communist thugs who ran Russia and the Soviet Union from 1917 to 1987. Moreover, the number of people murdered in the Soviet Union was exceeded only by the 76,702,000 people exterminated by Mao Zedong and the Communist thugs who ran Soviet China, better known as the People's Republic of China, or Red China. Keep in mind these were not casualties of civil or international wars. These were not victims of floods, earthquakes, hurricanes, or other natural disasters. Excluding abortion, these figures represent the number of people who were systematically exterminated in the Soviet Union and Soviet China by their own governments. Such figures dwarf the 35,000,000 military personnel killed in World War I and World War II combined!

Nikita Khrushchev: Communist & Third Soviet Dictator

Unlike the USA where there is automatic succession following the death of a sitting president, when the top leader of the Soviet Union died there was fierce competition among high level subordinates to succeed the deceased. Among the five Communist leaders who competed to succeed Stalin, Nikita Khrushchev emerged the winner. Like Lenin and Stalin before him, Khrushchev was essentially a thug.

Although the deliberate starvation of six million Ukrainians occurred while Stalin was in power, it was Nikita Khrushchev who devised and implemented the plan that led to their demise. There was repeated unrest among the Ukraine farmers following the forced collectivization of their farms. Nikita Khrushchev had demonstrated to Stalin that he was a ruthless killer by turning over some 500 men and women to the secret police for execution.[9] Favorably impressed by Khrushchev's total lack of respect for innocent human life, Stalin assigned Khrushchev the task of quelling the rebellious Ukraine farmers.

While Stalin may have expected the typical widespread torture and mass executions reserved for rebels, political competitors, counter-revolutionaries, religious leaders, and other enemies of the state, Khrushchev devised the plan to murder millions of men, women, and children through the slow, agonizingly painful method of starvation. Subsequent records indicated that in 1932, the year the starvation began, there was enough food to keep the Ukraine people fed for more than two years, but 90 percent of the food produced in the Ukraine was exported to other areas of the USSR.[10] Thus, the 1932-33 famine was not the result of unfortunate, naturally occurring climatic conditions; instead, it was the result of a diabolical "redistribution" scheme - the trademark of Communism!

The forced removal of peasants from their farms and placement onto government operated collectives was an unmitigated disaster. The farmers were constantly rebelling and production was poor. As W. Cleon Skousen[11] points out in his book, *The Naked Communist*, only 12 percent of Americans engaged in farming in 1958, but they produced enough food on their private farms to feed all Americans plus export food throughout the world. But under the Soviet system of socialized farming 50 percent of the people needed to work on farms in order to feed the Soviet population at a mere subsistence level. Communism could not remotely compete with free enterprise. But Stalin and Khrushchev blamed the farmers, and not their grotesque, slave master mentality and socialized method of farming for the ongoing crop production failures.

Khrushchev returned several times to the Ukraine to dispense Soviet-style justice to the farmers who desperately craved a modicum of freedom. He frequently left a trail of dead bodies in his wake. Life under Joseph Stalin's collectivization and Nikita Khrushchev's supervision was so repressive that when Nazis invaded Ukraine during WWII, the farmers greeted the Nazis as liberators! The Nazis found many mass graves containing the dead bodies of farmers, priests, and other Ukrainians. In just one section 10,000 bodies were found in some 90 massive burial plots. The victims, each with their hands tied behind their backs, had been shot in the head.[12] Welcome to Soviet Ukraine, where Communists make Nazis look like saviors!

Following the successful starvation deaths of six million Ukrainians, Stalin promoted Khrushchev to the Central Committee of the Communist Party in Moscow. Like the "Boston Strangler," the "Night Stalker," the "Hillside Strangler," and other notorious serial killers, serial mass murderer Nikita Khrushchev earned the nickname "The Butcher of the Ukraine" for terror-izing, torturing, starving, and summarily executing millions of Ukrainians, some of whom may have been his former friends and neighbors.

Khrushchev was the First Secretary of the Communist Party of the Soviet Union from 1953 to 1964, when he was forced from office by his fellow Communists. Lenin, Stalin, and Khrushchev were followed by several other Soviet leaders, all of whom were cold-blooded dictators, but none matched their lust for innocent blood. In succession, Nikita Khrushchev was followed by Leonid Brezhnev, Yuri Andropov, Konstantin Chernenko, and lastly by Mikhail Gorbachev. Gorbachev presided over the collapse of the Soviet Union in 1991, and Boris Yeltsin became President of Russia. The other member nations of the defunct Soviet Union, as well as members of the Soviet-dominated Warsaw Pact, adopted various forms of government as Moscow's noose began to loosen.

Question: Vladimir Lenin's collectivization of farming caused the starvation deaths of five million Russians in 1921-22. To help bring relief to the starving Russians, foreign aid was provided by organizations such as the Red Cross, the Nansen Committee, and the American Relief Administration. The Russians who helped arrange the foreign aid to bring some relief to the starving Russian people were:

A. Awarded a "Meritorious Service Medal" by Lenin.
B. Arrested and sentenced to death by Lenin.
C. Promoted by Lenin as Commissars of Food & Nutrition.
D. Promoted by Lenin to positions as Farm Managers.

Answer: B. The Russians who helped arrange foreign aid to help starving Russians were arrested and sentenced to death by order of Vladimir Lenin. However, F. Nansen personally intervened on behalf of the Russian intellectuals and Lenin commuted their sentences to banishment from Soviet Russia.[13]

Lenin's forced collectivization of farms was expanded under Joseph Stalin, which is said to have precipitated the "Great Famine" of 1932-33. While the famine of 1921-22 under Lenin was acknowledged by the Soviets, Stalin's deliberate starvation of six million men, women, and children during the "Great Famine" of 1932-33 has been denied.[14]

Alexander Kerensky's Warning To Sovereign America: The Bolsheviks Are Coming? No! The Bolsheviks Are Here!

"These people want to destroy the system we live under…They are still seeking to overthrow the system and to create a socialist future." And, "When you're a radical, what you are thinking of is power. It's about power. You adopt this position, you take that issue, but it's all about power…They want to know what they can get away with…You get power and you change everything." - David Horowitz, a former leftist radical raised by Communist parents[15]

After the fall of the Czar in 1917, Alexander Kerensky became the Minister of Justice, and later the second Prime Minister of the short-lived Russian Provisional Government. From this vantage point Kerensky observed first-hand how the Bolsheviks seized power in Russia through deceit and force. To escape imprisonment or death at the hands of predatory Communists, he escaped to Paris, but fled to the USA in 1940 when the Nazis invaded France. He lived briefly in Australia, but settled in the USA, spending much of his time in New York and California.

Although Alexander Kerensky was a socialist, until his death in 1970 he tried to warn Americans that Communists were attempting to seize power in the West through the same deceptive methods they employed in Russia. He warned that, in the West, just as in Russia, Communists were working to destroy liberty while pretending to defend liberty.[16] For example, when the Bolsheviks were discrediting the newly formed Provisional Government and paving the way for a Bolshevik takeover, they promised to distribute land and food to the peasants. But when they later seized power from the freely elected Constituent Assembly the Bolsheviks confiscated homes, businesses, farms, and starved to death millions of people. Their promises of "Bread, Peace and Freedom" brought mass starvation, civil war, and slave labor camps.[17] In 1917 people were unfamiliar with such diabolical deception, but henceforth students of history should have been forewarned by the Russian experience.

Unfortunately, Kerensky's warnings were heeded by too few Americans. Moreover, the warnings were rather belated, for the Sovietization of American government, education, and the media was already well under-way, and the vast majority of Americans were already being programmed to unwittingly embrace the mistakes of history, not avoid them. Being trained to ceaselessly demand Soviet-style "social justice," along with Soviet-style bureaucracies to pursue it, Bolshevik Democrats and Menshevik Republicans have created Soviet-bloc cities, counties, and states, as well as dominant Soviet-bloc enclaves within the U.S. Government. The list of huge, Soviet-style federal bureaucracies created to exercise authority not granted by the U.S. Constitution, or strictly forbidden by it, have Sovereign Americans in a state of alarm.

In 1932 William Z. Foster, the National Chairman of the Communist Party, USA, authored his infamous book, *Toward Soviet America*. Americans who are familiar with this book can see that William Z. Foster's dream of a Soviet America, while underway for most of the 20th century, has been placed on the fast track at the start of the 21st century. Liberals, Communists, progressives, and other Soviet Americans are enjoying one victory after another. Free speech among American "bourgeoisie" is progressively limited or banned because it violates Article 52 of the Soviet Constitution - which calls for a "separation of church and state;" violates campaign finance laws that restrict freedom of political speech prior to important national elections; violates Lenin-inspired "politically correct" speech codes that may offend one of the many Soviet American proletariat groups, thus deputizing the "dictatorship of the proletariat" as unchallengeable speech police.

In his 2002 book, *When I Was A Kid, This Was A Free Country*, G. Gordon Liddy[18] wrote, "Indeed, it is startling to realize how much the federal govern-ment is encroaching on our freedoms. The latest United States Government

Manual lists more than five hundred different federal agencies having thousands and thousands of federal bureaucrats. You and I are being taxed to pay their salaries, all so they can regulate our lives in countless ways." Seven years later, in 2009, President Barack Obama would add 10,000 new employees to the federal government - every month - while federal policies have destroyed millions of jobs in the private sector!

G. Gordon Liddy is, of course, correct. The federal government tells us what kind of light bulbs we must have in our homes and how much water our toilets must contain. We are required to provide intimate details regarding our income to the IRS, an agency that confiscates far more of our money than did King George III of Great Britain. We must get permission from the federal government to purchase a firearm from a federally-regulated fire-arms dealer. They tax our cigarettes, gasoline, and telephones - to name just a few. They regulate our private property through environmental laws and indoctrinate our children through federal educational mandates.

They have overshadowed local governments and private organizations with federal welfare, federal health care programs, federal retirement programs, federal disability programs, and an endless list of other expensive, inefficient, unconstitutional, centrally-controlled programs. The federal government has seized control of banks, mortgages firms, and auto manufacturers. They regulate workplace safety and regulate pay through federal minimum wage laws. Indeed, the destruction of Sovereign America and the progress made toward the construction of an unconstitutional, Leninist-style Soviet America has been stunning, and disheartening!

Chapter Two

Understanding The Psychology Of
Soviets, Socialists & Other Sociopaths!

"Twenty-two years ago in Brooklyn, I rented a room from a well-to-do, white political operative. I suspect he was a Communist, because while socialists occasionally lapse into honesty, this guy could lie in his sleep." - Nicholas Stix[1]

Dr. Michael Stone[2] of Columbia University is a forensic psychiatrist. His work is featured on the television program titled, *Most Evil*, which is presented under the heading "Investigation Discovery." In analyzing psychopathic serial killers, Dr. Stone characterized them as possessing "a lust for power over others." Their killing sprees are further motivated by a strong desire for attention, and they enjoy the celebrity status they achieve through the mayhem they create. Indeed, many serial killers have become legendary.

Consider, for example, serial killers such as David Berkowitz the "Son of Sam," John Wayne Gacy the "Killer Clown," Albert DeSalvo the "Boston Strangler," Ted Kaczynski the "Unabomber," John Allen Mohammad and Lee Boyd Malvo the "Beltway Snipers," Kenneth Bianchi and Angelo Buono the "Hillside Stranglers," William Bonin the "Freeway Killer," Richard Ramirez the "Night Stalker," and Dennis Rader the "BTK Killer." Rader was also known as the "BTK Strangler." BTK stood for Bind, Torture, and Kill. Each one of these serial killers achieved notoriety and their only "claim to fame" is the cold-blooded manner in which they killed a long list of innocent people.

According to forensic psychiatrists, when torturing or killing their victims, psychopathic serial killers experience a sense of superiority over others, but feel no sense of empathy, no sense of compassion, and no sense of remorse. They simply cannot put themselves in the shoes of the people they kidnap, torture, mutilate, and murder. The callous disregard psychopathic serial killers display towards their victims was made evident by convicted serial killer Keith Jesperson who said, "Taking a human life was nothing. I had done it so many times."

Convicted serial killer Edmund Kemper, while still a teenager, murdered his grandparents. Released from incarceration after five years, he murdered several female college hitchhikers. He dismembered some of his victims and ate their body parts. Eventually he murdered and decapitated his mother. In describing this psychopathic serial killer a psychiatrist said, "He delighted in killing." In other words, like other serial killers, he was a predator who savored "a lust for power" over his prey!

George Noory interviewed psychologist Vonda Pelto[3] on his *Coast to Coast AM* late night radio program to discuss her book, *Without Remorse: The Story of the Woman Who Kept Los Angeles' Serial Killers Alive.* After counseling serial killers in the Los Angeles County Men's Central Jail from 1979 to 1982, Dr. Pelto said she left that facility a changed person. From her professional contacts with serial killers she learned that they looked and acted just like everyone else. Armed with this knowledge, she grew much more suspicious of other people inside and outside the jail system. As a result of her experiences she is much more careful in public, and she advises others to not go out alone at night. When Dr. Pelto asked one serial killer how he felt when he killed other people, he said he felt "nothing." When asked if killing a human was like killing an animal, he said "no" because he did feel some consideration for animals. Clearly, as a human predator, he felt no remorse for his human prey.

At the beginning of the interview with psychologist Vonda Pelto, George Noory played an audio clip of an interview with Jeffrey Dahmer, a homosexual serial killer who murdered 17 people. Jeffrey Dahmer preyed primarily on black and Asian men and boys, and engaged in rape, torture, necrophilia, dismemberment, and cannibalism. During the interview Dahmer was asked why he tortured and murdered people, and he said he enjoyed the "control" he could exercise over others. This, of course, is consistent with the conclusion of forensic psychiatrist Michael Stone who stated that serial killers possess "a lust for power over others."

Some Serial Killers End Up In Prison; Others End Up In Government!

What happens when psychopathic serial killers charm, manipulate, or bully their way into positions of governmental power? To answer that question all we have to do is study 20th century history. All we need to do is take note of the 61,911,000 innocent men, women, and children who were collectively liquidated by Soviet leaders Vladimir Lenin, Joseph Stalin, and Nikita

Khrushchev; the 76,702,000 people exterminated by Mao Zedong and the thugs who ran Communist China; the 20,946,000 eliminated by Adolf Hitler; the 2,035,000 slaughtered by Pol Pot; and the 112,000 innocent people murdered by Fidel Castro - to mention just a few!

The important question is, of course, how do we prevent such psychopathic serial killers from ending up in powerful positions within the U.S. Government? The answer: Watch carefully for the symptoms of the psychopathic mind among politicians and bureaucrats. In addition to the symptoms of moral insanity listed later in this chapter, we could also look at the policies and practices Lenin, Stalin, Khrushchev, Mao, Hitler, Pol Pot, and Castro supported when holding positions of governmental power.

Firstly, it should be noted that all of these psychopathic serial mass murderers were socialists. As socialists, they all demonized a specific group of people they claimed were "rich" and insensitive to the needs of the common man. Having built up sufficient public hatred, they confiscated their money and property and exterminated their victims with a vengeance. While the mass killings occurred, they used the confiscated money and property to build powerful political empires to rule over those they did not exterminate. Clearly, they all had "a lust for power over others," just like their street-level serial killing brethren. Like convicted serial killer Edmund Kemper, they "delighted in killing."

As an act of premeditated mass murder, they all supported civilian disarmament through various gun control schemes. Conveniently for Hitler, his predecessors installed various gun control laws to make the establishment of his killing machine a bit easier. With the exception of Adolf Hitler, all were Communists! All of the governmental serial mass murders believed they must build and maintain a powerful central government to control health care, education, banking, finance, farming, manufacturing, family planning, social interactions, working conditions, incomes, etc., of the people unfortunate enough to live under their control. Each of these predatory socialists installed fellow socialists in top positions in the news media, entertainment industry, and educational institutions. Clearly, as predators, they used government power to micro-manage every important activity of their prey - under the guise of protecting and "liberating" them, of course!

Except for Joseph Stalin, all of these serial mass murderers were, of course, steadfast supporters of abortion. Stalin's lack of support for abortion was not due to an aversion to extinguishing innocent human life, but rather it was based on his desire to have a large workforce to build and operate his factories, farms, and slave labor camps. The global abortion holocaust, which began in Communist Russia in 1920, continues unabated in numerous Soviet-wannabe nations to this day. Predators, whether human or non-human, often start with the most vulnerable from among their prey, then they work their way up the food chain. Among children, no one is more defenseless than the pre-born and the newborn. Among adults, no one is more defenseless than the frail, the elderly, and the disarmed.

For those who possess "a lust for power over others," no institution is more attractive to them than the institution of government. Government, more than any other institution, can be perverted to grant almost unlimited power over others. It can be perverted to grant the power of life and death over the innocent as well as the guilty. When government is populated by people who possess "a lust for power over others," government power grows like a cancer - metastasizing to schools, colleges, hospitals, banks, farms, restaurants, vehicles, homes, families, and individuals. When government is populated by people who possess "a lust for power over others," innocent men, women, and children die by the millions, sometimes by the tens of millions. For this reason, government power over the people must always be kept to an absolute minimum! It is more than a matter of liberty; it is a matter of life and death!

Health Care Serial Killers!

As you may know the builders of Soviet America have been using millions of nonpaying illegal aliens, wealthy shyster trial lawyers, strangulating government regulation, a corrupt media, and a corrupt education establishment to bankrupt the American health care industry. Why? To drive up health care costs to such an extent that American-style health care becomes unaffordable for many Americans so they will actually demand an end to American-style health care and the imposition of a Soviet-style health care system.

But Katherine Ramsland[4] has written a book titled, *Inside the Minds of Health Care Serial Killers,* which her web site says "is the first book to examine the phenomenon of doctors, nurses, nurse's aides, and other health care practitioners who have murdered their patients." My question to you, the reader, is this: What happens to our health care system when serial killers in government completely take over a health care industry that is staffed with serial killing doctors, nurses, nurse's aides, and other serial killing health care practitioners?

Hint: They have already sanctioned serial killing in abortion clinics. And they have sanctioned the "mercy killing" of Terri Schiavo, who was deliberately dehydrated to death. In both cases government sided with the perpetrators, not the innocent victims. In addition, the builders of Soviet America advocate a Soviet-style national health care system like that in Canada and England. In both these nations older people are refused life-saving treatment due to government rationing, and many people die simply waiting for treatment after they have been placed on very lengthy government waiting lists.

Where Do We Go From Here?

Let's take a closer look at the criminal mind, or the mind of the sociopath. Closer examination may be important given that the Soviet Union, Soviet China, Soviet Cambodia, Soviet Cuba, and all blood-stained Soviet-style nations, including Soviet America, are the products of the criminal mind! For this reason it would be wise to follow the advice of the ancient Chinese military strategist Sun Tzu, who taught his followers to "Know thy enemy!" While many may be aware of this truism, few people know the full quote, which is as follows: "Know thy enemy and know yourself; in a hundred battles, you will never be defeated. When you are ignorant of the enemy but know yourself, your chances of winning or losing are equal. If ignorant both of your enemy and of yourself, you are sure to be defeated in every battle."

Moral IQ

Most people are familiar with the term intelligence quotient, or IQ, as assessed by standardized intelligence tests. The IQ score shows an individual's intellectual abilities relative to those of others who have taken the same test. By knowing a person's IQ we can speculate whether that person is an intellectual idiot, a genius, or somewhere in between.

In addition to testing general intelligence to gain an overall IQ score, we could also test for specific kinds of intelligence, such as social intelligence, creative intelligence, or moral intelligence. A score on a test of moral intelligence would render a moral IQ score that would be interpreted very much like a score on a test of general intelligence. A person's moral IQ score would show his relative standing when compared to the scores of others who had taken the same moral IQ test.

The intelligence quotient, or IQ, is normally distributed, with some people being very dull, some very bright, but most falling somewhere in the middle. A very bright person would have a much richer intellectual life than a very dull person. Likewise, a person with a high moral IQ will conceptualize moral constructs that are beyond the reach of those with a low moral IQ.

The morally intelligent person can "see" and manipulate moral constructs that the morally deficient person cannot visualize in his mind's eye. To the morally deficient sociopath who may have a low moral IQ (moral moron), a very low moral IQ (moral imbecile), or an extremely low moral IQ (moral idiot), the morally intelligent person sees moral constructs that cannot be seen by him; therefore, the morally intelligent person "sees things that are not there." Because the morally deficient person cannot perceive them, spiritual and moral constructs do not exist in his psychological world - and he behaves accordingly. He behaves like a sociopath.

Because political perspective is derived from moral perspective, those who can see spiritual and moral constructs that others cannot see are often labeled "extremists" or "religious extremists." Such "extremists" can see constructs such as "right versus wrong," whereas the sociopath will say that such constructs simply do not exist. To the sociopath "right and wrong," the "sanctity of human life," as well as constructs such as "honesty, fidelity, and mercy," etc. are all fabrications of religious extremists (or fascists) who want to impose restrictions on society that are based on mere hypothetical constructs. To the sociopath such moral constructs are useful only to the extent that they can be employed to manipulate, control, and exploit the people who embrace them.

Thus, the sociopath, who possesses a diminutive moral IQ, will maintain a morally based political perspective that is nearly opposite that of the morally intelligent person. Consequently, it is from the pool of moral morons, moral imbeciles, and moral idiots that we get socialists such as Vladimir Lenin, Joseph Stalin, Nikita Khrushchev, Adolf Hitler, Mao Zedong, Pol Pot, Fidel Castro, and other morally deficient dictators.

Armed with the above information, let's examine behaviors that may help us identify and understand the individual who possesses an extremely low moral IQ. Keep in mind that moral IQ is independent of general IQ. Therefore, an individual may be a genius with a very high general IQ, but this same person may also be a moral imbecile with a very low moral IQ. The reverse may also be true.

The Moral Insanity Of The Sociopath

"At best liberalism is a mental disorder. At worst it is pure evil." - Michael Savage[5]

In the early 1800s a researcher named J. C. Prichard[6] identified a character disorder which he referred to as "moral insanity" and "moral imbecility." According to Prichard, "In cases of this nature the moral or active principles of the mind are strangely perverted or depraved;" The term moral insanity was later replaced with the term psychopath. The root "psycho" was derived from psyche, which may be translated into the terms mind, spirit, or soul. Thus, the psychopath's problematic behaviors were believed to stem directly from the core of his personality, or the essence of his soul. Because the psychopath has difficulty adapting to the demands placed upon him by society, the term psychopath evolved into terms such as sociopath and antisocial personality.

The sociopath is considered morally insane because he displays little or no evidence of possessing a conscience. He can lie, cheat, steal, and kill in a cavalier fashion. Although many people may lie on occasion when under pressure, the sociopath lies often, with ease, and with no shame, remorse, or guilt. He may display some regret when caught, but the perceptive observer will detect a lack of sincerity in the emotion displayed. The socio-path has been described as deceitful, shrewd, selfish, ruthless, predatory, and **superficially charming**. He tends to reject authority, discipline, and traditional moral values. He does not learn from mistakes - except to be more careful to avoid getting caught again, and he is quick to blame others or society for his misdeeds. As psychiatrist James A. Bussell[7] has written, the sociopath "scoffs at the Golden Rule," and he "sneers at patriotism."

In outlining the characteristics of the sociopath we find he is **histrionic** and **deceitful**. The sociopath is compelled, by his very nature, to disguise himself with "social masks" to hide his moral insanity from unsuspecting prey. For the sociopath every day is Halloween. In whatever disguise the sociopath assumes, he changes masks effortlessly and wears them convincingly. In practice he is a "Master of Deceit," - a label J. Edgar Hoover[8] assigned to the chronically deceitful Communist. From a moral perspective, the sociopath truly is "morally insane."

The sociopath is remarkably **shrewd**. Whether on Wall Street, Main Street, or Mean Street, the sociopath is always street smart. Always the predator, he has a watchful eye and quickly "sizes up" his prey at a glance. The absence of a conscience serves him quite well. Unburdened by the internal conflict of weighing right versus wrong, the sociopath sees only the concrete, self-serving choice. This allows him to quickly spot "opportunities" that are overlooked by people whose perspective is clouded by abstract moral principles.

He is also egocentric, narcissistic, hedonistic, and arrogant. In short, the sociopath is a supremely **selfish** character. Your life and the lives of your family members have no intrinsic value to the sociopath. He will extinguish your life and the lives of all your family members for a few dollars, or for a few moments of revenge or pleasure. There is no sacrifice that you or anyone else can make that is too great to satisfy his most fleeting desires. The impulse to satisfy oneself is felt as irresistible to the sociopath. For this reason the sociopath is often sexually promiscuous and overly self-indulgent with alcohol and other drugs.

Previously called the psychopath, the sociopath is the classical, **pathological liar**. (Some differentiate the psychopath from the sociopath.) When wearing the mask of the truth-teller he lies with a straight face. He feigns indignation when someone detects inconsistency or hypocrisy or questions the sincerity of his performance. Simple lying, cheating, and stealing are considered "kid stuff." The hardcore sociopath may kidnap, rob, rape, torture, mutilate, and murder. His victims are men, women, and even innocent, defenseless children - both born and unborn, and he exhibits no sign of shame nor guilt when he mutilates, tortures, and exterminates. He often wears the mask of the social charmer, but there is no crime he will not commit if he believes he can profit from it and get away with it. He is morally insane.

The sociopath is **irresponsible**. According to the sociopath, the underlying cause of his immoral, unethical, and criminal behaviors are to be found outside himself. When caught he portrays himself as a helpless victim who is not responsible for the endless stream of choices he makes every day of his life.[9] Whether he operates at the upper, middle, or lower levels of the socioeconomic scale he will blame society, circumstances, or other people for his behavior.

Antisocial personality[10] disorder is a diagnostic label used more recently to identify the sociopath. As the label implies, the sociopath is anti-social, or anti-society. He is against society's authority figures, its laws, regulations, and rules of social order. He is a predator, and many laws have been established to punish ruthless predators that prey upon honest, law-abiding citizens. Therefore, the sociopath will eventually come into conflict with society's laws.[11] For the sociopath such laws are contrary to his nature, his instincts, his lifestyle, and his mode of operation. In a word, the sociopath is a **lawless** individual. Laws, including the U.S. Constitution, represent nothing more than inconvenient roadblocks to his predatory goals.

The sociopath is **ruthless**. This is the central characteristic from which all others originate. The sociopath lacks the humane inner core from which integrated human thoughts, feelings, and actions originate. Instead the psychological core of the sociopath is cold, callous, primitive, and sinister. Lacking a humane core, the sociopath must wear masks to hide this deficiency. On rare occasion, when the sociopath is confident that he is unobserved, the mask is removed. When the "mask of sanity"[12] is removed the sociopath appears very much like the schizophrenic whose personality has thoroughly disintegrated. The result is a truly zombie-like appearance. Unmasked, the eyes and facial expression reveal what appears to be an uninhabited human shell - uninhabited by anything that remotely resembles a human spirit or soul.

Lastly, the sociopath is **predatory** and **parasitic**. When presented with an unknown human or human-like face, the human infant will often display what is referred to as "stranger anxiety."[13] Thus, almost from birth our inner primitive self seems to warn us that we must be cautious of unfamiliar members of our own species. Instinctively many infants respond with anxiety and fear to vague, unknown, human-like creatures. In most cases it may be true that "a stranger is a friend we haven't met yet." However, in some cases a stranger is a sociopath we haven't met yet. Certainly, our Creator did not equip us with instinctive responses, such as stranger anxiety, unless they serve a useful purpose and have survival value. Of course, the "lust for power over others" stems from the sociopath's predatory and parasitic nature.

Human Predators Versus Human Prey

Our ancestors made enormous cultural progress when they advanced from hunter-gatherers to farmers. As hunter-gatherers their prey consisted of free-range animals that had to be pursued. Constantly chasing down animals was time-consuming, inconvenient, inefficient, frustrating, and sometimes dangerous. All that ended with farming. With Farming came the creation of barns, corrals, chicken coops, and fenced-in cow pastures. Animals of prey moved from free-range creatures to rigidly-controlled beasts of burden. Once-free animals now lived and died at the pleasure of the farmer or rancher, who provided their food, shelter, and medical care.

This, of course, is analogous to the manner in which human predators view their human prey. From the perspective of human predators we, too, must be transformed from free-range prey to rigidly-controlled farm-like animals. The history of humankind has been a constant battle between predator and prey. With the exception of the USA, the predators have always prevailed. The Soviet Gulag was the ultimate human farm! George Orwell understood the Soviet system well and likened it to an *Animal Farm*, and authored a 1945 book with that title.

Like the builders of the Soviet Union, the builders of Soviet America are busy building their Animal Farm. And, as Judge Andrew P. Napolitano noted in his book, *A Nation of Sheep*, far too many Americans sheepishly submit to repeated government shearing against their will! Far too many Americans have allowed the builders of Soviet America to construct their Animal Farm, knowing that it contains slaughter houses called abortion clinics designed to trim the herd.

The predatory nature of the sociopath explains why he is so persistent, so relentless, and so arrogant in building his Soviet America. He is a wolf, simply doing what he believes he was born to do according to his Darwinian worldview. As sheep, we must assume our roles in the natural order. Throughout nature predatory animals disguise themselves and "mask" their true intentions to capture their prey. Morality plays no role in the use of trickery by predatory animals, nor does it play a role in the hearts and minds of their human counterparts! A human wolf in sheep's clothing sees himself as shrewd, not immoral.

Because the predatory sociopath seeks to manipulate, control, and exploit his prey, he is attracted to government or any organization where enormous power can be exercised over others. With fellow traveling journalists and educators acting as Pied Pipers, it is through government that the sociopath can corral large herds of human prey with massive, authoritarian bureau-cracies and endless resource-robbing legislation and regulation. The dream of wielding near unlimited power over others certainly drove characters such as Vladimir Lenin, Joseph Stalin, Nikita Khrushchev, Adolf Hitler, Mao Zedong, Pol Pot, Fidel Castro, and other sociopaths to create socialist governments that micro-mismanage the lives of other people - under the ruse of protecting them - the same way a farmer protects the animals he views as his property. Clearly, the pursuit of socialism, fascism, and other dictatorial forms of government is symptomatic of the predatory sociopath who possesses "a lust for power over others."

Our Founding Fathers recognized the danger of such unrestrained govern-mental power, and therefore created a Constitution that greatly limits the scope and reach of the U.S. Government. However, with constant prodding by lawless journalists, educators, "religious" leaders, and civil rights leaders representing the sociopathic Left, morally deficient politicians, judges, and attorneys routinely ignore constitutional limitations (and their oaths of office) and distort the spirit and the letter of this restrictive document to constantly expand their power over us and gain unending access to our resources.

Clearly, we are not engaged simply in a war between Communism and capitalism. Instead, the current "culture war" is a contemporary mani-festation of the broad, age-old struggle between good and evil. You will find people with low moral IQs living simultaneously in both the worlds of Communism and capitalism, often using the profits of capitalism to finance Communism. This unholy alliance is the greatest threat to life, liberty, and property.

This is a war between predator and prey. It is a war between the morally insane and the morally mature - who are fighting for the hearts and minds of those who are morally moderate. This is a war between sociopaths who possess "a lust for power over others" and liberty-loving people who do not want to live as sheep on an Animal Farm constructed by human predators. It is a war between those who want us to live in Soviet America and those who want us to live in Sovereign America! Each of us must choose which side we will support. Not choosing is a default position that favors the predator!

Welcome to Soviet America!

Good-bye honest, ethical, and moral America!

------†††------

Pathological liar: "A person with a remarkable memory; he can even remember things that never happened." - Evan Esar[14]

------†††------

Special Note: The moral idiot, who is a sociopath, is not to be confused with the useful idiot, who is not a sociopath. The useful idiot is a person with a normal moral IQ who is deceived into supporting the goals and objectives of the moral idiot. The useful idiot is one who believes the cover story of the moral idiot and does not perceive the moral madman lurking behind the compassionate-looking mask. The useful idiot is often a naive, idealistic young person who, for example, sincerely wants to fight power-hungry capitalists by giving Communist-style power to government, not knowing power-hungry capitalists arrange the funding of Communism in order to gain Soviet-style governmental control over the useful idiot and everyone else. Useful idiots also tend to be older people who grew up in an earlier, more trustworthy era - before the corruption of American culture through the 1960s nihilistic counter-culture movement.

Both young and old useful idiots tend to be somewhat idealistic. And due to lack of experience with sociopaths, they tend to be more trusting and gullible. They tend to believe what they are told by the reporters on their television screens, as well as the journalists writing in newspapers and magazines, and the educators teaching and professing in classrooms and lecture halls across the USSA. They simply cannot fathom the idea that all these people may be deceiving them over and over again on nearly every important issue facing our nation and the world. To them, a sociopath is someone you want to avoid meeting in a dark alley at night, but not someone you look forward to seeing on your TV screen most every night. The useful idiot believes that no person could be so depraved that he or she would deliberately fool them day after day, year after year, and decade after decade. Unfortunately, that's exactly what the high-functioning sociopath expects the useful idiot to believe!

Chapter Three

Understanding The Philosophy Of
Soviets, Socialists & Other Sociopaths!

Nihilism: From Russia With "Free Love."

"People who have no weaknesses are terrible: There is no way of taking advantage of them." - Anatole France[1]

In the 1860s, about 60 years before the Bolsheviks seized power in Russia, a cultural revolution was slowly metastasizing across the Russian countryside. That cultural movement was known as nihilism. The Latin root for nihilism is nihil, which means "nothing." From the nihilist perspective, all thoughts, words, and deeds amount to nothing; hence, life has no meaning and no purpose. The root nihil is also found in the word "annihilate," which means to utterly destroy. Nihilists thus sought to destroy the existing traditional moral value system of Russia. They rejected the existing political, social, and religious order and sought to replace it with a new, radical, social order. The chaos generated by nihilism is said to have caused it to self-destruct as a movement by the late 19th or early 20th centuries.[2] However, its underlying philosophy permeated Russia and spread insidiously throughout the entire planet. Nihilism and its philosophical cousins remain alive and well in the 21st century.

Russian nihilism rejected the notion of truth, denied the existence of moral and ethical absolutes, and established that life had no intrinsic value. In brief, nihilism established a cultural standard that only a sociopath could love - or create! With this cultural standard marriage and family deteriorated, sexual perversion and abortion were promoted, crime and disease were rampant, and poverty and hunger became commonplace. Sadly, nihilists succeeded in transforming Russia into a huge, open, national, moral sewer.

For the true nihilist, cultural corruption is viewed as an end in itself. For those who embrace the "free love" lifestyle that emphasizes "wine, women, and song," or the more contemporary, "drugs, sex, and rock and roll," one may pursue nihilism for nihilism's sake. For those who believe that lying, cheating, stealing, and killing as a way of life are normal, acceptable behaviors, nihilism is not a problem to be solved, but a solution to an uptight, overly restrictive society. From the nihilist perspective, there should be no religious fanatics imposing their will upon others. Nihilists must be "free to be themselves," and no one should restrict their natural right to freedom of choice - regardless of the consequences - including the astronomical body count!

Socialism + Police State = Soviet-Style Communism!
Help Me + Protect Me = Enslave Me!

Pastor Ernie Sanders[3] has often stated that, "Communism is socialism with a police state." To justify socialism there must be unstable marriages, broken families, drug abuse, poverty, disease, and a sense of helplessness and hopelessness. People must be driven to the point where they (or some pre-selected revolutionary leaders) can cry out and demand, "Why doesn't somebody do something about this problem? Why is there no Soviet-style government bureaucracy to help these struggling families?" And almost magically, the Bolsheviks arrive to save the day with new, government-empowering programs.

Nihilism clearly established a philosophical and cultural basis conducive to the advancement of Marxism, subsequently paving the way for complete moral idiots such as Vladimir Lenin, Joseph Stalin, and Nikita Khrushchev to seize, maintain, and expand their power. After all, from a Soviet perspective, the cultural problems created and exacerbated by radical nihilists called for equally radical government solutions, and the iron-fisted Bolsheviks were more than happy to oblige. The Marxist tacticians building their Soviet America learned well from their Russian teachers - who taught them that a political opportunist with "a lust for power over others" should never let a good crisis go to waste, as stated by Rahm Emanuel, White House Chief of Staff in the Obama Administration.

To justify a police state there must be widespread street crime. People must fear liberal street gangs, and they must live under the threat of home invasion and possible car-jacking. They must fear rape, robbery, burglary, and, preferably, terrorism. But to achieve the necessary level of street crime the culture must be destabilized. And to destabilize the culture one must destabilize the family; and to destabilize the family there is no better formula than the one offered by nihilists. Under nihilism we find easy divorce and government welfare programs that generate unstable, father-less, gang-spawning liberal families; we find man-hating feminism, confusion of sex roles and sex identification, sexualized children and sanctioned pedophilia; we find alcohol and other drug abuse, depression, suicide, and homicide; we find failing schools, school shootings, joblessness, blighted neighborhoods, and a declining national self-image.

Again, the people are driven to demand solutions to nihilisms depravity, despair, and violence, and Leninists and Stalinists, conveniently waiting in the wings with strong-arm solutions in hand, come to the rescue. Yes, to justify both Soviet-style socialism and a Soviet-style police state, one must have deeply entrenched cultural rot, and nihilism and its philosophical cousins never fail to deliver - in Soviet Russia or in Soviet America!

So, from the tactical perspective of the political opportunist, nihilism is encouraged in order to corrupt the existing social order and pave the way for revolution. From this perspective nihilism serves as a necessary evil to justify another evil - a totalitarian police state. When people attempt to live according to moral principles, such as those found in the Ten Commandments and elsewhere in the Bible, overall, marriages and families tend to be stable. Consequently, children have little need to create liberal gangs as substitute families, and crime, poverty, and disease are kept at relatively low levels. But such stable, self-sustaining societies have little need for the massive, expensive, Soviet-style bureaucracies demanded by socialists. There is no need for Gestapo-style police forces to keep streets safe, for there is little street crime in a society inhabited by people who are self-governed by a set of morally-based principles.

Bourgeoisie + Proletariat = Communism
Thesis + Antithesis = Synthesis

The German philosopher Georg Wilhelm Friedrich Hegel created a far-reaching philosophical perspective, summarized in part as Hegelian dialectic. Within Hegel's dialectic it was postulated that a force or proposition, called a thesis, may be challenged by a counter-force or counter-proposition, called an antithesis, and the end product of the two conflicting forces or propositions will be a synthesis. Hegel's dialectic has been commonly summarized as "thesis + antithesis = synthesis."

In *The Communist Manifesto* Karl Heinrich Marx[4] borrowed Hegel's dialectic and applied it to conflicts, or class warfare, between the upper and lower classes. As a godless atheist, Marx was a materialist. Because he believed everything in the universe, including human history, was driven by conflict of opposing forces, he proposed his theory of dialectic materialism. For Marx the middle class, or bourgeoisie, represented the thesis, and the workers and peasants, or proletariat, represented the antithesis. When the bourgeoisie (thesis) is challenged by the proletariat (antithesis), the end product is Communism (synthesis).

In both Hegel's dialectic and Marx's dialectic materialism, the process of thesis + antithesis = synthesis is repeated over and over again. From the perspective of Karl Marx, the final product of this process is an idealistic "dictatorship of the proletariat." However, this end product has never been achieved in any Communist nation because the sociopathic thugs who always establish Communism never relinquish power to the proletariat. It's just one more promise they never keep, but it's a great selling point to be consumed by gullible, naïve, useful idiots.

In early American society where there was widespread free enterprise, private charity, and no Soviet-style, socialist government programs, one may offer the thesis that "free enterprise is good," but an anti-capitalist may counter with the antithesis that "socialism is better." The conflict between these two propositions results in a newly synthesized compromise position, resulting in a nation with a mixture of free enterprise and socialism. The process is repeated over and over again, with the thesis and antithesis producing more and more syntheses. This process, if continued over a long period of time, will slowly transform a nation governed by free enterprise into a nation dominated by socialism. And socialism, along with a police state, is necessary for the establishment of Soviet-style Communism.

The student of Marxism may see that in Czarist Russia the Czar represented the bourgeoisie, or thesis, the peasants represented the proletariat, or antithesis, and Communism represented the "dictatorship of the prole-tariat," or synthesis. However, Antonio Gramsci, the head of the Communist Party of Italy, injected a critical ingredient into the dialectic materialism of Karl Marx. According to Gramsci, if the bourgeois value system is shared by the proletariat, there will be no desire to overthrow the bourgeoisie. When sharing the same value system there is no antithesis, and therefore there can be no synthesis, and no Communism.

Because the proletariat will not overthrow a value system they support, they must be propagandized into rejecting the value system of the bourgeoisie and manipulated into developing their own antithetical value system. In brief, they must develop a revolutionary counter-culture. The proletariat must be raised to a feverish, revolutionary pitch and relentlessly pitted against the bourgeoisie until they eventually destroy and displace bourgeoisie culture, bourgeoisie institutions, and bourgeoisie leadership.

In Russia, Europe, Canada, Australia, and in America, the new, revolutionary value system injected into the universal proletariat has been none other than nihilism and its many variants! Thus, the thesis of cultural morality, confronted with the antithesis of cultural nihilism, leads to revolution and the synthesis of thuggish Communism. As history has demonstrated, when this formula is intelligently directed and persistently applied, nations can be conquered and the entire world transformed.

Furthermore, Gramsci correctly noted that throughout the West bourgeois values were deeply rooted in Christianity. Therefore, Christianity, its values, its leaders, and followers, must be corrupted, denigrated, destroyed, and replaced. Marxist values must displace Christian values, and it must do so in a manner that convinces the proletariat that they have embraced a new, higher form of spirituality. Also, the proletariat must believe they have done so by following their own leaders - people who have risen up from the depths of the proletariat community to challenge the evils of the bourgeois class.

The astute observer will recognize that the replacement of Christian values with its attendant private charities - supported by private donations and other private assistance - has been displaced throughout the West with a counterfeit Christianity based on Marxist principles. For example, through "social gospel" and "liberation theology," Marxists demand that "social justice" be accorded the less fortunate among us (the proletariat). And, "social justice" must be financed by the rich (the bourgeoisie) through Soviet-style "charity" (government programs) with Soviet-style, government-enforced "donations" or "investments" (heavy, progressive, income tax and other forms of confiscation). Through this formula Christendom is sustained, but only as a hollow illusion. It is systematically replaced with Marxism. True Christian charity, which can only be voluntary, is replaced with Marxist-style charity, which can only be involuntary. In others words, coercion is disguised as charity.

The Sovietization Of Western Culture

Thus, it appears the nihilistic Cultural Revolution in 1860s Russia was a template for the nihilistic cultural revolutions that occurred in Western

Europe, Canada, Australia, and in 1960s America. Throughout the West there were successful attempts to destroy the existing social order and replace it with a sociopathic, nihilistic ideology.

In America, for example, the Ten Commandments and right and wrong were replaced with the moral relativism of "values clarification." Creationism was replaced with Darwinism; fidelity replaced with "free love;" prenatal care replaced with abortion; self-reliance replaced with government dependence; self-defense replaced with increasing defenselessness; parental control replaced with government control; individuality and individual rights were replaced with proletariat group-think and group rights; private property rights replaced with animal rights, plant rights, and government rights; and the unity of the melting pot was replaced with the divisiveness of multiculturalism. Authentic education was replaced with indoctrination, journalism replaced with propaganda, and our republic was replaced with a democracy.

In addition, free speech and religious expression have been curtailed by Soviet-style totalitarian concepts and tactics such as "separation of church and state," political correctness, campaign finance laws, "hate crimes" laws, and tactics such as the so-called "Fairness Doctrine." Moreover, serious students of the Sovietization process know that all these assaults on our liberties represent just the tip of the Siberian iceberg that has struck America. Right in front of our eyes America has been, and continues to be, transformed, or perhaps we should say malformed, in a methodical, long-term, step by step process.

Yes, Senator John Edwards was correct when he said there are two Americas, but he failed to discuss the reality of these two nations. Like others who wish to divide America into "haves" (bourgeoisie) and "have nots" (proletariat), the Senator failed to discuss the waxing Soviet America with its malignant nihilism, humanism, cultural Marxism, and totalitarian government, and contrast it with the waning Sovereign America with its atrophic morality, ethics, Christian culture, and constitutional government.

Friedrich Wilhelm Nietzsche, a nihilist German philosopher, proclaimed in his writings that, "God is dead." In making this claim in such books as *Thus Spake Zarathustra*, Nietzsche laid the philosophical groundwork for hippies to make the same proclamation in their Marxist-inspired, nihilistic counter-culture movement in 1960s America. But God is not dead; nor is nihilism. Nihilism, and its kissing cousin, secular humanism, are both alive and well throughout the West. They are alive and well in Soviet American schools, colleges, churches, synagogues, businesses, newsrooms, and political organizations. They are alive and well in federal, state, county, and city governments.

Indeed, the grease of nihilism has been broadly brushed across America, paving a slippery road for Marxist ideology to slide easily into every nook and cranny of American society. Thus, just as the nihilization of Russian culture preceded and facilitated the Sovietization of Russian government, the nihilization of American culture is facilitating the Sovietization of American government. Moreover, the role of Pied Piper is played by nihilists, quasi-nihilists, nihilist sympathizers, Marxist dialecticians, and other culture warriors who disguise themselves as journalists, educators, screenwriters, religious leaders, and civil rights leaders.

Nihilists Prove Life Has No Intrinsic Value - For Them!

Russian nihilists produced more than just cultural rot throughout their beleaguered nation; many branched off to form a radical group known as the Narodnik movement. The Narodnik movement employed a "go to the people" campaign designed to inspire the peasants to revolt against the Russian Aristocracy. Some Narodniks, staying true to their nihilistic philosophical roots, advocated and engaged in assassination and terrorism. One of their most famous victims was Czar Alexander II, whom they assassinated in 1881 with a bomb tossed at his feet. The Narodniks were sloppy assassins, and failed at numerous attempts to murder Czar Alexander II - the man who emancipated the serfs in 1861. Unfortunately, they did succeed in killing and wounding many dozens of innocent bystanders, guards, and others in their many failed assassination attempts.

While the homicidal Narodniks (the Russian philosophical ancestors of William Ayers and the Weather Underground) were trying to instigate revolutionary change, their assassination of Czar Alexander II was counterproductive and severely hampered the reform movement. Before his assassination, Czar Alexander II had approved preliminary plans to establish an elected parliament, or Duma, which could review proposed reforms. But his successor, Czar Alexander III, immediately tore up those plans, thus delaying the creation of an elected parliament by more than 20 years. It was not until 1905 that a Duma would be formed by Czar Nicholas II, the grandson of Czar Alexander II. But Czar Nicholas II would also be murdered, in 1918, by nihilists who called themselves Bolsheviks instead of Narodniks.

The Triumph Of Soviet Nihilism:
Slave Labor Camps!

In 1973 Aleksandr Solzhenitsyn published a three-volume set of books titled *The Gulag Archipelago*. Unfortunately for Solzhenitsyn, he had the night-marish experience of spending 11 years working in the Soviet Union's forced slave labor camps. This system of slave labor camps, known as the Chief Administration of Corrective Labor Camps, or Gulag for short, was scattered throughout the USSR much like islands, thus giving rise to the addition of the adjective "archipelago" to the acronym "Gulag."

In 1973 the Soviet Secret Police discovered one of Solzhenitsyn's manu-scripts chronicling his personal impressions of the notorious system of camps, prisons, and detention centers designed for women as well as men, with some created specifically for children. Fortunately his punishment for telling the truth was expulsion, not incarceration nor death. Perhaps this was due to the fact that his account had already been published outside the USSR, thus putting an international spotlight on Solzhenitsyn and his story.

The Gulag was created by Vladimir Lenin shortly after the Bolsheviks seized power, and greatly expanded between 1924 and 1953 during the reign of Soviet dictator Joseph Stalin. Although the Gulag was started around 1918, reduced a few years after Stalin's death in 1953, variants remained operational until 1989. Because the Soviets destroyed many records to cover up their unspeakable crimes against humanity with the Gulag, the number of unfortunate souls to have passed through this system of hell holes is unknown, but estimates range as high as 30 million.

According to Nicolas Werth,[5] writing in *The Black Book of Communism,* various records indicate that from 1934 to 1941 about 7 million people entered the Gulag, and from 1934 to 1940, 300,000 people were known to have died in the Gulag. Records for other time periods are imprecise or unavailable. Nicolas Werth noted that, "On 1 January 1940 some 1,670,000 prisoners were being held in the 53 groups of corrective work camps and the 425 corrective work colonies. One year later the figure had risen to 1,930,000. In addition, prisons held 200,000 people awaiting trial or a transfer to camp." Beyond the Gulag, Nicolas Werth also reported that in just two years, from 1937 to 1938, approximately 680,000 people were executed by the Soviet GPU (Soviet Secret Police) or the NKVD (Soviet Security Police) Court. Welcome to the Soviet Union!

In describing the experiences of the "Ordinary People and the Concentration Camp System," Karel Bartosek[6] wrote the following in *The Black Book of Communism:* "The government opened the Lovech camp after closing the camp at Belene - a camp unforgettable to the Bulgarians, since the bodies of prisoners who died there were fed to the pigs." Bartosek notes that "Officially, the camp was created to deal with repeat offenders and hardened criminals. But according to eyewitness reports made in 1990, most of the inmates were in fact sent there without trial: 'You're wearing jeans, you've got long hair, you listen to American music, you speak the language of a country that is hostile to us, you've been talking to tourists... off to the camp with you!'" Given the description of the above "offenses," many of the people sent to this Soviet hell hole may have been quite young. To describe them in traditional Communist terms, these young people were "politically incorrect," and they had to pay for their counter-revolutionary behavior!

Karel Bartosek also reported a description of the Lovech camp provided by Tzvetan Todorov. According to this report, the head of the State Security forces in this camp would place a small mirror in front of those he selected for execution. As the selected prisoner would gaze into the mirror he would be told, "Here, take a last look at your face!" Each prisoner was then given a large sack, which in fact served as his own body bag and burial cloth. The prisoner was required to carry the sack off the camp site to a quarry, much "like Christ carrying his own cross up to Golgotha," according to Todorov. Upon arrival at the quarry each prisoner was "beaten to death by the brigadiers and tied up in the sack with some wire." When night fell their comrades were required to return their beaten bodies to the camp in a handcart. The bodies were stacked in piles behind the toilets. When the body count reached twenty, a truck would arrive and haul them away. Those who did not make their quota of dead bodies were later beaten by the head of the State Security force - who was in fact the police chief! This is how the Soviets celebrated "the triumphant of nihilism," which, of course, is the triumph of the sociopath!

In *The Gulag Archipelago* Solzhenitsyn described in excruciating detail a wide sample of the disease, destruction, and death that occurred in the Gulag from 1918 to 1956. His account is supported by the personal accounts of numerous residents of the Soviet Union, both bourgeois and proletarian, who survived the slave labor camps. Like Solzhenitsyn, they also discovered that the promised theoretical "dictatorship of the proletariat" espoused by Karl Marx was, in practice, a deadly "dictatorship over the proletariat."

In discussing Solzhenitsyn's *The Gulag Archipelago*, Eugene Rose,[7] before he became Father Seraphim, observed that in the 19th century Nietzsche predicted the world would see the "triumph of nihilism" in the 20th century. Because the Soviet slave labor camps were the product of Russian nihilism, the Soviet Gulag made Nietzsche nothing less than a doomsday prophet for the millions of innocent men, women, and children who were imprisoned, tortured, and savagely murdered in this nightmarish system!

There Is No Truth; All Is Permitted!

Because Nietzsche proclaimed that "God is dead," to the nihilist there is no God; therefore, there was no act of special creation and there is no afterlife. What we do between birth and death is of no real consequence beyond the material world. Thus, life has no meaning and no purpose other than the ones we fabricate in our feeble attempt to make sense of a senseless world. This means there is no right or wrong, and there is no truth. Truths are just fabrications. They exist only in our imagination. As Nietzsche has written, because "There is no truth; all is permitted."

Consequently, in the godless world of the nihilist lying, cheating, stealing, and killing are permitted. Starvation, slave labor camps, and gas chambers are permitted. Confiscation of property, income, savings, investments, and other personal assets are all permitted. Control of government, banking, finance, business, education, communication, transportation, and health care, are all permitted. Yes, manipulation, control, and exploitation of everyone and everything are permitted. "There is no truth; all is permitted."

For the quasi-nihilist who suspects there is a God, or believes there is a God but chooses to live life as if there is no God, God is seen as too distant, too detached, or perhaps too weak to intervene and rescue him from himself. He may thus taunt God with his self-destructive behavior, daring Him to intervene, daring God to show Himself and prove that He exists - and prove that He cares! And if God is not going to stop him, he is going to relish only the here and now, and he is going to experience all that the physical world has to offer. Thus, the quasi-nihilist, or aspiring nihilist, attributes to himself the ability to challenge, entice, and manipulate God for his own narrow-minded purposes. In this manner the quasi-nihilist demonstrates his arrogance. He demonstrates his low level of moral maturity.

By their own words and deeds the atheistic nihilist and the agnostic quasi-nihilist both demonstrate their blinding arrogance and low moral intelligence. The nihilist attributes to himself the ability to accurately perceive and understand the material world that he can see, and to deny the invisible world he cannot see. But quantum physics reveals a heretofore unseen world that the brightest scientific minds find completely baffling. Quantum physics reveals a world that cannot exist, a world that defies nihilistic logic.

So, the nihilist does not reject that which does not exist, he rejects that which he cannot perceive or comprehend. While he may have a general IQ of 160, it never occurs to him that he may have a moral IQ of only 60, or perhaps even 16. It does not occur to him that he may lack the moral intelligence to perceive and comprehend a world that is perceived and comprehended by others, especially when those others seem to exhibit a lower general IQ than he is able to present to the world.

Surrender Truth To Power

"The constant strategy of Communist repression, whose central aim was always the establishment of absolute power and the elimination of political rivals and anyone else who had any sort of real power in society, was to attack systematically all the organisms of civil society. Because the aim was a monopoly on power and truth, the necessary targets were all other forces with political or spiritual power." - Karel Bartosek, The Destruction of Civil Society, *The Black Book of Communism,* 1999[8]

Eugene Rose also wrote the following regarding nihilism: "It is the definitive abandonment of truth, or rather the surrender of truth to power, whether that power be nation, race, class, comfort, or whatever other cause is able to absorb the energies men once devoted to the truth." His assertion that we find in nihilism, "the surrender of truth to power," may explain key behavior of the liberal, progressive, Communist, Nazi, and other socialists who demonstrate the sociopathic tendencies one observes in adherents to nihilism's fundamental principles. They do not expend energy to pursue truth, so they direct that energy to pursue power. Power is an invisible, hypothetical construct, but it can be demonstrated in the tangible, material world. Therefore, invisible power may be pursued as a substitute for invisible truth.

Through power the godless nihilist can create his own heaven right here on Earth, given that heaven exists nowhere else for him. Only through power can the godless nihilist become his own god and create a Marxian utopia - a perverted, sociopathic version of heaven on Earth. Only through power can the nihilist demonstrate to the world his god-like control over life and death. Only through power can nihilists such as Lenin, Stalin, and Khrushchev plant fear in the hearts and minds of entire nations, the depth of which may rival the fear of God one may experience when unexpectedly facing imminent death. Only through power can the nihilist try to kill more people than are killed by a natural environment created by God. Only through power do liberals, Communists, Nazis, progressives, and other socialists reveal the full measure of their nihilistic moral madness, a madness that calls to mind the moral insanity of the cold-blooded sociopath!

The "surrender of truth to power" may take yet another form. In a nation undergoing the Sovietization process, the ever-growing repression of political correctness, "hate crimes" legislation, along with other tyrannical methods, free speech is systematically stifled. For example, today in pro-abortion Soviet America some priests, ministers, and Rabbis avoid discussing the Bible's characterization of a pregnant woman as one who is "with child." One may listen to some religious leaders for years and never hear them discuss the Bible's prohibition against homosexual behavior, fearing social, monetary, or perhaps legal, reprisals.

When priests, ministers, and rabbis stop condemning behaviors defined as sinful in the Bible and do so for fear of the nihilistic power structure, it becomes clear they have been intimidated to the point where they, too, "surrender truth to power." They surrender what they believe to be biblical truths to a nihilistic power structure that forbids such truths. Thus, one may conclude that Nietzsche's 19th century prediction of the "triumph of nihilism" in the 20th century has not only been realized, but nihilism's success in both the 20th and 21st centuries demonstrates his ability to render realistic forecasting based on his intimate understanding of the potential and pervasiveness of the criminal mind.

------†††------

"Lenin, who had nothing but contempt for so-called liberals, once said that a Communist should never trust a liberal in the clutch. But Lenin knew that the flaccid relativism that liberals profess in the moral sphere, their total lack of patriotic zeal, their hedonistic looseness, and their enmity for Christianity would be perfectly suited to weakening the fabric of Western society for a future Bolshevik takeover." - Michael Suozzi, Comrades on Campus, 1989[9]

Part Two:

The Long March Toward Soviet America

Power! It's All About
Predatory, Parasitic, Political, Power!

"Dictatorship is power based on force and unrestricted by any laws. The revolutionary dictatorship of the proletariat is power won and maintained by the violence of the proletariat against the bourgeoisie - power that is unrestricted by any laws." - Vladimir Lenin, first Communist dictator of the Soviet Union

"The constant strategy of Communist repression, whose central aim was always the establishment of absolute power and the elimination of political rivals and anyone else who had any sort of real power in society, was to attack systematically all the organisms of civil society. Because the aim was a monopoly on power and truth, the necessary targets were all other forces with political or spiritual power." - Karel Bartosek, The Destruction of Civil Society, *The Black Book of Communism,* 1999, p. 407

"In retrospect I see that I turned to Soviet Russia because I thought it had the solution of the problem of power...I have not changed my attitude about the dangers of excessive power. But now I realize that Bolshevism is not the way out because it is itself the world's biggest agglomeration of power over man...all of the Soviet Union is one gigantic company town in which the government controls all the jobs, owns all the homes, and runs all the stores, schools, newspapers, etc., and from which there is no escape...Russia cannot solve the problem of power because it is the ugliest manifestation of the problem." - Louis Fischer, former champion of the Soviet Union. From, *The God That Failed,* NY: Bantam Books, 1959, pp. 204-205

Chapter Four

Sovereign Americans
Are Beginning To Wake Up
In Soviet America!

"We must now face the harsh truth that the objectives of Communism are being steadily advanced because many of us do not recognize the means used to advance them...The individual is handicapped by coming face to face with a Conspiracy so monstrous he cannot believe it exists. The American mind simply has not come to a realization of the evil which has been introduced into our midst." - J. Edgar Hoover, FBI Director, *Elks Magazine*, August, 1956

As noted in Chapter One, in 1932 William Z. Foster,[1] the National Chairman of the Community Party, USA, wrote a book titled *Toward Soviet America.* In his book Foster described many Communist goals and objectives that would be pursued to realize the Communist dream of constructing a Soviet America. Few Americans took Foster seriously. Few Americans took the warnings of J. Edgar Hoover seriously. Those who did so were ridiculed. Their ridicule was compounded with extreme frustration as they watched one published Communist goal after another being achieved while the bulk of the American people lived in blissful ignorance and denial. Most Americans simply could not believe the Sovereign America founded by George Washington, Thomas Jefferson, and James Madison could ever be subverted and transformed into an American version of the now defunct Soviet Union. Surely a self-governing America could never resemble the Soviet slave state operated by genocidal maniacs like Vladimir Lenin, Joseph Stalin, and Nikita Khrushchev!

But increasing numbers of knowledgeable Americans today are asserting unequivocally that the evidence of an encroaching Soviet America can no longer be denied. Conservatives who once laughed at those who warned of an impending Soviet America are no longer laughing. Many have been left stunned and bewildered. Some report a sense of unreality regarding the events that are unfolding before their very eyes on a daily basis. Only now, more than fifty years later, are they beginning to understand what J. Edgar Hoover meant when he said the American mind has been presented with a criminal conspiracy that is so monstrous, so evil, that we cannot believe that it exists; we cannot believe that this evil is within our midst and accomplishing one diabolical goal after another, decade after decade - right in front of our eyes!

The evidence for the existence of the "evil" that J. Edgar Hoover spoke of more than fifty years ago is overwhelming and presented in detail throughout this book. But before the bulk of that evidence is presented, let's review some documented quotes from a wide variety of astute observers of the human condition who have concluded that William Z. Foster's dream of a Soviet America is, indeed, becoming a reality - and FBI Director J. Edgar Hoover's assessment was undoubtedly accurate.

Gerald Celente,[2] the Founder and Director of The Trends Research Institute, spoke to George Noory in 2008 on the late-night radio program *Coast to Coast AM*. After observing intrusive, heavy-handed federal involvement in the private U.S. banking system and the private financial affairs of the American people, Gerald Celente proclaimed that, "This is becoming the USSA - the United States of Soviet America!" Clearly, Gerald Celente was describing a fundamental characteristic of the "Soviet America" predicted by Communist William Z. Foster in 1932. In a return appearance five months later Gerald Celente[3] transposed a few words and stated that, "We're becoming the USSA - the United Soviet States of America." Seventy-six years earlier William Z. Foster predicted that Americans would one day live in "The United Soviet States of America," and he used those very words to title the last chapter of his book.

Michael Savage,[4] who has monitored this trend for many years, asked the following question on his radio talk show: "Aren't you afraid of a Soviet-style America?" Former U.S. Ambassador Alan Keyes[5] spoke to WorldNet-Daily.com regarding his "Loyal to Liberty" blog. In discussing the policies of the newly elected President Barack Obama, Alan Keyes stated that, "Given Obama's push to overturn constitutional government and make the U.S. a Soviet-style state, I think it's more important than ever that those of us who believe in liberty deliberate and work together."

Michael Reagan[6] reminded us that his father, President Ronald Reagan, called the old Soviet Union an "Evil Empire." Moreover, Michael Reagan expressed concern that America is following in the footsteps of the former "Evil Empire" and is now becoming a new "Evil Empire." He made this clear when he said, "My father wasn't afraid to call evil what it was - and neither am I. He defeated the 'Evil Empire' called the Soviet Union - but now we face a new 'Evil Empire.' It's called Socialism, and it's taken over our once-free nation through the victories of Obama, Pelosi and Reid." Other prominent Americans have also expressed concern that America is beginning to resemble the old Soviet Union. For example, when Pat Robertson[7] was discussing the First Amendment implications of an American student who had the microphone turned off when she spoke of God and Jesus Christ at her high school graduation, Pat Robertson said, "This brings us back to the bad days of Communism in the Soviet Union."

When Mark Levin[8] was discussing the so-called Fairness Doctrine on his radio talk show he stated that, "This is the old Soviet Union style thinking." On an earlier radio program Mark Levin[9] said the following regarding Democrat Senator Harry Reid: "He sounds like a Soviet commissar." Mark Levin's assessment of Senator Harry Reid may seem like hyperbole - until one considers the following warning issued by Conservative News Alerts[10] in February of 2009: "Now, according to the above report by *The American Spectator*, the House Energy and Commerce Committee, under the leadership of far-left [Democrat] Congressman Henry Waxman, is talking about Congressional mandated advisory boards of community watchdogs for conservative talk-radio! Sound familiar? It should. The Soviet Union used to call them commissars...political officers...politruk!"

When Denver radio talk show host Dan Caplis[11] spoke to Bill O'Reilly regarding efforts to ban Christmas decorations in Fort Collins, Colorado because they may offend non-Christians, Dan Caplis said, "This sounds like something out of the old Soviet Union." Authors Floyd and Mary Beth Brown[12] wrote that, "She [Rachel Maddow of MSNBC] is giving relentless coverage to left-wingers' calls for a Soviet-style inquisition [of Bush and Cheney]." In discussing Harvard University and Yale University, Thomas E. Brewton[13] wrote that, "Both institutions since the early 1900s have used the word truth in the same sense and to the same ends as the Soviets employed it in their propaganda journal 'Pravda,' a Russian word meaning truth."

In addition to the above, Ann Coulter[14] referred to Massachusetts as "the Soviet Union" when discussing Mitt Romney's bid for the White House in 2008. When discussing the debate between Hillary Clinton and Rick Lazio in their bid for a U.S. Senate seat in 2006, Ann Coulter[15] referred to New York as "the Soviet Union." Ann Coulter's characterization is interesting given that Massachusetts was the home state of William Z. Foster, the National Chairman of the Communist Party, USA, who wrote in 1932 that "George Bernard Shaw is right: the time will surely come when the victorious toilers will build a monument to Lenin in New York."[16]

When Rush Limbaugh[17] was discussing Obama's plans for America with Sean Hannity, Rush said, "I don't know where - what he [Obama] wants to try has worked. It didn't work in the Soviet Union." In discussing efforts to impose a government-run health care system upon the American people, Republican presidential candidate John Cox[18] said in 2007 that he rejects "Soviet-style Hillary Care." On her popular radio talk show Laura Ingraham[19] spoke of Representative Dennis Kucinich's efforts to restore the so-called Fairness Doctrine. Because it imposes federal restrictions on free speech Laura referred to it as the "Soviet Fairness Doctrine." She further stated that "Dennis Kucinich is more Marxist than he is James Madison." When responding to a report that a couple in New Mexico had been brought up on charges for refusing to provide photographic services to a civil ceremony of a same sex couple, Laura said, "This sounds like something out of the Soviet Union."[20]

In 1960 Billy James Hargis[21] wrote a book titled, *Communist America... Must It Be?* In his book Hargis warned that powerful forces were at work to create a Communist America. Nearly fifty years later we find concerned Americans, such as Glenn Beck,[22] making the following alarming statements: "We are now more Communist than China," and, "...both sides [Democrats and Republicans] are running towards bigger government. We're practically the Soviet Union."[23] Irwin Baxter,[24] of End Times Ministry, spoke to George Noory on *Coast to Coast AM* regarding the "Real ID Act." Signed into law by Republican George W. Bush in 2005, the "Real ID Act" requires Americans to possess the equivalent of a nationalized ID card. In light of the fact that Communists required Soviet citizens to possess a national ID card beginning in 1932, Baxter concluded that, "America is becoming worse than Red China; worse than Russia."

In *Communist America...Must It Be?* Billy James Hargis[25] further wrote that, "The American people need to see Communism for what it really is, whether disguised as liberalism, socialism, progressivism, or modernism." Nearly fifty years later Michael Savage[26] would state that, "It's chilling to see how much we've become like the ex-Soviet Union - thanks to liberalism!" Consistent with the "evil" identified by J. Edgar Hoover and the new "Evil Empire" recognized by Michael Reagan, Michael Savage[27] further reported that "At best liberalism is a mental disorder. At worst it is pure evil." (Underlines added for emphasis.)

In addition, on his radio talk show Rush Limbaugh[28] reported that liberal Democrats were using the power of the federal government to intimidate him. They were trying to silence him by distorting his words, publicly denouncing him, and sending a critical letter to the management of the Premiere Radio Networks. Rush characterized such behavior as follows: "...I think they've become Stalinist-like...this is not just liberalism. It's Stalinist, using the power of the state to intimidate citizens." Rush made a transcript of this program available to his listeners, and titled the transcript "Stalinists Have Taken Over the Left." On the last episode of the *Hannity & Colmes*[29] cable television show, Sean Hannity and Alan Colmes exchanged "going away" gifts. And it came as no surprise to conservatives when Alan Colmes, an uncompromising defender of liberalism, presented Sean Hannity with a revealing gift - a copy of *The Communist Manifesto!* (Underlines added.)

In 1958 former FBI agent W. Cleon Skousen[30] wrote a classic book titled *The Naked Communist.* The 1962 edition listed 45 goals Communists planned to achieve within the USA. (Most of those goals have been accomplished, just as nearly all the planks of *The Communist Manifesto* have been installed in the USA.) Communist goal number 15 was as follows: "Capture one or both political parties in the United States." Today, fifty years later, we find Cleveland radio talk show host Mike Trivisonno[31] stating that, "Sometimes I think this is Russia, and the Democrats are bringing back Communism." Trivisonno added that, "They [the Democrats] now want to turn the United States of America into Russia." A caller into Michael Medved's[32] radio talk show described the Democrats as "the new American Communist Party in a lot of ways."

Furthermore, on his radio talk show Pastor Ernie Sanders[33] reported that, "I refer to the Democratic Party as the Communist Party." Investigative reporter Alan Caruba[34] titled one of his articles, "Democrat Party: The CPUSA in Disguise?" (Note: CPUSA is the acronym for Communist Party, USA.) In this article Caruba wrote, "It's no secret that Democrats are liberal, but...what has been revealed is an intention to nationalize our nation's oil industry. That, simply stated, is Communism." In his article titled, "Communist Party strategists map out Obama's agenda," Aaron Klein[35] wrote, "The enactment of a 'single payer' socialist health care system; passing laws to make joining a labor union easier; raising the minimum wage and increasing labor union support - all these are just some of the policies the Communist Party USA has mapped out as crucial for [Democrat] Obama to push through during his term of office."

Radio talk show host Tammy Bruce[36] declared that, "The Democratic Party, with this shift, is the Marxist Party." While radio talk show hosts have focused on the transformation of the Democrat Party into a larger version of the Communist Party, evidence will be presented to demonstrate that members of the Republican Party have worked in concert with the Democrat Party to build a Soviet America. Recall the earlier statement by Glenn Beck that "…both sides [Democrats and Republicans] are running towards bigger government. We're practically the Soviet Union." However, it's no secret that, while claiming neutrality, the Communist Party, USA, always supports Democrat Party presidential candidates.

Author Kevin Trudeau[37] has written about the restrictions the Federal Trade Commission has placed upon his writings regarding "natural cures." After concluding that the FTC had engaged in censorship and had violated his First Amendment rights, Trudeau stated that, "This is Nazi Germany. This is Stalinist Russia." On the CNBC business program *Kudlow & Company* former Massachusetts Governor Mitt Romney,[38] a very bright and successful businessman, commented on the government's response to the economic downturn in the fall of 2008. He criticized the government's plan for massive confiscation and redistribution of wealth, preferring market forces to self-correct as they have done in the past. Governor Romney summarized his position by stating that, "From Adam Smith to Karl Marx; that's not the path America ought to take." In discussing his book, *The Professors,* David Horowitz[39] characterized the form of feminism taught in American colleges and universities today by stating that, "It's a Marxist form of feminism."

J. Neil Schulman[40] reviewed the federal attack on the Branch Dividians in Waco, Texas during the presidency of Democrat Bill Clinton. In that 1993 attack 86 "politically incorrect" men, women, and children were shot, gassed, and incinerated to death. The adult survivors were given very lengthy prison terms. In response to this un-American treatment J. Neil Schulman wrote the following: "So tell me. What are you supposed to do when it looks as if the federal government can cover up war crimes on its own citizens with a Soviet-style show trial of the victims, and nobody with a nationally respected voice seems to care?"

During Bill Clinton's first term as president he appointed his wife, Hillary, to head a task force to create a plan to replace America's free market health care system with a national, government-run system. At that time Steve Forbes of *Forbes* magazine appeared on a television program to discuss this issue. If memory serves me correctly, Steve Forbes referred to the Clinton plan as "Soviet-style" health care. Many years later, during the early days of the Obama Administration, Steve Forbes[41] discussed government and union efforts to push "Card Check" upon American businesses, stating that, "It's more of a Soviet-style way of doing union elections." He added that, "[It] goes against the grain of American tradition."

In Soviet America You Won't Worry About Property Or Imprisonment!

In 2005 the U.S. Supreme Court ruled in the Kelo decision that local governments could take private property from their owners - not for public purposes as stated in the Constitution, but for the purpose of bestowing it upon other private individuals or organizations that could generate tax revenue for government. In response to this decision Roger Hedgecock,[42] the former Mayor of San Diego, concluded that, "We're losing our country." He also angrily stated that, "Ownership of your home just passed from you to the government. Welcome to Russia!" Agreeing with Roger Hedgecock, Devvy Kidd[43] concluded that the U.S. Supreme Court "handed down a crushing blow to freedom with the *Kelo v. City of New London* decision." She further stated that, "As I have written in past columns, the quest for a one-world government under Communism is real and now it's right in the face of the American people."

Many who have been indoctrinated by the Soviet-bloc media and education establishments may fail to grasp the significance of the Kelo decision and may find no problem with government "confiscation and redistribution" of private property. But this court decision has placed many Sovereign Americans in a state of alarm because they are keenly aware that in the *Manifesto* Karl Marx[44] wrote, "In one word, you reproach us with intending to do away with your property. Precisely so; that is just what we intend." The Kelo decision, combined with the fact that the federal government has been confiscating, regulating, and restricting millions upon millions of acres of land to protect rats, mice, spiders, snakes, bugs, and various other "threatened and endangered" species without the constitutional authority to do so, tells even the most casual observer that Marxists are marching in lockstep *Toward Soviet America*!

Regarding private property, Foster[45] made the preposterous statement that the crime-infested Soviet Union was "fast becoming a crimeless country." Why? One reason is that with the abolition of property rights the Soviet government had confiscated (had stolen) all property, and therefore further crimes against property ceased. But what Foster was unwittingly telling the perceptive reader was that, in Soviet America you won't have to worry about crimes against your property - because you won't own any property! Foster[46] also admitted that, "from time to time" it becomes necessary to "confine a considerable number of political prisoners." But he assured the reader that there was no need to be concerned about these confinements.

Why? Because the confinement of political prisoners was only temporary, given that Communists engaged in "the liquidation of the last remnants of the exploiting classes in the Soviet Union."

So, in Soviet America political prisoners (incarcerated counter-revolutionaries) will not have to worry about long-term confinements because, as in the Soviet Union, Communists will empty prison cells by filling shallow graves. That Foster found this "liquidation" of political prisoners to be comforting, and believed it would help assure the reader of the superiority of a USSA over the USA, provides the reader with significant insight into the moral insanity of this cold-blooded Communist. It also tells the Sovereign American reader that Foster believed America was populated with a large number of readers who shared his vision of a genocidal Soviet America. Given the fact that, for many decades, nearly 4,000 pre-born babies have been exterminated every day in abortion clinics across Soviet America, it appears Foster's assessment was correct! This selfish destruction of innocent, defenseless human life continues unabated to this day!

After observing the rapidly accelerating deconstruction of Sovereign America and observing the Frankenstein of a nation that is being built upon the ruins, radio talk show host Mike Gallagher[47] used the following sound bite to promote his radio show: "Have I lost sight of what country we live in? Isn't this America?" Thomas Sowell,[48] a nationally syndicated columnist and senior fellow at the Hoover Institution, stated on *Hannity & Colmes* that we have now moved so far to the left that it may take a "military coup" to save America.

However, soon after Admiral Mike Mullen[49] assumed the position of Chairman of the Joint Chiefs of Staff, he publicly acknowledged that "We are part of a New World Order." As many Americans know, New World Order is a euphemism for a global, Soviet-style government. Therefore, it appears the highest levels of the U.S. military have already been placed under Soviet American control, and perhaps it has been that way for decades. Therefore, restoring America to a Constitutional Republic will require a massive movement at the grassroots level. As Bill Cunningham[50] warned on his Sunday night radio program, "They're not going to stop until it looks like the USSR…"

When Soviets Frame The Argument, Soviets Win The Argument!

The following has been attributed to Noam Chomsky: "The smart way to keep people passive and obedient is to strictly limit the spectrum of acceptable opinion, but allow very lively debate within that spectrum - even encourage the more critical and dissident views. That gives people the sense that there's free thinking going on, while all the time the presuppositions of the system are being reinforced by the limits put on the range of the debate."[51]

With the exception of a few good men and women, in past decades the vast majority of genuine conservatives and genuine libertarians have operated within the politically correct psychological framework imposed upon them by the builders of Soviet America. By framing important issues in terms acceptable to the Left, Sovereign Americans always seemed to take one step forward and three steps backward when engaged in important political battles. Consequently, Soviet Americans successfully infiltrated our institutions, corrupted our culture, damaged our economy, trashed our Constitution, eroded our sovereignty, brainwashed our children, stole our money, and confiscated much of our property - while blaming all the damage on the people who tried to stop them. That, my fellow Sovereign Americans, demonstrates what can be accomplished via Soviet-style psychological warfare!

By restricting themselves to innocuous labels such as "liberal" and "progresssive" to describe extremist leftists, Sovereign Americans have allowed Marxists, Leninists, and Stalinists to build their Soviet America in plain sight with minimal resistance - and oftentimes with useful idiot complicity! The above quotes, therefore, tell us that Sovereign Americans are finally breaking free of the politically correct psychological straitjackets placed around them by the builders of Soviet America. Sovereign Americans are beginning to recognize that as long as they allow the construction of William Z. Forster's Soviet America to remain an open secret, Sovereign Americans will most certainly lose the Cold War (culture war) now being fought on American soil. And if they lose the Cold War on the American front, like the defeated bourgeoisie of the Soviet Union, the defeated bourgeoisie of Soviet America will most certainly lose everything else as well.

Because Sovereign Americans are beginning to awaken, Soviet Americans now find it necessary to construct higher barriers through such measures as the "Soviet Fairness Doctrine." Through this doctrine the government, and not the talk show hosts, would dictate the content of talk radio programs - just as one would expect in the old Soviet Union and in a new Soviet America! Or, they may establish government mandated, community (Communist) "advisory boards" reminiscent of Joseph Stalin's Soviet commissars. Through the courts Soviet Americans have had the power, but not the constitutional authority, to trample freedom of religious expression on taxpayer-funded property. They are now proceeding to squelch free speech among radio talk show hosts - and much more!

Measuring Progress Toward Soviet America!

As noted earlier, the now discredited Democrat Senator John Edwards distinguished himself in many ways, including his insistence that there are "two Americas" - one for the rich and one for the poor. This book, too, explores the idea that there are two Americas, not as envisioned by John Edwards, but as envisioned by others. Firstly, there is the Sovereign America founded by George Washington, Thomas Jefferson, and James Madison. This is the America born on July 4, 1776, with the signing of the Declaration of Independence, and reinforced with the Articles of Confederation and the U.S. Constitution.

The Declaration of Independence, Articles of Confederation, and the U.S. Constitution are three tangible documents that provide incontrovertible evidence of the conception, birth, and life of the sovereign nation known as the United States of America. Moreover, one may objectively measure the extent to which the USA continues to exist as originally founded by comparing federal legislation and federal court rulings with the letter and spirit expressed in these founding documents, especially the Declaration of Independence and the U.S. Constitution. Some objective measurements in this regard will be presented in this book.

As discussed later in Chapter Nineteen, the title of Judge Andrew P. Napolitano's[52] book, *The Constitution in Exile,* tells us the U.S. Constitution has been discarded by those who have sworn to preserve, protect, and defend it. The book titled *Who killed the Constitution?* by Thomas E. Woods, Jr. and Kevin R. C. Gutzman[53] tells us the U.S. Constitution is not only dead, but it did not die from natural causes. If the U.S. Constitution is dead, then the Sovereign America founded by Washington, Jefferson, and Madison is also dead. This conclusion is consistent with William Z. Foster's[54] contention that "The capitalist State must be broken down and the Workers' State built from the ground up on entirely different principles, and this was done in the USSR." This statement by Foster provides a solid clue to help us answer the question, *Who killed the Constitution?* It also supplies us with a motive for their ongoing criminal activity!

Secondly, there is an emerging Communist America, conceived, in theory, by Karl Marx in 1848. In *The Communist Manifesto* Karl Marx outlined the steps necessary to establish Communism in a given nation. Those steps included ten "planks," such as plank number two that called for "A heavy progressive or graduated income tax," and plank number five that called for a "national bank." Both those planks were installed in the USA in 1913 (four years before the Russian Revolution of 1917) with the enactment of the personal income tax on February 3, 1913 and the establishment of the Federal Reserve banking system on December 23, 1913.

Consequently, one may present the installation of plank number two as verifiable evidence that a Communist America, as theorized by Karl Marx, was born on February 3, 1913. In addition, one may objectively measure the extent to which Communist America rivals, or has overtaken, the Sovereign America born on July 4, 1776. This can be accomplished by identifying the extent to which other Marxian planks and ideas have been incorporated into American government and American culture. This will be examined in subsequent chapters.

While Karl Marx may have conceived of a Communist America in 1848, William Z. Foster conceived of a specific kind of Communist America, and he called it Soviet America. Clearly, Soviet America was conceived in 1932 with the publication of Foster's book, *Toward Soviet America.* This is the Soviet-like America that Gerald Celente, Michael Savage, Glenn Beck, Laura Ingraham, Pat Robertson, and many others have begun to identify in recent years. Again, the extent to which the builders of Soviet America have accomplished their goal can be objectively assessed by identifying the extent to which the goals outlined by William Z. Foster have been achieved. That, too, is explored throughout this book. The birth of Soviet America, of course, would be the day any one of William Z. Foster's goals was first accomplished in the USA.

Also, as noted above, in the 1962 edition of *The Naked Communist* we find 45 goals Communists planned to achieve within the USA. While most of those goals have been advanced, this book focuses on several key goals. By examining the goals set forth by Karl Marx and William Z. Foster, along with the goals uncovered by W. Cleon Skousen, we can assess with reasonable accuracy the extent to which Sovereign America has been deconstructed and a Soviet America has been built upon the ruins.

Because the vast majority of Sovereign Americans ignored the work of William Z. Foster and disregarded the warnings of J. Edgar Hoover, Billy James Hargis, and W. Cleon Skousen, we now find writer Linda Kimball[55] sounding the following alarm in her attempt to mobilize her fellow Sovereign Americans: "In league with transnational progressives, New Left fanatics are stealthily lowering the 'iron curtain' upon the New Soviet Union - America and the West. Political activism by conservatives, Christians, and all traditional-values patriots is no longer just a civic and moral duty. It's now a matter of our very survival." According to Doug Giles,[56] more traditional values Americans are beginning to wake up: "Also, timid and sweet traditional value voters are not - not - talking about religion and politics any longer. Oh no, they're finally entering the verbal fray and starting to flap as they watch the USA morph into the USSA."

Welcome to Soviet America!

Good-bye Sovereign America!

Chapter Five

Re-Education In Soviet America!

Values Clarification:
Training American Children To Think Like Nihilists, Act Like Sociopaths, And Live Like Soviets!

"Give us the child for eight years and it will be a Bolshevik forever."
- Vladimir Lenin, first Communist dictator of the Soviet Union[1]

In Soviet America "The studies will be revolutionized, being cleansed of religious, patriotic and other features of the bourgeois ideology." - William Z. Foster, National Chairman of the Communist Party, USA, *Toward Soviet America,* 1932[2]

Question: Thomas Sowell, a senior fellow at the Hoover Institution at Stanford University, has investigated the widespread application of brainwashing techniques. Sowell reported that the brainwashing techniques he investigated were developed in totalitarian countries, with some techniques having roots in China under Mao Zedong. Mao, the Communist who established Communism in the nation of China, may be the deadliest genocidal maniac in human history, with a body count of over 76 million men, women, and children. This figure does not include victims of the abortion holocaust. According to Thomas Sowell the brainwashing techniques developed under Mao and other totalitarian dictators are in widespread use today in:

A. Cuban political prisons.
B. Iraqi military prisons.
C. American public elementary and secondary schools.
D. Mexican sweat shops in Los Angeles.
E. All of the above.

Answer: C. American public elementary and secondary schools.[3]

In preparing to write about the application of "values clarification" in America's public schools, I turned to the Index of Thomas Sowell's 1993 book titled, *Inside American Education: The Decline, The Deception, The Dogmas.*[4] Under the topic of "values clarification" I was stunned to find the following parenthetical words: (see Brainwashing). Perhaps even more sur-prisingly, under "Brainwashing" there were 24 separate topics wherein brainwashing in American schools was discussed, with "values clarification" being one of those 24 topics.

Thomas Sowell, a respected scholar and meticulous researcher, has pro-vided the reader with an in depth look at the deliberate damage inflicted upon the psyches of America's children in government-run schools. Most discouraging was the author's observation that, under "values clarification" our children are taught that "there is no right or wrong" way of thinking or behaving. (Sound familiar?) In "death education," sex education, drug education, and "nuclear education" programs, children are psychologically conditioned to reject parental authority and parental values, and embrace nihilistic thought processes based upon the notion that there is no such thing as "right and wrong."

In addition, the author devotes an entire chapter to "Classroom Brain-washing" wherein he documents how the goals of brainwashing are well established in government-run schools, and he describes in detail how "teachers" employ "classical brainwashing techniques developed in totali-tarian countries" to achieve these goals.[5] Thus, Marxist nihilists disguised as educators subject our children to mind-altering techniques similar to those used on military prisoners of war, incarcerated political prisoners, and other captive populations trapped behind what was once called the "Iron Curtain."

In government classrooms across the USSA our children are treated as political prisoners caught in the midst of a culture war waged against traditional American culture and the parentally transmitted value system that has heretofore sustained it. Attempts to discredit home schooling and private religious education are designed to ensure that very few political prisoners escape from behind the psychological Iron Curtain placed around government-run schools in Soviet America.

Through "values clarification" children are supposedly directed to clarify or better understand the values they embrace. However, as Thomas Sowell points out, values "confusion" would be a more accurate description of this brainwashing method. This conclusion is backed by reports of parents who testified before the Soviet-inspired U.S. Department of Education, with one parent stating that her son "came home one day very confused as to the rightness or wrongness of stealing" after being subjected to various psycho-logical conditioning programs at school, including "values clarification."[6]

By employing techniques that ensure children are "confused as to the rightness or wrongness of stealing," "re-educators" deprogram our children of the Commandment, You shall not steal, which was removed from government schools in 1980 by the U.S. Supreme Court. Clearly, through "values clarification" children are systematically deprogrammed of an important Commandment they may have learned at home or through religious training. They are cunningly deprogrammed of a principle that is necessary for the functioning of a sovereign individual and a sovereign nation. And of course, when students are psychologically reprogrammed to believe that stealing is no longer viewed as wrong, they are prepared to accept, perhaps even demand, the implementation of socialism - which requires theft by government on a truly massive scale!

Following comprehensive, nihilistic, psychological conditioning we find the following changes in our children: Respect for human life is replaced with acceptance of abortion, fetal stem cell research, euthanasia, and proletarian violence; honesty is replaced with acceptance of lying, cheating, and stealing; innovative individualism is replaced with conformist proletariat group-think; family self-sufficiency is replaced with government dependency; a sense of opportunity is replaced with a sense of hopelessness; responsibility is replaced with a sense of entitlement; American culture is replaced with foreign multiculturalism - whereby unity of the melting pot is replaced with diversity among hostile proletariat groups; patriotism is replaced with anti-Americanism - and diversity is transformed into a euphemism for anti-Americanism; clarity of thought is replaced with mental confusion; and a desire for border security, national security, and national sovereignty are replaced with acceptance of a vulnerable, dangerous, borderless, Socialist America submerged under a developing UN global Gulag.

The success of the nihilistic brainwashing of America's school children can be summed up by the following 1993 observation made by William J. Bennett:[7] "In 1940 teachers identified the top problems in America's schools as: talking out of turn, chewing gum, making noise and running in the hall." Contrastingly, Bennett noted that, "In 1990, teachers listed drugs, alcohol, pregnancy, suicide, rape and assault" as the most pressing problems in America's schools. There is no better summary of the difference between Sovereign America and Soviet America! There is no better summary of the "progress" made by the builders of Soviet America!

Moreover, critics of this sort of destructive psychological reorientation soon discover that psychological reprogramming is also readily applied outside the classroom as well. Millions of Americans have wandered outside the Soviet-bloc media to educate themselves on the frightful state of our schools. But when these enlightened citizens object to continued taxpayer financing of these Soviet-style re-education camps, they discover that they are accused of being "anti-education" or "insensitive to the needs of our children." Like critics living inside the former Soviet Union, they find themselves the target of psychological warfare. In Soviet America, to oppose brainwashing in Soviet-style re-education camps is to "oppose education."

Armed with the historical perspective of 19th and 20th century Russia, we can see that the nihilism that corrupted the Russian people and helped pave the way for a socialist totalitarian police state known as the Soviet Union, is now deeply entrenched within the USA. The war against American culture has many battlefronts, and on the battlefront of the American classroom the Soviets have been winning decisively for many decades! The only thing missing from our government-run schools is a red sign hanging above each entrance that says, "Welcome to Soviet America!"

Moral Idiot + Intellectual Idiot = Useful Idiot

In Soviet America "God will be banished from the laboratories as well as from the schools." - William Z. Foster, National Chairman of the Communist Party, USA, *Toward Soviet America,* 1932[8]

While "values clarification" and other psychological conditioning methods are employed to morally dumb down our school children with the basic tenants of nihilism, the "look-say" method of teaching reading, the "new math," and "outcome-based education," all ensure that our children will be dumbed down intellectually as well. This two-pronged approached is designed to produced children who are both morally and intellectually deficient. This ensures there will be plenty of useful idiots to play the role of proletarian in Foster's Soviet America.

As noted in Chapter Two, the naturally-occurring useful idiot tends to have a normal moral IQ; however, it can be discerned that the manufactured useful idiot is a person who has been programmed in school, through the media and the counter-culture to adopt the nihilistic perspective of the moral idiot. For example, in his book *Why Johnny Can't Tell Right From Wrong: Moral Illiteracy and the Case for Character Education,* William Kilpatrick[9] discusses "values clarification" in some detail, but most disturbingly he reports that with this method, "teachers act like talk show hosts, and where the merits of wife swapping, cannibalism, and teaching children to masturbate are recommended topics for debate." Consistent with Thomas Sowell's contention that "values clarification" is a deceptive title for a program that leads to values confusion, Kilpatrick states that, "For students, it has meant wholesale confusion about moral values: learning to question values they have scarcely acquired, unlearning values taught at home, and concluding that questions of right and wrong are always merely subjective."

Kilpatrick reminds us that in 1955 Rudolf Flesch wrote his classic indictment against government education titled *Why Johnny Can't Read*. And the reason Johnny can't read is because re-educators have replaced phonics with the "look-say" method of teaching reading. Unfortunately, this switch was made, and continues to dominate in government schools, in spite of the fact the phonics method has proven itself far superior to the "look-say" method.

As Jonathan Kozol[10] points out in his book, *Illiterate America*, government schools have failed the task of providing students with basic educational skills. Many students spend 12 years in the government-run school system and never learn to read beyond a very elementary level. They learn there is no such thing as right or wrong; they learn how to use a condom; and they learn how to support the global warming hoax; but they fail to learn basic reading, writing, and arithmetic. In discussing the relationship between illiteracy and crime, Kozol writes, "The prison population represents the single highest concentration of adult illiterates. While criminal conviction of illiterate men and women cannot be identified exclusively with inability to read and write, the fact that 60 percent of prison inmates cannot read above the grade-school level surely provides some indication of one major reason for their criminal activity."

As referenced above, with the Ten Commandments boldly engraved on the walls of the public U.S. Supreme Court building, in 1980 the U.S. Supreme Court ruled in *Stone v. Graham* that it was unconstitutional for the Ten Commandments to be posted on a public school bulletin board. With this decision the Court removed the Ten Commandments from all government-run schools. However, eight years later, in 1988, Phyllis Schlafly edited a book titled, *Child Abuse in the Classroom*, wherein parental testimony before the Soviet-inspired U.S. Department of Education was presented. Numerous testimonials established the fact that children were taught to disrespect their parents in government-run classrooms.

So, while the builders of Soviet America removed from our schools the Commandment, "Honor your father and your mother," they replaced it with questions such as the following that was asked in a "values clarification" class for third-graders: "How many of you ever wanted to beat up your parents?"[11] Also, the following question was asked in a fourth grade health class: "How many of you hate your parents?"[12] Clearly, materials that encourage respect for parents were removed and replaced with materials that foster disrespect for parents. It should therefore come as no surprise that students are often instructed to not inform their parents about what they are taught in school,[13] and boards of education are given instructions on how to discredit parents who dare to complain about this and other forms of anti-parental brainwashing taking place in their children's taxpayer-funded re-education classes.[14]

Pro-Homosexual Re-Education

"Present homo-sexuality, degeneracy and promiscuity as 'normal, natural, healthy.'" - Former FBI agent W. Cleon Skousen, Communist goal #26, *The Naked Communist,* 1962[15]

Re-education of our children in government-run schools did not end in the 1980s or 1990s, but continues unabated into the 21st century. As a matter of fact, it may be getting worse. For example, as researcher Rob Hood has reported, freshman students at a Deerfield, Illinois high school were required to sit through lectures presented by "homosexual, bi-sexual, and transgender students." Moreover, these freshmen students were also re-quired to sign a contract wherein they agreed to not discuss the contents of the lectures with anyone outside the classroom, including their parents. In other words, re-educators don't want parents and taxpayers to know that America's children are being psychologically reprogrammed to help advance Communist goal number 26 - as recorded in the Congressional Record in 1963.

Additional evidence demonstrates that the Soviet goal of normalization of homosexuality through re-education is advancing rapidly. As Rob Hood[16] noted, in 2006 the California State Assembly passed several pro homosexual bills, all of which were signed into law by Governor Arnold Schwarzenegger, a Menshevik Republican. One of these laws requires the editing of all public school textbooks and teaching materials to reflect only favorable per-spectives of homosexuality. Another bill authorizes educators to create "tolerance education" programs that forbid the "expression of traditional values" and further forbids communicating a "preference for traditional marriage." In other words, traditional American values are not tolerated in programs supposedly designed to teach tolerance. Welcome to Soviet America!

Reprogramming students to accept homosexual behavior as "normal, natural, healthy," has been widespread for decades, but now it is mandated by law in California schools. Government enforced mainstreaming of homosexuality in California public schools will, of course, spread throughout the entire Soviet American educational system. Regardless of one's personal views of homosexuality, one may ask why government-run, taxpayer-funded schools are advancing Communist goal number 26, while failing to teach reading, writing, and arithmetic?

Nihilistic Indoctrination

"Eliminate prayer or any phase of religious expression in the schools on the ground that it violates the principle of 'separation of church and state.'" Former FBI agent W. Cleon Skousen, Communist goal #28, *The Naked Communist,* 1962[17]

In writing *Welcome to Soviet America,* the 1962 edition of W. Cleon Skousen's book, *The Naked Communist,* was used as a source of information. In that edition Skousen warned Americans that Communists planned to eliminate prayer from public schools on the ground that it violated the principle of "separation of church and state." In 1962 the U.S. Supreme Court did precisely that. In *Engle v. Vitale* the Court ruled that prayer in public schools was unconstitutional on the basis that it violated the constitutional principle of "separation of church and state." Of course the Court, the media, and the education establishment conveniently failed to announce that this principle is found in Article 52 of the Soviet Constitution, but is found nowhere in the U.S. Constitution. They further failed to inform the American people that the First Amendment to the U.S. Constitution expressly forbids the federal government from prohibiting the free exercise of religion - anywhere in the USA! They also failed to announce that Communist goal number 28 had been achieved through this Court ruling. Welcome to Soviet America!

What happens when the U.S. constitutional principle of religious liberty is replaced with the Soviet constitutional principle of "separation of church and state" to fulfill William Z. Foster's goal of "banishing God" from the classroom? What happens when government removes God, prayer, and the Ten Commandments from our schools? What happens when government re-educators remove the Commandments, You shall not steal; You shall not bear false witness against your neighbor; You shall not murder; and Honor your father and your mother? (Exodus 20: 3-17). What happens when these Commandments are replaced with "values clarification" and situational ethics? What happens when children unlearn the "bourgeoisie" values taught by their parents and learn the nihilistic principle that "there is no such thing as right or wrong?" A few troubling statistics will answer those questions:

"...final FBI data from 1985-93 show that the number of adults age 25 or older committing murder decreased 20 percent. In the same period, homicides committed by 18- to 24-year-old males increased 65 percent. Homicides by 14- to 17-year-old males jumped 165 percent." - *The Arizona Republic,* May 22, 1995

"...8.8 percent of eighth and tenth grade students reported being robbed at school, 19 percent reported being threatened, and 9.5 percent said they were attacked." And, "...500,000 violent incidents occurred every month in public secondary schools in 1988." Also, "...57 percent of high school drug users said they bought their illegal substances at school." - William F. Jasper, *The New American,* August 8, 1994

"Moreover, 35 percent of juvenile inmates and 10 percent of students questioned believed it was 'OK to shoot a person if that is what it takes to get something you want.'" - Violence climbing rapidly among America's young and ruthless, *The Arizona Republic,* September 8, 1995

Citing the 1982 book *The Disappearance of Childhood* by Neal Postman, William F. Jasper[18] points out that, "as recently as 1950 'in all of America, only 170 persons under the age of 15 were arrested for what the FBI calls serious crimes (such as murder, forcible rapes, robbery, and aggravated assault).'" However, "between 1950 and 1979 the rate of serious crime committed by children increased by 11,000 percent!" Yes, that's eleven thousand percent!

The widespread, ongoing indoctrination of America's school children into the nihilistic value system of the sociopath helps us understand why America's schools are among the most debased and crime-ridden locations in the nation. It helps to explain the widespread depression, suicide, and drug and alcohol abuse among America's youth. It sheds light on why beatings, rape, and liberal gang violence occurs in many schools, and children avoid using school restrooms for fear of assault. It helps explain why our schools are failing: they are failing, in large part, because Marxist tacticians disguised as administrators and educators are psychologically damaging our students, defrauding their parents, and scamming the tax-payers who are forced to finance these Soviet-style re-education camps under the guise of education.

Decades ago we should have reinstated the crime preventing principle of "separation of school and state." Although it was noted in the late 1800s that government-controlled schools produced far more criminals than parent-controlled schools, the true explosion in crime occurred after the start of the nihilistic, Marxist, Cultural Revolution (anti-American counter-culture) of 1960s America - a Cultural Revolution predicted in 1932 by the National Chairman of the Communist Party, USA!

Comrade Carter Helps Foster
Build His Soviet America!

In Soviet America "The students will be taught on the basis of Marxian dialectic materialism, internationalism and the general ethics of the new Socialist society." - William Z. Foster, National Chairman of the Communist Party, USA, *Toward Soviet America,* 1932[19]

Question: Jimmy Carter, a Bolshevik Democrat from Georgia, was elected thirty-ninth President of the United States in 1976. During his four years in office he created the U.S. Department of Education. By creating this depart-ment within the U.S. Government Jimmy Carter fulfilled an important dream of:

A. George Washington, first President of the USA.
B. William Z. Foster, National Chairman of the Communist Party, USA.
C. Abraham Lincoln, sixteenth President of the USA.
D. John F. Kennedy, thirty-fifth President of the USA.
E. All of the above.
F. None of the above.

Answer: B. William Z. Foster, National Chairman of the Communist Party, USA.

In his 1932 book titled *Toward Soviet America*, William Z. Foster predicted that a Soviet America would have a "National Department of Education." Specifically, Foster wrote that, in order to advance the Marxist Cultural

Revolution, the new "American Soviet government" would place schools, colleges, and universities "under the National Department of Education and its state and local branches." And of course, to strip Americans of their repulsive "bourgeoisie ideology," classroom work would be "cleansed" of material that was religious or patriotic in nature. These studies would be replaced with "Marxist dialectic materialism, internationalism and general ethics of the new Socialist society." Foster also stated that our "obsolete methods of teaching" would be replaced with "a scientific pedagogy."[20]

It's not too difficult to see that Jimmy Carter's U.S. Department of Education, along with its federal mandates for state and local schools, serves to fulfill Foster's "National Department of Education and its state and local branches." It can be seen that teaching from a UN globalist perspective that emphasizes global solutions to environmental concerns such as global warming - as well as multiculturalism - fit well into Foster's "Marxist dialectic materialism" and his "internationalism." In addition "values clarification," with its nihilistic absence of right and wrong, is consistent with Foster's Communistic "general ethics for the new Socialist society."

In addition, Foster's stated goal of cleansing American schools of "bourgeois ideology" corresponds with the widespread cleansing of parental values from the minds of students through "values clarification" and other psychological conditioning programs. And all this is accomplished by Foster's Soviet American government in order to "further the cultural revolution," which, of course, is what Americans routinely refer to as the "culture war." Thus, more than forty years before it occurred, Foster predicted that, in Soviet America, the U.S. Government would create a National Department to bring state and local schools under centralized, governmental control, thus following the pattern set by Lenin and Stalin in the Soviet Union.

Foster's was dead right when he predicted that, in Soviet American schools, "The studies will be revolutionized, being cleansed of religious, patriotic and other features of the bourgeois ideology." Evidence of this cleansing was uncovered by Mel and Norma Gabler when they examined textbooks used by their children in government-run schools. According to Robert W. Lee, the Gablers, "found so many examples of immorality, obscenity, socialism, and anti-Christian, anti-American bias that they decided to register a complaint with the Texas State Board of Education's Textbook Committee."[21] And of course, the U.S. Supreme Court, along with the ACLU, has been working diligently to ensure that public schools in Soviet America are "cleansed" of all that is "religious," just as Foster had predicted.

Foster, a lifelong Communist, died in 1961 in Moscow, the political capitol of liberals, Communists, progressives, and other socialists who are working to fulfill Foster's dream of building a Soviet America. If William Z. Foster were alive today and still National Chairman of the Communist Party, USA, after viewing the fulfillment of his predictions he would most certainly be inspired to write a sequel to his book *Toward Soviet America*. The title of that sequel would, of course, be as follows: *Welcome to Soviet America*.

To no one's surprise, what Soviet American government officials, media pundits, and so-called educators will never tell you is that Jimmy Carter, a Bolshevik Democrat from Georgia, not only fulfilled a dream of Communist William Z. Foster when he created the U.S. Department of Education, but he also violated the Tenth Amendment to the U.S. Constitution. Because education was not delegated to the U.S. Government by the Constitution, the education of children is restricted to the states and to the people. In light of the fact that the U.S. Constitution is the supreme law of the land, federal interference in education constitutes an ongoing unlawful activity. And all unlawful behavior by federal officials must be terminated - in spite of the fact that this Illegal activity is proudly aided and abetted by the media!

We are told that ignorance of the law is no excuse for violating the law. So how can we excuse federal politicians and bureaucrats who routinely violate the law after taking a solemn oath to specifically uphold the law - as they must do before assuming office! Federal officials who continually engage in patently unlawful activities most certainly lack the moral authority to punish others for doing so. How can they punish people for modeling their behavior and following their example? Unfortunately, as author Peter Schweizer[22] has noted, the hypocritical "Do as I say, not as I do" attitude runs rampant among politicians and bureaucrats today. As each year passes the criminality of U.S. Government officials becomes more eerily similar to that of USSR Government officials! It truly hurts to say it again but, Welcome to Soviet America!

College Seniors:
Dumb & Dumber In Soviet America!

"Notably, at several elite schools (including Brown, Georgetown and Yale), where classes in basic history and economics are brushed aside in favor of trendier subjects like "queer theory," the seniors actually scored lower than the freshmen. That's right: students at these schools are paying up to $40,000 a year to become dumber." - Ashley Herzog, Ignorance is no excuse[23]

Ashley Herzog reported that a few years ago the Intercollegiate Studies Institute (ISI) randomly selected 14,000 freshmen and seniors and tested them in basic civic literacy. The results were stunning, and disheartening for Sovereign Americans, but very encouraging for Soviet Americans. Less than half of the college seniors tested were aware of the fact that the words "We hold these truths to be self-evident, that all men are created equal" are contained in the Declaration of Independence. Approximately half of the students were unaware that Jamestown was the first colony established in America. An astounding 78 percent could not define "public good," and 40 percent could not place the American Civil War in the correct time period. More than half the college seniors did not understand the concept of federalism, 47 percent "couldn't explain how wealth is generated in a free market system," and 40 percent "couldn't define the law of supply and demand."

If college students are not learning the basics of American history and American-style free market capitalism, what are they learning? According to David Horowitz, college students are learning how to become Marxists and how to hate America!

Using Colleges & Universities
To Build A Soviet America!

"I must report that our public colleges and many of our prestigious private colleges have become infiltrated with Communist and pro-Communist agents posing as college professors. Enjoying the blessings of America, they dig her grave. It is time for this situation to be exposed." - Michael Suozzi, Comrades on Campus, 1989[24]

"In the Soviet Union, we stop believing Communist Party propaganda at about the age of 10. Then I come to the United States and hear your Soviet experts parroting Soviet propaganda in universities that we dismissed in elementary school." - Lev Navrosov, a Soviet Jew who immigrated to the United States[25]

Indoctrination of our children does not stop at the 12th grade, but continues throughout their college years. For example, in 2007 Evan Coyne Maloney made a documentary film titled *Indoctrinate U.* In discussing the lack of tolerance for diversity of thought on Soviet American campuses, Kevin Mooney[26] wrote that, "Although most of America's institutions of higher learning were designed to foster debate and mold students into critical thinkers, a two-and-a-half-year investigation shows that a repressive political climate has taken hold in recent years - a climate where dissent is silenced and free speech is jeopardized." Thor Halvorssen, whose company supported the production of this documentary, stated that, "Universities have become a hostile environment for anyone interested in open discussions and critical thinking."

David Horowitz,[27] perhaps more than anyone else, has studied the extent to which our colleges and universities have become Marxist indoctrination centers. He has written several revealing books on this topic, including, *Indoctrination U.* Choosing a book title very similar to that of the above documentary film shows that Horowitz, like Maloney, has concluded that our colleges and universities have, indeed, become centers of indoctrination rather than centers of learning. In order to promote diversity of thought Horowitz created the "Academic Bill of Rights" which has been passed by student governments across the USA.

David Horowitz points out that, "In a democracy, the purpose of an education is to teach students how to think, not what to think..." Unfortunately, in classrooms today students are taught what to think, and are discouraged from learning how to think. An excerpt from Chapter Four of *Indoctrination U* provided by enounterbooks.com entices the reader with the following disturbing information: "An advanced stage of this intellectual corruption is manifest in courses and even entire departments that are devoted to indoctrination in sectarian dogmas. To take one at random, a course in 'Modern Marxist Theory,' taught by Martha Gimenez at the University of Colorado and listed in the university catalogue as Sociology 5055, describes its curriculum in this way: 'This seminar is designed to give students the ability to apply Marx's theoretical and methodological insights to the study of current topics of theoretical and political importance.' In other words, this is a course in how to be a Marxist. It is not - by its own description - an academic examination of Marxism that might also consider how Marxism has failed or why it might not provide 'insights' into current topics of importance."

David Horowitz discussed with Glenn Beck[28] his book titled, *One-Party Classroom: How Radical Professors at America's Top Colleges Indoctrinate Students and Undermine Our Democracy.* Horowitz explained that, based on his sampling of colleges and universities across the USA, he estimates that there are between 10,000 to 30,000 courses that teach students to "hate America." Students are taught that America is a racist, sexist, bigoted, homophobic country. (In other words, America is portrayed in standard

Marxist terms: as a nation composed of various proletariat groups that are oppressed by heterosexual white male bourgeoisie.) Furthermore, informed students who disagree with their Marxist professors are punished rather than challenged to engage in an intellectual discussion - as one would expect in an institution of higher learning!

In addition to fighting against classroom indoctrination with his "Academic Bill of Rights" for students, David Horowitz has created another interesting approach. Given that colleges and universities solicit financial donations on a regular basis from their alumni, Horowitz asks concerned citizens to help him notify alumni of the sad state of affairs at the institutions from which they graduated. Many alumni are unaware of the anti-intellectual corruption taking place at colleges and universities that are receiving their generous, out-of-pocket donations.

To hit corrupt colleges and universities where it hurts the most - in their pocketbooks - David Horowitz asks concerned citizens to donate to The David Horowitz Freedom Center. With these donations he sends copies of his book, *One-Party Classroom,* to various alumni across the country. Once alerted to the extent to which their alma mater has been corrupted, they are encouraged to demand American-style intellectual freedom before making future contributions. Horowitz points out that colleges and universities receive millions of dollars each year through private contributions; therefore, grassroots activism of this sort could have an attention-getting, attitude-changing, and behavior-altering effect.

Destruction Equals Progress

To build a Soviet America "The capitalist State must be broken down and the Workers' State built from the ground up on entirely different principles, and this was done in the USSR." - William Z. Foster, National Chairman of the Communist Party, USA, *Toward Soviet America,* 1932[29]

Keep in mind that the massive increases in murder, rape, and robbery in the USA are considered signs of "progress" by the builders of Soviet America. Massive increases in crime-creating one-parent families, abortion, and sexually transmitted diseases are also seen as encouraging signs that William Z. Foster's nihilistic Cultural Revolution has been an astounding success. By replacing phonics with the "look-say" method of teaching reading, by installing outcome-based education, by removing prayer, the Bible, and the Ten Commandments, and by employing psychological brainwashing techniques such as "values clarification," moral collapse and cultural destruction was assured - as envisioned by William Z. Foster.

Regardless of their emotion-laden denials, if Soviet Americans did not want to accomplish these destructive goals they would not have worked so hard to achieve them! They would have reversed course back in the 1950s, 1960s, or 1970s when the destructiveness of their policies became more evident with each passing decade. They would have reversed course in 1983 with the publication of *A Nation at Risk,*[30] a highly publicized study which concluded that, "If an unfriendly foreign power had attempted to impose on America the mediocre educational performance that exists today, we might well have viewed it as an act of war."

Sadly, too few people recognized in 1983 that the damage inflicted on our educational system was, indeed, an act of war. Even today most Americans fail to recognize that the classroom is a battleground in a culture war being waged by Soviet Americans who have imposed a foreign ideology upon America's school children. Most Americans fail to recognize the stated Communist goals of William Z. Foster and the documented Communist goals of former FBI agent W. Cleon Skousen.

Most Americans fail to recognize that the damage inflicted upon our educational system was well planned and well executed by hostile, destructive culture warriors (cold warriors) who are deceptively imposing a foreign ideology upon the American people in order to incrementally enslave them. Instead of reversing course in light of numerous revelations of devastating educational decline, the "Long March Toward Soviet America" continued, and it continues to this day.

As reading and math scores began to drop, and as school violence began to increase, the Soviet Americans who deliberately inflicted this damage told bourgeoisie taxpayers they must have more money to prevent further erosion. Year after year they use the same Hegelian dialectic: "thesis + antithesis = synthesis," or, as applied by Marxists: "problem + incorrect solution = greater problem." In "progressive" education this formula translates as follows: Sabotage education to create problems, pretend that more money is the solution, then use the money to incrementally build massive Soviet-style bureaucracies and front groups to worsen existing problems and to create new problems.

For example, sabotage reading by replacing phonics with the "look-say" method. When reading scores drop, complain that more money is needed for education. When more money is confiscated from useful idiot taxpayers and gullible parents, use it to finance "values clarification" classes that teach children there is no such thing as "right or wrong." When school violence increases as a result of this training, complain that more money is needed for education. When more money is confiscated from useful idiot taxpayers and gullible parents, use it to finance sex education classes. When teen pregnancy and sexually transmitted diseases increase among students as a result of this training, complain that more money is needed for education. Repeat until the "bourgeois" American value system collapses and a Soviet American system has been built upon the rubble. Don't laugh! They have successfully used this formula year after year for more than 50 years.

And how do they get away with it? By blaming all the damage on the "anti-education" people who try to stop or defund them. By blaming the "racist, sexist, bigoted, homophobes" who are "standing in the way of progress" - progress as defined by William Z. Foster! And by blaming "capitalism" and the "bourgeois" value system that kept crime and disease at astonishingly low levels prior to the nihilist, Marxist, Cultural Revolution of the 1960s.

There really is only one true solution: The total separation of school and state - and a return to private, American-style, parent-controlled education at all levels! The huge body count inside and outside abortion clinics tell us that, beyond all doubt, Soviet Americans have been winning the culture war (Cold War) on American soil for many decades, and complete victory is within their grasp! Yes, we must de-Sovietize the education establishment from top to bottom!

Rescuing Children & Young Adults From Soviet Inspired Re-Education Camps

"Get control of the schools. Use them as transmission belts for socialism and current Communist propaganda. Soften the curriculum. Get control of teachers' associations. Put the party line in textbooks." - Former FBI agent W. Cleon Skousen, Communist goal #17, *The Naked Communist,* 1962[31]

Do you agree with the following perspective put forth by Jeff Jacoby[32] in his article titled, Big Brother at School? "In a society founded on political and economic liberty, government schools have no place. Free men and women do not entrust to the state the molding of their children's minds and character. As we wouldn't trust the state to feed our kids, or to clothe them, or to get them to bed on time, neither should we trust the state to teach them."

There are many organizations working to de-Sovietize the system and restore American-style education. A few helpful organizations are provided below. The reader is encouraged to search the web for further resources:

1) **Alliance for the Separation of School and State**
   1071 N. Fulton Street, Fresno, California 93728
   Phone: 1-559-499-1776
   http://www.schoolandstate.org/home.htm

The leaders of this organization, like President Ronald Reagan, understand that government is not the solution to our problem, but rather government is the problem! They believe, and rightly so, that parents, not government, should control the education of their children. They report that eight million children across the nation are now being educated without the corrupting influence of government propagandists - and the number keeps growing!

2) **The David Horowitz Freedom Center**
   14148 Magnolia Blvd, #103,
   Sherman Oaks, California 91423
   http://www.HorowitzFreedomCenter.org

At this web site it is stated that the Mission of the David Horowitz Freedom Center is to defend America's free society through educating the public to preserve traditional constitutional values of individual freedom, the rule of law, private property, and limited government.

3) **Students For Academic Freedom**
   http://www.studentsforacademicfreedom.org

The subheading at their web site reads, "You can't get a good education if they're only telling you half the story." At this site college students can report, for example, if they have been given an unfair grade, subjected to one-sided lectures, given "stacked reading lists," or subjected to other forms of academic abuse. This site provides a lot of useful information!

4) There are numerous resources available to parents and students who would like to learn about home schooling. A few popular web sites are:

http://www.homeschool.com/   http://www.home-school.com/
http://www.homeschools.org/   http://www.hslda.org/

5) Lastly, below are several important organizations working to improve education.

http://www.eagleforum.org/links/   http://www.edaction.org/
http://www.stmarksacademy.net/   http://www.edwatch.org/

Welcome to Soviet America, where educational courses are carefully designed to reprogram students to become members of a poorly educated, morally challenged, Marxist-indoctrinated electorate that will vote repeatedly for morally challenged, Marxist politicians.

Good-bye Educated America!

Good-bye Moral America!

Good-bye Free America!

------†††------

"Liberty cannot be established without morality, nor morality without faith."
- Alexis de Tocqueville[33]

Chapter Six

The Gospel According To
Mao, Marx, Lenin & Stalin!

"We hate Christians and Christianity. Even the best of them must be considered our worst enemies. Christian love is an obstacle to the development of the revolution. Down with love of one's neighbor! What we want is hate... Only then can we conquer the universe." - Anatoly V. Lunarcharsky, Russian Commissar of Education[1]

Pre-Soviet American Culture

In early America the family, church, and local community made up the fabric of our social welfare system. When an individual needed assistance of any kind, the family was there to provide it. If the family needed help they turned to their local church. If the church needed assistance, the families and small business owners that made up the community pulled together to help. Consequently, individuals, families, and communities were essentially self-sustaining. If an individual was sick or unemployed, he was expected to do everything possible to get back on his feet because the longer he was out of work, the greater the burden he placed on his family, church, and community.

Welfare was personal, private, and conditional. Except for the elderly and the infirm, welfare was continued under the condition that recipients would do everything under their power to once again become productive. This system encouraged independence and interdependence, but discouraged dependence. There were few loafers and few criminals. The family, church, and community simply did not tolerate it. With this traditional "bourgeois" moral value system families remained intact because it brought emotional, spiritual, and material support to each member. Families and businesses were willing to contribute to their local churches and other community-based service organizations because they provided critical services that were seldom misused.

The above system represents the traditional early American model of community life. It is the model that served America well from the early 1600s to the early 1900s. Under this traditional model Americans lived in relatively safe cities and towns. Yes, there was crime, but it was generally limited. Criminals tended to prey upon other criminals, and less so upon innocent citizens. At night people often slept with open windows and unlocked doors. Most people had limited personal possessions, but few people felt poor. They had their dignity, their family, their friends, their church, and their community.

With industrialization and the growth of large cities, families, churches, and local community centers continued to play a central role in the lives of the residents. But in large cities there are many strangers, and the number of strangers increased as people traveled from city to city in search of work. But in spite of this great expansion and influx of strangers, the traditional American value system remained essentially intact. Still, there was relatively little street crime, even during the Great Depression that began in 1929!

The Sovietization Of Christianity!

"We will find our greatest success to the extent that we inculcate Marxism as a kind of religion: Religious men and women are easy to convert and win, and so will easily accept our thinking if we wrap it up in a kind of religious terminology." - Vladimir Lenin, first Communist dictator of the Soviet Union[2]

Question: How do Marxist dialecticians convert a Christian nation into a Communist nation?

Answer: By contaminating the Christian Gospel with a Communist message, and by placing a Christian mask over a Communist face.

Slowly and incrementally, the socialist model of social welfare replaced the traditional American model described above. In brief, government replaced the family, church, and local community. "Charity" was no longer voluntary and no longer private. No longer did individuals, families, and churches decide who needed help, what type of help was needed, nor for how long. Instead, socialist politicians, in their long march toward Soviet America, now decided who must contribute, how much they must contribute, to whom they must contribute, and for how long they must contribute. Sovereign America was slowly mutating into Soviet America! This was accomplished with little resistance as the Christian Gospel of Matthew, Mark, Luke, and John was surreptitiously replaced with the Social Gospel of Mao, Marx, Lenin, and Stalin.

As history has demonstrated, Communists are atheists who suppress religious expression by banning Bibles, removing religious symbols, and forbidding prayer. (Sound familiar?) After seizing power they close, confiscate, and loot churches and synagogues, and they ruthlessly execute religious leaders and their devout followers. (In Communist-controlled nations it is much safer to worship the State, its top leaders, its designated heroes, and its failed programs.) In spite of the well-documented, bloody, anti-religious bigotry of Communists, many active and passive followers of Communist dogma claim to be God-fearing Christians and Jews. Many are religious leaders, including priests, ministers, and rabbis.

But how can God-fearing Christians and Jews follow the Communist dogma of God-denying, religion-hating atheists? Are these Christians and Jews really closet atheists and scam artists who mask their atheism and criminal intent with religiosity in order to fleece the public? Could they be Communist moles that have infiltrated our churches and synagogues in order to subvert them from within? Are they timid Christians and Jews who have surrendered biblical truth to social and cultural pressure, fearing financial loss while cowering under the shadow of an increasingly tyrannical government? Or are they "moderates" who put one foot on each side of the culture war, tiptoeing back and forth, waiting to see who wins before choosing sides? Perhaps each of these questions could be answered in the affirmative.

There is, however, an additional alternative: Perhaps many are religious Christians and Jews who have been indoctrinated into thinking like Marxist-Leninists - and don't know it? How else do we explain the millions of liberal Christians and Jews who interpret the Bible as if it was written by Mao, Marx, Lenin, and Stalin? When confronted with ethical or moral problems, some Christians search their conscience and ask, "What would Jesus do?" But when religious liberals and progressives are confronted with ethical or moral problems, their solutions suggest they have asked themselves very different questions, such as, "What would Mao do? What would Marx do? What would Lenin do? What would Stalin do?" And after deciding what course of action these religion-hating atheists would take, they tell us, "This is what Jesus would do!"

How do we explain the fact that their solutions always seem to be eerily consistent with Communist dogma as outlined in *The Communist Manifesto*, the Soviet Constitution, and Communist books such as *Toward Soviet America*? How else can we answer the question, Why do liberal Christians and Jews work like religious fanatics to install in America the 45 "Current

Communist Goals" outlined in *The Naked Communist*? Why are they so comfortable installing the planks of *The Communist Manifesto* within the USA? Why do they ferociously attack anyone who questions their religious-like zeal for Karl Marx's "heavy progressive or graduated income tax," and label tax cuts as "Tax breaks for the rich?" Why can they not think outside the hammer and sickle when searching for solutions to any of our national problems?

There is no escape from the conclusion that liberal Christians and Jews think more like Vladimir Lenin than George Washington. Many think like Communists because they have been socially programmed or "re-educated" to do so. From the 1800s educational and media outlets have been saturating the minds of Americans with Soviet-style solutions to nearly every conceivable problem facing our nation - whether real or imagined; whether contrived or genuine. Over time Christians have been sufficiently programmed to ignore or reject the Gospel according to Mathew, Mark, Luke, and John and embrace the Gospel according to Mao, Marx, Lenin, and Stalin. But how did this re-education occur? Why did so many people stop thinking like Christian Americans and start thinking like Soviet Americans?

Question: Former FBI agent W. Cleon Skousen conducted a thorough study of Communist activities in the USA. He placed the results of his study in his classic book titled, *The Naked Communist*. In this book Skousen listed 45 goals that he labeled "Current Communist Goals." Current Communist goal number 27 was:

A. Elect Bolshevik Democrats to public office
   (like Jesse Jackson & Michael Moore).
B. Elect Menshevik Republicans to public office
   (like Arnold Schwarzenegger & Colin Powell).
C. Elect Bolshevik Libertarians to public office
   (like Bill Maher & Geraldo Rivera).
D. Infiltrate the churches and replace revealed religion with "social"
   religion. Discredit the Bible and emphasize the need for intellectual
   maturity which does not need a "religious crutch."

Answer: D. Current Communist goal number 27: Infiltrate the churches and replace revealed religion with "social" religion. Discredit the Bible and emphasize the need for intellectual maturity which does not need a "religious crutch."

Question: How was Communist goal number 27 achieved?

Answer: Through the social gospel movement and liberation theology!

Social Gospel:
Tricking Protestants Into Building A Soviet America!

"A young man or woman cannot be a Communist youth unless he or she is free of religious convictions." - Vladimir Lenin, first Communist dictator of the Soviet Union[3]

Harvard College, later renamed Harvard University, was founded in 1636 by Massachusetts Puritans. Harvard was named after its first benefactor, John Harvard of Charlestown, a Protestant Christian minister who left his personal library and half his estate to this new institution. Known as North America's first institution of higher learning, many of Harvard's early graduates became Puritan ministers. A 1643 brochure stated the purpose of Harvard University was, among other things, to avoid leaving "an illiterate Ministry to these Churches."[4]

Yale, the third oldest institution of higher learning in North America, was founded in 1701 by ten Protestant Congregational ministers. Named after Elihu Yale, a generous merchant benefactor, Yale was founded to create an institution "wherein Youth may be instructed in the Arts and Sciences [and] through the blessings of Almighty God may be fitted for Publick employment both in Church and Civil State."[5]

Thomas E. Brewton[6] points out that even before the Russian Revolution of 1917, a revolution was occurring at Harvard, Yale, and other colleges and universities across the USA. Most notably, the social sciences were slowly losing their Christian framework in favor of an atheistic, materialistic framework. Biblical principles were being subtly replaced with socialist principles, even at Christian theological seminaries. For example, Walter Rauschenbusch, a Rochester Theological Seminary professor, was one of the founders of the social gospel movement back in the 1800s. And, as Brewton points out, social gospel may be characterized as "socialism masquerading as Christianity." Moreover, much of what the early social gospel practitioners sought, such as the abolition of child labor, a shorter workweek, and government regulation of factories, was accomplished through labor unions and the New Deal of socialist President FDR. Thomas E. Brewton provides an excellent summary of social gospel at his web site (See note number six under Chapter Six notes). He also exposes Communist faculty and Soviet spies who taught at or graduated from Harvard University.

During this educational revolution Harvard, Yale, and most colleges and universities in the USA were pushed off their biblical foundations and landed on Marxist soil. Subsequently, these early Christian pillars have become unabashed transmission belts for atheistic Marxism. As Brewton has noted, "Veritas," the Latin word for truth, is found on the Harvard coat of arms, and "Lux et Veritas," meaning light and truth, is displayed at Yale. However, for more than a century both of these institutions "have used the word truth in the same sense and to the same ends as the Soviets employed it in their propaganda journal 'Pravda,' (a Russian word meaning truth.)"[7]

Liberation Theology: Duping Catholics Into Building A Soviet America!

"The struggle against the Gospel and Christian legend must be conducted ruthlessly and with all the means at the disposal of Communism." - Official statement, Radio Leningrad, 27 August 1950[8]

While leftist Protestants adopted the social gospel movement prior to the Russian Revolution of 1917, their Catholic counterparts were much slower in creating their Marxist version of Christianity; consequently, the world had to wait until the 1960s before "liberation theology" was introduced in South America. (During this same time period another Marxist revolution, often characterized as the counter-culture movement, was metastasizing across North America.) Like their Protestant cousins, through liberation theology leftists Catholics transformed the Christian Gospels into Marxist Gospels. Consequently, instead of helping the needy through local, private, voluntary, community-based services, demands were made for an increasingly powerful, centralized, Soviet-style government to provide social services.

Under liberation theology, the needy were displaced by the greedy and the seedy. There were few parasites in the traditional American welfare system because welfare was personal, private, and conditional. Exploitation simply was not tolerated. However, the Left reversed that value system. For example, the leftist National Welfare Rights Organization (which gave birth to ACORN) organized millions of single minority women and instructed them to become recipient's of taxpayer-funded welfare. The goal was not to help the women, but to overwhelm and collapse the system. So, the welfare recipients were exploited and the taxpayers were robbed of millions of dollars by these "compassionate liberals."

According to the City-Journal.org,[9] "From 1965 to 1974, the number of single-parent households on welfare soared from 4.3 million to 10.8 million, despite mostly flush economic times. By the early 1970s, one person was on the welfare rolls in New York City for every two working in the city's private economy." The end result was a massive, semi-permanent, non-working underclass that remains plagued with massive illegitimacy, drug abuse, crime, poverty, and dependency upon government and taxpayer - all reassuring signs of Soviet-style "progress."

The size, scope, and number of needy proletariat groups grew like tumors, and the justification for Soviet-style bureaucracies grew in equal proportion to the wealth transferred from the productive bourgeoisie to the ever-demanding "poor" proletariat. Concern for spiritual justice dispensed by God in the next world was replaced with "social justice" to be dispensed by government in this world. Consequently, over time a nation filled with Bible-based Christians worshiping God gave way to Marxist-based pseudo-Christians worshiping government.

More than 2000 years ago the scribes and Pharisees (the ancestors of today's liberals) tried to trick Jesus into choosing between God and government. Jesus wisely said, "Render therefore to Cesar [who represented government] the things that are Cesar's, and to God the things that are God's." (Matthew 22:21.) Today, through the social gospel movement and liberation theology liberals have succeeded in tricking tens of millions of Christians into believing that Jesus really meant to say, "The only way to render unto God is to render all unto government. Give your money not to the poor, but to government so Soviet-style bureaucracies can be created to redistribute wealth to the poor. Give your money not to the sick, but to government so that a massive, corrupt, Soviet-style health care system can be created that will make everyone poor."

So, while leftists have been demanding that conservatives respect their beloved Soviet constitutional principle of "separation of church and state," they have been surreptitiously transforming the church into a Soviet-like appendage of the state. However, those who are knowledgeable of both biblical principles and Marxist principles recognize the striking difference between the two.

Joseph Cardinal Ratzinger:
Liberation Theology Is Marxist!

"The philosophy of Marxism-Leninism - the theoretical foundation of the Communist Party - is incompatible with religion." - Official Statement, "Young Bolshevik," 1946[10]

Joseph Cardinal Ratzinger,[11] before he became Pope Benedict XVI, wrote a brilliant expose on liberation theology wherein he found it appropriate to use descriptive words such as "Marxist" and "Marxism" a total of 17 times on just nine pages. According to Cardinal Ratzinger, "An analysis of the phenomenon of liberation theology reveals that it constitutes a fundamental threat to the faith of the Church." The reader is invited to examine Cardinal Ratzinger's expose for himself or herself. But after reviewing his work one may conclude the following: Liberation theology is a fundamental threat to the Church for several reasons, including the fact that it embraces the Marxist dialectic of the class struggle, or more specifically, class warfare!

For example, instead of helping the poor directly, or encouraging the middle class and the rich to help the poor, the poor are pitted against the other classes. The poor are portrayed as inherently good victims and the more prosperous are portrayed as intrinsically evil exploiters. Moreover, the practitioner of liberation theology joins the "poor proletariat" in their Marxist-style class struggle against the "affluent bourgeoisie." This, of course, is classic Marxism, not Bible-based Christianity! Through this Marxist-style class warfare, Marxist dialecticians transform the Command-ment, "You shall not covet they neighbor's house...nor anything that is your neighbor's" into a new Commandment that says, "You shall covet your neighbor's house...and everything that is your neighbor's." Likewise, the Commandments "You shall not steal" and "You shall not bear false witness against your neighbor" are transformed into the Commandments "You shall steal" and "You shall bear false witness against your neighbor - because your bourgeois neighbor is exploiting you and therefore you deserve to exploit him."

Although Cardinal Ratzinger did not use this terminology, from his written work one may reach the following conclusion: In Bible-based Christian theology, as opposed to Marxist-based liberation theology, Christian leaders are to administer to the spiritual needs of each person as a unique individual, whether rich or poor, and not assign individuals to Marxist-inspired groups and pit one group against the other. For the liberation theologian, the problems and solutions are not spiritual, but instead the problems are material and the solutions are political! Consequently, the poor are transformed into a Marxist-style proletariat group and exploited by the liberation theologian to expand government control over the people in order to administer political solutions to material problems. Again, this is textbook Marxism!

Moreover, those who criticize the fabrication of this Marxist-style class struggle are smeared as "insensitive to the needs of the poor." Those who oppose the reprogramming of school children to accept homosexual behavior because it contradicts their Bible-based belief system are portrayed as "homophobic" and not as sincere devotees to biblical principles. Those who preach against gay marriage on biblical grounds are guilty of "hate speech." Consequently, "hate crimes" legislation is enacted to further erode the First Amendment rights of Bible-believing citizens under the pretext of protecting the rights of the homosexual proletariat.

In addition, those who oppose the creation of the illegal alien proletariat are, of course, portrayed as "xenophobic." Whites who question the preaching of black liberation theology are portrayed as "racists," while black critics are given the derogatory label of "Uncle Toms." To ensure victory over the bourgeoisie through class warfare, powerful cultural, political, and legal pressure is employed to clear the path for the construction and maintenance of a whole army of Marxist-style proletariat groups that are ushering in a seemingly unstoppable Soviet American political machine.

Black Liberation Theology:
Deceiving Blacks Into Building A Soviet America!

"The fight against religion must not be limited nor reduced to abstract, ideological preaching. This struggle must be linked up with concrete practical class movement." - Vladimir Lenin, first Communist dictator of the Soviet Union[12]

While the social gospel movement has been associated with Protestantism and liberation theology associated with Catholicism, many Protestant denominations proudly embrace liberation theology. Take, for example, the black liberation theology of the Reverend Jeremiah Wright, who served as Barack Obama's pastor for nearly 20 years. On *Hannity's America*, Sean Hannity interviewed the Reverend Eugene Rivers of the Azusa Christian Community in Boston. They discussed the black liberation theology espoused by Pastor Jeremiah Wright and other practitioners. According to the Reverend Eugene Rivers, black liberation theology is "...left-wing social science masquerading as theology." The Reverend Rivers further noted that, "This is warmed over, defunct Marxist structuralism applied to certain theological categories."

Barack Obama learned well from his black liberation theology mentors, such as the Reverend Jeremiah Wright who yelled from his pulpit, "God damn America!" For example, a few months after the election of Barack Obama to the presidency of the United States, Stanislav Mishin[13] wrote in the English version of *Pravda* that, "It must be said, that like the breaking of a great dam, the American descent into Marxism is happening with breath taking speed, against the back drop of a passive, hapless sheeple, excuse me dear reader, I meant people."

In his article titled, "American capitalism gone with a whimper," Mishin further stated that, Marxists had prepared America incrementally for about a century, and especially in the last two decades. He described Russia as the "initial testing ground" for Marxism. Consistent with what has been written in Chapter One, Mishin acknowledged that it was a "bloody test." He added that the Russian people did not surrender their freedoms and their souls without a fight, "no matter how much money Wall Street poured into the fists of the Marxists."

"Those lessons were taken and used to properly prepare the American populace for the surrender of their freedoms and souls, to the whims of their elites and betters." Stanislav Mishin added that, "Then their faith in God was destroyed, until their churches, all tens of thousands of different 'branches and denominations' were for the most part little more than Sunday circuses..." According to this Russian writer, "The final collapse [of American capitalism into Marxism] has come with the election of Barack Obama. His speed in the past three months has been truly impressive."

A little more than four months after Barack Obama became president, Jonah Goldberg,[14] author and editor-at-large of *National Review Online,* wrote the following: "The government effectively owns General Motors and controls Chrysler, and the president is deciding what kind of cars they can make." He added that the federal government now "owns majority stakes in American International Group, Fannie Mae, Freddie Mac and controls large chunks of the banking industry." Goldberg also noted that the Obama Administration "wants government to take over the business of student loans" (which it did) and is also "pushing for [and getting] nationalized health care." In addition, "the Environmental Protection Agency has ruled that it reserves the right to regulate any economic activity that has a 'carbon footprint.'"

Goldberg noted further that, "Just last week, House Speaker Nancy Pelosi said climate change requires that 'every aspect of our lives must be subjected to an inventory.' Rep. Barney Frank, chair of the House Financial Services Committee, has his eye on regulating executive pay." Goldberg also reminded the reader that during the campaign Obama said he wanted to "spread the wealth," and that is precisely what he is doing as president. But Jonah Goldberg, who authored the book *Liberal Fascism*, noted that the above unconstitutional government intrusions into the private sector are not descriptive of socialism, but rather they are suggestive of "Corporatism - the economic doctrine of fascism!"

Black Liberation Theology: The Black Proletariat Versus The White Bourgeoisie!

"It is impossible to conquer an enemy without having learned to hate him with all the might of one's soul." - Joseph Stalin, second Communist dictator of the Soviet Union[15]

James Cone,[16] a black liberation theology scholar and professor at New York's Union Theological Seminary, wrote the following regarding black liberation theology:

"Black theology refuses to accept a God who is not identified totally with the goals of the black community. If God is not for us and against white people, then he is a murderer, and we had better kill him. The task of black theology is to kill gods who do not belong to the black community." And, "...Black theology will accept only the love of God which participates in the destruction of the white enemy. What we need is the divine love as expressed in Black Power, which is the power of black people to destroy their oppressors here and now by any means at their disposal. Unless God is participating in this holy activity, we must reject his love."

Cone's statements that God must be for black people and "against white people," and God must participate "in the destruction of the white enemy," are clearly consistent with the Marxist-style class warfare mentality found in liberation theology. Such statements are certainly incompatible with the biblical concept of brotherly love. While liberation theology in general focuses on pitting the poor proletariat against the more prosperous bourgeoisie, black liberation theology pits the black proletariat against the white bourgeoisie. (Perhaps black liberation theology scholars are needed at the Union Theological Seminary in New York in order to achieve diversity. After all, only through diversity can administrators counter-balance all the white theology scholars at that university who teach that God must be for white people and "against black people," and God must participate "in the destruction of the black enemy.")

WorldNetDaily.com[17] noted that, in contradiction to Bible-based Christianity, in the black liberation theology espoused by James Cone, the black community does not serve God, but rather God is to serve the black community, and if God does not work to meet the material needs of the black community both here and now, then God is to be rejected. Clearly, when Christian Gospels are transmuted into Marxist Gospels in this fashion, concern for spiritual justice dispensed by God in the next world is replaced with "social justice" to be dispensed through "Black Power" in this world.

Yes, liberation theology, like social gospel, is Marxism disguised as Christianity. Fundamental to the practitioners of these heretical movements is the notion that spiritual justice administered by God must be replaced with "social justice" administered by government and its proxies. When examining the effectiveness of social gospel and liberation theology in facilitating the transformation of Sovereign America into Soviet America, one truly realizes that Sovereign Americans have underestimated the destructive potential of the dedicated, well-trained, Marxist dialecticians in our midst!

Welcome to Soviet America!

Good-bye Christian America!

------†††------

"You cannot bring about prosperity by discouraging thrift. You cannot help small men by tearing down big men. You cannot strengthen the weak by weakening the strong. You cannot lift the wage-earner by pulling down the wage-payer. You cannot help the poor man by destroying the rich. You cannot keep out of trouble by spending more than your income. You cannot further the brotherhood of man by inciting class hatred. You cannot establish security on borrowed money. You cannot build character and courage by taking away men's initiative and independence. You cannot help men permanently by doing for them what they could and should do for themselves." - The Reverend William J. H. Boetcker, Presbyterian clergymen, 1916[18]

Chapter Seven

Church, State & Religious Liberty
In Soviet America!

"The frustrating thing is that those who are attacking religion claim they are doing it in the name of tolerance. Question: Isn't the real truth that they are intolerant of religion?" - President Ronald Reagan

In 1962 the U.S. Supreme Court ruled in the case of *Engle v. Vitale* that prayer in America's public schools was unconstitutional when directed by a state government. In 1963, in *Abington v. Schempp*, the U.S. Supreme Court ruled that it was unconstitutional for the state to sponsor Bible reading or the praying of the Lord's Prayer in public schools. This decision was rendered in contradiction to the fact that both the U.S. Senate and the U.S. House of Representatives open each session with prayer. With the Ten Commandments boldly engraved on the walls of the public U.S. Supreme Court building, in 1980 the U.S. Supreme Court ruled in *Stone v. Graham* that it was unconstitutional for the Ten Commandments to be posted in a public school classroom. With this decision the Court removed from our schools the Commandments, "Honor your father and your mother; You shall not steal; You shall not bear false witness against your neighbor;" and "You shall not murder." (Exodus 20:3-17.)

In 1992 the U.S. Supreme Court ruled in *Lee v. Weisman* that it was unconstitutional for the state to sponsor prayer at school promotional activities and graduation ceremonies. In 2000 the U.S. Supreme Court ruled in *Santa Fe Independent School District v. Doe* that student-led, student-initiated prayer before a football game was unconstitutional. William Rehnquist, Antonin Scalia, and Clarence Thomas, the three dissenting justices in this ruling, wrote that the majority opinion rendered by the other six justices "bristles with hostility to all things religious in public life." (If you read Chapters 1 and 5 you should easily answer the below question.)

Question: Collectively, in the above five cases the U.S. Supreme Court ruled that prayer, Bibles, and the Ten Commandments must be banned from government schools because such cases represented violations of the constitutional principle of "separation of church and state." The phrase "the church is separated from the state" is found in which document?

A. Mayflower Compact.
B. Declaration of Independence.
C. U.S. Constitution.
D. Soviet Constitution.

Answer: D. Soviet Constitution.

The Soviet Constitutional Principle Of Separation Of Church & State

What Is Article Fifty-Two?

"Separation of church and state" cannot be found anywhere in the U.S. Constitution, nor in the Declaration of Independence, nor in the Mayflower Compact; however, Article 52 of the 1977 Soviet Constitution[1] stated the following: "Citizens of the USSR are guaranteed freedom of conscience, that is, the right to profess or not to profess any religion, and to conduct religious worship or atheistic propaganda. Incitement of hostility or hatred on religious grounds is prohibited. In the USSR, the church is separated from the state, and the school from the church." Similar Articles were placed in previous Soviet Constitutions as well!

What Is The First Amendment?

In contrast to Article 52 of the Soviet Constitution, the First Amendment to the U.S. Constitution states the following: "Congress shall make no law respecting an establishment of religion, or prohibiting the free exercise thereof; or abridging the freedom of speech or of the press; or the right of the people peaceably to assemble, and to petition the government for a redress of grievances."

As shown above, the "Establishment Clause" of the First Amendment to the U.S. Constitution clearly states that, "Congress shall make no law respecting an establishment of religion." It further states that Congress shall make no law "prohibiting the free exercise thereof." Nowhere in the U.S. Constitution do we find the words "separation of church and state," nor do we find a principle upon which the fabrication of such a phrase could be justified. What is clearly stated is that the federal government may not establish a religion, and it may not prohibit Americans from freely engaging in religious activities - such as praying, Bible reading, or posting of the Ten Command-ments.

A careful reading of the U.S. Constitution reveals that it places restrictions on the U.S. Government, but places no restrictions on "We the People." In order to transplant the Soviet constitutional principle of "separation of church and state" and construe it in the U.S. Constitution, the "justices" on the U.S. Supreme Court had to ignore or distort both the wording of the U.S. Constitution and the Founder's original intent. In each of the above five decisions outlined in the above paragraphs, the U.S. Supreme Court violated the following clearly stated constitutional principle: Congress, and thus the federal government, shall not prohibit the free exercise of religion - anywhere at any time. No exceptions are listed. In addition, the federal government may pass no law "abridging the freedom of speech." From an American perspective, voluntary, spoken prayer, as traditionally said at school graduations, football games, and in public school classrooms, would most certainly be deemed the type of "free speech" which the federal government may not abridge.

The U.S. Constitution was drafted in 1787, and the Bill of Rights was added in 1791. But in each of the above decisions the U.S. Supreme Court concluded that, from 1791 to 1962, everyone, including those who authored the First Amendment, did not understand the meaning of the words in the First Amendment. We are to believe that for 171 years the First Amendment was misunderstood, and that the Court finally corrected the mistaken interpretations of George Washington, James Madison, Alexander Hamilton, Benjamin Franklin, and the other 35 signatories to the U.S. Constitution. Many of the framers of the U.S. Constitution engaged in prayer on govern-ment property - a practice that continues to this day in the U.S. Senate and U.S. House of Representatives.

Ignoring the wording of the First Amendment, the original intent, and the recorded words and actions of the framers of the U.S. Constitution, the U.S. Supreme Court came to the preposterous conclusion that the Christians who drafted the First Amendment intended to establish a "wall of separation" to keep religion out of government. What kind of mind would conclude that America's Christian Founders, who believed government could not succeed without biblical principles, would keep biblical principles out of the govern-ment they just created? Read just a few quotes from some of our Founding Fathers and ask yourself, did they believe that prayer, the Bible, and the Ten Commandments had no place in government?

1. "Our Constitution was made for a moral and religious people. It is wholly inadequate for the government of any other." - **John Adams**, second President of the United States of America.

2. "God who gave us life gave us liberty. Can the liberties of a nation be secure when we have removed a conviction that these liberties are a gift of God? I tremble for my country when I reflect that God is just, and that His justice cannot sleep forever." - **Thomas Jefferson**, third President of the United States of America.

3. "We have staked the whole future of American civilization, not upon the power of government, far from it. We have staked the future of all our political institutions…upon the capacity of each and all of us to govern ourselves, to control ourselves, to sustain ourselves according to the Ten Commandments of God." - **James Madison**, fourth President of the United States of America, "Father of the U.S. Constitution," and author of the First Amendment!

4. "Lastly, our ancestors established their system of government on morality and religious sentiment. Moral habits, they believed, cannot safely be trusted on any other foundation than religious principle, nor any government be secure which is not supported by moral habits." - **Daniel Webster**, U.S. Senator and U.S. Representative.

The Jeffersonian Principle
Versus The Soviet Principle!

In establishing the doctrine of "separation of church and state" the U.S. Supreme Court made reference to a letter written by Thomas Jefferson in 1802. In this letter, written to a group of Baptists and Congregationalists in Danbury, Connecticut, Jefferson was responding to searing criticisms launched against him, including charges that he was an atheist, and even an infidel. Jefferson, as a newly elected president, was essentially telling them to back off, stating that there should be "a wall of separation between church and state." Jefferson was therefore telling them they could not use their religious standing as a basis for criticism of a political figure, given that church and state are separate institutions. Of course, as American citizens they could criticize Jefferson and other political figures; however, as religious leaders they could not impose church doctrine or their religious standards upon a political figure.

Moreover, those who conveniently misconstrue Jefferson's "wall of separation" should take note of his 1805 Second Inaugural Address[2] wherein he stated that, "In matters of religion I have considered that its free exercise is placed by the Constitution independent of the powers of the General [federal] Government. I have therefore undertaken on no occasion to prescribe the religious exercises suited to it, but have left them, as the Constitution found them, under the direction and discipline of the church or state authorities acknowledged by the several religious societies."

John W. Whitehead[3] has noted that this Address by Jefferson clearly shows that his "wall of separation between church and state" was, also, a wall of separation around the church to protect it from any infringements by the federal government. Note that Jefferson stated the federal government had no authority over "religious exercises" (such as praying, Bible reading, or displaying the Ten Commandments); however, individual state governments (many of which had established churches during Jefferson's lifetime) could exercise "direction and discipline" over religious expression as "acknowledged by the several religious societies."

Jefferson's understanding of "separation of church and state" was thus consistent with that of the other Founders who feared the federal government may follow in the footsteps of the British Government and establish a national religion or national church, perhaps something akin to the Church of England. The Establishment Clause prevents this from occurring. Most importantly, Jefferson's Second Inaugural Address is consistent with statements of James Madison,[4] the author of the First Amendment who said, "There is not a shadow of right in the General [federal] Government to intermeddle with religion...This subject is, for the honor of America, perfectly free and unshackled. The government has no jurisdiction over it."

From the words plainly written in the First Amendment, together with the words of Jefferson and Madison, it is abundantly clear that we the people are free to engage in religious activities anywhere, whether on private property or public property, and the federal government may not prohibit such activities. The imposition of the Soviet constitutional principle of "separation of church and state" upon the American people is a clear violation of the First Amendment to the U.S. Constitution.

While Jefferson's "wall of separation between church and state" protected religious expression from federal interference, the U.S. Supreme Court twisted the meaning of Jefferson's words and presented them from the Soviet perspective. Consequently, as in the Soviet Union, citizens of Soviet

America could no longer pray, read Bibles, or post the Ten Commandments on government property. And of course, in the Soviet Union all property was government property. Given the ongoing destruction of private property rights in the USA, when the construction of Soviet America has been completed, all property will eventually become federally owned or federally regulated property in this country as well.

It must also be noted that, in his superb 1982 book, *The Second American Revolution*, John W. Whitehead reported that Thomas Jefferson not only founded the University of Virginia, but he also encouraged students to meet, pray, and worship together on campus. Jefferson further encouraged students to meet and pray on campus with their professors. Whitehead also noted that Jefferson authored the first plan of public education, which was adopted by the city of Washington. In this public educational plan for the city of Washington, Thomas Jefferson recommended the employment of the Bible and the Isaac Watts Hymnal as teaching aides to help students learn how to read.

In light of Jefferson's encouragement of students to pray on the public University of Virginia campus - even with their professors, and his educational plan that included the use of the Bible (which contains the Ten Commandments) to teach reading in public schools, how could any honest, rational person conclude that Thomas Jefferson believed in a "wall of separation" that prohibited prayer, Bible reading, and the posting of the Ten Commandments in public schools or on any government property? How could anyone conclude that the federal government could prohibit the free exercise of religion in this manner when the U.S. Constitution states, in plain English, that the federal government may not prohibit the free exercise of religion?

> "Destroy a nation's morality,
> and it will fall in your lap like ripe fruit from a tree."
> - Vladimir Lenin, first Communist dictator of the Soviet Union[5]

By deceitfully removing from government schools the Bible and the Ten Commandments - along with their prohibitions against murder, stealing, and lying; by replacing those prohibitions with the nihilistic program of "values clarification" which tells our students there is no such thing as "right and wrong;" by flooding our children's senses with media violence and pornography; by creating an abortion industry that communicates the message that it is OK to choose death for innocent children; by discouraging mothers from careers as full-time, child-guiding homemakers; by removing fathers from the home via no-fault divorce; and by creating fatherless, gang-spawning families with federal welfare programs; the builders of Soviet America have succeeded in weakening our ability "to govern ourselves, to control ourselves, to sustain ourselves according to the Ten Commandments of God," as envisioned by James Madison and the other Founding Fathers.

Weakening our ability in this fashion, of course, paves the way for an ever-expanding, micro-managing, Soviet-style dictatorship that can be rationalized on the grounds that someone must govern us, control us, and sustain us - now that we can no longer govern, control, and sustain ourselves! Of course, such a diabolical plan could only be fabricated and implemented by sociopaths who possess "a lust for power over others."

Can Taxpayers Exercise Their Constitutionally-Protected Right To Freedom Of Religious Expression On Taxpayer-Funded Property? In Sovereign America, Yes! In Soviet America, No!

When reviewing the above Court decisions regarding the Establishment Clause of the First Amendment to the U.S. Constitution, consider the following: Forbidding students, or anyone else, from praying, reading the Bible, or posting the Ten Commandments on government property simply does not pass any test of common sense - from an American perspective. Firstly, it means a taxpayer cannot pray on taxpayer-funded property. This could only make sense to those who view religious liberty from the perspective of Karl Marx, Vladimir Lenin, Joseph Stalin, and Nikita Khrushchev, but not from the perspective of George Washington, John Adams, Thomas Jefferson, and James Madison. This could only make sense to those who are guided by principles found in the Soviet Constitution - and could never make sense to individuals inspired by the principles found in the U.S. Constitution!

Secondly, to say that a student praying on government property violates the Establishment Clause is to say that the student is a federal official attempting to establish a national religion or a national church. But the praying student is not a government official, and may not even be a member of any religion or a member of any church. To assert that a private, taxpaying citizen engaging in voluntary prayer on taxpayer-funded property somehow violates a constitutional restriction that was placed on federal officials is clearly symptomatic of dishonest or irrational thought processes. As stated in the U.S. Constitution for anyone to read, the student is someone who possesses a right to religious expression that cannot be prohibited by Congress, and therefore cannot be prohibited by the President, the U.S. Supreme Court, or any other federal officials.

Keep in mind that, as stated earlier, even today U.S. Senators and U.S. Representatives pray on government property every time they begin a session, and the U.S. Supreme Court building has the Ten Commandments boldly posted for all to see. In rendering the above five decisions, the majority members of the U.S. Supreme Court have demonstrated well beyond a reasonable doubt that they are dishonest, ignorant, or delusional. Employing the Soviet constitutional principle of "separation of church and state" in order to prohibit the free exercise of religion anywhere in the USA is a clear violation of a U.S. constitutional principle that has been enshrined by the words, "Congress shall make no law respecting an establishment of religion, or prohibiting the free exercise thereof." (If you read and can recall the material in Chapter Five, you should have no problem answering the below question.)

Question: As stated earlier, in 1962 the U.S. Supreme Court banned prayer in state-run public schools, stating that it violated the constitutional principle of "separation of church and state." Later the U.S. Supreme Court also banned Bibles and the Ten Commandments from public schools. However, in his classic book, *The Naked Communist,* former FBI agent W. Cleon Skousen warned Americans that Communists operating within the USA planned to:

A. Sell copies of *The Communist Manifesto* in public schools.
B. Elect Bolshevik Libertarians to public school boards.
C. Replace crosses with hammers and sickles in all Catholic schools.
D. Eliminate prayer or any phase of religious expression in the schools on the ground that it violates the principle of "separation of church and state."

Answer: D. In 1962, the same year the U.S. Supreme Court banned prayer in public schools on the ground that it violated the constitutional principle of "separation of church and state," former FBI agent W. Cleon Skousen warned Americans that Communists had established the goal to "Eliminate prayer or any phase of religious expression [such as Bible reading or the posting of the Ten Commandments] in the schools on the ground that it violates the principle of 'separation of church and state.'" In the 1962 edition of his book Skousen listed this as goal number 28 under the posting of his 45 "Current Communist Goals." Sadly, most of the 45 Communist goals listed by this former FBI agent have either been accomplished or are well on their way toward accomplishment. Welcome to Soviet America!

So, whenever you hear anyone, such as a judge, attorney, politician, educator, religious leader, civil rights leader, reporter, journalist, pundit, etc., supporting the banning of prayer, Bibles, the Ten Commandments, or other forms of religious expression from public schools or any government property because such activity violates the principle of "separation of church and state," remind yourself - and them - that they are pushing a principle found in the Soviet Constitution, but not in the U.S. Constitution. Remind yourself - and them - that they are supporting the implementation of a principle that was, and remains, a cherished goal of Communist operatives who are successfully building their Soviet America through the ruthless and relentless application of deception - backed by government force!

Question: In an ongoing attempt to warn the American people of the 45 Communist goals listed by W. Cleon Skousen, including the Soviet roots of the principle of "separation of church and state," the following news and information sources have routinely publicized the above information in an attempt to thwart the construction of a Soviet America:

A. *The New York Times, Los Angeles Times, Washington Post,* et al.
B. ABC, CBS, NBC, CNN, MSNBC.
C. *Time, Newsweek.*
D. All of the above.
E. None of the above.

Answer: E. None of the above. Welcome to Soviet America!

Question: Bolshevik Democrat Bill Clinton nominated Ruth Bader Ginsburg to the U.S. Supreme Court in 1993. Her nomination was approved 96 to 3 by the U.S. Senate. As a member of the U.S. Supreme Court she has consistently supported the Soviet constitutional principle of "separation of church and state." Before Ruth Bader Ginsberg joined the Court, she served as a volunteer lawyer, Board member, and General Counsel to:

A. Center for Soviet American Progress (CSAP).
B. People for the Soviet American Way (PSAW).
C. American Civil Liberties Union (ACLU).
D. Soviet American Civil Liberties Union (SACLU).
E. Soviet Americans United for Separation of Church & State (SAUSCS).

Answer: C. American Civil Liberties Union (ACLU).

Question: The American Civil Liberties Union was founded by:

A. Thomas Jefferson, 3rd President of the USA.
B. Roger Nash Baldwin, a Communist.
C. Abraham Lincoln, 16th President of the USA.
D. Ronald Reagan, 40th President of the USA.
E. None of the above.

Answer: B. The ACLU was founded by Roger Nash Baldwin, a self-pro-claimed supporter of Communism who said, "I have continued directing the unpopular fight for the rights of agitation, as director of the American Civil Liberties Union. I seek the social ownership of property, the abolition of the propertied class and sole control of those who produce wealth. Communism is the goal."

Baldwin visited the Soviet Union several times, and in 1927 he wrote *Liberty under the Soviets*, wherein he praised the USSR. When Joseph Stalin signed a non-aggression pact with Adolf Hitler in 1939, Baldwin denounced this act and expelled Communists from the ACLU. Among those expelled were Elizabeth Gurley Flynn, a founding member of the ACLU and the first woman to serve as Chairperson of the Communist Party, USA (CPUSA). William Z. Foster, a National Chairman of the CPUSA and author of *Toward Soviet America*, was also expelled from the ACLU by Baldwin. (Do you believe Baldwin, who stated Communism was his goal, was sincere or employing a deceptive, psychological warfare tactic when he expelled Communists from the ACLU after they helped found the ACLU?) After Baldwin retired from the ACLU he maintained an office in the United Nations - an organization enthusiastically endorsed by Communists in both Soviet America and in the Soviet Union! Baldwin died in 1981.[6]

One thing is certain, from its inception the ACLU has remained true to its Communist roots, even after Baldwin expelled known Communists. As Devvy Kidd[7] has written, the ACLU has been aggressively implementing the Communist agenda. According to Kidd, "For the past few decades, the ACLU has been on a major crusade to destroy Christianity in America," and to also "promote filth under 'freedom of speech and expression.'" From among the 45 Communist goals placed into the Congressional Record in 1963 by Representative Albert Herlong, Jr., Devvy Kidd stated that the ACLU has worked tirelessly to pursue the following dirty dozen Communist goals "in their quest to destroy America's culture and traditions:"

Goal #16: Use technical decisions of the courts to weaken basic American institutions, by claiming their activities violate civil rights.

Goal #17: Get control of the schools. Use them as transmission belts for socialism and current Communist propaganda. Soften the curriculum. Get control of teachers' associations. Put the party line in textbooks.

Goal #22: Continue discrediting American culture by degrading all form of artistic expression. An American Communist cell was told to "eliminate all good sculpture from parks and buildings," substituting shapeless, awkward and meaningless forms.

Goal #23: Control art critics and directors of art museums. "Our plan is to promote ugliness, repulsive, meaningless art." [Such as a Crucifix stuffed into a jar of liberal urine?]

Goal #24: Eliminate all laws governing obscenity by calling them "censorship" and a violation of free speech and free press.

Goal #25: Break down cultural standards of morality by promoting pornography and obscenity in books, magazines, motion pictures, radio and television.

Goal #26: Present homo-sexuality, degeneracy and promiscuity as "normal, natural and healthy."

Goal #27: Infiltrate the churches and replace revealed religion with "social" religion. Discredit the Bible and emphasize the need for intellectual maturity, which does not need a "religious crutch."

Goal #28: Eliminate prayer or any phase of religious expression in the schools on the grounds that it violates the principle of "separation of church and state."

Goal #31: Belittle all forms of American culture and discourage the teaching of American history on the ground that it was only a minor part of "the big picture." Give more emphasis to Russian history since the Communists took over.

Goal #32: Support any socialist movement to give centralized control over any part of the culture - education, social agencies, welfare programs, mental health clinics, etc. [Including health care, of course.]

Goal #40: Discredit the family as an institution. Encourage promiscuity and easy divorce.

Question: How can the U.S. Supreme Court employ "transnationalism" and substitute the Soviet constitutional principle of "separation of church and state" for the U.S. constitutional principle of religious liberty?

Answer: While Sovereign America is a Constitutional Republic, Soviet America is a dictatorship. Therefore, as in the Soviet Union, Soviet American dictators are not restricted by national laws, including the supreme law of the land. (Solution: The lawless must be rendered powerless.)

Question: Given the historical fact that the Soviet Union collapsed in 1991 and the Soviet Constitution is no longer operative, why must Americans continue to have their religious liberty restricted by the Soviet constitutional principle of "separation of church and state?"

Answer: Because, although the Soviet Union has disintegrated, Soviet America is flourishing; consequently, Soviet constitutional principles will remain operative within the USSA until the American version of the "Evil Empire" also collapses.

There's Only One American-Style Solution: De-Sovietization!

If government and religious liberty cannot co-exist on taxpayer-funded property, we should terminate government ownership and control of that property instead of terminating traditional, American-style religious liberty!

If we must live under Article 52 of the Soviet Constitution, and thereby abide by its principle of "separation of church and state," then why must we also follow the example set by the Soviet Union's dictators and remove church from the state? Instead, let's return to our American roots. Let's return to the basic American principles that call for respect for individual liberty and its corresponding limited, non-intrusive government. Yes, let's remove the state from the church instead of the church from the state! Let's return God, the Bible, prayer, and the Ten Commandments to our schools and remove intrusive, repressive, government. Just as Lenin nationalized private schools in order to Sovietize education within the USSR, let's privatize all government schools in order to de-Sovietize education throughout the USSA! All public schools belong to us anyway. We paid for them with our tax dollars!

And, just as the ACLU and other Soviet-style organizations now monitor our schools to make sure church does not intrude upon the state, we could have an American version of the ACLU monitor the schools to make sure the state does not intrude into our schools! (Organizations such as the American Center for Law and Justice, or ACLJ, come to mind!) Indeed, the principle of "separation of church and state," when viewed from an American perspective (when viewed from a truly Jeffersonian perspective) would be very liberating to all freedom-loving Americans! Education has been in steady decline in the USA since the government took "the church" out of the state. By de-Sovietizing education, we could also reverse the embarrassingly low achievement levels of the students now trapped in government-run schools.

Demand this American-style solution from all federal, state, county, and city politicians. Demand that this proposed solution be addressed by all newspaper and magazine editors, radio talk show hosts, TV talking heads, and educators.

Recap Of Previous Material

Article 52 of the Soviet Constitution stated that, "the church is separated from the state and the school from the church." Therefore, in the Soviet Union prayer, the Bible, and the Ten Commandments were forbidden on government property; and, of course, all property was government property in the USSR. By contrast, the U.S. Constitution states the federal government shall not establish a religion, and shall not prohibit the free exercise of religion. In other words, the U.S. Constitution states that the federal government shall not prohibit prayer, Bible reading, or displays of the Ten Commandments - anywhere at any time. No exceptions are enumerated nor implied.

However, Thomas Jefferson wrote in a private letter that there should be, "a wall of separation between church and state." Because Thomas Jefferson encouraged students to pray in government schools, encouraged students to pray with their professors in government schools, and he encouraged the use of the Bible (which contains the Ten Commandments) to teach reading in government schools, it is obvious that Jefferson's "separation of church and state" did not prohibit such behavior. Madison stated, for example, that the American people are "perfectly free and unshackled" with respect to religion and that "the government has no jurisdiction over it." These and other statements demonstrate beyond all doubt that both Jefferson and

Madison correctly understood the U.S. Constitution prohibited the federal government from restricting religious expression among the American people.

Thus, when government officials, including those sitting on the U.S. Supreme Court, forbid such behavior, they can only do so from the Soviet constitutional principle of "separation of church and state" and not Jefferson's personally expressed principle of "separation of church and state." Such behavior does not violate any expressed or implied principle within the U.S. Constitution. When members of the U.S. Supreme Court adopted the Soviet constitutional principle of "separation of church and state" and fraudulently applied it the U.S. Constitution, they fulfilled Communist goal number 28, as documented by W. Cleon Skousen in his book, *The Naked Communist:* "Eliminate prayer or any phase of religious expression in the schools on the ground that it violates the principle of 'separation of church and state.'" Clearly, we cannot stamp "Made in America" on "separation of church and state." It was manufactured in the Soviet Union and surreptitiously imported into the USA by those who are building their Soviet America. It's time for the de-Sovietization process to begin!

A Few Helpful Resources

1. **Alliance for the Separation of School and State**.
(See Chapter Five, page 76, for details.)

2. **Freedom of Education.Net**.
(www.freedomofeducation.net/separation-of-school-and-state.shtml.)

This organization offers numerous enriching articles supporting the notion that, in a free country, freedom of education is as basic as freedom of speech and freedom of religion. Freedomofeducation.net drives home this point with the following quote of John Holt: "A person's freedom of learning is part of his freedom of thought, even more basic than his freedom of speech." Freedomofeducation.net provides enlightening answers to such questions as: Why separate schools from the state?

"Hate Crimes" Legislation: Prosecuting (Persecuting) Christians For Bible-Based Speech!

"Present homo-sexuality, degeneracy and promiscuity as 'normal, natural, healthy.'" - Former FBI agent W. Cleon Skousen, Communist goal #26, *The Naked Communist,* 1962[8]

"...the dictatorship of the proletariat will produce a whole series of restrictions of liberty in the case of the oppressors, exploiters and capitalists." - William Z. Foster, National Chairman of the Communist Party, USA, quoting Vladimir Lenin[9]

"We hate Christians and Christianity. Even the best of them must be considered our worst enemies. Christian love is an obstacle to the development of the revolution. Down with love of one's neighbor! What we want is hate...Only then can we conquer the universe." - Anatoly V. Lunarcharsky, Russian Commissar of Education[10]

Could a 75-year-old grandmother be jailed for the "crime" of displaying or reciting Bible-based messages while on public property? No! This could never happen in America! But it can happen, and it did happen, in Soviet America. In Philadelphia, Pennsylvania eleven Christians were arrested and jailed for singing and preaching in a public park at a homosexual street festival - in violation of Pennsylvania's "hate crimes" law. Several of these Christians were grandmothers. One was 75 years old.[11] Five were charged with five felonies and three misdemeanors which added up to 47 years in jail.[12] After several months a judge dismissed the charges - perhaps due to extreme public pressure over such repressive government behavior - the type one would expect to find in the Soviet Union.

You know you are living in Soviet America when promoting principles found in the *Holy Bible* will land a grandmother in the jail house, but advocating principles found in *The Communist Manifesto* will put a <u>community organizer</u> in the White House! In light of this observation, consider the following words of FBI Director J. Edgar Hoover in 1970:[13] "The Communist Party conducts training schools...for new members, advanced members, cadres, teachers, trade-union members, Negroes, youth, Party leaders, et cetera. The object, of course, is to make better <u>Communist organizers</u>, agitators, and propagandists out of Party members." (Underline added.)

Alas, in New York a pastor had a Bible verse placed on a billboard. City officials had it removed citing "hate crime" rhetoric. In San Francisco pro-family groups were denied their First Amendment right to advertise in the local media because they offered homosexuals an opportunity for change[14] - but not the kind of change Barack Obama spoke about in his presidential campaign. In New Mexico a couple faced thousands of dollars in fines because they refused to provide photographic services to a lesbian couple on the basis that such a union violated their deeply held religious beliefs.[15]

Just as the builders of Soviet America are forcing a Soviet-style health care system on the American people - similar to the systems adopted in Canada, France, and the United Kingdom, they are also forcing Soviet-style anti-free speech laws upon Bible-believing Americans, similar to the laws passed in Canada, France, and the United Kingdom. For example, a newspaper publisher in Canada and another man who placed an ad both faced jail time and were fined $4,500. What was their crime? The newspaper ad contained several Bible verses addressing homosexuality.[16] According to Bob Unruh of WorldNetDaily.com, "In the United Kingdom... a pastor was detained for 'homophobia' for reading from the biblical book of Romans, a Christian campaigner was arrested for handing out tracts and a Roman Catholic archbishop was investigated for criticizing homosexual partnerships."[17]

Bob Unruh[18] also noted that Peter LaBarbera of Americans for Truth reported that legislators in both Canada and France were fined for publicly criticizing homosexuality. Pastor Ake Green of Sweden was jailed for a month for preaching "that homosexuality is a sin." A British couple was told they could not adopt a child because "their Christian faith might 'prejudice' them against a homosexual child..." Clearly, Janet Folger, President of Faith2Action, was correct when she described "hate crimes" legislation as "hate free speech" legislation.[19] Indeed, it may also be characterized as "hate Bible-based speech" legislation.

Those who express their Bible-based beliefs regarding homosexuality are not only intimidated, fined, arrested, and jailed, some are threatened with death! Before his death (by natural causes) D. James Kennedy of Coral Ridge Ministries had stated in a letter that, "I have received seething hate mail and horrible threats of death and other violence in the past, and will probably continue to do so as long as I preach God's truth about homosexuality."

In addition, radio talk show host Dr. Laura Schlessinger had made plans to expand to television. However, the "speech police" were successful in intimidating Proctor & Gamble and others into dropping their support for the television show. A Bible-believing Jew, Dr. Laura Schlessinger had been labeled "homophobic," "hateful," and "intolerant" because of her Bible-based beliefs regarding homosexuality. One protester outside Paramount held a sign that read, "Dead bigots can't hate." According to D. James Kennedy, "The FBI had concluded that the security threat against Dr. Laura is real, and Kraig T. Kitchen, CEO of Premier Radio Network, which owns Dr. Laura's show, says, 'We have a legitimate fear for her life.'"

Who needs protection from whom? Who is full of hate, the people who believe the words found in the Bible, or those who threaten to kill people because they believe the words contained in the Bible? Obviously President Ronald Reagan was correct when he said, "The frustrating thing is that those who are attacking religion claim they are doing it in the name of tolerance. Question: Isn't the real truth that they are intolerant of religion?"

In presenting homosexuality as "normal, natural, healthy," the builders of Soviet America have employed a tactic they use quite often: they project their own hatred onto their Bible-believing Christian and Jewish prey. They manifest their hated by charging Christians and Jews with "hate speech" when they simply recite or display certain passages from the Bible.

Yes, the builders of Soviet America hate everything America and Americans stand for, and Christians of all ages are learning that Foster's "restrictions of liberty" imposed by the "dictatorship of the proletariat" does not stop with the removal of nativity scenes, the banning of Christian symbols, or the prohibition against saying "Merry Christmas" during the Christmas season. It does not stop with banning Bibles, prayer, and the Ten Commandments from government-run schools and other taxpayer-funded property. That's just the beginning!

Christians are also learning that homosexuals, atheists, and others have been fashioned into a Marxist-style "dictatorship of the proletariat" so they can "produce a whole series of restrictions of liberty" which clearly violate the free speech rights and religious liberty of Bible-believing Christians and Jews - as protected by the First Amendment to the U.S. Constitution. Moreover, laws that provide special rights or protections for any group clearly violate the Fourteenth Amendment that guarantees equal protection under the law to all Americans - whether gay, straight, black, white, male, female, Christian, or anti-Christian!

And of course, everyone possessing a rudimentary understanding of the U.S. Constitution knows beyond all doubt that federal "hate crime" laws are a violation of the Tenth Amendment. Nowhere in the U.S. Constitution has the federal government been delegated the authority to punish American citizens for what they think, say, or feel about other people. Such Orwellian "thought crime" laws could never be passed in Benjamin Franklin's Constitutional Republic, but they could easily be adopted in William Z. Foster's People's Republic!

Welcome to Soviet America!

Good-bye Free-Speech America!

Chapter Eight

Self-Defense & The Second Amendment In Soviet America!

"At the outset the Bolsheviks took measures to destroy everything that made the Cossacks a separate group: their land was confiscated and redistributed among Russian colonizers or local peasants who did not have Cossack status; they were ordered, on pain of death, to surrender all their arms (historically, as the traditional frontier soldiers of the Russian empire, all Cossacks had a right to bear arms); and all Cossack administrative assemblies were immediately dissolved." - Nicolas Werth, *The Black Book of Communism: Crimes, Terror, Repression,* 1999[1]

"In view of the experiences of the civil war against the Cossacks, we must recognize as the only politically correct measure massive terror and a merciless fight against the rich Cossacks, who must be exterminated and physically disposed of, down to the last man." - Bolshevik Party Central Committee, 24 January 1919[2] (Underline added.)

What Is The Second Amendment?

"A well regulated militia being necessary to the security of a free state, the right of the people to keep and bear arms shall not be infringed." - Second Amendment to the U.S. Constitution

What Is The Purpose Of The Second Amendment?

"When a strong man, fully armed, guards his own palace, his goods are in peace." - *Holy Bible,* Luke 11:21

The purpose of the Second Amendment to the U.S. Constitution is to publically acknowledge and legally protect the natural, inalienable right of the people to possess, carry, and use the firearms they deem necessary to defend themselves, their families, and their freedom against criminals in both the public and private sectors. Furthermore, it may be said that the purpose of the Second Amendment is to prevent political predators who possess "a lust for power over others" from fabricating laws that would disarm the American people and render them incapable of defending their lives, preserving their liberty, protecting their property, and safeguarding their prosperity.

Gun Freedom:
A Prerequisite For American-Style Liberty!

"Criminals don't fear the law, but they do fear armed citizens." - Wayne LaPierre, *Guns, Crime, & Freedom,* 1994[3]

Consider the following statement by U.S. Representative Henry A. Waxman,[4] a Bolshevik Democrat from California: "If someone is so fearful that, that they're going to start using their weapons to protect their rights, makes me very nervous that these people have these weapons at all!" But there should be no reason for Representative Waxman to feel nervous about the American people "using their weapons to protect their rights" - unless he believes that he and his comrades are enacting unconstitutional laws that are violating their rights. Keep in mind that this is precisely why our Founding Fathers placed the right to keep and bear arms in the Bill of Rights, so politicians like U.S. Representative Henry A. Waxman would feel nervous about threatening our rights. Our Founders made this abundantly clear, as can be seen in the following five statements:

1. "As civil rulers, not having their duty to the people duly before them, may attempt to tyrannize...might pervert their power to the injury of their fellow citizens, the people are confirmed by the article in their right to keep and bear their private arms." - **Tench Coxe**, Pennsylvania Federalist.

2. "Guard with jealous attention the public liberty. Suspect anyone who approaches that jewel. Unfortunately, nothing will preserve it but down-right force. Whenever you give up that force, you are ruined." And, "The great object is that every man be armed...everyone who is able may have a gun." - **Patrick Henry**, First Continental Congress.

3. "What country can preserve its liberties if their rulers are not warned from time to time that their people preserve the spirit of resistance? Let them take arms!" - **Thomas Jefferson**, primary author of the Declaration of Independence, and third President of the United States of America.

4. "To preserve liberty it is essential that the whole body of the people always possess arms and be taught alike, especially when young, how to use them." - **Richard Henry Lee**, Signatory, Declaration of Independence.

5. "Before a standing army can rule, the people must be disarmed; as they are in almost every kingdom of Europe. The supreme power in America cannot enforce unjust laws by the sword, because the whole body of the people are armed..." - **Noah Webster**, author of several colonial textbooks, including the first American dictionary.

The above five quotes represent just a few of the numerous statements generated by our Founding Fathers wherein they conveyed the need for an armed citizenry to prevent predatory politicians from robbing the people of their natural, God-given rights. Among those rights are the right to life, liberty, and property - all of which are under constant threat by those who are building their Soviet America.

Let's explore the issue of gun control in some detail. We'll start by reviewing four quotes from the builders of the Soviet Union, Soviet China, and Nazi Germany. Then we'll compare them to quotes from four of the Founding Fathers of Sovereign America.

Gun Control:
A Product Of The Communist & Nazi Mind!

If You Think Gun Control Is A Good Idea,
Meet Four People Who Think Just Like You Do!

1. "...one of the basic conditions for the victory of socialism is the arming of the workers [proletariat] and the disarming of the bourgeoisie [middle class]." - **Vladimir Lenin**, first Communist dictator of the Soviet Union who disarmed, starved, imprisoned, tortured, and murdered millions of defenseless men, women, and children.

2. "If the opposition [to Communism] disarms, well and good. If it refuses to disarm, we shall disarm it ourselves." - **Joseph Stalin**, second Communist dictator of the Soviet Union who disarmed, starved, imprisoned, tortured, and murdered tens of millions of defenseless men, women, and children.

Collectively, Vladimir Lenin, Joseph Stalin, Nikita Khrushchev and their comrades murdered 61,911,000 defenseless men, women, and children. That's almost double the 33,100,000 people living in Canada in 2010. None of these victims were casualties of foreign war. Instead, they were casualties of the armed domestic culture war waged by officials of the Soviet government against their own disarmed people!

3. "Political power grows out of the barrel of a gun." - **Mao Zedong**, first Communist dictator of Soviet China who disarmed, imprisoned, tortured, and murdered tens of millions of defenseless men, women, and children. The body count of Mao Zedong and his comrades is a mind-boggling 76,702,000. That's more than twice the population of Canada in 2010. Again, these are domestic casualties of the Soviet Chinese culture war, and not casualties of troops fighting foreign wars or repelling foreign invaders.

The unfathomable body counts generated in the Soviet Union and Soviet China demonstrate what happens when "ordinary citizens" are disarmed and subsequently "protected" against counter-revolutionaries by a Soviet-style Department of Homeland Security! When the Patrick Henrys in the Soviet Union and Soviet China declared, "Give me liberty or give me death," the gun control serial killers who should have been in prison instead of government, were more than eager to give them death!

4. "The most foolish mistake we could possibly make would be to permit the conquered Eastern peoples to have arms. History teaches that all conquerors who have allowed their subject races to carry arms have prepared their own downfall by doing so." - **Adolf Hitler**, first and only fascist dictator of Nazi Germany who disarmed, imprisoned, tortured, and murdered millions of defenseless men, women, and children. Adolf Hitler (whose nickname was "Wolf," an animal that is a true predator) is responsible for systematically exterminating 20,946,000 men, women, and children - none of whom died in combat or on the battlefield.

Gun Freedom:
A Product Of The Sovereign American Mind!

If You Think Gun Freedom Is A Good Idea,
Meet Four People Who Think Just Like You Do!

1. "...the right of the citizens to bear arms in defense of themselves and the State, and to assemble peaceably together...shall not be questioned." - **George Washington**, first President of the United States of America, and "Father of our nation!"

2. "Arms in the hands of citizens [may] be used at individual discretion...in private self-defense..." - **John Adams**, second President of the United States of America, and contributing author to the Declaration of Independence.

3. "No free man shall ever be debarred the use of arms." And, "The strongest reason for the people to retain the right to keep and bear arms is, as a last resort, to protect themselves against tyranny in Government." - **Thomas Jefferson**, third President of the United States of America, and primary author of the Declaration of Independence.

4. "Besides the advantage of being armed, which the Americans posses over the people of almost every other nation...forms a barrier against the enterprises of ambition." - **James Madison**, fourth President of the United States of America, and "Father of the U.S. Constitution."

Whenever a politician, government agent, political activist, journalist, reporter, radio talk show host, TV talk show host, educator, celebrity, author, or anyone else presents you with a position for or against gun control, check the above quotes. A quick check will tell you whether that person agrees with Lenin, Stalin, Mao, and Hitler, or whether that person agrees with Washington, Adams, Jefferson, and Madison. In other words, you can determine if that person thinks like a Communist or Nazi (or perhaps a useful idiot), or like a true American who respects the natural right of individuals to defend themselves, their families, and their freedom. (Perhaps you could show the above eight quotes to those who support gun control and ask them to explain why they have sided with Lenin, Stalin, Mao, Hitler, and other homicidal, genocidal dictators!)

We must insist that the current meanings of the words in the U.S. Constitution remain consistent with the historical meanings of the words in the U.S. Constitution - and not those of the Soviet Constitution and not those fabricated in the creative imaginations of judicial "legislators." We must insist that the current meanings of the words in the U.S. Constitution remain consistent with the documented words of George Washington, John Adams, Thomas Jefferson, and James Madison, and not those of Karl Marx, Vladimir Lenin, Joseph Stalin, or Nikita Khrushchev! The U.S. Constitution was written by Americans, not by Soviets!

Gun Control:
A Product Of The Soviet American Mind!

"Whenever standing armies are kept up, and the right of the people to keep and bear arms is, under any colour or pretext whatsoever, prohibited, liberty, if not already annihilated, is on the brink of destruction." - St. George Tucker, Virginia Supreme Court, 1833[5]

George Washington, the "Father of America," clearly stated that, "Guns are America's liberty teeth, we need them every hour!" William Z. Foster, the "Father of Soviet America," also recognized this truism. Foster knew that, to remove America's liberty, conquerors must first extract her liberty teeth! For this reason Foster[6] said, "...the revolt of the workers [proletariat] cannot succeed in the face of the highly-destructive arms possessed by the capitalists [bourgeoisie]." In other words, Foster was informing his fellow travelers that a Soviet America would not be possible as long as their intended victims - the American middle class - remained armed. Hence, the bourgeoisie must be disarmed, and various gun control schemes would be implemented until that goal was achieved. To establish and maintain a Soviet America "the right of the people to keep and bear arms" must be infringed!

For this reason socialist politicians are obsessed with disarming law-abiding, taxpaying citizens through various unconstitutional gun control schemes; however, they have no intention of disarming themselves, their private body guards, or their taxpayer-funded security personnel. Like health care, education, food services, and other important issues in Soviet America today, self-defense is also viewed as two-tiered by socialist politicians. Like all thieves, socialist politicians who rob us of our money, our property, and our freedom, do not want their victims to be armed, but they have few reservations about arming themselves.

As a member of the U.S. House of Representatives, Earl Landgrebe[7] had the opportunity to study the motivation of his fellow politicians and lobbyists up close and personal. After doing so he stated the following back in 1973: "What the liberals fear is privately owned guns - not guns owned by the government. The liberal position on privately owned guns is entirely consistent with the liberal position on all private property; there shouldn't be any; all private property should be controlled, regulated or confiscated by the omnipotent state. The liberals have no objections to guns - only guns they do not control. They are seeking a legal monopoly on guns...in order to eliminate any final opposition to a socialist government. This is the purpose of the gun control lobby - not the reduction of crime, which could be easily achieved by harsher penalties for criminals - but the elimination of citizen opposition to their socialist plans."

In light of the fact that about one in four liberals will admit to owning a gun, Representative Landgrebe was also correct when he said, "The liberals have no objections to guns - only guns they do not control." Because liberals believe that lying is a virtue, the actual number of pro-gun control liberal gun owners may be much higher than one in four.

Gun Control:
A Product Of The Menshevik Republican Mind!

Congressman Landgrebe's statement that liberals push gun control "in order to eliminate any final opposition to a socialist government" is consistent with the above statement of William Z. Foster. But it is also consistent with a statement by Sarah Brady, a Menshevik Republican and fanatical supporter of civilian disarmament through gun control. Sarah Brady, who has been actively involved in organizations such as The Brady Campaign to Prevent Gun Violence and The Brady Center to Prevent Gun Violence, has unequivocally stated that, "Our task of creating a Socialist America can only succeed when those who would resist us have been totally disarmed."[8]

Aaron Zelman,[9] A Dachau Concentration Camp survivor and founder and executive director of Jews for the Preservation of Firearms Ownership (JPFO), wrote the following in the *American Survival Guide*: "These Sarah Brady types must be educated to understand that because we have an armed citizenry, that a dictatorship has not yet happened in America. These anti-gun fools are more dangerous to liberty than street criminals or foreign spies. You cowards - you gun haters - you don't deserve to live in America. Go live in the Soviet Union if you love gun control so damn much."

Recall the above quote of Sarah Brady: "Our task of creating a Socialist America can only succeed when those who would resist us have been totally disarmed." Recall further that William Z. Foster, National Chairman of the Communist Party, USA, wrote in 1932 that a Socialist America was a steppingstone toward the ultimate goal of a Soviet America.[10] Therefore, this statement of Sarah Brady indicates that she does, indeed, understand that a dictatorship has not yet happened in America because the American people are armed - and that is precisely why she wants them disarmed. She stated plainly that she wants a Socialist America, and a Socialist America would require an unconstitutional, dictatorial government. Furthermore, she did not move to the Soviet Union, as Aaron Zelman had suggested in 1990, the year before the USSR collapsed. Instead, it appears Sarah Brady and her socialist comrades want the Soviet Union to move here! By striving to build a Socialist America they are knowingly or unknowingly paving the way for a Soviet America!

Sarah Brady's statement indicates that she fears resistance, perhaps armed, justifiable resistance, from Sovereign Americans who wish to live in the Constitutional Republic created by Washington, Adams, Jefferson, and Madison, and who do not want to live in the Socialist American stepping-stone envisioned by Communist honcho, William Z. Foster. Her statement further suggests that her primary task is to build a Socialist America, and gun control is simply a means to achieve that end. Given that Congressman Earl Landgrebe said liberals "are seeking a legal monopoly on guns...in order to eliminate any final opposition to a socialist government," and Sarah Brady said, "Our task of creating a Socialist America can only succeed when those who would resist us have been totally disarmed," perhaps The Brady Campaign to Prevent Gun Violence should be renamed "The Brady Campaign to Prevent Gun Violence Against the Builders of Socialist America!"

Gun Control:
A Product Of The Bolshevik Democrat Mind!

"Probably all laws are useless; for good men do not need laws at all, and bad men are made no better by them." - Demonax the Cynic[11]

In light of Representative Landgrebe's statement, consider the following double standard exhibited by one arrogant, authoritarian, socialist politician: In violation of the Second Amendment and in violation of his oath of office, Senator Jay Rockefeller, a Bolshevik Democrat from West Virginia, took a leadership role in supporting the 1994 ban on so-called "assault weapons." This ban included such weapons as the Colt AR-15 rifle - which is the civilian version of the M-16 rifle used by the U.S. military. However, while he succeeded in passing legislation that prevented other Americans from possessing this type of weapon, Senator Rockefeller kept an AR-15 rifle in his home. In addition, he admitted that he kept his "assault weapon" at his Washington, D.C. residence. However, when informed that it was against the law to keep such a weapon in your home in the District of Columbia, he changed his mind and said he stored his AR-15 rifle in Virginia.[12] (Do you believe him? Neither do I.)

Senator Rockefeller's desire to be well-armed while working to disarm law-abiding, taxpaying citizens can best be understood in light of his views of the government's relationship to "We the People." When Bolshevik Democrats were trying to force a Soviet-style health care system upon the American people in 1994 under the Clinton Administration, Senator Rockefeller[13] said, "We are going to push through this health care reform regardless of the views of the American people." In other words, Senator Rockefeller wanted to force socialized medicine upon the people even though 85 percent of Americans reported that they were satisfied with the private medical care they were receiving at that time. In light of Senator Rockefeller's effort to deprive Americans of "assault weapons" while pushing socialized medicine upon us against our wishes, we must conclude Representative Earl Land-grebe was correct when he said liberals "are seeking a legal monopoly on guns...in order to eliminate any final opposition to a socialist government."

Let's examine the self-defense double standard of two more politicians who are pushing a Socialist America upon "We the People:"

Firstly, "We're going to hammer guns on the anvil of relentless legislative strategy. We're going to beat guns into submission." - Senator Charles Schumer, a Bolshevik Democrat from New York.[14]

Secondly, "Banning guns addresses a fundamental right of Americans to feel safe." - Senator Diane Feinstein, a Bolshevik Democrat from California.[15]

When Senator Schumer says he wants to "hammer guns" and "beat guns into submission," what he is really saying is that he plans to "hammer" the Second Amendment to the U.S. Constitution and "beat" our natural, inalien-able, God-given right to keep and bear arms "into submission!" Adding a few words to Senator Diane Feinstein's sentence adds enormous clarity and understanding to her true intent: "Banning guns addresses a fundamental right of [Soviet] Americans to feel safe [from Sovereign Americans]."

Consider also the following additional statement by Senator Feinstein[16] after passing a gun ban bill: "If I could have gotten 51 votes in the Senate of the United States for an outright ban, picking up every one of them... 'Mr. and Mrs. America, turn 'em all in,' I would have done it. I could not do that. The votes weren't here."

So, if Senator Feinstein could muster enough votes, she would deprive all taxpaying American citizens of their natural, God-given, constitutionally-protected right to keep and bear arms. She would violate her oath of office and render every American defenseless against violent criminal attack. She would clear the path for a disarmed citizenry to be placed under the rule of a heavily armed, Soviet-style, socialist government.

Senator Feinstein's desire to have Congress enact laws to confiscate the self-defense weapons of the American people is clearly in direct conflict with many recorded statements of America's Founding Fathers. For example, Samuel Adams, a member of the First and Second Continental Congress, stated that, "The Constitution shall never be construed... to authorize Congress to prevent the people of the United States who are peaceable citizens from keeping their own arms." Her statement is also in conflict with that of Thomas Jefferson, primary author of the Declaration of Independence and third President of the United States of America, who said, "The constitutions of most states (and of the United States) assert that all power is inherent in the people; that they may exercise it by themselves; that it is their right and duty to be at all times armed."

Although the above positions of Senators Schumer and Feinstein violate the U.S. Constitution, violate their oaths of office, and show a callous disregard for the personal security and hard-fought liberty of the American people, those statements also reflect an arrogant, tyrannical, "better than thou" attitude. Why? Because both of these socialist politicians have secured concealed carry permits for themselves[17] and are toting the types of personal firearms they wish to deny the rest of us "ordinary citizens." Additionally, they both reside in states where it is extremely difficult for ordinary citizens to obtain concealed carry permits, and they work in the District of Columbia where it is nearly impossible for others to secure such permits. And, they carry personal firearms in spite of the fact that they both are protected by highly trained, well-armed, taxpayer-funded, Capitol police.

Because these and other socialist hypocrites are protected by the Soviet-bloc media, we do not know how many politicians arm themselves while working to disarm the rest of us. However, we may be guided by the following words of Senator Ben Nighthorse Campbell, a Colorado Republican: "You'd be surprised how many senators have guns." In addition, we do know that in attempting to disarm us they are violating the Constitution and they are violating their oaths to support the Constitution. The shameful double standard of Senator Rockefeller, Senator Schumer, Senator Feinstein, and an unknown number of closet hypocrites, demonstrates once again that

Representative Landgrebe was correct when he said, "The liberals have no objections to guns - only guns they do not control."

Gun Control: A Product Of Colluding Public & Private Sector Criminal Minds!

"Laws that forbid the carrying of arms...disarm only those who are neither inclined nor determined to commit crimes...Such laws make things worse for the assaulted and better for the assailants; they serve rather to encourage than to prevent homicides, for an unarmed man may be attacked with greater confidence than an armed man." - Thomas Jefferson, quoting Casare Beccaria, author of *On Crimes and Punishment,* 1764

In the early 1900s armed thugs in the Red Hook district of Brooklyn, New York made their living by robbing docks, warehouses, and passersby. To defend themselves, law-abiding citizens began carrying firearms, and crime started to drop in the area. Fearing injury and loss of income, local liberal gangsters asked New York State Senator, Timothy D. Sullivan, a Bolshevik Democrat, for help.

Agreeing with Casare Beccaria and Thomas Jefferson that gun control laws that forbid the carrying of arms "make things worse for the assaulted and better for the assailants," "Big Tim" Sullivan concluded that passage of a strict gun control law would be the best way to protect his liberal gangster friends from armed, law-abiding citizens. Selling it to the people of New York as a way to "fight crime," in May of 1911 the Sullivan Law was passed in the New York State Legislature. This early gun control law prohibited almost all law-abiding, taxpaying citizens from possessing firearms that may be carried for self-defense. This was achieved by requiring a permit, to be issued by the local police department, in order to own or carry a firearm small enough to be concealed. As in New York today, only the political and economic elite were issued gun permits following the enactment of the Sullivan Law.[18, 19]

As planned, nearly all law-abiding, taxpaying citizens obeyed this criminal-inspired law and disarmed. Consequently, New York's street-level gangsters resumed robbing citizens without fear of armed resistance. Inspired by the "success" of the Sullivan Law, corrupt politicians in the federal government and many city and state governments began to push gun control laws throughout the nation. After following Timothy D. Sullivan's formula for "fighting crime," as expected, crime escalated across the nation, especially in Democrat-controlled cities with the most restrictive gun control laws.

Aided & Abetted By
Soviet-Bloc Media Hypocrites!

Contemporary New York gangsters can thank not only Bolshevik Democrat Timothy D. Sullivan for creating a safe work environment for robbers, burglars, rapists, and murderers, they can also thank the propagandists at *The New York Times*. Consider the following two quotes from this leading Soviet-bloc newspaper:

"The only way to discourage the gun culture is to remove the guns from the hands and shoulders of the people who are not in the law enforcement business." - *The New York Times*, September 24, 1975

"Gun violence won't be cured by one set of laws. It will require years of partial measures that will gradually tighten the requirement for gun owner-ship, and incrementally change expectations about the firepower that should be available to ordinary citizens." - *The New York Times*, December 21, 1993

In light of the above statements in *The New York Times*, take note of the following article: "The problems with gun control," by Charley Reese.[20] According to Reese, the purpose of gun control is not to reduce crime; instead, gun control is a tool of the elite to control what *The New York Times* calls "ordinary citizens." To support his claim, Reese points out that [thanks to the Sullivan Law] ordinary people who are really exposed to violent crime cannot get a permit in New York to carry a concealed handgun for self-defense. However, one person who was granted a permit to carry a concealed weapon was "the publisher of *The New York Times*."

So, like Senators Rockefeller, Schumer, Feinstein, and other elitists, the publisher of *The New York Times* believes his life is worth defending, but the lives of us "ordinary citizens" are not worth defending! While the publisher of *The New York Times* used his newspaper to state that guns should be restricted to those in law enforcement, as an elitist he exempted himself from that restriction. And, while he used his newspaper to advocate the disarming of law-abiding citizens - leaving us defenseless against violent criminal attack - he armed himself with the weapons he wanted to deny us "ordinary citizens."

In addition to the obvious hypocrisy, elitism, and callous disregard for the security of what his newspaper calls "ordinary citizens," there is another disturbing aspect to this anti-Second Amendment stance. The second quote from *The New York Times* is disturbingly consistent with a quote by George Mason. Specifically, in *The New York Times* it was stated that, "It will require years of partial measures that will <u>gradually</u> tighten the requirement for gun ownership, and incrementally change expectations." Two hundred years earlier George Mason, author of the Virginia Bill of Rights, warned that, "[When] the resolution of enslaving America was formed in Great Britain, the British Parliament was advised by an artful man, who was governor of Pennsylvania, to disarm the people; that it was the best and most effectual way to enslave them; but that they should not do it openly, but weaken them, and let them sink <u>gradually</u>." (Underlines added.) As discussed in more detail below, it is clear that 20th and 21st century liberal tyrants are imitating 18th century British tyrants and loyalist tyrants!

The Soviet-Bloc Media:
Disarming & Robbing Americans Of Truth!

In the December, 1993 issue of their newsletter, *Media Watch,* the Media Research Center (MRC) published the results of their analysis of all gun control stories reported from December 1, 1991 to November 30, 1993 on *ABC's World News Tonight,* the *CBS Evening News, CNN World News,* and *NBC Nightly News.*

When analyzing the Brady bill issue, MRC found that for every person who supported gun freedom, these four news outlets presented three persons who supported the Brady bill gun control measure. When reporters quoted persons in the Brady bill gun control debate, they quoted gun control advocates 69 percent of the time, gun freedom advocates 22 percent of the time, and neutral sources 8 percent of the time.

Among gun control stories that did not include the Brady bill issue, MRC found that 59 percent supported gun control, 37 percent were classified as neutral, and a mere 4 percent discussed the issue of gun owner's rights. When news stories covering the Brady bill were analyzed, 69 percent supported this gun control bill, 31 percent were found to be neutral, and none, or Zero percent, could be classified as defending the Second Amend-ment rights of law-abiding citizens to keep and bear arms!

In a second MRC study titled, *Network News Spinning Gun Control Debate,* released on January 5, 2000, Ben Johnson reported that liberals continued their lopsided reporting on the issue of gun control. This study analyzed the morning and evening newscasts of ABC, CBS, CNN, and NBC from July 1, 1997 to June 30, 1999. Of the 653 news stories analyzed, 357 advocated more gun control, 260 were considered neutral, and only 36 supported gun freedom. Thus, overall, the number of news reports supporting gun control outnumbered news reports supporting gun freedom by a ratio of 10 to 1. For evening news programs the ratio dropped to 8 to 1; however, for morning news programs the ratio of pro-gun control reports to pro-gun freedom reports was an astounding 13 to 1.

On December 27, 1994, Phil Donahue discussed the growing militia movement and the Second Amendment with representatives of the Michigan, Ohio, and Montana militias. On his now defunct television program, Phil and company placed the text of the Second Amendment on the television screen for viewers to read. However, the words "of the people" were conveniently missing.[21] This "Sovietized" version of the Second Amendment strengthened the pro-gun control position of Phil and his comrades, whereas an accurate rendering would have supported the pro-gun freedom position of the militias.

With the key words "of the people" conveniently missing from the Second Amendment, most audience members and millions of television viewers were misled to believe that the Second Amendment protects the right of states, but not the right of the people, to keep and bear arms. However, the fact that the right to keep and bear arms was acknowledged as an inalienable individual right can be found in historical documents containing the words of George Washington, John Adams, Thomas Jefferson, James Madison, Tench Coxe, Patrick Henry, Richard Henry Lee, Noah Webster, Samuel Adams, George Mason, Alexander Hamilton, Fisher Ames, and other Founding Fathers, many of whom contributed to the framing of the U.S. Constitution, including the Second Amendment.

In his 1984 book, *That Every Man Be Armed: The Evolution of a Constitutional Right,* Stephen P. Holbrook,[22] a noted attorney and constitutional scholar, wrote the following: "In recent years it has been suggested that the Second Amendment protects the 'collective' right of states to maintain militias, while it does not protect the right of 'the people' to keep and bear arms. If anyone entertained this notion in the period during which the Constitution and Bill of Rights were debated and ratified, it remains one of the most closely guarded secrets of the eighteenth century, for no known writing surviving from the period between 1787 and 1791 states such a thesis." Moreover, in her 1994 book, *To keep and Bear Arms: The Origins of an Anglo-American Right,* Dr. Joyce Lee Malcolm,[23] a professor of political history at Bentley College in Massachusetts, wrote, "The argument that today's National Guardsmen, members of a select militia, would constitute the only persons entitled to keep and bear arms has no historical foundation."

The dishonesty of the media in promoting a view of firearms that encourages people to embrace the "crime fighting" tactics of Timothy D. Sullivan and his liberal gangster friends was summed up in the following words of J. Neil Schulman[24] in his 1994 book, *Stopping Power: Why 70 Million Americans Own Guns:* "A favorite media practice is to focus only on the bad things firearms are used for. If a handgun is used for murder or mayhem, it's headline news. If that same handgun is used by a restaurant patron to stop a takeover robbery, the story is buried."

Robert W. Lee[25] exposed a strikingly irrational perspective penned by *Time* magazine to mold the minds of the American people so they would support civilian disarmament through gun control: "Meanwhile, advocates of gun control continue to blame guns, rather than the humans who wield them irresponsibly, for gun-related deaths. For example, *Time* magazine declared in its July 17, 1989 issue: 'At any one time, the nation harbors a large tribe of those crying and struggling with the loss a gun has caused.' (Will a future *Time* evaluation of education lament the large tribe of students crying and struggling with the misspelled words their pencils have caused?)"

What happens when defenders of the Second Amendment challenge members of the Soviet-bloc media regarding their dangerous and dishonest reporting? Wayne LaPierre[26] answers this question in his 1994 book, *Guns, Crime, and Freedom:* "Dare to challenge a media position, or call them to task for dishonest or unfair practices, and you risk personal attack. Your motives are impugned, your character assaulted, and even your sanity is called into question." LaPierre further wrote of media efforts to block the speech of those who support the constitutionally-protected right of the people to keep and bear arms: "The abuse of the media is not limited to inserting their own personal agendas into their own presentations; they block opportunities for opposing views to be presented and may even refuse to accept paid advertising that takes issue with their worldview...Access to public airways was arbitrarily denied the NRA because our viewpoints differed from those of gun-hating media in Metro Washington."

Recall that the street-level gangsters in the Red Hook district of Brooklyn, New York, sought gun control in order to disarm their victims so they could safely rob them of their wallets, jewelry, and the valuable items found in warehouses and on the docks. Likewise, liberal media gangsters seek gun control in order to disarm their victims so they can safely rob them of the truth. Unfortunately, as we have seen in the Soviet Union, Soviet China, Soviet Cambodia, and Soviet Cuba, robbery of this sort does not stop with the truth. And it does not stop after their victims are disarmed and robbed of their natural right to self-defense. Instead, such robbery is preparatory work that creates a safe work environment for the calculating thieves who will eventually rob their victims of their money, their property, their freedom, their dignity, their humanity, and oftentimes their lives! Knowledgeable Americans can see that this scenario is now unfolding before their very eyes in a country that is now beginning to eerily resemble the nation envisioned by Communist boss William Z. Foster[27] in his 1932 book - *Toward Soviet America!*

A Tale Of Two Nations!

"But if anyone does not provide for his own, and especially for those of his household, he has denied the faith and is worse than an unbeliever." - *Holy Bible,* First Timothy 5:8

In the 1970s terrorists targeted Israeli schools, school buses, and a kindergarten. In 1974 terrorists gunned down 34 Israeli school children in a school bus. Realizing that their school children were virtually defenseless against violent criminal attack, the Israeli government chose the only effective solution possible - they provided an armed defense for their children. Consistent with the traditional American view that the people have a natural, inalienable right to keep and bear arms to defend themselves, their families, and their freedom, Israeli teachers, principals, nurses, parents, grandparents, and other responsible adults were trained and equipped with firearms. After the school children were guarded in this fashion, two attempts by terrorists to infiltrate the schools were thwarted, and the school shootings stopped.

Following the Israeli success in ending terrorist school shootings by arming teachers and other responsible adults, the U.S. Congress did precisely the opposite. Indeed, they passed a law that would ensure American school children would be rendered defenseless in the event of a school shooting by domestic terrorists. Instead of choosing a tactic proven to reduce school shootings, they chose a tactic proven to increase school shootings. In 1996 Bolshevik Democrat Bill Clinton signed into law an unconstitutional piece of legislation that made it a federal crime for teachers, principles, parents, grandparents, and other responsible adults to possess a firearm within 1,000 feet of a public, parochial, or private school. Instead of employing a tactic that stopped school shootings in Israel, the disciples of Timothy D. Sullivan within the U.S. Government employed a tactic that was used to protect armed New York gangsters.

Keep in mind that the Marxist propagandists operating side by side with the teachers within the government-run school system indoctrinate our children with the liberal, nihilistic, "values clarification" mantra that literally tells our children that, "There's no such thing as right or wrong."[28] They ask our school children discussion questions such as, "How many of you ever wanted to beat up your parents?"[29] They ask them, "How many of you hate your parents?"[30] And, the message abortionists convey to our children under the guise of "health education" is as follows: If you are inconvenienced by innocent, defenseless human life, you can choose to terminate that life!

For emotionally troubled students who have been indoctrinated in this nihilistic fashion for 8, 10, or 12 years, the creation of "gun-free school zones" are viewed as nothing more than an invitation to commit mass murder! And, that invitation was accepted on April 20, 1999 at Columbine High School in Littleton, Colorado; it was accepted again on April 16, 2007 at Virginia Polytechnic Institute and State University (Virginia Tech) in Blacksburg, Virginia; and that invitation was accepted at numerous other bloodstained academic institutions across Soviet America.

In discussing the tragedy of school shootings, Sovereign Americans such as Thomas Sowell[31] asked the obvious question not asked by the Soviet-bloc media: How were school shootings stopped? As in Israel, they tend to be stopped, of course, by other people with guns. Unfortunately, as is almost always the case, armed police arrive just in time to draw chalk marks around the dead bodies of unarmed teachers and defenseless students.

If you think the police can help our children under fire in their classrooms, think again. Nearly 800 law enforcement officers assembled outside Columbine High during the killing spree, but they were of no help to those inside the school. SWAT teams arrived at the school 20 minutes after 911 calls were made, and SWAT team members did not locate the dead gunmen inside the school until 46 minutes after 911 calls were placed. Thus, Eric Harris and Dylan Klebold, the two mass murderers of Columbine High, were free to shoot students and teachers at will for 46 minutes before they were shot to death - not by the police - but by their own suicidal actions!

Before taking their own lives Harris and Klebold killed 12 and wounded 21 defenseless people. While domestic terrorists gunned down 34 Israeli school children before teachers and others were armed, perpetrator Seung-Hui Cho killed 32 people on the Virginia Tech campus after teachers and others were disarmed. Like Harris and Klebold, Cho took his own life - after having unrestricted access to a campus full of unarmed students, administrators, and professors.

In his outstanding 1998 book, *More Guns, Less Crime: Understanding Crime and Gun Control Laws*, John R. Lott, Jr.[32] examined mass public shootings in America. In summary, he concluded that states that made it easy for law-abiding citizens to carry handguns during the 1977 to 1992 period "virtually eliminated mass public shootings after four or five years. These results raise serious concerns over state and federal laws banning all guns from schools and the surrounding area. At least permitting school employees access to guns would seem to make schools less vulnerable to mass shootings." In a later study by John R. Lott, Jr. and William Landes,[33] it was found that of 16 school shootings which took place between 1977 and 1995, 15 occurred in states that have restrictive gun control laws, and only one shooting occurred in a state where law-abiding citizens are not prohibited from carrying concealed handguns for self-defense against violent criminal attack.

We must ask ourselves, who is it that fears guns in the hands of law-abiding citizens? A 1983 National Institute of Justice survey of 2,000 felons in state prisons across America found that 74 percent agreed with the statement that, "one reason burglars avoid houses when people are home is that they fear being shot during the crime." And, 69 percent stated that they knew at least one fellow criminal who had been "scared off, shot at, wounded, or captured by an armed victim." The majority, or 57 percent, agreed that, "most criminals are more worried about meeting an armed victim than they are about running into the police." Clearly, all criminals fear guns in the hands of law-abiding victims. Hence the need for gun control laws to allay the fears of criminals in both the public and private sectors.

Gun Control: A Product Of Homicidal & Genocidal Predators Who Possess "A Lust For Power Over Others."

"Your best life preserver is personal ownership of a military-style semi-automatic rifle." - Aaron Zelman, Dachau Concentration Camp survivor, and founder and executive director of *Jews for the Preservation of Firearms Ownership* (JPFO)

The *Guinness Book of World Records* reported that "the worst genocide" in terms of the percentage of a nation's population was inflicted upon the people of Cambodia. Of the 7 million inhabitants of this small nation, "more than a third" were killed by Khmer Rouge soldiers. Under the leadership of Communist Pol Pot, the soldiers collected weapons from the Cambodian people in house-to-house searches. As the weapons were confiscated the soldiers informed the citizens that, "We are here now to protect you, and no one has need for a weapon anymore."[34] When the soldiers finished disarming the population, the "I'm here to protect you" attitude was changed to "I'm here to kill you." Pol Pot's well-armed soldiers then proceeded to murder between 2 to 3 million unarmed men, women, and children from 1975 to 1979.

Pol Pot and his fellow Communists appointed themselves the social engineers of the new Cambodia, perhaps envisioning a Soviet-style Cambodia. As in the Soviet Union, the people were forced to surrender their money and property, abandon their homes, and work on collective farms in the countryside. Educated people, those who spoke a foreign language, or anyone who appeared to be an intellectual was exterminated. Citizens who wore eyeglasses, a wristwatch, or possessed any professional or technical skill were liquidated. New arrivals to Cambodia and all capitalists and suspected capitalists were marked for death.

In his classic 1994 book, *Death by Government,* R. J. Rummel[35] wrote: "In total, during the first eighty-eight years of this [20th] century, almost 170 million men, women and children have been shot, beaten, tortured, knifed, burned, starved, frozen, crushed, or worked to death; buried alive, drowned, hung, bombed, or killed in any other of the myriad ways governments have inflicted deaths on unarmed, helpless citizens and foreigners. The dead could conceivably be nearly 360 million people." (Underline added.) Rummel further stated that, during the 20th century 15 governments had exceeded the one million mark each in the number of people they killed in "peacetime." Collectively, these 15 predatory governments (which had essentially declared war upon their own citizens) killed about 151 million unarmed men, women, and children - a figure that is more than four times as great as the 35 million military personnel killed in World War I and World War II combined!

Liberal Tyrants Are Imitating
British Tyrants & Loyalist Tyrants!

"Let none but Americans stand guard tonight." - George Washington

We have always had two Americas. Among the thirteen original colonies there were those who wanted America to be a free and sovereign nation. But at the same time there were those who wanted the colonies to remain under the rule of a tyrannical foreign power headed by King George III. These two disparate groups have coexisted throughout our history. Contemporary political descendents of the colonists who wanted America to remain subordinate to international powers continue their struggle into the 21st century.

When James Watt served as Secretary of the Interior under President Ronald Reagan, he boldly stated that, "I never use the words Democrats and Republicans. It's liberals and Americans." Leftists, of course, become defensive when called un-American or un-patriotic. However, liberals are the political descendents of those who were called "loyalists" at the time the "rebels" wrote the Declaration of Independence. The loyalists wanted the colonies to remain dependent upon King George III, and their liberal descendents have actually formulated numerous versions of a "Declaration of Interdependence" in order to undo the liberty established through the blood, sweat, and tears of the colonial patriots and every generation of patriots that has followed.

The colonists who opposed independence and the establishment of a Sovereign America were called loyalists because they remained loyal to King George III of England, the tyrannical madman who was slowly dying from a degenerative brain disease. The loyalists saw themselves as loyal, but they were loyal to a foreign power. They were not loyal to Sovereign America but to British America. During the Cold War of the 20th century the loyalists, now called liberals, once again pledged their loyalty not to Sovereign America but surreptitiously to the Soviet Union. Today they remain loyal to the principles upon which the Soviet Union was founded, and are using those same principles to build their Soviet America.

With the collapse of the USSR liberals want the USA to be loyal to yet another foreign power, the United Nations. The UN, of course, is an organization composed of foreign powers headed by Communists, socialists, fascists, and a variety of tinhorn dictators. But liberals love the UN because it pursues the same goal as the now defunct USSR: The destruction of the sovereignty of the USA and all the other nations of the world and their inclusion into a one world, Soviet-style government. Clearly, the difference between liberals and conservatives mirrors the difference between North Koreans and South Koreans, or perhaps former East Berliners and West Berliners!

In America You Have A Right
And A Duty To Keep And Bear Arms!

"I call on every officer and man...to live and act as becomes a Christian soldier, defending the dearest rights and liberties of his country." - George Washington

"Whatever you think about guns, without them there never would have been any liberty in the United States." - *Washington Times*, May 11, 1993

Given the above statement from the *Washington Times,* one may conclude that firearms were absolutely necessary for the colonists to establish liberty. How else could they have challenged and defeated the mightiest army in the world in the 18th century? However, once liberty is established it must be safeguarded; therefore, the people must preserve the right to keep and bear arms in order to maintain that liberty! It's just common sense! Anyone who threatens the right of the people to keep and bear arms also threatens the right of the people to maintain the liberty our Founding Fathers fought, suffered, and died to establish. They threaten the very liberty millions of Americans fought, suffered, and died to preserve, protect, and defend in numerous wars and other military conflicts around the globe over a period of more than 200 years. The right to keep and bear arms is more than a right, it is a duty! We owe it to our forefathers. We owe it to ourselves. We owe it to our children and grandchildren.

The American Revolution was sparked when British troops headed for Lexington and Concord. The British had two main objectives: The first was to arrest Samuel Adams and John Hancock at Lexington. The second was to disarm American patriots by confiscating their store of weapons and munitions at Concord. However, on the evening of April 18, 1775, Paul Revere and William Dawes rode through the countryside warning their fellow citizens that "The regulars [British] are coming!" Armed with this knowledge and their ever-present muskets, the colonial Minutemen challenged the British as they approached Lexington the very next day. Shots were exchanged, and American patriots embarked on their long, bloody struggle to protect their rights and gain their freedom.

Predictably, after the Revolutionary War had begun, the British Colonial Office had presented a proposal that stated "the Militia Laws should be repealed and...the Arms of all the People should be taken away." That, of course, is precisely what liberals are demanding today. That is precisely what Senator Diane Feinstein has demanded. Wisely, the courageous colonists refused to surrender their muskets to the British Government or their loyalist proxies. Fortunately for all freedom-loving Americans, after 8 years of war, the patriots achieved their victory over the British forces and their loyalist allies.

The British sought to disarm colonial American patriots for the same reason that liberals now want to disarm contemporary American patriots: they wish to rule over us with an iron fist, and do so without resistance. In his book, *A People's History of the United States,* Howard Zinn[36] writes, "victory over the British army was made possible by the existence of an already armed people." It is clear that liberal dictators do not want to make the same mistake British dictators made more than 200 years ago. Keep in mind that American colonists refused to surrender their arms to the British Government in 1775 - twelve years before the U.S. Constitution was drafted and sixteen years before the Second Amendment and the Bill of Rights were created. They knew their right to self-defense was a natural, God-given right that was not dependent upon a piece of paper, nor any government!

Our Founding Fathers knew that the colonial militia, composed of non-governmental citizens, helped the colonial Army defeat the British super-power of King George III because they were well-armed and refused to be disarmed through laws that violated their natural, inalienable right to self-defense. They also knew that their hard-fought freedom would soon disappear if the right to keep and bear arms was not secured. Based on their experiences with the British and their study of world history, our forefathers understood government very well and sought to protect the people from corrupt government by adding the Second Amendment to the Bill of Rights.

History of the 20th century tells us that our Founding Fathers were correct in their assessment of government and the need to acknowledge and protect the right of the people to keep and bear arms. As noted by R. J. Rummel,[37] during the 20th century 61,911,000 innocent men, women, and children were collectively liquidated by Soviet gun control fanatics Vladimir Lenin, Joseph Stalin, and Nikita Khrushchev; 76,702,000 people were disarmed and exterminated by Mao Zedong and the gun control thugs who ran Communist China; 20,946,000 were eliminated by Adolf Hitler and his band of gun control Nazis; 2,035,000 people were disarmed and murdered by gun control Communist Pol Pot; and 112,000 people were disarmed and exterminated by Communist and gun control fanatic Fidel Castro - to mention just a few!

Sovereign America: The Land Of The Free; Soviet America: The Land Of The UN-Free!

"[Self-defense is] justly called the primary law of nature, so it is not, neither can it be in fact, taken away by the laws of society." - Sir William Blackstone

In the 1940s and 1950s "right-wing extremists" in America first warned that the United Nations posed a threat to U.S. sovereignty and our personal liberty. Back then, most Americans just laughed. But today you will find no one laughing at the National Rifle Association, Gun Owners of America, Citizens Committee for the Right to Keep and Bear Arms, Second Amendment Sisters, the Law Enforcement Alliance of America, the American Policy Center, and numerous other pro-Constitution, pro-self-defense, pro-liberty groups.

Through the United Nations, Soviet Americans have been working with other liberals, progressives, Communists, fascists, and a variety of tinhorn dictators in nearly 200 nations to, among other things, impose UN taxation without representation; place the U.S. military under UN command; impose a UN World Court - with no trial by jury; place U.S. environmental policies and U.S. parks under UN control; place U.S. education policies under UN control; allow foreign UN bureaucrats to monitor parent-child relations in the USA in order to "protect children's rights;" impose UN gun control restrictions, and many other intolerable atrocities against the natural, constitutionally-protected rights of Sovereign Americans.

Much of what the UN advocates has already been implemented by liberals in the USA and in other nations around the world. But most Americans are ignorant of the atrocities taking place right under their very noses because the Soviet-bloc media will not report these threats to their freedom. In an attempt to protect our constitutionally-protected right to keep and bear arms from UN interference, in the recent past the National Rifle Association asked its members to sign an "Official Citizen's Petition." The NRA petition stated that the UN has "no right to meddle in the internal affairs of the United States."

Also, in the recent past the American Policy Center created a "Keep US Free" project. A key element of this project was a petition to the U.S. Congress titled, "Declaration of Independence from the United Nations." The Citizen's Committee for the Right to Keep and Bear Arms sponsored a petition titled, "Don't Let The United Nations Take Our Guns Petition." More recently Representative Ron Paul, a Sovereign American from Texas, has attempted to remove the USA from UN membership by introducing his "American Sovereignty Restoration Act," known as H.R. 1146. Unfortunately, most U.S. Representatives show little or no interest in restoring U.S. sovereignty.

Soviet America Is Replacing Sovereign America!

"The saddest epitaph which can be carved in memory of a vanished liberty is that it was lost because its possessors failed to stretch forth a saving hand while there was still time." - George Sutherland, Supreme Court Justice

Bolshevik Democrats such as Senators Schumer and Feinstein have reversed the relationship of government to "We the People." Our Declaration of Independence and Constitution establish the principle that politicians are the servants and we the people are the masters. Abraham Lincoln, our 16th president, acknowledged this relationship when he said in America we have, "government of the people, by the people, and for the people." President Lincoln was even more explicit when he stated that, "The people are the masters of both Congress and the courts, not to overthrow the Constitution, but to overthrow the men who pervert it."

Ronald Reagan, our 40th president, concurred when he said, "The Founding Fathers understood that only by making government the servant, and not the master, only by positing sovereignty in the people and not in the state can we hope to protect freedom and see the political commonwealth prosper." Why did our Founding Fathers set up a Constitutional Republic wherein the people were the masters and government was the servant? George Washington, our first president, answered this question more than 200 years ago when he said the following regarding government: "Like fire, it is a dangerous servant and a fearful master."

Therefore, how could socialist politicians come to the preposterous con-clusion that they, as our servants, could disarm us, their masters? They could only reach such an un-American conclusion by abandoning the per-spective of the Sovereign American and replacing it with the perspective of the Soviet American. During the construction of Soviet America, the U.S.

Congress has transformed itself into an entity more akin to the defunct Soviet Politburo than a constitutionally-restricted legislative body. In Soviet America, as in the Soviet Union, government officials set themselves up as masters (predators) and reduce the people to the level of servants (prey). Therefore, every time government officials advocate another gun control law that makes it more difficult for us to defend ourselves, our families, and our freedom, they are providing us with political sign language that says,

Welcome to Soviet America!

Good-bye Safe and Secure America!

------†††------

It is no coincidence that the people who are deceitfully robbing us of our money and our property, are precisely the same people who are working to rob us of our ability to protect our money and our property. It is no coincidence that the people who are deceitfully robbing us of our liberty and our sovereignty, are precisely the same people who are working to rob us of our ability to defend our liberty and our sovereignty. It is no coincidence that the people who are deceitfully robbing us of truth, prosperity, and social harmony, are precisely the same people who are working to rob us of our ability to promote truth, prosperity, and social harmony.

------†††------

"How can you rightfully ask another human being to risk his life to protect yours, when you will assume no responsibility yourself?" - Jeff Snyder, *Nation of Cowards: Essays on the Ethics of Gun Control*, 2001[38]

Chapter Nine

The Abortion Holocaust:
From Russia – Without Love!

"Any country that accepts abortion as legal is not teaching its people to love, but to use any violence to get what they want. This is why the greatest destroyer of love and peace is abortion." - Mother Teresa[1]

Warning: Unvarnished descriptions of abortion are provided below. Therefore, people of conscience who are unfamiliar with the details of abortion may find this chapter disturbing. This cannot be avoided. To sanitize the crime of abortion would be a disservice to every truth-seeking reader. It would also be a disservice to every victim of abortion.

What if it was common knowledge that there were hundreds and hundreds of locations across the country where babies were chemically burned to death - very slowly - on a daily basis, and no anesthetic was administered to these young victims before they were tortured to death in this manner? What if you knew, beyond all doubt, that at these same locations babies were having their arms and legs ripped from their bodies, their skulls crushed, and this gruesome act was inflicted upon these youngsters with no anesthetic? What if you had access to documented cases describing how babies were having their brains sucked out of their skulls - without the benefit of anesthesia - and found that, after dismemberment, the body parts of these young victims were being sold for profit?

What if you knew, beyond all doubt, that in this nation such monstrous acts were being committed against more than one million babies each and every year - decade, after decade, after decade? What if you read confirmed reports informing you that people of conscience were arrested and jailed for peacefully protesting on public sidewalks outside the locations where these barbarous acts occurred? What if many of the mothers of these young victims suffered from severe depression, drug abuse, suicide, as well as short-term and long-term medical complications - some of which were fatal - all as a direct consequence of the gruesome ways in which their pre-born children were tortured to death?

What if the courts decided that the infliction of such torturous deaths upon helpless, innocent babies was a constitutional right to be freely exercised by the perpetrators? What if, in this same nation, high level government officials, scientists, educators, and investigative reporters tried to hide the details of these gruesome acts from you and the public at large; turned a deaf ear to the mothers who suffered debilitating psychological, spiritual, and physical trauma as a consequence of these acts; supported the people who exterminated tens of millions of babies in this manner; and routinely demonized private citizens who tried to fully inform the public about this ongoing holocaust?

Armed with the above "What if" questions, in your opinion, what country is described in the previous paragraphs? Would you conclude that this was a description of the Soviet Union? Could this be a description of Nazi Germany? Or would you conclude that this was a description of Soviet China, or Soviet Cuba? You could correctly be tempted to answer "Yes" to any of these questions, but you would have to answer "No" to the following question: "Is this a description of America?" That's correct, the answer is "No," this is not a description of America.

It is certainly not a description of the America envisioned by the Founders who signed the Declaration of Independence, a document that states in black and white that we are endowed by our Creator with an unalienable right to life. It is not the America founded by the signatories to the U.S. Constitution, which states that even a criminal cannot be deprived of life without due process of law. It is not a description of the America in which I grew up. No folks, this is not a description of America, but it is, however, a chillingly accurate description of Soviet America!

Clearly, Soviet America does not remotely resemble the Sovereign America founded by George Washington and James Madison, but it does eerily resemble the Soviet Union operated by Vladimir Lenin and Nikita Khrushchev! Not surprisingly, the Soviet American killing machine described above is enthusiastically endorsed by the Communist Party, USA. Unfortunately, it is also an integral part of the political platform of the Democrat Party, USA. Anyone who does not support the Soviet American killing machine described above cannot rise to the highest positions of power within the Communist Party or within the Democrat Party. Period!

From Nazi Germany To Soviet America!

"The technique of saline abortion was originally developed in the concentration camps of Nazi Germany." - David C. Reardon[2]

Through abortion liberals kill their own children before they are born - at a rate of about 3,700 each day in Soviet America. Some abortions are performed by injecting saline (salt) solution into the womb. Through this method the child is chemically poisoned and burned to death. The chemical burning of the child's flesh may cause kicking and thrashing in the womb before the salty solution poisons the child to death. This process induces labor and a dead baby is delivered, usually within a day or so. This slow, excruciating painful death may take an hour or more, and, of course, no anesthetic is administered to the child before he or she is subjected to this cruel, but not unusual, form of punishment - which is arbitrarily administered for the crime of inconveniencing the mother.

This is not an unusual form of punishment because, according to David C. Reardon, the saline solution abortion technique employed by liberals in Soviet America was developed in fascist Germany's Nazi concentration camps. (However, some sources claim the saline solution abortion method was developed in the 1930s by Romanian surgeon Eugen Aburel Bogdan.) So, while leftists like to slap the "Nazi" and "fascist" labels on the opponents of abortion, in reality it is the abortion-loving liberals, and not the pro-life conservatives, who are following in the footsteps of Adolf Hitler, Adolf Eichmann, and Joseph Goebbels - on this and many other life-and-death issues. While Nazis may or may not have originally developed the saline solution abortion method, it is an historical fact that Nazis encouraged, performed, and even compelled abortions. Therefore, aggressive feminist support for all forms of abortion forces the thoughtful observer to take a closer look at the term "Femi-Nazi."

With partial birth abortion liberals kill their children while they are in the process of being born. When the child is partially delivered and just seconds away from taking his or her first breadth, the abortionist cuts a hole in the back of the neck, inserts a tube into the child's skull, and literally sucks the child's brains out until the skull collapses. Again, this gruesome procedure is administered with no anesthetic. In surgical abortions - a common method of abortion in Soviet America today - the arms and legs are torn from the child's body while in the womb, and the head is crushed and ripped from the torso. The body parts are then aspirated from the womb. And of course, this ghastly procedure is also performed with no thought of inducing anesthesia.

Liberal Body Count Versus Nazi Body Count!

"During the Nazi occupation of Europe, SS forces committed mass murder of prisoners and civilians in unprecedented numbers. The loss of life has been estimated at 5 to 6,000,000 Jews, 7,000,000 Russian civilians, 2,600,000 Russian prisoners of war, 4,200,000 Polish civilians, and many hundreds of thousands of civilians in other countries. At the same time, some 130,000 Germans were killed by the Gestapo for opposing the Hitler regime." - Frederic V. Grunfeld[3]

Adding up the numbers put forth above by Frederic V. Grunfeld, we may conclude that Nazis systematically exterminated about 20 million people across Europe during World War II. This figure does not include troops killed on the battlefield, or civilians who could be classified as "collateral damage." The figure of 20 million includes only those men, women, and children who were systematically executed by firing squads, gas chambers, massive ovens, medical experimentation, deliberate starvation, and other Nazi extermination camp methods.

However, it is estimated that, from 1973, liberals may have exterminated nearly 50 million pre-born children in their abortion clinics across the USSA during their ongoing war against everything American, including its people and its culture. So, from an historical perspective, in Soviet America alone liberals may have exterminated more than twice as many innocent people as were exterminated by the Nazis - a group of genocidal maniacs liberals mimic while claiming to disdain. Pro-life activist Pastor Ernie Sanders[4] estimates the number of abortion casualties may be twice as high as the publicized figure of 50 million as a consequence of routine under-reporting by abortionists. If Pastor Ernie Sanders is correct, Soviet Americans (American liberals, progressives, and Communists) may have exterminated five times as many people as the Nazis through abortion alone!

A Crime Against Humanity
Is Not A Crime In Soviet America!

"...the saline (salt) solution, burns babies alive in the mother's womb...she delivers a dead, burned baby. In those instances where the baby is born breathing, it is placed into a plastic bag and smothered to death." - La Verne Tolbert, Inside the Soul of Planned Parenthood[5]

After World War II, captured Nazi leaders were prosecuted by Nuremberg Military Tribunals for various crimes against humanity. Many were indicted and convicted by the Nuremberg War Crimes Tribunal for "encouraging and compelling abortions" which were determined to be "a crime against humanity."[6, 7] Many had concluded that abortion was considered both a crime against humanity and a war crime for several reasons. Firstly, the Nazis had forced women to have abortions against their will. Secondly, in many cases the Nazis had forced the abortions because they wished to exterminate "non-Aryan" races.

However, John Hunt[8] thoroughly investigated these charges and reported that James McHaney, the prosecutor who drew up the indictments, stated that, "But protection of the law was denied to unborn children of the Russian and Polish women in Nazi Germany. Abortions were encouraged and even forced on these women." (Underline added.) John Hunt therefore concluded that all abortions were considered both a crime against humanity and a war crime because "protection of the law was denied to unborn children."

The tens of millions of babies poisoned, burned, crushed, stabbed, and shredded to death in abortion clinics across Soviet America are among the most innocent and defenseless victims in a culture war that began to escalate conspicuously in the 1960s. With a daily body count of nearly 4,000 victims through abortion alone, Soviet Americans have established themselves as determined, deadly, cold-blooded, culture warriors.

When (and if) this culture war is concluded, will liberals, progressives, Communists, and other Soviet Americans face the same justice as their Nazi counterparts did in the 1940s? Or will their list of victims continue to expand beyond the abortion clinic? I guess that depends on who wins this culture war - which is, in fact, a continuation of the Cold War on American soil. While this war is being fought, your tax dollars continue to provide Planned Parenthood with about 350 million dollars in federal funding each year[9] although this organization routinely engages in what the Nuremberg War Crimes Tribunal correctly described as "a crime against humanity."

Having the power to force people of conscience to subsidize organizations such as Planned Parenthood with their tax dollars partially exposes the diabolical genius behind Karl Marx's "heavy progressive or graduated income tax."[10] The defenders of human life voluntarily contribute their private funds to pro-life organizations. Unfortunately, through Marxist-style taxation and Marxist-style redistribution of wealth, the defenders of life are simultaneously forced to involuntarily contribute to public funding that helps sustain the pro-abortion opposition they wish to defeat.

Of course, abortion is not the only method liberals pursue to extinguish the lives of undesirable people. Sometimes liberals kill their own children shortly after they are born by refusing life-saving medical care or nourishment for a "defective" or unwanted child. When parents, grandparents, and others become elderly and burdensome, liberals seek to exterminate them through euthanasia. So far they have not succeeded in installing euthanasia nation-wide, but they are pursuing it with all the fervor of Nazi eugenicists. If legalized, the body count from euthanasia could rival that of the abortion holocaust. Don't think it can't happen here? Remember Terri Schiavo, who was slowly starved and dehydrated to death while the government prevent-ed her parents from saving her life. This could never happen in America, but it could happen, and did happen, in Soviet America! Senior citizens, the disabled, and the infirm must take note.

In Soviet America, Crime (Including Homicide) Really Does Pay!

If It's Not A Child, You're Not Pregnant! - Bumper Sticker[11]

So, like their predecessors in Nazi Germany and the Soviet Union, liberals have exterminated tens of millions of innocent, defenseless babies in abor-tion clinics across Soviet America since 1973. Currently, liberals exterminate about 1.3 million unborn children each year in Soviet America, and, along with exterminators in other nations, they collectively kill more than 40 million unborn children worldwide each year. But why do liberals kill their own children through abortion? The answer: Convenience! And why do liberals kill other people's children through abortion? The answer: Profit! For those who possess "a lust for power over others" as described in Chapter Two, there may be an additional motive: They may simply "delight in kill-ing!"

According to Representative Mike Pence,[12] a conservative Republican from Indiana, Planned Parenthood performs approximately 305,000 abortions each year in its 850-plus facilities across Soviet America. Moreover, this abortion provider rakes in over $1 billion per year from clinic operations, government grants and contracts, private contributions from limousine liberals, wealthy corporations, and tax-exempt foundations. Sadly, your tax dollars provide Planned Parenthood with about $350 million each year in federal funding! That's more than $1 billion in just three years from tax-payers alone! Indeed, abortion is a very profitable business.

Pain (Torture) OK For The Innocent, But Not For The Guilty!

"According to one study, aborted foetuses have been heard to cry from 21 weeks and some doctors believe that distress can be felt as early as 13 weeks." - Roger Highfield[13]

In January of 2008, thirty-five years after their infamous *Roe v. Wade* decision that legalized abortion in the USA, the U.S. Supreme Court heard arguments regarding the possibility that some Death Row inmates may experience pain when receiving a lethal injection as punishment for their homicidal behavior. During this procedure convicted murderers are first injected with an anesthetic to prevent the perception of pain. This is followed by an injection of a paralytic drug to prevent voluntary muscle movement. Lastly, the inmate receives a lethal dose of a chemical that stops the heart from beating.

When the drugs are administered correctly the inmate dies a quick and painless death. However, if an insufficient amount of the anesthetic is administered the inmate may experience excruciating burning pain from the heart stopping drug - and the inmate could not notify officials of this pain due to the administration of the paralytic drug. Whether or not any condemned inmate has ever suffered pain due to an insufficient dosage of an anesthetic is not known, but, it is theoretically possible.[14]

In April of 2008 the U.S. Supreme Court ruled that, as currently administered, lethal injection does not violate the Eighth Amendment prohibition against cruel and unusual punishment. Interestingly, former ACLU member and pro-abortion "Justice" Ruth Bader Ginsberg dissented. So, liberals express a high level of anxiety over the remote possibility that, if not administered correctly, a convicted murderer may briefly suffer an extreme level of pain from a lethal injection. However, these same liberals display a total and absolute disregard for the near certain probability that an innocent pre-born child will suffer an extreme level of pain, sometimes over a protracted period of time, when subjected to a late-term abortion - whether the procedure is administered correctly or incorrectly. Given that a lethal injection of saline solution is used to terminate late-term pregnancies, and it takes an hour or so for the poisoned and chemically burning child to die, why do liberals not consider this to be a form of "cruel and unusual punishment" for the crime of inconveniencing a liberal mother? Why do liberals enthusiastically embrace and aggressively defend this form of torture?

As a result of *Doe v. Bolton*, the companion decision to *Roe v. Wade*, the U.S. Supreme Court legalized abortion through all nine months of pregnancy; that is, through the entire 36 week gestation period. However, Doctor Paul Ranalli, a neurologist at the University of Toronto, has reported that an unborn child of 20 weeks gestation has developed all the nervous system components necessary to experience pain. Moreover, the electrical activity of the nervous system of a pre-born child of 20 weeks gestation can be recorded by standard electroencephalography, or EEG. Doctor Robert J. White, a professor of neurosurgery at Case Western Reserve University agrees with Doctor Ranalli, and has stated that a pre-born child of 20 weeks gestation "is fully capable of experiencing pain... Without question, [abortion] is a dreadfully painful experience for any infant subjected to such a surgical procedure."[15]

Professor Nicholas Fisk of England studied the hormones released by pre-born children of 19 weeks gestation and found that they release pain and stress-related hormones when subjected to painful and stressful stimuli. In Germany, Doctor Joachim Partch found that pre-born children as young as 16 weeks gestation released similar pain and stress-related hormones. Even more disturbing is the report of Dr. K. J. S. Anand, an assistant professor of pediatric anesthesia at Emory University in Atlanta. According to Doctor Anand pre-born children may experience greater pain, not less pain, than prematurely born children and adults. This conclusion was based on the observation that pre-born children develop the nervous system components necessary to experience pain well before they develop the components necessary to mitigate pain. So, while pre-born children may experience pain beginning at 16 weeks gestation, they do not begin to develop the ability to blunt pain until the age of 28 weeks gestation.[16] For this reason unborn children of 20 weeks gestation or older are routinely administered an anesthetic prior to prenatal surgery.[17]

Consequently, the unrestricted level of pain experienced by a pre-born child during a surgical abortion, or during an hour-long or two hour-long saline solution abortion, may be as close as any human can come to experiencing the absolute horror of hell on Earth. When it comes to torture and death, the cold-blooded, premeditated cruelty of liberal abortionists places them on the same moral plane as Nazi death camp doctors and Soviet Gulag administrators. Unlike America, in Soviet America it is perfectly OK to deliberately inflict prolonged, unfathomable pain upon the most innocent among us, but it is not OK if there is the remotest possibility that temporary pain may be accidentally inflicted upon convicted murderers.

Defenders of life have tried to pass the Unborn Child Pain Awareness Act, introduced in both the House and the Senate.[18, 19] This legislation would require abortionists to inform a woman of the medical evidence demonstrating that her unborn child will feel pain in the event she seeks an abortion while carrying a child of 20 weeks gestation or older. If requested by the woman, this legislation would further require the administration of an anesthetic to the unborn child, or information on how anesthesia may be obtained. Unfortunately, pro-life forces have been unable to pass this compassionate piece of legislation in either the U.S. House of Representatives or the U.S. Senate. Although enough votes were garnered in 2006 in the House, procedural tactics were employed by opponents and the legislation was stalled. Welcome to the cold-blooded Socialist America predicted in the 1960s by Nikita "The Butcher of the Ukraine" Khrushchev!

In Soviet America
Pain & Death Are OK For Pre-Born Children,
But Not For Wild & Commercial Animals!

"I recently spoke to a young pregnant woman named Victoria, who said, 'In this society we save whales, we save timber wolves and bald eagles and Coke bottles. Yet, everyone wanted me to throw away my baby.'" - Ronald Reagan,[20] Conservative Republican and fortieth President of the USA

Liberals have passed legislation to make it a federal crime to kill certain animals, whether born or unborn. The U.S. Fish & Wildlife Service has a long list of wild animals (and plants) on the Threatened and Endangered Species list. Consequently, it is a violation of federal law to kill a Giant Kangaroo Rat, Copperbelly Water Snake, Indiana Bat, Salt Marsh Harvest Mouse, Blunt-nosed Leopard Lizard, or the Delhi Sands Flower-Loving Fly. However, the same liberals who have placed rats, snakes, bats, mice, lizards, and flies within a protective legal cocoon, vehemently oppose legislation to make it a federal crime to torture and kill unborn babies.

In Britain "rats, guinea pigs and hedgehogs" as well as other "pre-born vertebrate animals" are protected from excessive pain by the Animal (Scientific Procedures) Act of 1986.[21] In the USA we find that, as far back as 1902, the federal government enacted the Humane Slaughter Act. As a result of this legislation it is illegal in America to even shackle an animal about to be slaughtered unless that animal has first been rapidly and effectively rendered "insensible to pain." In comparing this longstanding concern for the welfare of animals to the callous disregard for the excruciating pain inflicted upon pre-born children in the womb during late-term abortions, the National Right To Life Educational Trust Fund[22] has noted that, sadly, "An unborn child has less legal protection from feeling pain than commercial livestock."

Why do liberals have a protective attitude toward unborn animals but a sadistic and homicidal attitude toward unborn children? It is said that Nazi dictator Adolf Hitler was fond of dogs, but he was also obsessed with exterminating born and unborn people, and he did so by the millions? We also know that Soviet dictator Nikita Khrushchev earned the nickname "The Butcher of the Ukraine" by executing and starving to death millions of Ukrainians. Khrushchev also reinstituted abortion in the Soviet Union after the death of Joseph Stalin. However, Khrushchev proudly elevated dogs to the position of cosmonaut!

Recall from Chapter Two the work of psychologist Vonda Pelto, Ph.D.,[23] who authored the book, *Without Remorse: The Story of the Woman Who Kept Los Angeles' Serial Killers Alive.* When Dr. Pelto asked one incarcerated serial killer how he felt when he killed other people, he said he felt "nothing." When asked if killing a human was like killing an animal, he said "no" because he did feel some compassion for animals. Yes, there are many discernible threads tying Nazis, Soviet Russians, Soviet Americans, and incarcerated serial killers together, and their affection for animals and contrasting disregard for humans is one of the most disturbing. Truly, the criminal mind, when placed in top government positions, is both fascinating and frightening to behold!

No Child Left Alive!

"After I delivered her, I held her in my hands, I looked her over from top to bottom. She had a head of hair, and her eyes were opening. I looked at her tiny feet and hands. Her fingers and toes even had little fingernails and swirls of fingerprints. Everything was perfect. She was not a 'fetus.' She was not a 'product of conception.' She was a tiny human being…But these vital statistics did not mention her most striking trait: She was my daughter. Twisted with agony. Silent and still. Dead." - Nancyjo Mann, describing her saline solution abortion[24]

Liberals, progressives, and other socialists who make up the core of the Democrat Party know that when they commit abortion they are stopping a beating heart. They know they are extinguishing the life of an innocent, defenseless child. They know they are terminating the life of a unique individual who is genetically distinct from the mother; who may have a different blood type and different sex than the mother; and therefore they know they are not simply removing some ill-defined and useless appendage from the mother. They know they are killing a pre-born child who has two arms, two legs, two eyes, two ears, a nose, and a mouth - just like every other human being. They know the pre-born child has a functioning brain and nervous system, and therefore feels pain when subjected to any late-term abortion procedure.

They know that abortion not only kills a pre-born baby boy or girl, but also damages the mother psychologically, spiritually, and physically. They know the mother will have an increased chance of depression, drug abuse, and suicide. They know the mother will have an increased risk for breast cancer, uterine cancer, and infertility. Finally, they know they are employing procedures imported from Nazi Germany and the Soviet Union. Liberals and progressives know all this, but like their Nazi and Communist mentors, they do not care! They do not care anymore than Adolf Hitler, Adolf Eichmann, Josef Mengele, Vladimir Lenin, Joseph Stalin, Nikita Khrushchev, or Mao Zedong cared about the tens of millions of innocent men, women, and children they summarily arrested, jailed, tortured, and murdered.

Liberals do not care because they do not live in America; instead, psychologically, they live in Soviet America - and they want to force the rest of us to live in their Frankenstein of a nation. Only in Soviet America could the "mean-spirited" conservative opponents of the abortion holocaust, and not the "compassionate" liberal perpetrators of abortion holocaust, be targeted for re-education through "sensitivity training."

For Sale In Soviet America:
Body Parts From Aborted Babies!

"Back in the 1990s, Planned Parenthood's operation in Overland Park was apparently operating somewhat like a slaughter house - where every part was used except the silent scream of the unborn boy or girl." - Andrea Lafferty[25]

In addition to receiving payment for performing abortions, liberals also engage in the ghastly but lucrative practice of trafficking in body parts. For example, a Planned Parenthood clinic in Overland Park, Kansas, sells arms, legs, eyes, lungs, livers, pancreas, thymus, and other body parts to various firms for research. In one instance the life of a baby girl of 24 weeks gestation was terminated, her body dismembered, and her body parts sold to eight different research organizations. A 1999 price list, as one would find in a warehouse, was discovered with a baby spleen selling for $75.00, a thymus for $100.00, and gonads were listed at $550.00.[26]

It should be noted that in 2007 the District Attorney for Johnson County, Kansas, filed charges against this clinic in Overland Park. Planned Parenthood was charged with 29 counts of performing illegal late term abortions along with 29 counts of unlawful failure to determine the viability of late term abortions. In addition, 27 counts were filed for unlawful failure to maintain records, and 23 felony counts were lodged for creating false information.[27]

In Ohio, attorneys working with the Life Legal Defense Foundation are suing Planned Parenthood for covering up a statutory rape. In this case an adult soccer coach seduced and impregnated a thirteen-year-old girl. Before he was caught the perpetrator attempted to cover up his crime by coercing the young girl into having an abortion. Planned Parenthood performed the abortion, but did not notify the young girl's parents before doing so - as required by Ohio law. Nor did they notify law enforcement that the crime of statutory rape had been committed.[28]

Life Legal Defense Foundation suspects such cover-ups may occur routinely at Planned Parenthood clinics across Soviet America. For example, in their Spring, 2007 Lifeline newsletter we find the following: "Arizona: A twelve-year-old girl, impregnated by her foster brother, received an abortion at Planned Parenthood. The clinic notified neither parents, police, nor child protective services, but simply returned the girl home, where she was raped and impregnated again."[29] Pro-abortion feminists say they are champions of women's rights, women's health, and women's reproductive freedom. Ask yourself, are pro-abortion feminists truly protecting women's rights, or are they really protecting abortion provider profits? Are they protecting profits at any cost to women's psychological, physical, and spiritual health and welfare?

From Soviet Russia To Soviet America!

"After being the first country to legalize abortion in 1920 under Dicta-tor Vladimir Lenin, the former Soviet Union reversed its position in 1936, only to change its position again in 1955." - John-Henry Westen[30]

Clearly, when liberals, progressives, Communists, and other Soviet Ameri-cans perform or support abortion, they are following in the footsteps of Nazi eugenicists. They are engaging in or aiding and abetting behavior that the Nuremberg War Crimes Tribunal determined to be "a crime against humanity." However, it should also be noted that Russia, the first nation to adopt Communism, was also the first nation in the modern era to legalize abortion. Yes, Vladimir Lenin and his Bolshevik cohorts legalized abortion in 1920 - three years after the fall of the Czar in 1917, and two years before the establishment of the Soviet Union in 1922. Indeed, Communism and death have always been inseparable.

As the principles and practices of Communism spread across the planet, abortion became normalized nearly everywhere, including the European nations that, collectively, were previously referred to as "Christendom." Given the Sovietization of Europe, the label of Christendom no longer applies. Today, Christmas, Christian prayers, Christian symbols, and Christian traditions are openly denigrated and banned from the public arena across the USSA. Moreover, liberals now proclaim that America is not, and never was, a Christian nation, and we see a Soviet America joining Soviet Europe in adopting the cultural template first employed within the Soviet Union.

Together, Vladimir Lenin and his successor, Joseph Stalin, shot, hanged, beat, worked, and starved to death tens of millions of their own citizens. With the widespread extermination of adults causing a potential loss of manpower to operate future Soviet factories, collective farms, slave labor camps, and to pursue global conquest, Stalin ended legalized abortion in 1936. But upon Stalin's death in 1953 abortion was reinstated in 1955 under Nikita "The Butcher of the Ukraine" Khrushchev - the third genocidal sociopath to rule over the Soviet Union.

During the 20th century the world witnessed the mind-boggling body count that occurs when people with criminal minds are placed in the highest positions of political power. During the past century we saw innocent people, both born and unborn, tortured and murdered by the tens of millions in the Soviet Union, Nazi Germany, Soviet China, Soviet Cuba, Soviet

Cambodia, and other criminal-controlled nations. But most Americans never suspected that such psychopathic behavior could ever be imported and routinely exhibited within the USA. It is true that such behavior could never occur in America, but it could occur, and is now occurring, in Soviet America!

Media Engage In Soviet-Style Blackout To Hide Truthful Message: Liberal Violence Begets Liberal Violence!

"Until the birth of Steven, I had had abortions, and I considered them up to that point a form of birth control. And once I had Steven, I think the reality of the murderous act of abortion hit me front and center. And at that point, his life was expendable, too... I attempted to suffocate him... The bottle, literally, that I was using forcefully to suffocate him burst!" - Susan Walk[31]

In his book, *Abortion and the Conscience of the Nation*, President Ronald Reagan wrote, "We cannot diminish the value of one category of human life - the unborn - without diminishing the value of all human life...There is no cause more important."[32] Was President Reagan correct? Has abortion contributed to the devaluation of human life, perhaps to the extent that it leads to other forms of violent crime? Mother Teresa said, "Yes!" However, when she tried to convey this message in a speech, the Soviet-bloc media "blacked out" her life-promoting message. In an article titled "Mother Teresa's speech on Abortion 'blacked out,'" Morris Faulkner noted that Mother Teresa was the featured speaker at the National Prayer Breakfast in 1994. President Bill Clinton, Vice-President Al Gore, members of Congress, federal judges, diplomats, and members of the media attended this event.

Mother Teresa's message was simple and indisputable, that violence begets violence: "If we accept that a mother can kill her own child, how can we teach other people not to kill each other."[33] Thus, acceptance of the violent crime of abortion leads to the acceptance of other forms of violent crime. Why are so many students "choosing death" for their fellow students, as we have seen at Columbine, Virginia Tech, and elsewhere across the nation? Why are there so many news reports of mothers drowning, microwaving, and torturing their young children to death after they are born? Why are women leaving their babies in unattended vehicles in the dead of summer - resulting in dead, dehydrated babies? From where did these women get the idea that their children were disposable? How did they ever develop such a liberal attitude toward innocent, defenseless, human life?

Why has homicide become the number one cause of death for pregnant American women, and why are the fathers of the unborn children most often found to be the perpetrators of these double homicides? Is it because liberals have, over a period of more than 40 years, seared the conscience of America to such an extent that "choosing death" for the most innocent among us is simply a matter of choice? Is it because, through abortion, liberals have deeply embedded within the nation a culture of death? The answer is "Yes," and the culture of death is widespread. For example, teenage girls who have had an abortion are 10 times more likely to attempt suicide within six months after the abortion than teenage girls who do not have abortions. A study in 1987 showed that, among women who suffered psychological trauma after an abortion, 60 percent had thought about suicide and 28 percent had actually attempted suicide.[34]

A 13-year study analyzed all women between the ages of 15 to 49 who died in Finland from 1987 to 2000. This study found that women who had an abortion were 248 percent more likely to die from suicide, accidents, or homicide in the year following their abortion than women who had not been pregnant the prior year. Researchers also found that women who had an abortion were six times more likely to commit suicide than women who had experienced childbirth in the prior year, and they were twice as likely to commit suicide as women who suffered a miscarriage.[35]

A study of California women found a 154 percent higher suicide rate and an 82 percent higher accident rate among women who had an abortion when compared to women who did not have an abortion. Studies have also shown that women who have had an abortion are more likely to engage in substance abuse and other risk-taking behavior, and are more likely to report anxiety, sleep disorders, relationship problems, and psychiatric illness.[36]

Naturally, the Soviet-bloc media ignore the relationship between the violent, deliberate deaths of pre-born children and the subsequent violent, deliberate deaths of their mothers, just as they ignore and deny all the symptoms of Post Abortion Syndrome (PAS), also referred to as Post Traumatic Stress Disorder (PTSD).[37] Instead, liberals blame many of the homicides and suicides on guns, or the people who oppose abortion, but they do not blame the climate of death created by the gruesome, morbid, Soviet-inspired, Nazi-inspired, abortion industry.

Furthermore, it should be noted that Morris Faulkner pointed out that, while Mother Teresa's pro-life message was blacked out entirely by *The New*

York Times, this same newspaper printed the entire text of a speech given by Secretary of State James Baker at a previous National Prayer Breakfast. Most other large newspapers also participated in this news blackout. *The Washington Post* printed the story as an insignificant news item on one of its back pages, and the text of Mother Teresa's speech was not included. The major television newscasters followed suit. They spoke of Bill Clinton's attendance at the event, but they did not mention Mother Teresa and they ignored her life-saving message. Welcome to Soviet America!

The Soviet-Led International Sisterhood

"He [the abortionist] said he never feels bad or guilty about his work, which includes performing abortions on viable babies, babies who are old enough to live outside the womb." - Joanie Barrett, a founding member of Students for Life of America, at Wayne State University in Detroit, Michigan[38]

The above quote could have been placed in Chapter Two, Understanding the Psychology of Soviets, Socialists & Other Sociopaths! In that chapter we find a discussion of the television program *Most Evil,* along with the following paragraph: According to forensic psychiatrists, when torturing or killing their victims psychopathic serial killers experience a sense of superiority over others, but feel no sense of empathy, no sense of compassion, and no sense of remorse. They simply cannot put themselves in the shoes of the people they kidnap, torture, mutilate, and murder. The callous disregard psychopathic serial killers display towards their victims was made evident by convicted serial killer Keith Jesperson who said, "Taking a human life was nothing. I had done it so many times."[39]

Unfortunately, the "progress" Bolshevik Democrats have made in building their Soviet America is beginning to match the "progress" their mentor Bolsheviks made in Soviet Russia. For example, in a 2005 report by LifeSiteNews.com,[40] it was reported that 3.5 million Russian women became pregnant each year, but approximately 1.5 million women actually gave birth. Thus, roughly 60 percent of all pregnancies in Russia end in abortion. Predictably, the Soviet Union collapsed under the burden of its socialist programs in 1991; however, the new Soviet-style Russian government continues to be involved in health care. Consequently, one out of three Russian women who have an abortion eventually die from complications. Of an estimated 38 million Russian women of childbearing age, approximately 6 million are infertile. Not surprisingly, the medical community considers abortion to be a major contributor to the current crisis of infertility in Russia.

LifeSiteNews.com further reported that alcoholism, sexually transmitted diseases - including HIV, divorce, and domestic violence are all disturbingly high in Soviet Russia today. In addition, a 1995 study indicated that nearly half of all murders in Russia are the consequence of domestic violence. Thanks to the 1960s Marxist Cultural Revolution in America, women now living in Soviet America can feel a true sense of sisterhood with the women now living in Soviet Russia: Both are sharing the same spiritual, psychological, and physical morbidity that only a dysfunctional, morally-challenged, international, proletariat sisterhood could defend!

Progressives: Proudly Progressing Backwards!

"As early as 1973, Drs. Duff and Campbell made it clear that infanticide was happening in American hospitals. From the early 1970s onward the pro-infanticide advocates in this country began a concentrated assault to convince the nation that killing a newborn baby was sometimes the most compassionate course of treatment." - C. Everett Koop, M.D., former United States Surgeon General, and Francis A. Schaeffer, Christian theologian[41]

A survey of 157 medical schools in Soviet America and Soviet Canada found that in 1993, 98 percent required graduating students to take an oath. However, only one school required graduating students to take the original, or classical, Hippocratic Oath that included the following: "I will neither give a deadly drug to anybody who asked for it, nor will I make a suggestion to this effect. Similarly I will not give to a woman an abortive remedy." Unfortunately, a mere 8 percent of the more contemporary, revised oaths taken by medical students in the 1990s included a prohibition against abortion, and only 14 percent included a prohibition against euthanasia. Clearly, the sanctity of human life has lost most of its luster among leading educators within the medical community.[42]

Hippocrates, who was born in Greece in 460 BC, developed medicine into a true and independent profession. For this reason he was honored with the title "Father of Medicine." He was also honored by having his name attached to the once popular medical profession oath, known as the Hippocratic Oath, as discussed above. However, given that attitudes towards abortion and euthanasia have changed from prohibition in 460 BC to acceptance in 1920 AD, from a moral perspective the world has been going backwards instead of forward. Indeed, from a moral perspective, "progressives" have taken 1970s America backwards in time to 1930s Nazi Germany and to 1920s Soviet Russia. Only in Nazi Germany, Soviet Russia,

Soviet America, and other morally-challenged nations could the systematic slaughter of tens of millions of pre-born children be proudly hailed as "progress."

Psychological Warfare & The Soviet-Bloc Media!

"For two hours I could feel her struggling inside of me. But then, as suddenly as it began, she stopped. Even today, I remember her very last kick on my left side. She had no strength left. She gave up and died. Despite my grief and guilt, I was relieved that her pain was finally over. But I was never the same again. The abortion not only killed my daughter; it killed a part of me."
- Nancyjo Mann, describing her saline solution abortion[43]

Keep in mind that the Bolsheviks at ABC, CBS, NBC, MSNBC, CNN, *The New York Times, Washington Post,* the *Los Angeles Times*, *Newsweek*, *Time*, and every recent Democrat Party presidential candidate, all militantly defend the chemical poisoning and burning to death of pre-born children in the USSA and around the globe. They support the crushing of their tiny skulls, the ripping off of their arms and legs from the torso, and the piercing of their skulls and the aspiration of their brains. To enhance the horror of these procedures to a level found at Treblinka, Auschwitz-Birkenau, and other Nazi extermination camps, liberals and so-called "progressives" vehemently oppose any laws that require the administration of an anesthetic to prevent or buffer the pain inflicted upon their helpless, pre-born victims. And, of course, they support the selling of marketable body parts and the dumpster disposal of unmarketable body parts. (May God have mercy on their souls - provided He finds them not guilty by reason of moral insanity!)

As in the Soviet Union, the Soviet American media have ignored, and have thus covered-up, the gruesome details of the ongoing politically correct crime of abortion! Rather than exposing and condemning the abortion holocaust, the media are aiding and abetting the perpetrators. Consequently, self-proclaimed investigative reporters who portray themselves as "watchdogs," actually behave more like well-trained ostriches. Since 1973 they have turned blind eyes and deaf ears to the millions of victims of the abortion holocaust.

The Media Research Center (MRC) analyzes and meticulously documents how the Soviet-bloc media report important issues to the public. Analyzing reports on environmentalism, gun control, abortion, and most every other important issue, MRC found media bias to be consistent, widespread, and often profoundly outrageous. In studying abortion reporting MRC noted that defenders of life refer to themselves as "pro-life" and refer to their opponents as "pro-abortion." Perpetrators of the abortion holocaust, however, refer to themselves as "pro-choice" and refer to their opponents as "anti-abortion."

MRC analyzed news reports over a four-month period in 1988 when abortion was covered extensively by *ABC's World News Tonight*, the *CBS Evening News*, *CNN PrimeNews*, and *NBC Nightly News*. It was found that 97 percent of the time the perpetrators of the abortion holocaust were labeled "pro-choice," which is the label they have chosen for themselves, or they were given some other positive connoting label such as "abortion rights activists." Only once were they referred to as "pro-abortion," which is the label assigned to them by their opponents. However, the defenders of life were referred to as "pro-life," which is their preferred label, only 21 percent of the time. The remainder of the time they were labeled "anti-abortion," "anti-abortion activists," or were assigned some other negative connoting label as preferred by their opponents.[44]

Thus, the television news component of the Soviet-bloc media framed the issue of abortion from the perspective of the perpetrators of the abortion holocaust simply by adopting their language. This, of course, would tend to subtly shape public opinion in favor of abortion by incrementally programming viewers, slowly over time, to also frame the issue from the perspective of the perpetrators. This, however, is only one of the many psychological conditioning tools that can be employed by the Soviet-bloc media to desensitize mass audiences into accepting the unacceptable. Such psychological tools come in handy when nation building, as when one wishes to build a Soviet America!

By the way, while eagerly supporting heinously barbaric abortion practices on pre-born American children, liberals express outrage at the humiliation, abuse, and the appearance of torture of Iraqi war prisoners by U.S. troops at the Abu Ghraib prison facility. *The New York Times*, for example, ran more than 50 front-page stories criticizing the mistreatment of Iraqi war prisoners by U.S. troops. But how many front-page stories did they run to expose the torture, mutilation, and murder of the tens of millions of innocent, defenseless, aborted American babies? Why do they not place photos of prisoners abused at Abu Ghraib alongside photos of babies aborted in Soviet American abortion clinics? Why does *The New York Times* not follow the courageous example of the *Genocide Awareness Project* and print comparative images of the innocent victims of genocide in Nazi Germany, Soviet Russia, and Soviet America?

Why do liberals oppose water-boarding terrorists, which causes no physical pain and no physical harm; but support excruciatingly painful procedures such as saline solution abortion? Why do they subject their own pre-born children to this lethal form of torture? Why do liberals say that placing a caterpillar in the prison cell of a terrorist constitutes torture, but cutting a hole in the back of a child's skull, inserting a tube, and sucking the child's brains out does not constitute torture? Why do liberals always seem to identify with cold-blooded killers, but not with innocent victims? Is it just a coincidence that liberals oppose the death penalty for convicted murderers who rob others of their right to life, while liberals rob tens of millions of innocent, defenseless, pre-born children of their right to life?

Given that the Soviet-bloc media will show photos of abused Abu Ghraib prisoners, but not photos of aborted babies, one must go outside the Soviet-bloc media to compare the two classes of victims. One may do so quite easily by surfing the net and visiting various sites, such as the one set up by the *Genocide Awareness Project*.[45] Upon viewing photos of aborted babies, one discerns the chilling message liberals communicate to every pre-born child they can get their hands on: Welcome to Soviet America!

Encore: Using The U.S. Supreme Court To Build A Soviet America!

"I'm getting a chill up my spine because we're becoming more and more like the ex-Soviet Union." -Michael Savage,[46] radio talk show host and author

When the U.S. Supreme Court concluded in 1973 that a woman has a constitutional right to an abortion, Justice Harry Blackmun wrote the *Roe v. Wade* decision. However, as Judge Robert H. Bork[47] has noted, in his written decision Justice Blackmun cited no constitutional principle upon which the decision was rendered. This, of course, is clear evidence that we the people have a Constitution, and we have a government, but we do not have a constitutional government. If we do not have a constitutional government, then what kind of government do we have?

The perpetrators of the abortion holocaust and those who aid and abet the perpetrators have argued that there is an implicit right to privacy in the U.S.

Constitution. Therefore, they conclude, an implied right to an abortion is based upon an implied right to privacy. Consequently, although neither abortion nor privacy are discussed in the U.S. Constitution, liberals conclude the decision of a woman to have an abortionist torture her pre-born child to death is nonetheless protected by the U.S. Constitution.

Interestingly, the Soviet Americans who conclude that there is an implied right to an abortion in the Constitution based upon the implied right to privacy, have also concluded that there is no implied nor explicit "right of the people to keep and bear arms" in the Second Amendment to the U.S. Constitution even though this right is plainly printed in black and white. If people who seek an abortion have a constitutional right to privacy, how can government require us to seek permission and inform them, in writing, when we purchase or carry a firearm for personal, private self-defense? If we have a constitutional right to privacy, then how can government force us to tell them, by April 15th, how much money we earn every year, from where we acquired our money, where we invested our money, how much interest we earned on our money, and how we spent our money?

How can government tell us how much water we must have in our toilets - in the privacy of our bathrooms? How can government tell us what kind of light bulbs we must have in the privacy of our living rooms and bedrooms? How can government tell us what kind of personal ID cards we must carry in the privacy of our wallets? How can government secretly tap our private phones, secretly read our private mail, secretly monitor our private banking transactions, and secretly burglarize our private homes? Comrades, Why is there a constitutional right to privacy inside the abortion clinic but not outside the abortion clinic? Hey Bolshevik Democrats and Menshevik Republicans, Who do you think you are fooling?

Soviet American Hypocrites

The first U.S. troops arrived in Vietnam as military advisers in May of 1961 to prevent a Communist takeover of South Vietnam. The last U.S. troops left the U.S. Embassy in South Vietnam on April 30, 1975, two years after the 1973 signing of the Paris Peace Accords that formally ended combat activities by U.S. troops. Also in 1973, two years before the last U.S. troops left Vietnam, the U.S. Supreme Court rendered the *Roe v Wade* decision that essentially legalized abortion throughout America - as was done in Russia five decades earlier by Communist dictator Vladimir Lenin.

Consequently, while perpetrators of the abortion holocaust were literally throwing unmarketable body parts of aborted American babies into back alley dumpsters, they were simultaneously calling U.S. troops "Baby Killers" as they returned home from Vietnam. How do liberals explain this unconscionable, hypocritical behavior? To the dismay of American patriots, U.S. troops left a foreign land where they were fired upon by abortionists who were building a Soviet Vietnam, only to return home to be spat upon by abortionists who were building a Soviet America!

Some Pro-Life, Pro-American Victories!

"I call heaven and earth as witnesses today against you, that I have set before you life and death, blessing and cursing; therefore choose life, that both you and your descendants may live:" - *Holy Bible*, Deuteronomy 30:19

People of conscience have achieved some measure of success in their counterattacks against the Soviet American abortion industry. For example, in 1976 Congress passed the Hyde Amendment, introduced by Representative Henry Hyde, a conservative Republican from Illinois. The Hyde Amendment forbids the use of federal funds to finance abortions through the federal Medicaid program. The Hyde Amendment has been modified from time to time to provide exceptions, as in cases of rape, incest, or medical threats to the life of the mother. In 1980 the Hyde Amendment faced legal challenges from pro-abortion forces, but it was found to be constitutional by the U.S. Supreme Court. Prior to the passage of this life-saving Amendment, pro-life taxpayers were forced to pay for the abortions of 300,000 Medicaid recipients.

To counter efforts by abortionists to force people of conscience to participate in this documented crime against humanity, Congressman Dave Weldon, a conservative Republican from Florida who is also a physician, joined with Congressman Henry Hyde to pass the Hyde-Weldon Conscience Protection Amendment in 2004. This Amendment forbids abortion holocaust perpetrators from forcing health insurance companies, hospitals, physicians, and other health care professionals to involuntarily aid and abet those who commit abortion. Consequently, people of conscience cannot be forced to perform abortions or finance abortions, and they cannot be coerced into providing abortion referrals or abortion information.[48] Thanks to Congressmen Hyde and Weldon, as of 2004 people of conscience can declare themselves "Conscientious Objectors" in the endless war liberals are waging against unborn American children!

Also, in 2003 the Republican Congress banned partial birth abortion, and the U.S. Supreme Court upheld the congressional ban in 2007. Thus, while the abortion holocaust continues, this one horrific procedure is no longer legal in the USSA. In addition, as a testament to the ongoing efforts of pro-life groups to educate the public, the number of abortions have been declining across Soviet America since 1981. By exposing the gruesome facts hidden by the Soviet-bloc media and education establishment, the defenders of life have educated countless Americans, and, in the process, they have saved millions of innocent lives!

Clearly, the mass graves and slave labor camps of the Soviet Union are not the only symbols of the triumph of nihilism; we can also see that the astronomical body count produced by thousands of abortion clinics across the globe serve as further evidence that the philosophy of the sociopath has spread far beyond the borders of the Russian Narodniks!

Welcome to Soviet America, where innocent, defenseless human life is viewed as disposable.

Good-bye to Sovereign America, where "Life, Liberty, and the Pursuit of Happiness" were once proudly encouraged and celebrated by government, media, and the education establishment!

------†††------

"Before I formed you in the womb I knew you; before you were born I sanctified you; I ordained you…" - *Holy Bible*, Jeremiah 1:5

Chapter Ten

Health Care Perestroika
In Soviet America

Health Care Saboteurs
Seizing Soviet-Style Control Over Health Care!

In Soviet America there will be "a national Department of Health" that will provide "free medical service." - William Z. Foster, National Chairman of the Communist Party, USA, *Toward Soviet America,* 1932[1]

"We are going to push through this health care reform regardless of the views of the American people." - Senator Jay Rockefeller, Bolshevik Democrat from West Virginia[2]

Russia was the first nation on the planet to adopt Communism. This explains why Russia was also the first nation in the modern era to legalize abortion. So, it should come as no surprise that Russia was the first nation to make "free" and "universal" health care a constitutional right.[3] In the Soviet Union this right was enshrined in Article 42 of the Soviet Constitution, which stated, in part, that "Citizens of the USSR have the right to health protection. This right is ensured by free, qualified medical care provided by state health institutions."

The free, universal, government-run health care system in the Soviet Union was assessed just prior to the collapse of the USSR in 1991.[4] Under the Soviet system it was found that infant mortality was 2.5 times higher than in the USA, and maternal mortality was almost seven times higher. A summary of the Soviet health care system indicated that it was suffering from "chronic underfunding, antiquated and deteriorating facilities, inadequate supplies and outmoded equipment, poor morale and few incentives for health care workers, and consumer dissatisfaction." After the collapse of the USSR, Russia attempted to decentralized and partially privatize health care. Today "Bolshevik Big Brother" government remains involved in health care, which includes CMI, or Compulsory Medical Insurance (Sound familiar?) The current system is worse than the old Soviet system, which helps explain why Russians now have one of the lowest average life spans on the planet.[5]

156

An in depth study of Soviet health care was also conducted during the first few years of Mikhail Gorbachev's perestroika, or restructuring. Researchers Daniel S. Schultz, M.D. and Michael P. Rafferty, M.D.[6] found a two-tiered system of health care in the Soviet Union. Firstly, there was an "open" system for the general public, and secondly there was a "closed" system for the Soviet elite. Of course, the closed system for the Soviet elite received a disproportionate amount of funding, and doctors working in this system had a much lighter workload. In the open system for the lowly proletariat, doctors could spend seven minutes with each patient, but five minutes of that time were squandered filling out bureaucratic paperwork required by Soviet bosses. Clearly, under the Soviet system Communist bosses, their families and friends, and those who performed services highly regarded by the government, all received much better care than the lowly proletariat. This system, of course, is precisely the opposite of that which was promised to the "dictatorship of the proletariat" by Vladimir Lenin and his fellow Bolsheviks who built the Soviet system.

And of course, the final health care system that will eventually be set up in Soviet America will mirror that of the Soviet Union, Soviet Cuba, Soviet England, and other two-tiered systems. A two-tiered Soviet-style system is guaranteed in Soviet America - given that the Democrat members of Congress who supported the federal takeover of the private health care system in the USA have exempted themselves, the president, and other federal employees from the system they have created for the lowly Soviet American proletariat. Obama, Pelosi, and Reid said they created a good plan for us, but it's just not good enough for them!

However, Representative John Fleming,[7] a conservative Republican from Louisiana, introduced House Resolution 615. This resolution required all members of Congress who vote for a government-run health care system to give up their participation in the "closed" Federal Employees Health Benefits Program (FEHBP) and enroll in the same nightmarish "open" system they have created for the rest of us - the lowly proletariat. Congressman Fleming, who is also a physician and a conservative, understands the problem from the political, medical, and philosophical perspectives. Of course, when con-fronted with this resolution Bolshevik Democrats provided a predictable response: Nyet!

It should also be noted that the highly touted "free" health care in the USSR was not really free. Soviet citizens could find free health care in the Soviet Constitution, but not in Soviet hospitals. (Such constitutional disconnects are often found in Soviet America as well, demonstrating that the same mindset was at work in both the USSR and the USSA.) For those who wanted their prescriptions filled, wanted their much needed operation placed on a surgery schedule, or wanted to actually receive some other routine medical care, money must first be slipped "under the table" to government health care workers.

The fee of 500 rubles was required for standard treatment - an amount that was equivalent to two and a half months salary for the average Soviet citizen. Simply getting admitted into a hospital may cost 25 rubles, or a family member may be required to donate a unit of blood. If you want to know what "free" health care will look like when liberals have completed construction of their Soviet America, just take a close look at the health care available in yesterday's Soviet Union or today's Soviet Russia. The reader can also examine other nations that have eagerly embraced the obvious mistakes made in Russia.

Health Care Refugees:
Running Away From Soviet-Style Health Care!

"Thirty thousand Canadians are passing up free medical care at home to go to some other country where they have to pay for it. People don't do that without a reason." - Thomas Sowell[8]

Today we find health care refugees from Soviet Canada, Soviet England, Soviet Cuba, and other such nations. All are pouring into the USA and elsewhere to escape their "free," Soviet-style, "universal" health care systems. Like backyard mechanics and other do-it-yourselfers, some who cannot escape are forced to become their own doctors and dentists. For example, the dental waiting lists are so long in the United Kingdom that some British patients resort to pulling their own infected teeth with a pair of pliers.[9] Others trapped in this Soviet-style health care nightmare simply die while waiting month after month for free medical care that never materializes.

Walter E. Williams[10] noted that, according to the World Health Organization 25,000 British cancer patients die unnecessarily each year due to lack of adequate medical care through the NHS, or Britain's National Health Service. Williams further noted that 12 percent of specialists surveyed acknowledged that they had withheld kidney dialysis to patients in need of this lifesaving medical treatment; however the treatment was withheld for financial reasons - not medical reasons! Walter E. Williams further noted that in the

United Kingdom large numbers of people are languishing on waiting lists - not just medical waiting lists. Instead, many are placed on waiting lists while waiting to be placed on waiting lists! Yes, you read that correctly! Reading unvarnished facts about government-run health care often brings to mind past excursions into "Ripley's Believe It Or Not!"

In the USA a person diagnosed with cancer will wait approximately four weeks before treatment begins. In the United Kingdom a cancer patient must wait ten months, or about forty weeks, for their free cancer treatment to begin.[11] So, why are liberals, progressives, Communists, and other socialists replacing a health care system with a four-week treatment wait with a health care system with a forty-week treatment wait? If a patient in the UK must wait ten times longer for cancer treatment than a patient in the USA, why is this deadly delay considered to be a sign of "progress?" Such extreme treatment delays can only be seen as progress when viewed from the macabre perspective of the homicidal, the genocidal, the suicidal, and the delusional.

Glenn Beck[12] reported that Americans have a better survival rate for 13 of the 16 most common forms of cancer when compared to Europeans who depend on public health care. While American men with prostate cancer have a 91.9 percent survival rate, those in France have a 73.7 percent chance of survival. In the United Kingdom the survival rate drops down to 51.1 percent. Also, every year 100,000 operations are cancelled in the United Kingdom - after a long nerve-racking wait just to get on the waiting list. Beck also noted that one million British patients are waiting to be admitted to a hospital, and 200,000 are waiting to get on the waiting list - just as Walter E. Williams had reported!

The Brits are not the only ones with long waiting lists. While John Stossel reported that nearly one million Canadians are waiting to receive "free" health care at any given time, Glenn Beck noted that, of the 33 million people living in Canada, 800,000 are on those medical waiting lists for more than 18 weeks - that's 4 ½ months! According to Glenn Beck, every year tens of thousands of foreigners leave their homeland where government has made health care free, and they come to America where government has made health care expensive. Why? If the government-run health care systems in these nations are superior to the private-run systems in the USA, shouldn't tens of thousands of Americans be fleeing to these nations every year - instead of vice versa? Why the one-way street? Worldwide, people are voting with their feet and their pocketbooks, and they are clearly voting against government-run health care.

John Stossel[13] agrees. Many Canadians flee to the USA because they prefer to pay for expeditious private health care than wait for free, but dangerously sluggish, government-run health care. They flee their Soviet-style health care system because they know that, for American women suffering from breast cancer, approximately one in four will die from the disease. However, among women receiving "free" government-run health care in France, one in three will die, and in the United Kingdom nearly one out of every two women with breast cancer will die from this disease. So, why are liberals forcing Americans to make the same mistake the Russians, Canadians, French, and British have made by adopting a "free," government-run, Soviet-style health care system? Why do liberals want Americans to be subjected to a health care system that makes the IRS look compassionate and the Post Office look efficient?

Unfortunately, liberals have succeeded in duping Americans into incrementally Sovietizing our health care system through the creation of Medicare, Medicaid, and SCHIP - the State Children's Health Insurance Program. Predictably, they used Soviet-style psychological manipulation to achieve this objective. After all, Medicare is for the elderly (the senior proletariat), Medicaid is for the poor (the poor proletariat), and SCHIP is for the children (the youth proletariat). How could any moral American not enthusiastically embrace each of these compassionate-looking steppingstones that lead us directly *Toward Soviet America*?

Glenn Beck offered his television viewing audience a few thought-provoking questions. Firstly, he asked if they would rather send their children to a private school or a public school. Then he asked if they would prefer to use a private restroom or a public restroom. Now, if they would prefer a private school to a public school and a private restroom to a public restroom, why would they want to replace their private health care system with a public health care system? Perhaps Glenn Beck's most poignant observation was the fact that our ancestors left Europe and came to America precisely because they wanted to escape the kind of government programs now being foisted upon us, our children, and our grandchildren "regardless of the views of the American people!"

When trying to convince a crowd that a massive federal health insurance program would not destroy the private sector health insurance industry, President Obama said "If you think about it, UPS and FedEx are doing just fine, right? No, they are! The Post Office is always having problems." But with that statement Obama undercut his own argument for a massive government-run health insurance program. Why does he want the same government that runs the Post Office to greatly expand control over health care when he acknowledges that "The Post Office is always having problems," but private sector postal carriers such as UPS and FedEx are "doing just fine?"[14] Yes, the same federal government that has been guarding our borders is now guarding your health.

The Illegal Alien Proletariat:
Foot Soldiers In The Cold War
Against American-Style Health Care!

"In Los Angeles, 60 hospitals have closed their emergency rooms over the past decade, which imposes another kind of cost." - Phyllis Schlafly, A New Argument Against Immigration[15]

Did you notice that the Soviet Constitution stated that, "Citizens of the USSR [not illegal aliens] have the right to health protection?" Given that the Soviet Union collapsed in financial ruin without having the burden of providing free health care to 20 million illegal alien proletarians, what does that extra, unnecessary financial burden portent for the USA? Numerous hospitals across American have collapsed in financial ruin due to the federal requirement to provide "free" heath care to millions of illegal alien proletarians who have crossed our federally mismanaged borders.

Why has the federal government forced non-federally operated hospitals to provide health care to nonpaying patients while the federal government floods those same hospitals with millions of nonpaying illegal alien proletarians? A child can see that this is a formula for widespread financial disaster. Are they intentionally trying to bankrupt our American-style health care system in order to justify their dream of imposing a Soviet-style, federally operated system? The answer is obvious. What will happen when the liberals who created these health care problems actually take control over the entire system - as they claim they must do to solve the problems they have deliberately created?

In September of 2007 Rush Limbaugh[16] discussed the issue of health care on his popular radio program. He noted that the Los Angeles Times[17] printed an article stating that nearly two dozen private hospitals in Los Angeles and Orange counties were on the verge of bankruptcy or closure. It was further noted in the article that some community clinics and hospitals in these areas had already closed, and that these additional closures would put an enormous strain on existing hospitals. While much information was provided in the article, Rush exposed the fact that the authors failed to state the reason these hospitals were on the verge of financial collapse. The reason, of course, is the flood of uninsured patients, most of whom are nonpaying illegal alien proletarians who entered the country under the myopic eye of the taxpayer-funded U.S. Department of Homeland Security - the same Department whose vision improves when searching law-abiding American citizens at airports across the country. Why the tight, Soviet-style security within the USA - and the deliberately inadequate security at our borders? What are they telling us?

Liberals want the American people to be alerted to the health care crisis, but they are carefully hiding the fact that nonpaying illegal alien proletarians are the primary cause of the financial crisis facing numerous hospitals. Under-standing the cause may motivate exceedingly large numbers of taxpaying Americans to demand that, after decades of mismanagement, the federal government finally fulfill its constitutional obligation and secure our borders. But we should not expect liberals at the *Los Angeles Times* to inform the American people that liberals are using nonpaying illegal alien proletarians as a wrecking ball to deliberately destroy American-style health care in order to create an excuse to replace it with a substandard, Soviet-style health care system which, like our borders, they intend to micro-mismanage.

Sean Hannity[18] of the FOX News Network narrated a weeklong series that investigated the destructive effect of the federally-created illegal alien crisis. Hannity reported, for example, that Antelope Valley Hospital in California is in serious financial trouble and may be forced to close if the current trend continues. The reason, of course, is the never-ending stream of nonpaying patients. It is difficult to comprehend, but 40 to 45 percent of the patients seeking services at this hospital are nonpaying illegal aliens. How could any business operate in the black when nearly half the customers demand products and services with no intention of paying for them?

This is government-mandated theft!

This is government sabotage!

The three million nonpaying illegal alien proletarians seeking medical services in California have wreaked havoc on many budgets - both public and private. Consequently, the County of Sacramento was considering reducing services or cutting staff at area hospitals. To help alleviate the problem, Doctor Gene Rogers, the Medical Director of the Medically Indigent Services Program for Sacramento County, recommended to the

County Board of Supervisors that they cease providing non-emergency and elective medical care to nonpaying illegal aliens. He informed his superiors that, while [unconstitutional] federal law required emergency and certain other medical services to be provided to nonpaying illegal aliens, it was a violation of federal law to provide non-emergency and elective medical care unless the State legislature passed legislation allowing such services.

No one listened, so Dr. Rogers filed a whistleblower lawsuit. As one would expect in a government-run system, Dr. Rogers lost his job for trying to place his hospital in compliance with federal law. Now, Antelope Valley Hospital remains on the verge of financial collapse, County taxpayers continue to get stuck with the unpaid medical bills of con-artist foreigners, federal law continues to be violated by the County, the federal government continues to invite more nonpaying illegal aliens into the country, and anyone who tries to take corrective action is labeled xenophobic or racist by psychological warfare commissars! This is not mismanagement; this is not benign neglect or simple malfeasance; this is unceasing, aggressive, methodical, sabotage!

According to Pamela Hughes[19] of KTAR.com in Phoenix, Arizona, the federal government has set aside $250 million in taxpayer money each year for the last four years to reimburse border hospitals for the medical treatment of nonpaying illegal aliens. Hughes further noted that Doctor Michael Christopher, the chief of staff at St. Joseph's Hospital and Medical Center in Phoenix, said the $250 million in federal assistance amounts to "pennies on the dollar." St. Joseph's alone spends "millions upon millions each year" for the medical treatment of nonpaying illegal alien patients. Dr. Christopher opined that the federal government created this problem and has forced it upon states and hospitals. Consequently, hospitals across the nation have closed because nonpaying illegal aliens have left them "fiscally insolvent." In assessing the direction of this federally-created fiscal nightmare Doctor Christopher added that, "...we're not terribly hopeful."

Every border county in Arizona and California is in serious financial trouble due to what may be called a federal illegal alien crime syndicate. In addition, an online search indicated that many hospitals, including those far from our borders and deep within the heartland, are facing similar financial problems, and many are now closed or under threat of closure. However, like the liberals at the *Los Angeles Times*, liberals across the nation reported hospital closings due to financial problems, but many failed to inform their readers of the primary cause of these fiscal problems. Unfortunately, from New York to California, through journalistic malpractice liberal "reporters" have lured the

American people into a Soviet-style health care trap that would make any KGB disinformation officer proud. Welcome to Soviet America!

By the way, keep in mind that federal involvement in health care can only be justified for military personnel, military veterans, and other current and former federal employees. All other federal involvement in American health care is unconstitutional, and therefore illegal. It is a clear violation of the Tenth Amendment. This would hold true even if federal involvement did not amount to sabotage. By sabotaging our health care system, the liberal elite can claim that our private, American-style system does not work, and these same saboteurs must come to our rescue with a Soviet-style system from which only they will escape.

The Illegal Alien Proletariat:
A Clear & Present Danger!

"In the present crisis, government is not the solution to our problem; government is the problem." - President Ronald Reagan[20]

The federally-created illegal alien proletariat not only threatens our health by forcing the closure of numerous emergency rooms and hospitals across the nation, they also threaten our very lives and the lives of our children and grandchildren in more sinister ways. Keep in mind that, unlike legal immigrants, none of the illegal aliens walking our streets have been screened for the many contagious diseases that are prevalent in the Third World nations from which many have been transplanted!

In addition, none of these aliens have been screened by law enforcement. So, we have 12 to 20 million medically unscreened illegal aliens walking our streets, and unknown numbers of robbers, rapists, burglars, murderers, liberal gang members, drug dealers, child molesters, habitual drunk drivers, and identity thieves in our neighborhoods as well. According to Sean Hannity's report, as many as nine million Americans have their identities stolen every year, and most identity thieves are illegal aliens! (Of course, liberals don't like to call these identity thieves illegal aliens. They prefer to call them "undocumented workers.") To add insult to injury, federal IRS and Social Security privacy laws prohibit members of these agencies from notifying victims that their identities have been stolen! Thank you Uncle Scam! Yes, this is precisely the kind of Soviet-style mentality we want making critical, life-and-death health care decisions for us and our family members!

Doctor William Campbell Douglass II[21] of Baltimore, Maryland, has expressed deep concern for the health of his grandchildren in light of the known diseases that innumerable medically unscreened illegal aliens are bringing into our homeland - thanks to the U.S. Department of Homeland Security! According to Dr. Douglass the list includes tuberculosis, chagas disease, leprosy, dengue fever, whooping cough, cysticercosis, morgellons, and polio. In addition, cholera, typhoid, and plague are known to be existent in the home countries of some illegal aliens. Some of these diseases were previously unknown in the USA. Others were vanquished long ago, but are now reappearing. Many are lethal, some are incurable, and several bring a slow, painful, nightmarish death to their victims. Again, thank you Uncle Scam! Sure, we can't wait to turn our entire health care system over to federal officials who are knowingly exposing our children and grandchildren to these horrendous diseases.

Don't hold your breath waiting for so-called "investigative reporters" from the Soviet-bloc media to warn you of the terrifying health threat posed by the millions of medically unscreened illegal aliens occupying our homeland. And don't wait for them to warn you of the threat to your family posed by the millions of illegal aliens unscreened by law enforcement. On the contrary, consistent with Marxist theory, they portray the illegal aliens as proletarian victims, while health and safety conscious Americans are portrayed as racist, xenophobic, bourgeoisie! Again, Welcome to Soviet America!

As these diseases begin to spread across the USA, what effect will they have on our financially beleaguered health care system? What effect do Bolshevik Democrats and Menshevik Republicans expect to achieve by deliberately introducing and reintroducing such horrifying and deadly diseases within America's unsuspecting population? What can we do when the government deliberately and unnecessarily exposes our children and grandchildren to numerous deadly diseases, then tells us they must inject them with government-mandated vaccines laced with mercury, aluminum, and other debilitating and highly toxic chemicals in order to protect them from these diseases? What can we do when politicians, the media, and educators employ psychological weapons of mass deception and label us as "racists" when we tell them we want this moral madness to stop?

Moral Bankruptcy
Leads To Financial Bankruptcy!

"Contrary to popular opinion, 'free' health care is actually the most expensive kind - paid for in massively higher taxes and regulations that drive up medical costs exponentially." - Joseph Farah[22]

When government forces private hospitals to provide free health care, then floods those same hospitals with millions of nonpaying illegal alien proletarians, the cost of health care goes up dramatically! It goes up for several reasons. Most importantly, when the word spreads both inside and outside the USA that world class health care is free to anyone, including anchor baby moms and other scam artists, this incentive attracts an endless stream of nonpaying patients across our federally mismanaged borders. But no health care is really free. As this federally-created magnet draws more and more nonpaying patients, the cost to paying patients begins to skyrocket. Clearly, health care is growing more and more expensive for those who pay for it because federal saboteurs are making it increasingly available to more and more proletarians who don't pay for it!

The nonpaying patients are knowingly passing their costs onto patients who pay their own health care. They also pass the costs onto private insurance companies, who pass their costs onto their increasingly cash-strapped customers. In addition, nonpaying patients pass their costs onto taxpayers who are forced to bear yet another unnecessary financial burden by paying the unpaid bills left at hospitals and medical clinics. This is government-sponsored theft. In Marxist terminology, it is the tactical use of the proletariat by a Soviet-wannabe government to financially destroy and eventually displace the bourgeoisie - or the American middle class. So far, their plan is working quite well! More and more useful idiots are asking government health care saboteurs to seize greater control over the health care system they are methodically destroying.

Joseph Farah points out that when doctors and hospitals send medical bills to insurance companies or to the government, health care costs continue to rise. However, when both these institutions stay out of the billing process, the price of health care drops. Farah makes his point by noting that while most medical procedures have been increasing in cost over time, Lasik eye surgery has been decreasing in cost over time. Why? Lasik eye surgery has been decreasing in cost because it is not covered by private insurance nor by Medicare - which is taxpayer-funded government insurance. Yes, free health care really is the most expensive kind! "Free" health care contributed to the financial collapse of the Soviet Union. It has been slowing bankrupting Soviet England, Soviet France, Soviet Canada, and it is now bankrupting hospitals (and taxpayers and paying patients) across Soviet America.

Farah also points out that we rarely hear discussions about ways to reduce health care costs. Of course, those who are working to drive up health care costs would be engaging in self-defeating behavior if they offered solutions to the financial problems they have worked so hard to create. Clearly, the number one reason for the health care crisis in America is health care sabotage. Stop the government saboteurs and the chronic aiding and abetting by the media and you will cure what ails America's health care system.

One Hundred Million Dollar Theft Is Not A Crime In Soviet America!

"Her [Hillary Clinton's] agenda is total socialism, if not Communism, but healthcare is the only issue she can get away with promoting publicly... 'It's all about the children,' she says, 'We have to provide healthcare for the low income children.' Mrs. Clinton's idea of 'low income children' is a 24 year old living at home with a family income of up to $80,000.00 annually. Obviously, this is not about the children. It's about government control over your healthcare in the hands of politicians who won't stop until they have control over every aspect of your life." - J. R. Dieckmann[23]

In April 2007 Carol Plato[24] presented the costs of providing government mandated medical care to the illegal aliens (the illegal alien proletariat) that government politicians (Bolshevik Democrats and Menshevik Republicans) have invited to fleece responsible Americans (the bourgeoisie). Representing Martin Memorial Medical Center, Carol Plato spoke before the Florida House Committee on State Affairs. According to Plato, her facility has provided two illegal aliens with $1.5 million each in unreimbursed medical care.

The hospital spent $30,000 of its own money to return one of the illegal aliens to his home country of Guatemala. Because they ended this particular scam in this manner, they are being sued by the family of the illegal alien and the hospital is now facing $250,000 in legal fees. Welcome to Soviet America! Welcome to Sociopathic America!

According to Plato, in 2007 the Florida Hospital Association estimated that providing "free" health care to illegal aliens costs Florida hospitals approximately $100,000,000. Yes, that's one hundred million dollars in the State of Florida alone! Plato added that "a large percentage of the babies born at our facility are from illegal parents," and "...our health care costs are severely affected by this."

She stated that the Mexican Consulate and U.S. Immigration provided no assistance when contacted. When questioned, Plato added that federal immigration officials said they would do nothing to stop this scam unless the illegal alien commits a crime. In other words, entering the USA illegally is not a crime, and ripping off Florida hospitals for $100,000,000 is not a crime - at least not in Soviet America! Try ripping off the Marxist-inspired IRS for $100,000,000 and see what happens!

These diabolical politicians and bureaucrats do not belong in our health care system; they belong in our prison system!

Separation Of Church & State
Applies To All Government Property!

"Medicaid and Medicare combined made an estimated $23.7 billion in 'improper payments' last year, according to government audits." - Kaitlynn Riely[25]

Keep in mind that, in Soviet America, government and religious liberty cannot co-exist on taxpayer-funded property. Beginning in 1962 trans-nationalists re-educated the American people and instructed us that George Washington, John Adams, Thomas Jefferson, and James Madison did not understand the First Amendment to the U.S. Constitution because they believed it prohibited the federal government from restricting religious liberty. To correct the "mistake" of our Founders, liberals borrowed the principle of "separation of church and state" from Article 52 of the Soviet Constitution and applied it to all taxpayer-funded property in the USSA. Consequently, prayer, Bibles, and the Ten Commandments have been banned from taxpayer-funded schools and all other taxpayer-funded property.

So, if (or when) the builders of Soviet America finish constructing their government-run, Soviet-style health care system, you can forget about bringing priests, ministers, rabbis, Bibles, crosses, holy water, prayer books, et cetera, to friends and relatives who may be lying on their deathbeds in taxpayer-funded hospitals. The Soviets will not tolerate it! Of course, they will wait until we no longer have private health care facilities to which we can escape. At that point attorneys from the Elizabeth Gurley Flynn-created ACLU will be more abundant in hospitals than bedpans! Again, it may not happen immediately, but you can bet your last tax dollar it will happen eventually! Never underestimate the criminal mind! That's how we got into this mess in the first place!

President Reagan was 100 percent correct when he said, "In the present crisis, government is not the solution to our problem; government is the problem." Firstly, government has sabotaged our private health care system by overloading it with millions of nonpaying illegal aliens who have closed countless emergency rooms and numerous hospitals. Secondly, government has sabotaged our health and that of our children and grandchildren through unnecessary exposure to 12 to 20 million medically unscreened illegal aliens. Thirdly, government has subjected our children and grand-children to vaccines laced with dangerous chemicals. Fourthly, government has strategically refused to restrict frivolous law suits against health care workers and hospitals in order to drive medical costs through the roof. Fifthly, they refuse to permit American citizens to purchase health insurance across state lines, thus limiting choices, restricting competition, and driving up costs. Lastly, following the old Soviet medical model, they place layer and layer of restrictive red tape upon the health care industry - thus driving up administrative costs.

In spite of all this, Obama tells us his government-run, Soviet-style health care system will reduce the cost by controlling costs. But they have never reduced costs! The federal government controlled about 50 percent of America's health care before passage of the so-called comprehensive health care reform bill. So, why have they not already reduced costs in govern-ment-run systems like Medicare and Medicaid, both of which experience massive, chronic corruption and are going broke under government micro-mismanagement?

Do the American people really believe that the government officials who have been deliberately driving up health care costs for decades will reverse course and suddenly work to reduce costs - without reducing the quality and the quantity of the health care received? Do the American people really want health care saboteurs taking complete control of our health care system? Instead of completely Sovietizing health care, let's de-Sovietize the system instead. Let's kick the federal saboteurs out of our private health care system and give control back to the states and the private sector - as required by the Tenth Amendment to the U.S. Constitution!

Smooth Operator: Obstructing American-Style Reform In Order To Demand Soviet-Style Reform!

"Proponents claim the present system leaves 47 million people without insurance and unable to get it. Bull. Almost half of these uninsured could afford coverage but choose not to obtain it; almost half only remain uninsured for four months; and millions are noncitizens." - David Limbaugh, More Health Care Lies[26]

Senator Jim Demint, a conservative Republican from the state of South Carolina, appeared *On The Record* with Greta Van Susteren.[27] Senator Demint, who authored the book, *Saving Freedom: We Can Stop America's Slide Into Socialism,* was highly critical of President Obama's efforts to have the federal government take over health care. Senator Demint noted that the health care plan pushed by Obama has no tort reform and actually adds more liability - which of course drives up the cost of health care.

Throughout this chapter and throughout this book it has been stated that the builders of Soviet America sabotage the private sector so they can put forth government plans to "fix" the systems they have sabotaged. By repeating this process over and over again, government eventually takes over and micro-manages every aspect of the private sector.

In a health care discussion with Greta Van Susteren, Senator Jim Demint described a variation of this tactic wherein Senator Barack Obama had sabotaged efforts at liberty-preserving health care reform, thus setting the stage for President Barack Obama to later demand liberty-crushing health care reform. Senator Demint stated the following:

"The fact is Greta, he's [Obama's] not for reform. He voted against everything we put up for health care reform when he was in the Senate. What he wants is for the government to take it over. Just like General Motors and AIG." Senator Demint added the following: "Republicans have put forth much more health care reform than the Democrats...in the last several years since I've been in the Senate. Obama voted against everything that would have helped make it more affordable and accessible for people to have their own insurance when they can't get it at work. He's saying we don't want to do anything. The facts are against him. We tried to reform the system, now he wants the government to take it over. We need to stop him."

In Sun Tzu fashion, Barack Obama was against health care reform before he was for it!

Why did Senator Obama vote against every bill designed to reduce the cost of health care and to make it more affordable and more accessible? Why did President Obama not add tort reform to his government health care takeover plan in order to reduce the cost of health care and make it more affordable and accessible? Why does he not stop illegal aliens from bankrupting and closing down countless emergency rooms and hospitals across America - which drives up the cost of health care for American citizens? The answer is obvious: The builders of Soviet America must destroy it so they can restructure it. The trillion dollar question is: Will the American people stop the health care saboteurs from completely taking over health care? Can the American people remove government saboteurs from the health care system? Can we repeal and replace the current federal takeover plan?

In addition, while Obama said the federal government must become more involved in health care to reduce costs, the facts do not support this claim. As noted by David Limbaugh,[28] greater federal involvement would increase, not decrease, health care costs. Limbaugh noted that the Congressional Budget Office (CBO) concluded "the plan would fall $239 billion short of covering its initial cost estimates of $1 trillion." Also, government estimates for proposed programs are always far below actual costs. For example, Limbaugh reported that, in 1965 government planers projected Medicare Part A would cost taxpayers $9 billion. However, the actual costs were $67 billion, or seven times higher than projected.

"Even worse," Limbaugh noted, government projections for the Medicaid special hospital subsidy was projected at $100 million in 1987, but the actual cost to taxpayers was $11 billion! That's more than 100 times higher than the government had projected. Given the history of government greatly underestimating the cost of their Soviet-style programs (in order to dupe taxpayers into supporting them), what happens to the American economy - and to the American taxpayer - if Obama's projected cost of $1 trillion for his federal takeover of health care is seven times higher - or more than 100 times higher than projected? Could America remain fiscally viable with an additional taxpayer burden of $7 trillion just for this program? What if the Medicaid model is followed? The American taxpayer could be saddled with an additional $100 trillion in taxes! America would collapse in financial ruin - just like the USSR! Thank you Comrade Obama!

In talking with Sean Hannity[29] on the FOX News Network, Senator John McCain, a Menshevik Republican from Arizona, called for tort reform. According to McCain about $100 billion is spent annually on defensive medicine. In addition, a neurosurgeon may spend as much as $200,000 annually for malpractice insurance. All these lawyer-generated costs are passed on to health care consumers. McCain also pointed out a glaring inconsistency conveniently overlooked by the self-proclaimed "watchdogs" in the Soviet-bloc media: Obama said the government takeover of health care will reduce health care costs, but at the same time he is calling for increased taxes on "the rich" to pay for his plan.

As Brent Baker[30] of the Media Research Center pointed out, Sharyn Alfonsi of ABC and Katie Couric of CBS presented positions calling for increased taxes on the rest of us as well. Instead of exposing this scam, these "watch-dogs" at ABC and CBS were found aiding and abetting the perpetrators by calling for a federal tax to be added onto the price of soft drinks to help pay for Obama's government-run health care plan. But if his plan will reduce costs, then taxes should be correspondingly reduced, not increased. What a scam!

Day after day the electronic and print media were filled with reports of the need for health care reform, but the media never pointed out the glaring fact that those who continued to demand Soviet-style reform were the same diabolical creatures that concocted the need for reform. Moreover, as reported by Christopher Neefus,[31] a *New York Times/CBS News* poll showed that 72 percent of the poll respondents supported a government-run health insurance plan that would compete with private sector plans. However, 48 percent of the poll respondents had voted for Obama, but only 25 percent had voted for McCain. So the sample employed to conduct the poll contain-ed nearly twice as many Obama supporters than McCain supporters, thus skewing the results heavily in favor of a government-run insurance plan. Welcome to the world of Soviet-style psychological warfare!

Government Health Care Has Been Making Us Sick For Decades!

"Swinging open the door, I stepped into a nightmare: the ER overflowed with elderly people on stretchers, waiting for admission. Some, it turned out, had waited *five days*. The air stank with sweat and urine. Right then, I began to reconsider everything that I thought I knew about Canadian health care." - Dr. David Gratzer, a Canadian-trained physician who practices medicine in the USA. From, The Ugly Truth About Canadian Health Care[32]

Doctor Len Horowitz,[33] who calls himself the "King David of natural healing," reports that AIDS, fibromyalgia, chronic fatigue, Gulf War Syndrome, multiple sclerosis, lupus, Guillian Barre, asthma, allergies, autism, hyper-activity, attention deficit disorders, numerous types of cancer, and other illness are attributable to vaccines. In early 2008 Dr. Horowitz was a guest on the *Coast to Coast AM* overnight radio program hosted by George Noory.[34] On this program Dr. Horowitz claimed that babies are needlessly injected with the Hepatitis B vaccine, exposed to heavy metal toxicity and amino acid poisons. He added that vaccines make children more susceptible to autoimmune diseases - including cancer. Dr. Horowitz emphasized the link between autism and vaccines. As many Americans are aware, autism has increased at a truly alarming pace in recent years. Although not recorded in the *Coast to Coast AM* archives, Dr. Horowitz said the govern-ment mandate to inject our children with vaccines known to contain such health destroying substances is nothing short of "genocide."

Dr. Horowitz is not alone in his concern over vaccines. For example, a visit to the web site of the *Autistic Society*[35] reveals some shocking and depressing information. Posted at that site is an article by John Hanchette[36] of the *Niagara Falls Reporter*. According to Hanchette about one in every 5,000 children in the USA was afflicted with autism 20 years ago. By the year 2000 the ratio was one in 500, and by 2002 it was one in 250. In the year 2003 nearly one in every 155 male toddlers was afflicted with autism. In early 2010 the *Autistic Society* reported that one in every 110 children in America is diagnosed with autism. Hanchette points out that over a period of 15 years the number of autism cases in California increased by 440 percent, and that the special educational requirements of each autistic child costs states about $2 million for the first 18 years of life. How can this mind-boggling crisis be explained?

Like Dr. Len Horowitz, John Hanchette lays the blame on government-mandated vaccines laced with the neurotoxin mercury. During the 1990s the number of vaccines given to our children was increased from 20 to 40, and this increased dosage pushed the amount of mercury injected into our children to a level that is many times higher than permitted by EPA stan-dards. Although the federal government and the pharmaceutical industry knew that our children were at risk of being injected with a collection of vaccines laced with a dangerously excessive amount of this neurotoxin, they continued to vaccinate 8,000 children each day over a period of nearly four years.

This is not the kind of health care Americans should expect from fellow Americans, but this is precisely the kind of health care Americans must expect from the cold-blooded, pro-abortion, pro-euthanasia, pro-population control fanatics who are building their Soviet utopia! This is the kind of health care one would expect from health care saboteurs who want to overload and bankrupt the system with chronically ill and special needs children. Keep in mind that, during the 1990s, while the Clintons were saying the federal government must take complete control of our health care system "for the children," that same government was knowingly using a chemical weapon of mass destruction against our children. So, the next time pro-abortion, pro-euthanasia, pro-population control liberals say they must control our health care "for the children," you'll know exactly what they mean!

John Hanchette also cites a study that showed children who received mercury-laced vaccines were nearly 27 times more likely to develop autism than children who did not. Armed with this information, one begins to understand why Doctor Len Horowitz used the word "genocide" in his discussion of federally mandated vaccines. In light of the "clear and present danger" the federal government poses to the health of the American people, we must fight against the federal takeover of our health care system - and we must fight as if our very lives depended on it! Instead of separating church from state, let's separate health care from state! (When you truly understand how government psychopaths threaten our health and safety, you begin to realize why they want to take our guns away - and act as if their lives depended on it!)

A Liberal Exposes
A Government-Created Health Threat!

"Nor were the problems I identified unique to Canada - they characterized all government-run health care systems. Consider the recent British controversy over a cancer patient who tried to get an appointment with a specialist, only to have it canceled - 48 times. More than 1 million Britons must wait for some type of care, with 200,000 in line for longer than six months." - Dr. David Gratzer, a Canadian-trained physician who practices medicine in the USA. From, The Ugly Truth About Canadian Health Care[37]

For those who believe the vaccine health threat is a partisan issue, they simply need to check out an article written by Robert F. Kennedy, Jr.[38] The article, titled "Deadly Immunity," contains some very scary information. For example, Kennedy, a very liberal Democrat, reported that members of the federal Centers for Disease Control (CDC) and the Federal Drug Administration (FDA) held a secret meeting with leaders of the pharmaceutical industry to discuss the link between mercury-laced vaccines and autism.

After reviewing numerous studies linking thimerosal - a preservative used in vaccines that contains 50 percent ethylmercury - to autism, those attending the meeting concluded a link could be established. However, the group did not discuss ways to alert and protect the public from further harm, but instead they put together a plan to cover up their findings. In addition, they continued to subject the American public and others around the world to mercury-laced vaccines to protect the financial interests of the pharmaceutical industry. In further exposing the true depth of their moral insanity, Kennedy reported that members of this secret cabal decided to hide from the public studies that exposed the link - and further ordered new pseudo studies to be conducted for the sole purpose of whitewashing the link between vaccines and autism. This is your tax dollars at work! This is your federal health protectors - the CDC and FDA - at work! If you have any questions, read the article yourself!

Doctor Joseph Mercola[39] has investigated the link between mercury-laced vaccines and autism, and has posted a link to the Kennedy article, as well as other revealing articles, at his web site. He also posted a link to a YouTube.com interview of Robert F. Kennedy, Jr. by Joe Scarborough of MSNBC's *Scarborough Country*. According to Dr. Mercola, "Today, there is little doubt that thimerosal, a preservative that is 50 percent ethylmercury, is a contributing factor in many cases of autism. It is a well-established fact that exposure to mercury can cause immune, sensory, neurological, motor, and behavioral dysfunctions - all similar to traits defining, or associated with, autism."

People can argue that there are two sides to the vaccine-autism debate. But no one can justify the wanton disregard for the health of the American people by government agents in the public health sector who hide damaging information, fabricate false data, and continue to administer highly suspect vaccines. Yes, we need health care reform. But the only reform that will improve the health of the American people will be the type of reform that removes government saboteurs from our health care system. By adding more government saboteurs through a government takeover of health care we place ourselves on a one-way street toward national suicide!

Bolshevik Big Brother Is Watching You!

"The majority of France's state-owned hospitals are managed in a way that is reminiscent of the old USSR..." - Conservative News Alerts[40]

Nothing engages a predator more than an opportunity to closely monitor the behavior of its prey!

Keep in mind that just about everything you do affects your health. Everything you eat, everything you drink, and everything you smoke, affects your health. Everything you choose to not eat, not drink, and not smoke impinges upon your health. How you sleep, how long you sleep, when you sleep, and where you sleep impacts your health. What you choose to wear and what you choose not to wear may affect your health.

If you choose to not exercise, if you choose to exercise, what type of exercise you choose, all influence your health. Your employment affects your health, your lack of employment affects your health, and your leisure choices affect your health. Your social habits and sexual habits may have a lasting impression on your health. Where you live, how you travel, and where you travel, all have an impact on your health.

In other words, every lifestyle choice you make may directly or indirectly affect your health. As a matter of fact, what you think, what you feel, and what you believe can have a positive or negative impact on your health. Certainly you've heard of the placebo effect? And we all know that both acute emotional trauma and chronic stress can impact one's health. Consistent with this theme, for many generations *Reader's Digest* has been telling us that "Laughter is the best medicine." Therefore, when government is in charge of your health care everything you think, feel, say, or do can potentially fall under federal jurisdiction.

If you don't think government can dramatically affect your life based simply on the thoughts and feelings you express within a medical context, you haven't been paying attention. As John Velleco[41] of Gun Owners of America has reported, more than 150,000 veterans have been stripped of their Second Amendment rights in recent years because they reported nightmares or other symptoms of combat-related stress or depression within a counseling setting.

Moreover, these rights were stripped away without due process of law. Of course, this could never happen in America, but it can happen, and has happened, in what may justifiably be called Soviet America! To correct this injustice Senator Richard Burr, a conservative Republican from North Carolina, has introduced S.669, the Veterans Second Amendment Protection Act. As one would expect in America, Senate Bill 669 requires government health care workers to respect a veteran's right to due process of law. If an individual is clearly a danger to himself or others, subsequent loss of the constitutionally-protected right to armed self-defense must take place in an open courtroom - not behind closed doors in a government-run medical facility.

Criminals are guaranteed due process of law under the Fifth Amendment to the U.S. Constitution. Therefore, veterans who have committed no crime certainly must not be punished with the loss of a constitutionally-protected right without due process of law. Only in a Soviet-style America could law-abiding veterans be ranked lower than robbers, rapists, and murderers! Only in Soviet America do we find Bolshevik Democrat lawyers rushing to the U.S. Naval detention facility at Guantanamo Bay, Cuba, to establish and protect the "constitutional rights" of incarcerated foreign terrorists, while stripping away the constitutional rights of American veterans!

Unknown to many Americans, the Obama Administration used the pseudo "economic stimulus plan" passed in early 2009 to help set up a Bolshevik Big Brother health care monitoring system. According to Bob Unruh[42] of World-NetDaily.com, the bill contained a provision that requires all Americans to participate in a government-run electronic medical records program - just like they have at the VA! Yes, as in the Soviet Union, no one in Soviet America can refuse to submit to this heavy-handed government invasion of privacy.

Bob Unruh reported that, "…documentation on abortions, mental health problems, impotence, being labeled as a non-compliant patient, lawsuits against doctors, and sexual problems could be shared electronically with, perhaps, millions of people." He further noted that an organization called Consumer Watchdog stated the following: "Reportedly Google is pushing for the provisions so it may sell patient medical information to its advertising clients on the new 'Google Health' database." Yes, nothing engages a predator more than an opportunity to closely monitor the behavior of its prey! Now we know why leftist Chris Matthews of MSNBC gets a thrill up his leg when he thinks about Barack Obama!

You say you don't want that mercury-laced vaccine the CDC says is not laced with mercury? Sorry! The choice is not yours to make. It's only your body when you want an abortion. You can only be pro-choice when you choose death. Yes, it's a private decision to be made between you and your doctor. But your doctor now works for the government, and the doctor must do what the Health Care Commissar says must be done. Your Bolshevik Big Brother is trying to protect you from that flu epidemic - which, like human-caused global warming - may be just a bunch of hot air!

Yes, choosing to have an abortion is a matter of privacy, according to liberals. But now if a woman chooses to have the abortion - or any other medical procedure, liberals say it's no longer a privacy issue. Once the decision is made to have the abortion it becomes the government's business and it must, by law, be placed into electronic medical records for review by unnamed doctors, nurses, clerks, bureaucrats, government researchers, and others. When it comes to choosing whether or not you wish to participate in Big Brother's medical monitoring scheme, those who claim to be pro-choice - say you no longer have a choice!

The federal Office of Health Information and Technology will maintain the intrusive "health records database" under the federal Department of Health and Human Services - a federal department predicted by Communist William Z. Foster in 1932. According to Austin Hill,[43] within the health care sections of Obama's so-called stimulus bill - which was read by few, if any, in Congress before it was passed - the federal government has assumed the power to provide "appropriate information to help guide medical decisions at the time and place of care." Not only will the federal government "help guide medical decisions," but doctors who "spend too much" on certain patients may be assessed "penalties."

In other words, after telling us for several decades that a concern for privacy dictates that abortion and other medical procedures are to be made between a woman and her doctor, liberals suddenly changed their minds. Agents of the federal government may now "help guide medical decisions." And they can't "help guide medical decisions" unless they are cognizant of your medical history and your current medical choices.

Question: Why do government officials want to read your medical records, but show no interest in reading the medical legislation they fashion into law?

For an eye-opening - and frightening - expose of the sinister mindset behind the government takeover of health care, the reader is encouraged to visit the following web site: http://www.DefendYourHealthCare.us. At this web site Betsy McCaughey, founder of the Committee to Reduce Infection Deaths and a former New York lieutenant governor, discusses how Obama and the Democrats will reduce health care to seniors by cutting Medicare by $500 billion - and removing the process from public scrutiny. (These are the same Democrats who always scare seniors into voting for Democrats by telling them Republicans want to cut their Social Security.) McCaughey provides a brief but chilling account of how the Democrat plan will limit - even prohibit - health care for seniors, the disabled, and others deemed unworthy by cold-blooded government commissars.

Please show me where in the U.S. Constitution the federal government has been granted such intrusive, dictatorial power? Austin Hill concluded that, "Essentially, we now have the beginnings of a governmental agency that eventually will, by force of law, determine which persons will be eligible for health care, and what treatment they will receive." According to Austin Hill and other astute observers of the federal government, this language lays the groundwork for the government to assert, at a future date, that certain individuals may have a duty, or an obligation, to die! Or do you believe the pro-abortion, pro-euthanasia, pro-health care rationing, pro-population control, pro-Soviet crowd would never subject the "useless eaters" among the lowly proletariat and the much-hated bourgeoisie to such inhumane treatment? Remember Terri Schiavo?

It is as clear as a bell that predators have determined the "herd" must be reduced. You may be too old, too weak, or too sickly. You may be too self-destructive, too time-consuming, or just too much trouble. Most important-ly, you may be too expensive. You must sacrifice for "the greater good" as any good Marxist would say. With control of your medical records and your medical choices, those who have "a lust for power over others" now have Soviet-style power over you! Thanks to the pervasive, prolonged, and strategic use of psychological warfare, the pro-choice electorate has chosen to no longer live in America. Therefore, you no longer live in America. Welcome to your new home. Welcome to Soviet America!

American-Style Solutions
To Government-Created Problems!

"Communists weren't defeated with the fall of the USSR, they simply went underground then popped up here in America and hijacked the Democrat Party." - J. R. Dieckmann[44]

One: Stop the federal government from using nonpaying illegal aliens to sabotage the financial solvency of our American-style health care system.

As noted above, with this tactic the builders of Soviet America have closed or financially devastated numerous emergency rooms and hospitals across the country, and have forced responsible people to pay higher health care costs in the process. Demand secure borders and no jobs, no sanctuary, and no amnesty for the federally-created illegal alien proletariat.

Two: Stop the federal government from using medically unscreened illegal aliens to directly sabotage the health of the American people.

As discussed above, according to Doctor William Campbell Douglass II, the 12 to 20 million medically unscreened illegal aliens in our country un-necessarily expose us, our children, and our grandchildren to tuberculosis, chagas disease, leprosy, dengue fever, whooping cough, cysticercosis, morgellons, and polio. In addition, cholera, typhoid, and plague are known to be existent in the home countries of some illegal aliens.

Three: Stop the federal government from using poorly tested and highly suspect vaccines. As discussed above, these vaccines sabotage our health, create more health care problems than they solve, and threaten to overload our American-style health care system with disabled and chronically ill patients.

As discussed in this chapter, Doctor Len Horowitz contends that AIDS, chronic fatigue, Gulf War Syndrome, fibromyalgia, multiple sclerosis, lupus, Guillian Barre, asthma, allergies, autism, hyperactivity, attention deficit disorders, numerous types of cancer, and other illness are attributable to vaccines.

Four: Stop the federal government from using the legal profession to sabotage our ability to afford American-style health care. Demand real tort reform.

Getting lawyers out of the equation would substantially reduce health care costs. As columnist Charles Krauthammer[45] (who is also a physician) has reported, according to a Massachusetts Medical Society study, five out of six doctors stated that about 25 percent of the tests, procedures, and referrals they ordered were made just to avoid lawsuits. The Pacific Research Institute concluded that $200 billion is wasted each year on defensive medicine. Krauthammer stated that, "Just half that sum could provide a $5,000 health insurance grant - $20,000 for a family of four - to the uninsured poor (U.S. citizens ineligible for other government health assistance)." According to Krauthammer we need to "abolish the entire medical malpractice system" and create a pool that malpractice patients can access for financial compensation. A relatively small tax on all health-insurance premiums could fund the pool. Moreover, medical experts, not lawyers and untrained jurors, would decide each case, and careless doctors would face loss of their medical license instead of multimillion dollar law-suits.

Five: Stop the government from sabotaging our ability to purchase afford-able American-style health insurance across state lines.

According to Ann Coulter,[46] "You could fix 90 percent of the problems with health insurance by ending the federal law allowing states to ban health insurance sales across state lines." In some states one insurance company may control 80 percent of the market. Simply put, we have insufficient American-style free market forces at work in the health insurance industry. Vigorous competition always drives down the cost of a product or service. In addition, government forces insurance companies to cover services that most Americans have no interest in insuring, such as early childhood development programs and sex-change operations. President Reagan was correct: Government is not the solution to our problem; government is the problem.

Six: Stop the federal government (and the media) from using false and misleading data to sabotage confidence in our American-style health care system. This type of fraud is immoral, unethical, and should be illegal.

We are told that between 46 and 50 million Americans are without health insurance. But what we are not told is that when you remove from the equation illegal aliens, legal foreigners, and people who can afford health insurance but chose not to buy it; when you remove people who are eligible for SCHIP or Medicaid but chose not to enroll; and when you remove people who are between jobs and without health care insurance for a short period of time - usually four to six months - you end up with a figure of about 15 million chronically uninsured people. That's about 5 percent of the total U.S. population.

So, as Doctor Eric Novack[47] points out, why has the federal government created a health insurance plan that threatens the health care of nearly 100 percent of the American people when only a tiny percent are in need of genuine help? What about a voucher plan targeting only this specific population? Why not leave the rest of us alone? Why have politicians excluded themselves from the program they have unnecessarily created for the rest of us? In addition, Dr. Novack said the federal plan will not reduce health care costs, will not improve health care for the American people, but it does give the federal government the power to dictate the health care options of the American people. No thanks! I'd rather live in James Madison's Sovereign America - not William Z. Foster's Soviet America!

Seven: As recommended by J. R. Dieckmann,[48] we could open neighborhood medical clinics. They could be a mixture of privately operated and county operated facilities. We must keep the federal saboteurs out of our private and local health care systems. Our health, welfare, and liberty hang in the balance!

Welcome to Soviet America!

Good-bye private American-style health care!

Hello public Cuban-style health care!

Chapter Eleven

The Soviet-Bloc Media!

"We have no freedom of the press for the bourgeoisie. We have no freedom of the press for the Mensheviks and Socialist-Revolutionaries, who represent the interests of the beaten and overthrown bourgeoisie. But what is there surprising in that? We have never pledged ourselves to grant freedom of the press to all classes, and to make all classes happy." - Joseph Stalin, second Communist dictator of the Soviet Union[1]

"It should be clear by now that my focus here is not freedom of speech or of the press...This freedom is all too often an exaggeration...At the very least, blind references to freedom of speech or the press serve as a distraction from the critical examination of other communication policies." - Mark Lloyd, "Chief Diversity Officer," Federal Communications Commission, Obama Administration[2]

In decades past, conservative pundits seemed to perpetually enter, exit, and re-enter a state of disbelief and disappointment when, once again, they observe unethical and malicious displays of psychological manipulation by the leftist media. However, many Sovereign Americans are beginning to face the facts. They are beginning to recognize that the leftist media are not objective; nor are they simply biased. Instead, the leftist media are corrupt, and there's a big difference between bias and corruption.

Moreover, they are beginning to learn that the leftist media are not liberal. Instead, they are Marxist; they are Leninist; they are Stalinist, but they are not liberal. By definition a liberal is someone who is tolerant and open minded. But the American liberal is intolerant and closed minded. The American liberal embraces both socialism and fascism - the political philosophies of narrow-minded tinhorn dictators and intolerant genocidal maniacs. Therefore, media leftists only wear the mask of the tolerant and open minded liberal.

So-called liberals do not show occasional favoritism or intermittent infatuation, as one would expect if they were simply biased. Instead, they consistently engage in Soviet-style psychological manipulation of the masses. They routinely provide protection for politicians who advocate Marxist principles and they launch savage, merciless, venomous attacks against those who oppose them. That is not the kind of behavior one would expect from people who are simply biased. However, that is precisely the kind of behavior one would expect from people who are corrupt. That is precisely the kind of behavior one would expect from people who are Marxists, Leninists, or Stalinists. That is precisely the kind of behavior one would expect from morally-challenged people who wish to build a Soviet America.

Many conservatives and libertarians are beginning to realize the undeniable reality that the Soviet American media are just as corrupt and just as leftist as one would find in the Marxist-controlled media of Soviet China, Soviet Cuba, or the now defunct Soviet Union. For all the above reasons, the term "liberal media" must be replaced with far more accurate terms such as the leftist media, Marxist media, Leninist media, Stalinist media, Soviet-bloc media, Soviet American media, or the corrupt media!

The Soviet-Bloc Media: Media We Cannot Believe In

"Infiltrate the press. Get control of book-review assignments, editorial writing, policy-making positions." And, "Gain control of key positions in radio, TV and motion pictures." - Communist goals #20 and #21, respectively, as documented by former FBI agent W. Cleon Skousen[3]

Following the directive put forth by Karl Marx in *The Communist Manifesto*, Soviet Americans seized control of the media establishment generations ago. Consistent with what has been stated in previous paragraphs, collectively, all their print and electronic Marxist media outlets may appropriately be referred to as the Soviet-bloc media. This may be contrasted with the Sovereign American media, which only began to blossom with the advent of talk radio in the 1980s and the Internet in the 1990s. The Sovereign American media seek internal fairness and balance. However, due to the extreme corruption of the Soviet American media, the Sovereign American media spend much of their time and effort exposing and countering Soviet-bloc media propaganda and disinformation.

The goal of the Soviet-bloc media is to facilitate the construction of a Soviet America. This is accomplished, in part, by aiding and abetting fellow Bolshevik Democrats in the Soviet-bloc education establishment, business community, religious community, civic community, and in all levels of government. This objective is also accomplished by destroying "counter-revolutionaries" such as former Alaska Governor Sarah Palin, Ohio's "Joe the plumber," not to mention Menshevik Republicans such as Dan Quayle,

George W. Bush, or anyone else who may pose a threat to Bolshevik Demo-crat control over the Soviet America they are steadfastly constructing.

The Soviet-Bloc Media & Psychological Warfare: A Case Study!

"...for the last year, we have been brainwashed, propagandized, and insultingly lectured to by the news media..." - Newt Gingrich[4]

Former Speaker of the House Newt Gingrich was asked by Greta Van Susteren of the FOX News Network to give his assessment of media coverage of Governor Sarah Palin during the 2008 presidential campaign. Mr. Gingrich said, "This is like watching Pravda." Pravda, of course, was the official newspaper of the Communist Party of the Soviet Union. It was used as a vehicle to inform and educate the public and indoctrinate readers with the principles and practices of Communism. Pravda means "truth" in Russian. But those familiar with Communism know the words truth and Communism are thoroughly incompatible. Some Americans are slowly waking up to the reality that the word truth is employed in today's Soviet American media with the same level of accuracy as was displayed in yesterday's Soviet Russian media.

Media Psychological Warfare Target: Sarah Palin

"She [Governor Sarah Palin] had no idea how evil the news media could be." - Glenn Beck[5]

"...as my own experience [with Communists] shows, that those who told the truth became the victims of an unprecedented smear attack..." - Ronald Radosh, former American Communist[6]

Mr. Gingrich focused on *The New York Times*, *Saturday Night Live*, and others. He stated that Katie Couric misquoted Henry Kissinger in her inter-view with Sarah Palin, and Charlie Gibson misquoted the Bush Doctrine in his interview with Sarah Palin. Both, he concluded, manipulated the facts in this manner in order to fabricate a false and unflattering impression of Governor Palin. Mr. Gingrich stated that the coverage of Governor Palin has been "vicious" and "dishonest." Mr. Gingrich further noted that in a period of three weeks *The New York Times* ran two front-page smear pieces on Cindy McCain, the wife of Senator John McCain, while Barack Obama's wife Michelle has been given puff pieces by the media. Mr. Gingrich said the "elite media" have given up any pretense of objectivity. He also stated that *The New York Times* "...has been the most unendingly dishonest newspaper in America this year."

Mr. Gingrich was also responding to an interview of Governor Sarah Palin by Drew Griffin of CNN. Byron York of the *National Review* wrote, "Watching press coverage of the Republican candidate for vice-president, it's sometimes hard to decide whether Sarah Palin is incompetent, stupid, unqualified, corrupt, backward, or... all of the above. Palin, the Governor of Alaska, has faced more criticism than any vice-presidential candidate since 1988..." Earlier in the day both Bill O'Reilly and Rush Limbaugh pointed out that Byron York was clearly criticizing media coverage of Sarah Palin that presented a false, negative picture of this conservative vice-presidential candidate.

But when Drew Griffin presented Byron York's article to Sarah Palin and television viewers, he distorted Byron York's position and indicated that the conservative author was stating that he could not tell if Governor Palin "is incompetent, stupid, unqualified, corrupt, backward, or all of the above." Armed with this distortion, Drew Griffin was presenting Sarah Palin and his audience with the false impression that she was not only being mocked by the Marxist media, but also by Byron York, a writer with strong conservative credentials. This, folks, is just one clear example of Soviet-style psychological manipulation of the voting public.

For decades media Marxists prided themselves in their promotion of women. From the 1960s they engaged in a massive psychological conditioning campaign to insure women marched to the beat of the feminist proletariat drum. "Get out of the home and get out of your maternity gowns! Excel in business, medicine, politics, or any other field of endeavor you desire and displace those sexist bourgeois men!" So, they were riding high when Hillary Clinton announced her bid for the presidency of the United States. As the presumptive Democrat presidential nominee, Hillary had received glowing reports from the Soviet-bloc media. Everyone expected the media to continue their protection of Hillary and slap down any serious opponents, but instead the reverse occurred.

When Senator Barack Obama entered the Democrat primary and began to attract large numbers of voters, the media switched their allegiance from the Bolshevik feminist to the Bolshevik black. Many proletarian feminists were stunned by the sudden turn of events and felt a deep sense of betrayal. It was fascinating to behold. And to the shock of Oprah Winfrey's loyal feminist audience, she abandoned Hillary Clinton, the feminist candidate for president, and endorsed Barack Obama, a black male candidate. The Democrat presidential primary alone provided abundant evidence that the Marxist media pursue a distinct political agenda, even within the ranks of their own Democrat Party.

When focusing on Sarah Palin, the Marxist media no longer seemed interested in encouraging and promoting highly successful women. As Mr. Gingrich noted, Sarah Palin is a very accomplished woman, but he could not recall anyone in the elite media asking her one substantive question, or any question about her many accomplishments or her career in Alaska. Instead, they focused on her clothing, shopping habits, her children, and her ability to be vice-president while raising a family. This was very sexist behavior by a media that claims to be in the forefront of the fight against anti-female sexism.

Greta Van Susteren[7] interviewed Sarah Palin nearly one week after the 2008 election and discussed leaks from inside the McCain camp regarding reported mistakes made by Sarah Palin when preparing for the vice-presidential debate. For example, the media seized upon reports that Palin referred to Africa as a nation rather than a continent, and she reportedly seemed unclear as to the what nations are involved the North American Free Trade Agreement. Van Susteren said, according to a member of the McCain camp who was present during the debate preparation, those mistakes never happened. Governor Palin agreed that those reports of mistakes were false, but what she found frustrating was the absence of interest in setting the record straight. Although Governor Palin did not mention the media, she was certainly speaking of the media and anyone else who should have been concerned about accurately reporting the facts.

So, the media went on the offensive against Republican Sarah Palin when false and unverified reports of mistakes were leaked to the press. However, as discussed below in this chapter, the same media played deaf, dumb, and blind when Democrats Barack Obama and Joe Biden made a series of profound mistakes, and they even rose to their defense when presented with obvious blunders.

Sarah Palin is living the dream feminists claim they want women to enjoy. For this reason former Senator Fred Thompson said if Sarah Palin had been a liberal, Hollywood liberals would have been scrambling to make a movie of her life to document her struggles and achievements. Clearly, Thompson was correct. Because Sarah Palin is a "bourgeois" woman saddled with those "oppressive" traditional American middle class values, her struggles and achievements are ignored and she remains targeted for destruction by a media industry that claims to celebrate women's accomplishments.

Because Sarah Palin chose life instead of death for her special needs child; because she hunted moose instead of tracking down sexist Republican men; because she supported the NRA instead of the ACLU; and because she chose Sovereign America over Soviet America, she is viewed as an existential threat. As a young woman, she succeeded at becoming a beauty pageant contestant, a TV sportscaster, a member of the Wasilla city council, mayor of the city of Wasilla, the first female governor of the state of Alaska, a mother of five children - and a loving wife! But because she accomplished all this while rejecting feminist proletarian principles, she represents a clear and present danger to the builders of Soviet America. She must to be destroyed - at all costs, even if it means tearing off completely the flimsy mask of the professional journalist and truly exposing the vicious predator hidden beneath.

As noted by the AgustaChronicle.com,[8] as governor of the state of Alaska, Sarah Palin enjoyed an 80 percent approval rating among Alaskans. But after she entered the national scene, in just a few weeks the Marxist media drove her negatives higher than her positives in national surveys. An Augusta Chronicle staff writer wrote, "The media are making politics unlivable. Plain and simple. What does it say that the most popular governor in America was nominated to be vice-president - and by the time the national media were done with her, her negatives were higher than her positives? We think that says more about the media than Sarah Palin."

This should come as no surprise given that the Project for Excellence in Journalism found that 39 percent of the media coverage of Sarah Palin was negative, 33 percent were mixed, and only 28 percent were deemed positive. That shows the astounding power of the press to manipulate public opinion to a degree envied by marketing psychologists - and KGB disinformation officers!

What kind of mind would engage in full-scale psychological warfare against Sarah Palin, a wholesome, Christian, vice-presidential candidate with years of executive experience in the political arena? What kind of mind would treat presidential candidate Barack Obama, a "Chicago Machine" Marxist with no executive experience in the political arena, as some sort of new age messiah? What kind of mind would lie, distort, and conceal information in order to repel voters away from a candidate who thinks like George Washington, the father of the USA, and attract them toward a candidate who thinks like Vladimir Lenin, the father of the USSR? What kind of mind would do so in such a brazen and unapologetic manner? The mind of a professional journalist would not engage in such behavior. The mind of a compassionate human being would not engage in such behavior. However, the mind of a propagandist would find this behavior not only routine, normal, and expected, but also laudatory! Welcome to the world of Soviet-style psychological warfare. Welcome to Soviet America!

Protecting Joe Biden From Himself: More Media Voter Manipulation

Now let's take a look at media treatment of Democrat Joe Biden, Republican Sarah Palin's counterpart in the 2008 presidential election. Let's also examine media behavior towards presidential candidates Republican John McCain and Democrat Barack Obama.

In the 2008 presidential election a major concern of voters was Barack Obama's inexperience. To counter this valid criticism Senator Joe Biden was selected as Obama's running mate. Given that Biden had nearly 40 years experience in government and politics, his job was to add political weight to the ticket. However, according to Karl Rove, during the vice-presidential debate with Governor Sarah Palin, Senator Joe Biden made 16 factual errors. Former Speaker of the House Newt Gingrich counted 14 inaccurate statements by Biden in that same debate. For example, Mr. Gingrich noted that, in the vice-presidential debate Joe Biden said he would talk to people in a particular restaurant to better understand the concerns of the middle class. But Mr. Gingrich said the restaurant named by Biden went out of business in 1986. However, no one in the Marxist media exposed that conspicuous lie, nor did they show any interest in any of his other numerous false statements.

Furthermore, when interviewed by a reporter, Senator Biden stated that after the stock market crash of 1929 President Franklin D. Roosevelt appeared on television and addressed the nation. However, Roosevelt was not president in 1929 when the stock market crashed, and television had not yet been invented. The media also ignored Biden's claim that "Jobs" is a three letter word, and gave scant attention to Biden when he asked a wheelchair-bound paraplegic to "stand up" during a political rally.

Again, the Soviet-bloc media were unimpressed by these preposterous blunders by a Democrat vice-presidential candidate with decades of experience. So, although Republican Sarah Palin had made few - if any - factual errors during the campaign, she was characterized by the media, as Byron York had observed, as "incompetent, stupid, unqualified, corrupt, backward, or...all of the above." But while her Democrat counterpart Joe Biden had made numerous, preposterous, inexcusable errors, the Marxist media seemed to portray him as a Democrat version of the astute Dick Cheney.

Barack Obama: Marxist Media
See No Evil, Hear No Evil, Say No Evil

Not only did the Soviet-bloc media turn a blind eye and a deaf ear to Senator Joe Biden's endless parade of factually incorrect statements, they were equally deaf, dumb, and blind to the numerous gaffes and sometimes preposterous blunders made by Democrat presidential candidate Barack Obama. Let's take a look at some of the obvious errors and whoppers told by Barack Obama - which were ignored by the same leftist media that excoriated John McCain for the few mistakes that he had made, and which trashed Sarah Palin for mistakes she had not made!

L. Brent Bozell,[9] the President of the Media Research Center, has documented many of Obama's problematic statements during his 2008 campaign for the White House. Firstly, when campaigning in the state of Oregon Obama said he had been to "57 states," but had not been to Hawaii or Alaska. How can a U.S. Senator with degrees from Columbia University and Harvard Law School not know the USA has 50 states? Was something in his mind as well as on his mind? When in New Mexico Obama said, "On this Memorial Day, as our nation honors its unbroken line of fallen heroes - and I see many of them in the audience here today - our sense of patriotism is particularly strong." Was Obama telling us that he can see dead people?

In Missouri Obama said the U.S. military needed to transfer some Arabic translators from Iraq to Afghanistan. According to Obama, "We only have a certain number of them and if they are all in Iraq, then it's harder for us to use them in Afghanistan." Obama must have been getting advice from some misinformed voices in his head because Afghans do not speak Arabic! But this is just the tip of the iceberg!

When in Sunrise, Florida, Obama said, "How's it going, Sunshine?" While in South Dakota he referred to Sioux Falls as "Sioux City." When explaining why Hillary Clinton beat him in Kentucky during the Democrat primary, Obama explained that Arkansas, Bill Clinton's home state, was closer to Kentucky. But actually Illinois, Obama's home state, is closer to Kentucky. A glance at a map of the USA reveals that Kentucky is actually a border state of Illinois. When in Selma, Alabama Obama said his birth was inspired by the 1965 civil rights movement in that city. But Obama was born in 1961.

Most disturbing is Obama's claim that his uncle "was part of the American brigade that helped to liberate Auschwitz." But Auschwitz was liberated by the Red Army of the Soviet Union, not by the U.S. military. Obama also claimed that his grandfather knew some of the U.S. troops that liberated Auschwitz and Treblinka. Again, both of these Nazi death camps were liberated by Soviet military forces, not U.S. forces!

These whoppers make Bill "I never inhaled" Clinton look honest, not to mention sober!

In his nightly monologues during the 2008 presidential campaign, TV talk show host Jay Leno repeatedly portrayed Republican John McCain as an old geezer - with no fear of leftists charging him with age discrimination. And Leno repeatedly portrayed Republican Sarah Palin as a shallow dunce - with no fear that leftist feminists would charge him with sexism. Although he did crack jokes about Joe Biden, Leno suggested there was insufficient material to crack jokes about Barack Obama - and he said that with a straight face! Given the numerous campaign gaffs recorded by the Media Research Center, L. Brent Bozell would certainly disagree. When an Obama joke was told by Leno, it did not reflect poorly on Obama, but did poke fun at others, such as the media love affair with Obama. For example, Leno joked that MSNBC was "Obama Headquarters." Patrick J. Buchanan[10] would agree, stating that the media smeared McCain and Palin, but overlooked mistakes by Obama and Biden. Buchanan further stated that the media protected Obama when he made mistakes and they acted like his "press secretary - almost!"

Jay Leno was wrong! Barack Obama creates material for late-night jokes almost on a daily basis. For example, in his first press conference as president-elect, Barack Obama made reference to Nancy Reagan, the wife of Republican President Ronald Reagan, implying that she had conducted séances in the White House. But Nancy Reagan had consulted an astrologer, not a medium, while in the White House. However, Hillary Clinton, wife of

Democrat President Bill Clinton, reportedly worked with a spiritual adviser who led Mrs. Clinton through imaginary conversations with the deceased Eleanor Roosevelt, wife of Democrat President Franklin D. Roosevelt. Thus, no séances were actually conducted, by Nancy Reagan or Hillary Clinton.

Marxist Media Tell Voters: Menshevik McCain Bad; Bolshevik Obama Good!

The Project for Excellence in Journalism analyzed 2,412 news stories covering the candidates in the 2008 presidential campaign. They studied 48 news outlets that included newspapers, broadcast news, cable news, and web sites. When comparing coverage of John McCain and Barack Obama, it was found that coverage of McCain was twice as negative as the coverage of Obama.

In summary, 57 percent of the McCain coverage was rated negative while only 29 percent of Obama's coverage was rated negative. While 29 percent of McCain's coverage was neutral, 35 percent of Obama's coverage was neutral. Lastly, while only 14 percent of McCain's coverage was found to be positive, 36 percent of Obama's coverage was deemed positive. So, McCain received twice as much negative coverage as Obama, and Obama received about 2 ½ times as many positive stories as McCain.[11]

A Reporter We Can Believe In

Barbara West,[12] another accomplished "bourgeois" woman, is a health reporter and news anchor at WFTV in Orlando, Florida. As a true reporter and not a propagandist pretending to be a reporter, she asked Senator Joe Biden some direct, relevant questions not asked by representatives of the Soviet-bloc media. On October 23, less than two weeks before the 2008 presidential election, Barbara West directed the below exchange with the Democrat Party's candidate for vice-president of the United States:

Barbara West: You may recognize this famous quote: "From each according to his ability, to each according to his needs." That's from Karl Marx. How is Senator Obama not being a Marxist if he intends to spread the wealth around?

Senator Biden: Are you joking? Is this a joke?
Barbara West: No.

Senator Biden: Is that a real question?
Barbara West: That's a question!

Senator Barack Obama, Senator Joe Biden, and the entire Soviet-bloc media pretended that questions of Marxism were grossly inappropriate. However, in his book, *Dreams from My Father*, Obama wrote that, while attending Occidental College in Los Angeles, California, he "chose his friends carefully" and did so "To avoid being mistaken for a sellout." So whom did he choose? In his own words Obama wrote that he chose, "The more politically active black students. The foreign students. The Chicanos. The Marxist professors and structural feminists."

In other words, Barack Obama chose to befriend people who would most likely belong to a Soviet American proletariat group, or may be one of their Bolshevik leaders. Obama sought out Marxist professors to avoid being mistaken for a "sellout," which of course would be someone who does not share William Z. Foster's dream of building a Soviet America. He wanted both campus proletarians and campus Bolsheviks to know that he was a fellow traveler, a fellow Soviet American. As shown in Chapter Sixteen, Obama has had a lifelong affinity to Marxists.

Through his carefully planned associations Barack Obama advertised that he was no George Washington. He was no Thomas Jefferson. He was no James Madison. He wanted fellow Marxists to rest assured that he was not one of those "bitter" Sovereign Americans who "clings" to his Declaration of Independence, his U.S. Constitution, his Bible, or any other document that may contain principles embraced by the racist, sexist, bigoted, homophobic, religious, selfish, capitalist bourgeoisie! No, he was not a member of the oppressive middle class; instead, he was one of them. He, too, was a revolutionary. He, too, followed in the footsteps of Karl Marx, Vladimir Lenin, Joseph Stalin, and Mao Zedong.

Clearly, while Senators Obama and Biden tried to laugh off Obama's long standing affinity to Marxism, this is no laughing matter. As Vladimir Lenin, Joseph Stalin, Nikita Khrushchev, Mao Zedong, Pol Pot, and Fidel Castro have demonstrated over and over again, Marxism is a deadly serious matter! And Barbara West conveyed the appropriate level of sincerity in her interview with Senator Joe Biden. Observe for yourself the demeanor of Barbara West and compare it to the defensive giddiness of Senator Joe Biden during the interview. It is available at YouTube.com under the heading, "Real Reporter Asks Real Questions - Obama Campaign Angry." (See note number eleven under Chapter Eleven notes for web address.)

The Soviet-Bloc Media:
Do Not Trust - Until You Verify!

When dealing with the Soviet Union President Reagan said, "Trust, but verify." So, when dealing with the Soviet-bloc media, the Soviet-bloc education establishment, or any other Soviet-bloc tricksters, one may be tempted to trust, but do so only to the extent that you can "Trust, but verify." Trust the media in Soviet America to the same extent you would trust the media in the former Soviet Union. Neither may be viewed as simply biased. They must be viewed as equally corrupt. Therefore, never trust ABC, NBC, CBS, CNN, and MSNBC. Never trust *The New York Times*, *Los Angeles Times*, or *The Washington Post*. Never trust *Time*, *Newsweek*, or any other member of the Soviet-bloc media - until you can verify the information via legitimate sources of news and information! Trusting without verifying is how we got into this mess in the first place!

Surveillance Of The Soviet-Bloc Media By MRC

"In our state, naturally there is and can be no place for freedom of speech, press, and so on for the foes of socialism. Every sort of attempt on their part to utilize to the detriment of the State - that is to say, to the detriment of all the toilers - these freedoms granted to the toilers, must be classified as a counter-revolutionary crime." - Andrey Vyshinsky, Soviet prosecutor under Communist dictator Joseph Stalin[13]

As previously noted, in 1987 L. Brent Bozell founded the Media Research Center, or MRC. This non-profit educational foundation was created to investigate liberal bias in the media and share documented findings with the public. Because it began in the late 1980s, MRC was able to study media reporting of the Soviet Union before its collapse in 1991, including the relationship of the USSR to the USA. MRC also published the results of studies conducted by other organizations, such as the National Conservative Foundation.

In 1990 MRC published a classic book titled, *And That's The Way It Isn't: A Reference Guide To Media Bias.*[14] For those of us old enough to have watched the *CBS Evening News* before Dan Rather became the anchor, we can recall that Dan Rather's predecessor, Walter Cronkite, always ended his newscast by saying, "And that's the way it is," followed with the current date of the newscast. However, studies reported by MRC have demon-strated beyond all doubt that Cronkite, as well as other leftist journalists and reporters, slanted the news heavily to the left. Therefore, leftist reporters should have ended their newscasts with, "And that's the way it isn't." For this reason MRC's title selection was certainly ingenious.

TASS was the official Communist news agency that collected and distributed news and information to all Soviet news sources within the USSR, including newspapers, radio stations, and television stations. Referring to the book *Reluctant Farewell* by Newsweek's Moscow Bureau Chief Andrew Nagorski, it was reported that the vast majority of news stories generated by leftist American journalists stationed within the Soviet Union were simply stories rewritten from those released by the Communist-controlled TASS and other Soviet news sources. Consequently, leftist American journalists working within the Soviet Union essentially operated as distributors of Soviet propaganda. (In other words, leftist American journalists in the USSR operated the same way as leftist American journalists in the USSA!)

MRC reported that there was a "cozy relationship" between the Soviet Government and leftist American reporters stationed within the Soviet Union. These "journalists" tended to trust the Soviet Government more than the Russian people as sources of information, and they had a particular disdain for Russian dissidents who rejected the Soviet system of government. Moreover, instead of portraying this bloodstained, Gulag-infested, KGB-monitored, Communist dictatorship as vastly inferior to the USA, the USSR was portrayed by liberal reporters as America's moral equivalent. (Yes, Michael Savage, "Liberalism is a mental disorder.")

According to MRC, in the 1980s the Soviets began to utilize American networks to promote Soviet propaganda. However, rather than exposing or rejecting this propaganda, the networks increasingly gave Soviet spokesmen and government officials greater access to the American public. When the Soviet Air Force shot down a civilian Korean airliner, KAL-007, that had strayed into Soviet airspace on September 1, 1983, nearly twice as many network stories presented the Soviet position (that the plane was on a spy mission for the USA) over the American position (that the Soviets tracked it for many hours and knew it was a civilian air liner that had strayed off course, but they shot it down anyway). The 269 passengers and crew were never seen again.

In November of 1985 Soviet Leader Mikhail Gorbachev and President Ronald Reagan met at the Geneva summit. When the National Conservative Foundation analyzed coverage by the ABC, CBS, and NBC evening news teams, it was found that Reagan's efforts to expose Soviet human rights violations were essentially ignored. Moreover, when they were discussed, the networks often provided excuses for the Soviet abuses and even offered praise for presumed improvements. When reporting on the Strategic Defense Initiative, or SDI, the networks gave the Soviet position more than three times as much coverage as the American position.

When Ronald Reagan and Mikhail Gorbachev met again in Washington, D.C. in December of 1987, MRC found that ABC, NBC, and CBS evening news teams favored the Soviet perspective over the American perspective on the issues of détente, glasnost, and Afghanistan. They also presented the Soviet view that the USSR, a Communist dictatorship, was morally equivalent to the USA. (Perhaps they based this on Soviet leader Nikita Khrushchev's 1960s prediction that America would soon become a socialist nation, and combined it with American Communist William Z. Foster's 1930s prediction that someday America would be transformed into a "Soviet America." A Soviet America would, indeed, be the moral equivalent of the Soviet Union!)

Surprisingly, the media reversed its previous pro-Soviet stance on SDI and Soviet human rights abuses and now favored the American view. However, although the Soviet Union had a well-deserved reputation for cheating on past agreements with the USA, the media focused very little attention on this fact. But when they did cover the issue, half of the time was devoted to convincing the American people that the long history of Soviet cheating should be excused and it should not prevent the USA from signing the Intermediate Nuclear Forces (INF) treaty.

MRC reported that a close examination of media reporting found that the media displayed a "Blame America First" tendency; they were likely to report on aggression and human rights abuses by American allies, but tended to ignore similar behavior by Soviet allies. Moreover, during the 1980s the media tended to condemn efforts by America to liberate counties from repressive Marxist regimes. Lastly, a National Conservative Foundation study found that *The New York Times*, *The Washington Post*, *Time* magazine, and *Newsweek* magazine collectively ran five times more stories of atrocities committed by the democratically-elected government of El Salvador than by the Communist dictatorship of Nicaragua.

Welcome to Soviet America!

Good-bye Media-Trusting America!

------†††------

"For the most part, America's daily newspapers are promoting the Communist Line." And, "From all appearances, the American Press has accepted the Soviet definition of freedom, and jumps to do the bidding of the Kremlin with dismaying zeal." - Billy James Hargis, *Communist America...Must It Be?* 1960[15]

Chapter Twelve

Marxist Class Warfare
& The Black Proletariat!

Soviet America's Most Reliable Proletariat!

A major objective of Communists "is to hoodwink the Negro, to exploit him and use him as a tool to build a Communist America." - J. Edgar Hoover, Director of the FBI from 1935 to 1972[1]

Slavery and abortion are two crimes against humanity that will haunt America throughout eternity. While the abortion holocaust continues to stain the land with innocent blood, mercifully, formal slavery has been banished. Fortunately, the old slave master (defended by white Democrats) was abolished in the mid 1800s (by white Republicans). When Republican President Abraham Lincoln issued the Emancipation Proclamation in 1862 slavery began to lose its legal status.

In 1865 the Thirteenth Amendment outlawed slavery throughout the Union. Although blacks had gained their freedom, for many generations after the signing of the Thirteenth Amendment they continued to be brutalized and terrorized by racist individuals and organizations. The U.S. Supreme Court decision in *Brown v. Board of Education* in 1954, the Civil Rights Act of 1964, and the Voting Rights Act of 1965 put an end to the Jim Crow laws that sanctioned racial segregation and the outright mistreatment of blacks.

The above victories over racism were achieved through a working partnership between courageous blacks and whites. From among the many individuals who fought for the civil rights of blacks, two powerful groups were to play divergent roles during the 20th century and beyond. The first group, often motivated by biblical principles, sought true, American-style liberty for blacks. They wanted to end racism and pursue their vision of America as a land of equal opportunity for every citizen regardless of race, ethnicity, or nationality.

The second group, however, saw an opportunity to exploit an inherent weakness in the earlier American system. Given the horrendous mistreatment of blacks by whites, blacks were seen as an ideal group to assume the role of proletariat by those who envision not "one nation under God," but rather "many nations under government." Through government enforced "diversity" various propagandized factions could be pitted against one another, and especially against whites - who were to assume the role of Karl Marx's bourgeoisie.

Borrowing the biblical words of Jesus, Abraham Lincoln stated in a speech before he became president, that a house divided against itself could not stand. This principle is not lost among Marxists who wish to see America fall, and have therefore divided America into as many factions as possible. Each faction, or proletariat group, is pitted against the bourgeoisie, or the middle class, whose value system forms the foundation of the Sovereign America built by Washington, Jefferson, and Madison. As America divides into many factions through "diversity," it eventually falls into many pieces, and a Soviet America is being built upon the ruins.

For the Marxist inspired group, America's racist past presented them with a priceless opportunity to set into motion class warfare on a nationwide scale. Black resentment over past injustices could be exploited and directed against contemporary whites, including those who have no ancestors who practiced slavery, and even those who fought to end racist practices. By constantly reminding blacks and whites of past atrocities, and by endlessly portraying blacks as current victims of white racism, blacks could be manipu-lated into a chronic state of anger and hostility towards whites.

Simultaneously, whites would be manipulated into a constant state of guilt, with black anger and hostility employed to intimidate whites into a com-pliant, submissive, and eventually subordinate role. Whites who protest against this dangerous form of psychological manipulation are portrayed as racists who are standing in the way of "social justice" and "social progress." Blacks who adopt the middle class values of the white bourgeoisie and refuse to play the role of proletarian are viewed as counter-revolutionaries and are therefore intimidated into compliance with such labels as "Uncle Toms." Some independent thinking blacks are called "Oreos" that are "black on the outside, but white on the inside." U.S. Supreme Court Associate Justice Clarence Thomas, for example, serves as an example of one who refuses to assume the Soviet-inspired roles of Bolshevik, Menshevik, or proletarian.

Dictatorship Of The Black Proletariat
Over A Black Counter-Revolutionary

"If you gave Clarence Thomas a little flour on his face, you'd think you had David Duke talking." - Carl Rowan, leftist black columnist[2]

"But they [Communists] had never been able to conquer their fear of the individual way in which I acted and lived, an individuality which life had seared into my bones." - Richard Wright, a black writer who joined, but later rejected, the Communist Party[3]

When speaking to a group of students, the conservative U.S. Supreme Court Associate Justice Clarence Thomas addressed the issue of maintaining ideas very different from those of most blacks in America. Justice Thomas described this as a challenge, given that the vast majority of blacks are liberal and have assumed the role of proletarian as assigned to them by their Bolshevik Democrat handlers. Justice Thomas noted that as a young boy, he was told there were neighborhoods he could not go into because he was black. If he wandered into certain white neighborhoods he would risk verbal or even physical assault.

Today, in the 21st century, liberals are telling Justice Thomas there is a "neighborhood of ideas" that he cannot go into because he is black. Essentially, liberals are telling Justice Thomas and all other blacks that they cannot go into the neighborhood of ideas espoused by George Mason, Patrick Henry, Noah Webster, and other like-minded individuals. Instead, they must restrict themselves to the neighborhood of ideas embraced by the present day followers of Karl Marx, Vladimir Lenin, and Joseph Stalin. If Justice Thomas avoids the Marxist neighborhood of ideas and dwells in the Mason neighborhood of ideas, he risks verbal or possibly physical assault - by liberals! However, by maintaining his conservatism Justice Thomas refuses to have intellectual and behavioral limitations imposed upon him by a Soviet American version of the "dictatorship of the proletariat," whether that dictatorship is black or white.

Some Operational Principles
Underlying The Black Proletariat!

"The Negro masses will make the very best fighters for the revolution." - William Z. Foster, National Chairman of the Communist Party, USA, *Toward Soviet America*, 1932[4]

Recall in Chapter Three that Italian Communist Antonio Gramsci injected a critical ingredient into the dialectic materialism of Karl Marx, namely that, if the bourgeoisie value system is shared by the proletariat, there will be no desire to overthrow the bourgeoisie. Instead, the proletariat will aspire to become integrated into the bourgeois middle class. When both groups share the same value system there can be no antithesis (no revolutionary anti-American counter-culture) to challenge the existing thesis (traditional American culture); and therefore there can be no synthesis (no blending of revolutionary anti-American counter-culture with traditional American culture to incrementally produce Communism - or a Soviet America).

Because proletarians will not overthrow a value system they support, they must be propagandized into rejecting the value system of the bourgeoisie and manipulated into developing their own "diverse" antithetical value system. Therefore, the black proletariat must be propagandized into rejecting the Sovereign America founded by 18th century slave owners such as Washington, Adams, Jefferson, and Madison - who paved the way for liberty. In addition, they must be further deceived into demanding the Soviet America inspired by 20th century slave masters such as Lenin, Stalin, Khrushchev, and Mao - who paved the way for genocide. We must conclude that, for the builders of Soviet America, private slave masters who paved the way for liberty are bad, but government slave masters who paved the way for genocide are good! Like Sovereign Americans today, why do Soviet Americans not reject both private and government slave masters?

To help build a Soviet America, black proletarians must be manipulated and controlled so they do not identify with the white bourgeoisie. Instead, they must always "think black, feel black, and act black." This explains why some black students who accept the role of proletarian refuse to perform scholastically; stating that doing well in school is equivalent to "acting white." In Soviet America blacks must not think outside the psychological straitjackets fabricated for them by Soviet American dialecticians. They are not to think like Adam Smith and they are not to be influenced by Clarence Thomas - who entices all young people to travel freely into any "neighborhood of ideas" they find appealing and rewarding. Instead, blacks must think like Karl Marx and they must be influenced by the Reverend Jeremiah Wright - who, like Karl Marx, instructs his followers to reject "middleclass-ness," or the white bourgeoisie value system.

In addition, the black proletariat must be emotionally stoked to a feverish, revolutionary pitch and relentlessly pitted against the white bourgeoisie until they eventually destroy and displace the bourgeoisie culture, bourgeoisie institutions, and bourgeoisie leadership. Both the Marxists at the top of the socioeconomic ladder and the proletarians at the bottom of the ladder want the white, bourgeoisie, middle class destroyed. This, of course, benefits only the Marxists at the top of the ladder for the proletarians at the bottom will have no middle class to escape into, nor will their children and grandchildren. Superb psychological manipulation drives them to destroy future opportunities for true liberty and prosperity - while falsely believing they are pursuing both!

Paradoxically, we find that contemporary American descendents of slaves are leading the charge to empower the new slave master. Yes, as strange as it may seem, many of those who are fighting to install a new form of slavery in the 20th and 21st centuries are descendents of those who fought against slavery in the 19th century. Perhaps many blacks truly prefer to "escape from freedom," as described by social psychologist Erich Fromm.[5] Those who wish to escape from freedom may do so by cultivating a Soviet-style slave master government, thus creating the opportunity to surrender to a Bolshevik Big Brother who will provide them with a small monthly income, housing, food stamps, education, health care, and "political protection," at least temporarily! A Bolshevik Big Brother will allow them to escape the anxiety that one may experience when confronted with the freedom to supply one's own material wants and needs.

The wholesale manipulation, control, and exploitation of a population composed of several hundred million people would, of course, require enormous control over government, the media, and the education establishment - as proposed by Karl Marx in *The Communist Manifesto!* Hence the need for an endless stream of authoritarian legislation by Marxist political operatives, prejudiced reporting by the media, and biased lectures at colleges and universities. Clearly, the theories of Marx and the tactics of Gramsci have been successfully employed in the development and maintenance of Soviet America's black proletariat.

It was also noted in Chapter Three that Gramsci pointed out that in America and the West bourgeoisie values were deeply rooted in Christianity. Therefore, Christianity and Christians must be corrupted, denigrated, destroyed, and replaced. Hence the need for Supreme Court decisions that replace the American constitutional principle of freedom of religion with the Soviet constitutional principle of freedom from religion. To build a Soviet America Marxist values must displace Christian values throughout the culture, and it must be done in a manner that convinces the proletariat that they have embraced a new, higher form of spirituality.

Therefore, traditional Christian theology must be corrupted with Marxist ideology, thus calling for the insinuation of "liberation theology" and the "social gospel" movement into the black community and beyond. Instead of encouraging their flock to be free from sin, they tell their flock they are free to sin. Hatred of whites equals hatred of oppression. Hatred of America equals hatred of injustice. Hatred of capitalism equals hatred of exploitation. From this insinuation we find the black community pulled sharply to the left by such figures as the Reverend Jesse Jackson, the Reverend Al Sharpton, and the Reverend Jeremiah Wright, all of whom call for "social justice" through the forced confiscation and redistribution of other people's (bourgeoisie) money and property, as outlined by Karl Marx!

Also, the proletariat must believe they have been "enlightened" by following their own leaders - people who have risen up from the depths of the proletariat community to challenge the evils of the bourgeoisie class. They must never be told that they are pawns in a sinister game constructed by some of the best criminal minds the white race has ever produced, including Karl Marx, Antonio Gramsci, and their contemporaries who wish to re-enslave them and the rest of the world under the ruse of "liberating them."

Of course, as we have seen in the Soviet Union, Soviet China, Soviet Cuba, and elsewhere, the dictatorship of the proletariat always seems to possess real power only during the revolutionary stage. Once the bourgeoisie is defeated and the Bolshevik elite acquire unchallengeable power, the proletariat is no longer needed. While, in theory, Karl Marx envisioned an interim dictatorship of the elite to be followed by a dictatorship of the proletariat, the elite never relinquish power to the proletariat once it has been acquired.

Instead, proletarians find themselves laboring in Gulags; working on collective, government-owned farms and factories; or standing before firing squads for speaking out against their new slave master. The promise of a ruling class known as the dictatorship of the proletariat never has, and never will, materialize. Clearly, the dictatorship of the elite possesses "a lust for power over others" and they would never relinquish that power to anyone else, especially those who are so shortsighted that they would allow themselves to be manipulated into destroying any chance of ever enjoying genuine liberty!

Strategic Destruction Of The Black Family To Facilitate Construction Of The Black Proletariat

"Abolish the family! Even the most radical flare up at this infamous proposal of the Communists...The bourgeois family will vanish as a matter of course when its complement vanishes, and both will vanish with the vanishing of capital." - Karl Marx, *The Communist Manifesto,* 1848[6]

As the Reverend Jesse Jackson[7] was preparing for an interview on the television program *FOX & Friends Weekend*, he spoke to another black male guest sitting next to him. Jackson was talking about recent statements made by then Democrat presidential nominee Barack Obama, referring specifically to Obama's call for black men to take responsibility for the children they father. Unaware the microphone had been turned on, Jackson was "caught on tape" saying that Obama was "talking down to black people...telling niggers how to behave." Spoken like a true liberal "man of the cloth!" It should be noted that before the Reverend Jesse Jackson made these statements, he was on record encouraging blacks to stop using the "N-word." He was also highly critical of actor Michael Richards for using that word when working as a standup comedian.

Given the epidemic of crime-creating fatherless families within the black community, why did Jackson say Obama was "talking down to black people" when he called for men to be responsible for the children they bring into this world? Regardless of skin color, the vast majority of young drug dealers, murderers, robbers, burglars, rapists, and gang members locked up in prisons across the nation come from fatherless families. As most anyone could have predicted, the cultural phenomenon of fatherless families exploded after the introduction of federal welfare - the brainchild of Bolshevik Democrats. This federal debacle provided an array of financial incentives for young women to have children out of wedlock. In effect, federal welfare transferred an enormous amount of money from the taxpaying bourgeoisie to the black proletariat - provided they produced dysfunctional, crime-creating, fatherless families.

Although federal welfare had been reformed in 1996, the damage had already been done. The phenomenon of fatherless families had become normalized throughout America, and had become deeply ingrained within the black community. Without the massive damage inflicted upon the black community by rewarding self-destructive behavior, Jackson and many other hucksters masquerading as civil rights leaders would never have become "rich and famous." Although federal welfare programs created by Bolshevik Democrats are responsible for the most destructive problems facing the black community since the 1960s, it is the opponents of welfare, the conservatives, who are blamed for the damage. Thus, their explanation is rooted in Marxist ideology that states that all proletarian problems are caused by the bourgeoisie, and could never be caused by Soviet-style government programs created by conniving Bolsheviks.

The tactic of creating family-destroying programs, then blaming the destruction on the people who tried to stop them, has been repeated over and over again by the Bolshevik leadership that controls the black proletariat and all other proletariat groups. As clearly shown in numerous studies, the rate of fatherless families, crime, drug abuse, and imprisonment among blacks was far lower before trillions of taxpayer dollars were confiscated and redistributed by Bolshevik Democrats on an endless stream of social welfare programs. Clearly, in terms of family unity and crime, blacks were far better off before the Marxist-inspired, Cultural Revolution of the 1960s. Thus, it is not poverty or bourgeois white racism that lies at the heart of the problems within the black community; instead, it is their Bolshevik Democrat leadership, both black and white, which has systematically destroyed the black family and the black community since the mid 1960s.

As Marx wrote in *The Communist Manifesto*, "Do you charge us with wanting to stop the exploitation of children by their parents? To this crime we plead guilty. But, you will say, we destroy the most hallowed of relations, when we replace home education by social." Keep in mind that for the Marxist, one stops the exploitation of children by parents simply by separating children from their parents, thus leaving children vulnerable to a culture that has been systematically corrupted by liberal nihilists.

The process of separation is accomplished through a whole arsenal of anti-family tactics. They include welfare programs that encourage fatherless families; easy divorce laws; mandatory, government-controlled education that disparages parental authority; a feminist philosophy that rejects traditional male/female relations and keeps women in the workplace and away from home and children; and high taxation rates that force mothers to work in order to supplement the income of responsible fathers. The most casual observer may easily discern that all of the above tactics have been implemented with stunning success by those who are methodically building their Soviet America. And it should come as no surprise that all of the above family destroying tactics have been advocated either by Karl Marx in *The Communist Manifesto* or by William Z. Foster in *Toward Soviet America!*

Clearly, federal welfare was a key building block for those creating their Soviet America. Firstly, by allowing the federal government to become involved in welfare, the feds began to compete with and nearly displace state, county, city, private, and many religious welfare programs. Thus, the local governmental and private American-style systems of welfare were replaced with a centralized government-run system reminiscent of the old Soviet Union. Secondly, it was suspiciously consistent with Marx's call to destroy the family and place it under government control. Of course, what is seldom noted by social commentators is the glaring fact that federal involvement in welfare is patently unconstitutional - a clear violation of the Tenth Amendment.

Dictatorship Of The Black Female Proletariat Over The White Female Bourgeoisie: Do As I Say, Not As I Do!

"...the dictatorship of the proletariat will produce a whole series of restrictions of liberty in the case of the oppressors, exploiters and capitalists." - William Z. Foster, National Chairman of the Communist Party, USA, quoting Vladimir Lenin[8]

Following Jesse Jackson's use of the word "niggers" on *FOX & Friends Weekend*, the women on ABC's television program *The View*[9] discussed the use of the "N-word." Whoopi Goldberg and Sherri Shepherd, both of whom are black, told Elizabeth Hasselbeck, who is white, that it was OK for blacks to use the N-word but it was not OK for whites to use that word. Elizabeth said she believed no adult should use that word and suggested its usage would be passed on to children with damaging effects. At one point in the discussion Sherri said to Elizabeth, "Don't tell me I can't use that word." And when speaking to Barbara Walters, who is white, Sherri said, "I don't want to hear it come out of your mouth!" In other words, when in the presence of Sherri, Barbara could be found guilty of "using the N-word while white!"

Clearly, Sherri was communicating to the white women that, "It's wrong for you to put that restriction on my speech, but it's OK for me to put that same restriction on your speech." To no one's surprise, Jesse Jackson did not later complain that Sherri Shepherd was "talking down to white people...telling honkies how to behave." But we may ask the question, Did Sherri Shepherd's statements communicate the following to the white women on that television program: "Don't tell me, a black proletarian, what I can or cannot say; instead, under the rules of engagement for the 'dictatorship of the black proletariat' I will tell you, the white bourgeoisie, what you can and cannot say?" Her verbal behavior was certainly consistent with the Marxist dialectic paradigm that was permeating the land during the 1960s Counter-Cultural Revolution, although she was probably unaware of the Marxist roots of her cultivated behavior.

Contrastingly, when Barbara was addressing Sherri, she began a sentence with, "Is it OK..." So, while Sherri was "talking down" to Elizabeth and Barbara, Barbara was deferential and "talking up" to Sherri. Barbara, a white woman, was actually asking Sherri, a black woman, to tell her what speech was appropriate or inappropriate (politically correct or politically incorrect, to put it in cultural Marxism terms) for both blacks and whites regarding the use of the N-word.

In talking directly to Elizabeth, Whoopi spoke the following words: "Listen to me...You have to understand...You don't understand...I need you to under-stand...You have to understand...You have to listen to the fact that we're telling you...You have to say...You must acknowledge..." Obviously, the statements Whoopi directed towards Elizabeth were authoritarian in nature. Whoopi was plainly "talking down" to Elizabeth. She spoke to Elizabeth as if she were scolding a child. Perhaps this is why Elizabeth did, in fact, cry when Whoopi finished speaking. Whoopi was communicating to Elizabeth what many parents have communicated to their children: "Do as I say, not as I do."

Both Whoopi and Sherri demonstrated the classic "Do as I say, not as I do" parental dictum. It stems from the notion that "rank has its privileges" and insubordination will not be tolerated. The same double standard employed by parents is also found in the military, corporate structures, and in other social hierarchies. By telling the white women, "Do as I say, not as I do," Whoopi and Sherri were asserting the same "top down" authority found in all hierarchical settings, whether formal or informal. As Peter Schweizer[10] revealed in his book, *Do As I Say (Not As I Do): Profiles in Liberal Hypocrisy*, Ted Kennedy, Ralph Nader, Barbara Streisand, Michael Moore, Al Franken, Hillary Clinton, Noam Chomsky, Nancy Pelosi, George Soros, Gloria Steinem, and Cornel West have all demonstrated the "Do as I say, but not as I do" double standard commonly found among people who feel superior or entitled.

It is the quintessential double standard of the dictator, whether benevolent or malevolent. It is a double standard one would expect to find in Stalin's dictatorship of the Bolshevik or in Marx's dictatorship of the proletariat. It is the double standard one would expect to find in a "dictatorship of the black proletariat" during the intermediate and final stages of construction of William Z. Foster's Soviet America. Whether they are aware of it or not, Whoopi and Sherri are cultural revolutionaries in a slow motion, Marxist revolution. Under the dictatorship of the black proletariat, Whoopi and Sherri were telling the white women on *The View* that there is a "neighborhood of ideas" that whites may not go into - "By Order of the Speech Police!"

Elizabeth stated that we all live in the same world, therefore we should all avoid using the N-word. Whoopi and Sherri disagreed, and both argued that they, as blacks, lived in a very different world (a different neighborhood of ideas) than Elizabeth and other whites. Perhaps Whoopi and Sherri were unwittingly arguing that they lived in Soviet America, a nation of "diversity" consistent with Marxist proletarian principles, while Elizabeth lived in Sovereign America, a melting pot based upon the "bourgeois" American notion of "One nation under God."

During this episode of *The View* we saw abundant evidence that two America's do indeed exist, and they could never coexist! Whoopi stated to Elizabeth that she lived in a different America because, when she was young, her mother could not vote in the USA even though she was born in America. So, Whoopi lives in an America that resents the fact that blacks could not vote in the past, and therefore blacks and whites now live in different psychological worlds. But Elizabeth lives in an America that celebrates the fact that blacks can vote in the present, and therefore blacks and whites now live in the same world.

The above interaction on this episode of *The View* provides a real-world example of Hegel's "thesis + antithesis = synthesis," Marx's dialectic materialism of class warfare - including his dictatorship of the proletariat, and Gramsci's proletarian rejection of the bourgeoisie value system - all working to build Foster's Soviet America. While Whoopi and Sherri unwittingly played their roles as proletarian dictators, and Barbara unwittingly played her role as a defeated, subordinate bourgeois woman, Elizabeth behaved like an insubordinate "counter-revolutionary" who refused to play the role of a defeated bourgeois woman.

For her insubordination Elizabeth was browbeaten to the point of tears. While Whoopi, Sherri, and Barbara unwittingly played the roles they were counter-culturally programmed to play, Elizabeth, like Justice Clarence Thomas, refused to be confined to a specific "neighborhood of ideas" constructed by politically correct speech commissars, Marxist dialecticians, and others who are working to build their Soviet America. Although she was outnumbered and bullied, like Rosa Parks, Elizabeth Hasselbeck refused to move to the back of the bus!

In addition, the double standard noted above may help explain how some black liberals can label whites racist, whether they engage in racist behavior or not, while excusing themselves of racism. According to this liberal double standard, blacks cannot be racist because only people in positions of power can be racist. And because they claim to not be in power, they cannot be guilty of racism even when brazenly displaying racist behavior.

But according to this line of reasoning the Grand Dragon of the Ku Klux Klan could not be a racist when visiting, for example, Somalia, given that white people are not in power in that African nation. Moreover, a member of the KKK could only be a victim of racism but never a perpetrator of racism while visiting or residing in any black-led nation - even if that KKK member was lynching blacks! Of course, this line of reasoning is simply illogical. Contrary to the assertion of powerlessness, one would expect to find such a non-sensical and transparent form of rationalization employed only by those who possess considerable power, and therefore do not expect to be publicly challenged.

Marx, Foster & Khrushchev Prediction: The Proletariat Will Bury You!

In 1956 Soviet dictator Nikita Khrushchev,[11] "The Butcher of the Ukraine," proclaimed to Americans and other Westerners, "We will bury you!" Because this statement was made during the Cold War and both the USA and the USSR possessed nuclear weapons, it was assumed Khrushchev was proclaiming the Soviets would bury Americans and other Westerners under nuclear rubble. However, in 1963 Khrushchev[12] added the following to his earlier statement: "Of course we will not bury you with a shovel...Your own working class will bury you." Khrushchev was referring to statements in *The Communist Manifesto* wherein Karl Marx wrote, "What the bourgeoisie produces, above all, are its own grave-diggers." William Z. Foster[13] echoed the words of Marx when he wrote that, "Capitalism has provided its own executioners and grave diggers, the proletariat." In other words, under the direction of Bolsheviks the working class, or proletariat, will rise up and deal a deathblow to the middle class capitalist, or bourgeoisie, and replace it with a "dictatorship of the proletariat."

NAACP: We Will Bury The N-Word

While Khrushchev wanted to bury the American middle class in 1956, in July of 2007 the leadership of the National Association for the Advancement of Colored People, or NAACP, decided to bury the N-word, a derogatory term created by the colonial American middle class perhaps as early as 1786. A mock burial was held by the NAACP in Detroit, Michigan,[14] and similar ceremonies were held in Pearland, Texas[15] and Denver, Colorado.[16] Clearly, there are many blacks who want to kill the N-word and bury it once and for all. In doing so, they wish to bury a monumentally hurtful remnant from our racist past.

However, as demonstrated on *The View*, there are blacks who wish to keep the N-word alive. They wish to continue its use within segments of the black community while chastising whites for following their example. Clearly, those who wish to bury the N-word wish to bury a hurtful symbol of racism, while those who wish to keep the N-word alive wish to keep a hurtful symbol of racism alive. Elizabeth believed that both blacks and whites should not use the N-word. This is precisely the position of the NAACP and many other blacks across the nation. So, when Whoopi and Sherri chastised Elizabeth they were also chastising the NAACP. It is Whoopi and Sherri who are out of step with the NAACP on this issue, not Elizabeth! Should we expect Sherri to speak to the leaders of the NAACP the same way she spoke to Elizabeth and say, "Don't tell me I can't use that word?"

Marx, Foster & Khrushchev Were Correct: The Black Proletariat Are Burying The White Bourgeoisie!

"Since at least the Great Depression, American reds [Communists] have sought to manipulate 'blacks' into fighting their revolution for them." - Nicholas Stix[17]

People unfamiliar with Marxism may ask, Why do Soviet Americans in government, the media, and in academia claim to be opposed to racial discrimination, while they demand that whites be discriminated against in education, employment, and throughout society? Why are blacks who criticize whites called civil rights activists, while whites who criticize blacks are called racists? People who have not studied Communism may ask, Why are whites presumed to be guilty of crimes against blacks when all the evidence points to their innocence, as in the fraudulent Tawana Brawley case or the fabricated Duke rape case? Why is this type of chronic, danger-ous, anti-white racism enthusiastically displayed by the leftist media?

Moreover, why are blacks presumed to be innocent of "hate crimes" against whites when all the evidence points to their guilt, as in the case of the car-jacking, kidnapping, robbery, rape, torture, and mutilation murders of Christopher Newsom and Channon Christian? The two victims were tortured and brutalized in a manner seldom seen outside an abortion clinic; however, beyond the Knoxville, Tennessee area the Marxist media focused very little attention on this gruesome crime. After Marxist media dialecticians learned that black proletarian predators had tortured, mutilated, and murdered two white, bourgeoisie prey in a manner that would have made Hitler vomit, it appears that, after yawning, their only question was, "What else can we do to frame the bourgeoisie white Duke Lacrosse players and inflame the black proletariat?"

Why? Why do the Soviet-bloc media sensationalize phony crimes such as the Tawana Brawley case and the Duke Rape case, knowing they are helping to frame innocent whites, while they ignore actual, vicious crimes commit-ted by blacks against whites? Walter E. Williams[18] explores this issue in some detail in his article, "Media conceal black interracial crimes."

In his article Walter E. Williams further noted that, "According to the 2004 FBI National Crime Victimization Survey, in most instances of interracial crimes, the victim is white and the perpetrator is black. In the case of interracial murder for 2004, where the race of victim and perpetrator is known, more than twice as many whites were murdered by a black than cases of a white murdering a black." Keep in mind that in America whites far outnumber blacks (Whites = 66%; Hispanics = 15%; Blacks = 13%; Asians = 4.5%). So, one would expect results quite different from those found in the 2004 FBI National Crime Victimization Survey. Williams criticized Jesse Jackson, Al Sharpton, politicians, and the news media for their failure to address the issue of black-on-white crime. Williams stated that such a double standard is dangerous because "it contributes to a pile of racial kindling awaiting a racial arsonist to set it ablaze. I can't think of better recruitment gifts for America's racists, either white or black."

Walter E. Williams is correct: white and black liberal support for, and denial of, black-on-white crime serves to provide fuel for both white and black racists. Thus, while liberals of all colors claim they fight against racism, they are major contributors to both black and white racially motivated crime. By falsely portraying blacks as being disproportionately victimized by whites when reporting on interracial crime - when the reverse is true, they provide black racists with the excuse they seek to victimize whites. This conspicuously lopsided and unfair reporting is also noted by white racists and it provides them with the rationalization they seek to victimize blacks. Such blatant psychological manipulation by Soviet-bloc dialecticians is clearly designed to inflame racial hatred and resentment among both black proletarians and white bourgeoisie.

Who wins? The builders of Soviet America win, for an ongoing race war provides them with the excuse they seek to maintain a massive Soviet-style "Justice Department" and well-financed federal law enforcement agencies. And, while everyone is distracted by street-level interracial crime, we focus less attention on the shenanigans of the Bolshevik elite. Who loses? The losers are those blacks, whites, Hispanics, Asians, Native Americans, and all others who wish to live in peace, prosperity, and liberty! The losers are all those who reject the construction of a Soviet American police state and the continued destruction of Sovereign America.

Those who understand the role of the black proletariat in Soviet America know that the two Knoxville, Tennessee victims were viewed by the Soviet-bloc media as white bourgeoisie and the five sadistic executioners were simply assuming their rightful roles as black proletarians. The perpetrators were fulfilling their roles as members of the "dictatorship of the proletariat" as envisioned by Karl Marx. They were fulfilling William Z. Foster's[19] prediction that "The Negro masses will make the very best fighters for the revolution." They were also behaving in a manner consistent with Foster's[20] statement that, "Capitalism has provided its own executioners and grave diggers, the proletariat." The executioners of Christopher Newsom and Channon Christian were also operating in a manner consistent with Foster's[21] statement that capitalists can only be removed from power with force, and that, as occurred in the Soviet Union, in Soviet America the bourgeoisie must be "liquidated."[22]

Moreover, Foster[23] also stated that, "The wonder is not that the Negro is beginning, at least, to think along Communist lines, but that he did not embrace that doctrine en masse long ago." So, as far back as 1932 when Foster published his book *Toward Soviet America,* he concluded that blacks were already beginning to "think along Communist lines," with a lot of help from white "liberals," of course! Add to Foster's statements the 1848 statement of Karl Marx, as noted earlier: "What the bourgeoisie produces, above all, are its own grave-diggers."

Therefore, such "revolutionary" behavior by the proletariat against the bourgeoisie is stealthily encouraged by publicly ignoring it and publicly denying it. The propagandists in the Soviet-bloc media thus send a clear message to the black proletariat: "Keep up the good work. We'll cover for you." The message sent to the white bourgeoisie is quite different: "Accept your role as a defeated bourgeoisie or be labeled a racist."

So, if whites do nothing about media encouragement and denial of black-on-white crime, they lose through increasing victimization as black racists become more emboldened. If they fight against black racism and expose biased, anti-white reporting they are portrayed as racists. In Soviet America the bourgeoisie cannot tell the truth and get away with it! But as the Reverend Jesse Lee Peterson said to radio talk show host Bill Cunningham, white Americans must stand up against the ruthless onslaught of mis-reporting by the anti-white Marxist media and the race hucksters they support. Surrender is not an option! Jesse Lee Peterson,[24] who is black, complimented Bill Cunningham, who is white, for standing tall and con-fronting this issue head-on.

Measuring The Effectiveness Of The Soviet-Bloc Media In Provoking Violent, Anti-White Racism Among The Black Proletariat

"How many have overlooked the real cause of racism? It seems the main-stream media has played a *direct* role. When that is admitted, and the proper actions taken, we will see a significant decrease in racism." - Kevin Roeten, Media Stoking the Fires of Racism - Part I[25]

Of course, the Soviet-bloc media cannot take full credit for the progress made in inciting the black proletariat to rob, rape, torture, mutilate, and murder the white bourgeoisie. Members of the Soviet-bloc education establishment must assume considerable responsibility given that they teach our students that white America is inherently racist, and, when deciding a course of action students should remember that "there's no such thing as right and wrong." In addition, Bolshevik Democrat and Menshevik Republican politicians, judges, and lawyers; progressive civil rights activists; Marxist liberation theologians and social gospel preachers; and other leftists who habitually and falsely portray blacks as victims and whites as per-petrators of racism must all be given credit for transforming countless numbers of blacks into enforcers of cultural Marxism, executioners, and grave diggers - each and every year.

In his insightful article "The Color of Crime" Patrick J. Buchanan[26] wrote about observations he made regarding a *Washington Post* report on crime among black Americans. Citing the newspaper article, Buchanan noted that blacks are more likely to be victims of crime than are whites or Hispanics; they are more likely to be victims of serious violent crimes such as rape, assault, and robbery. In addition, blacks are more than twice as likely as whites to be victims of crimes involving firearms. Most strikingly, it was noted that "Nearly half the people murdered in the United States are black." Given that blacks make up about 13 percent of the population but nearly 50 percent of the murder victims, it is clear that they are disproportionately affected by violent crime. However, the Post also noted that when blacks are murdered, in more than 90 percent of the cases they are murdered by other blacks.

However, Buchanan noted that while the Post portrayed blacks as victims of crime, it failed to mention white victims of crime. Moreover, there was no mention of the fact that whites are disproportionately victimized by blacks - which is precisely opposite the impression cultivated by the Soviet-bloc media and education establishment. Buchanan listed some of the major findings in a study conducted by the New Century Foundation in 2005. The study is titled "The Color of Crime: Race, Crime and Justice in America."[27] A direct examination of those major findings (available online as a free PDF download) reveals some stunning figures which serve to measure the effectiveness of the Soviet-bloc propagandists in inciting interracial violence among the black proletariat. For example:

- Blacks are seven times more likely to commit murder than persons of other races, and eight times more likely to commit robbery.

- Blacks are nearly three times more likely to use a gun and twice as likely to use a knife during the commission of a violent crime.

- Blacks commit 85 percent and whites commit 15 percent of the interracial crimes involving blacks and whites. (Keep in mind that blacks make up about 13 percent of the U.S. population and whites compose roughly 66 percent.)

- Blacks target whites more often than they target other blacks. When committing violent crimes blacks target whites 45 percent of the time; they target other blacks 43 percent of the time; and they target Hispanics 10 percent of the time. When whites commit violent crimes, they target blacks only 3 percent of the time.

- It was estimated that blacks are 39 times more likely to commit violent crimes against whites than vice versa, and 136 times more likely to commit robbery.

- Blacks are 2.25 times more likely to commit so-called "hate crimes" against whites than vice versa.

Larry Elder,[28] author of the book, *The Ten Things You Can't Say In America*, discussed the issue of interracial crime with Travis Smiley. (Larry Elder should have titled his book, *The Ten Things You Can't Say In Soviet America*.) Elder noted that blacks are more likely to victimize whites than vice versa, while discussing the issue of black racism. Travis Smiley suggested that blacks cannot engage in racist behavior against whites because blacks lack power. Larry Elder responded by saying, "That is one of the most idiotic things I've ever heard...What an absurd thing to say!" (The spirited discussion is available on YouTube.[29])

After reviewing the above figures Patrick J. Buchanan noted that blacks complain because they have difficulty hailing a cab. But reluctance of cab drivers to stop and pick up blacks may not be due to white racism, but rather it may be due to white awareness of black racism and the black propensity to disproportionately target whites for robbery and other violent crimes.

As the above reports show, blacks also target other blacks when committing violent crimes, and when blacks are murdered, in more than 90 percent of the cases they are murdered by other blacks. This tells us that when blacks complain about black-on-black crime but not black-on-white crime, they are hurting the black community as well as the country as a whole. Why? Because as Mother Teresa[30] said regarding abortion, "Any country that accepts abortion as legal is not teaching its people to love, but to use any violence to get what they want. This is why the greatest destroyer of love and peace is abortion."

Likewise, black acquiescence of, or outright encouragement of, black prole-tarian violence against the white bourgeoisie has boomeranged back against the black community. When removing the taboo against killing unborn babies and loosening any restriction against killing whites, the black prohi-bition against killing other blacks is severely weakened. The result is violent crime at a level no morally sane person should tolerate. Clearly, the Marxist Cultural Revolution of the 1960s has increased death and mayhem to a level only a Soviet American revolutionary could appreciate! Welcome to Soviet America!

The deadliest threat to the African-American is not the KKK. It's not AIDS, war, or the white bourgeoisie. Instead, the deadliest threat to the African-American is the Soviet American, whether black or white!

Jena 6: A Case Study
In Media Racism & Psychological Manipulation!

"A newspaper is not only a collective propagandist and a collective agitator, it is also a collective organizer." - Vladimir Lenin, first Communist dictator of the Soviet Union[31]

Two stories were told regarding the "Jena Six" fiasco. Firstly, there was the story crafted by the Soviet-bloc media for wholesale consumption by a gullible public. This was the story designed to inflame the black proletariat and pit them against the white bourgeoisie. This was the dangerously deceitful story designed to manipulate blacks into believing they are justified in victimizing whites - while manipulating whites into believing they deserve to be victimized.

In the Soviet American version whites hung nooses under a "whites-only" tree - a tree under which only white students at Jena High School could congregate. The nooses served as a warning to blacks to stay away from the "whites-only" tree. This reckless taunting by racist white students justifiably infuriated blacks, given the fact that blacks were lynched by racist whites, especially in the Southern states during the slavery and Jim Crow years. In response to this white racist behavior a schoolyard fight broke out between blacks and a white student.

Six black students were charged with attempted murder although the white student appeared to have recovered quickly from his wounds; therefore, the black students must have been charged with attempted murder simply because they are black. Also, the white students who hung the nooses from the "whites-only" tree were not disciplined. In response to this injustice perhaps as many as 20,000 blacks from around the nation came to this small Louisiana town of 3,000 people - 90 percent of whom are white, in order to stage a protest! Moreover, $500,000 was raised for the defense of the "Jena Six" who are being railroaded by overzealous, racist prosecutors. One of the black students was later seen on the internet with $100 bills sticking out of his mouth, and two others served as presenters of a Hip-Hop Award on Black Entertainment Television.

Now here's the real story - based on information provided by Patrick J. Buchanan,[32] who praised and cited Craig Franklin of the *Jena Times* and Charlotte Allen writing for *The Weekly Standard*. Information was also provided by Jason Whitlock of the *Kansas City Star*, whose account was posted on the web site of Michelle Malkin. Buchanan noted further that a few honest and brave reporters can still be found among a dwindling pool of reporters displaying such characteristics.

Here's some of what the Marxist media deceptively chose not to report:

There was no fight. A gang of 8 to 10 black students attacked and severely beat a white student in the Jena High gym. In preparing their premeditated attack, they barricaded an exit so their intended victim could not escape. When attempting to escape through another exit, the white student, Justin Barker, was struck on the head from behind by Mychal Bell. As the victim fell unconscious, the other black students joined in and stomped and kicked Justin Barker in the head. When the assistant principle found Barker lying on the floor, he thought he was dead.

Six of the black assailants were arrested and charged with attempted second-degree murder. None of the assailants reported that the noose incident served as inspiration for the attack. None of the witnesses reported hearing any attackers complain of the noose incident. While there was racial tension in the town of Jena, the noose incident - which occurred three months earlier - was unrelated to this attack. Only afterwards was the noose incident resurrected to rationalize the racially-motivated crime committed by the six black assailants.

In addition, the media conveniently failed to report that the "whites-only" tree was a fabrication. Although most of the students who sat under this tree were white, blacks had also convened under the tree at times. More-over, the white students who hung the nooses did so to tease other white students who were on the rodeo team, and to poke fun at a rival school whose football team employed a western theme. The naive white students, who got the idea of fashioning nooses from watching the western movie *Lonesome Dove* on TV, had no idea the nooses could be offensive to blacks. When the white students learned of this they were remorseful. The nooses were seen by few students because they were displayed very briefly.

In addition, the noose hanging white students were disciplined by school officials in spite of their naiveté. They were required to spend nine days at an "alternative facility." They also received two weeks of in-school suspension as well as Saturday detentions. Moreover, the white students were required to attend a Disciplinary Court and they had to submit to mental health evaluations by licensed professionals.

While the black attackers (proletariat) received $500,000 from their liberal supporters, the white victim (bourgeois) received a bill for more than $5,000 from the hospital for emergency room services. It appears Communist boss William Z. Foster was correct when he wrote "The Negro masses will make the very best fighters for the revolution" and "Capitalism has provided its own executioners and grave diggers, the proletariat." Welcome to Soviet America!

Liberal Democrats
Fought For Slavery & Racial Discrimination
Against Blacks In The 19th & 20th Centuries!

As stated earlier, there is good reason the builders of Soviet America seek control over all sources of news, information, and education. Just like the builders of the Soviet Union, truth is seldom on their side. For example, through the Soviet-bloc news media and education establishment Democrats are portrayed not as predatory Bolsheviks who manipulate, control, and exploit the proletariat, but instead they are portrayed as legitimate champions of the downtrodden. Conversely, Republicans are portrayed as racist, sexist, homophobic, mean-spirited, bigoted, bourgeoisie. Unvarnished American history tells a much different story, and perhaps no one has accurately summarized the history of anti-black racism among Democrats more cogently than Roger Hedgecock, a former mayor of San Diego.

As Roger Hedgecock[33] points out in his article, "Drenched in blood of slavery," eleven years before the Civil War began, Congress passed the Fugitive Slave Law in 1850. Under this law runaway slaves were required to be returned to their masters, given that slaves were viewed as legal property. The Fugitive Slave Law required law enforcement officers to assist in recapturing and returning runaway slaves. Those who refused faced a fine of $1,000. Today that is the equivalent of a $100,000 fine!

The Republican Party was formed in the 1850s to challenge the injustices of the Democrat Party. The enactment of the Fugitive Slave Law by Democrats was one example. After Republicans countered the Fugitive Slave Law by enacting laws at the state level, Democrats denounced these laws at their 1860 national convention.

In addition, it was the Southern Democrats who created Jim Crow laws that made it legal to segregate blacks from whites after the Civil War. From 1877 to 1954 blacks were legally forced to sit in the back of the bus. They were legally forced to use separate restrooms and drinking fountains. They were legally separated in restaurants and forced to attend separate schools. As noted at the beginning of this chapter, in 1954 the U.S. Supreme Court ruled in *Brown v. The Board of Education* that racial segregation in public schools was a violation of the Fourteenth Amendment. Consequently, racial segregation of all schools and all public facilities was determined to be unconstitutional.

The Civil Rights Act of 1964 put the last nails in the coffin of the racist Jim Crow Laws. Unfortunately, Southern Democrats, such as Al Gore's father, opposed this law. However, it was passed by Northern Democrats and Republicans. Without Republican votes the Civil Rights Act of 1964 would never have become law. Roger Hedgecock further noted that, given the historical fact that Democrats have consistently fought for slavery and racial discrimination and Republicans have consistently fought against these injustices, if there is a call for reparations it must be the Democrats, and not the Republicans, who should reach into their wallets and purses.

Furthermore, it was the Democrats who levied poll taxes in the Southern states. Unable to pay poll taxes most blacks and many poor whites were denied their right to vote. In 1966 the U.S. Supreme Court ruled that citizens could not be forced to pay a poll tax in order to vote. Roger Hedgecock noted that the infamous Ku Klux Klan was founded by a Democrat and it remained a Democrat-operated domestic terrorist organization throughout its morbid history. It was the Democrats who, through their membership in the KKK, ran around in white sheets and pointy hats to hide their identities as they burned crosses and lynched innocent blacks. "No Republican has ever been a member of the KKK," Hedgecock noted!

It was a Republican president, Abraham Lincoln, who freed the slaves - over the objections of the Democrats. It was John Wilkes Booth, a Democrat, who assassinated Lincoln after he freed the slaves. Hedgecock further noted that, after the assassination of President Lincoln it was "the Republican-led Congress (over the objections of the Democratic Party minority)" that passed the Thirteenth Amendment which abolished slavery; passed the

Fourteenth Amendment that acknowledged freed slaves have the same rights as all other citizens; and passed the Fifteenth Amendment which guaranteed freed slaves the right to vote.

Predatory Democrats Have Not Changed!

The early slave masters controlled the food, shelter, education, employment, health care, transportation, energy usage, communication, and just about every other significant activity of their slaves. Shorty after passage of the Civil Rights Act of 1964 both Northern and Southern Democrats began working surreptitiously to not only re-enslave blacks, but to enslave us all. Just like the Democrat slave masters of the 19th century, the Democrat wannabe slave masters of the late 20th and early 21st centuries have been working to achieve dictatorial control over the education, employment, health care, housing, transportation, communication, energy usage, farming, manufacturing, banking, finance, and every other significant activity of every American through a Soviet-style, slave master government. Yes, the more things change, the more they stay the same!

Because the newly evolving slave masters are government officials, they wield far more power than the old slave masters who were private citizens. The predatory, authoritarian mentality of the early Southern Democrat has never left the Democrat Party. They just changed their masks and their message, and greatly expanded their goal. Through the relentless application of Soviet-style psychological class warfare, Democrats have convinced most blacks and many whites, Hispanics, and others that "Freedom is Slavery" and "Slavery is Freedom!" This type of psychological manipulation is truly "Orwellian" given that George Orwell[34] described in his novel *Nineteen Eighty-Four* how a despotic "Big Brother" controlled a brainwashed population with slogans such as "War is Peace," "Freedom is Slavery," and "Ignorance is Strength."

New Jim Crow Laws - For Soviet America!

Just as Democrats passed gun control laws to disarm blacks during and immediately after the slavery era, they now push gun control laws to disarm all "ordinary" Americans. Clearly, today Democrats view all Americans the same way they viewed black Americans during the slavery and Jim Crow era. Southern Democrats had passed gun laws designed to disarm newly freed blacks, but not to disarm themselves. Today we find Bolshevik Democrats such as Senators Charles Schumer, Diane Feinstein, Jay Rockefeller, and others pushing gun control laws to disarm all "ordinary" Americans, but not themselves!

Yes, while working to disarm others these same Bolshevik Democrats, such as Senators Charles Schumer and Diane Feinstein, personally arm themselves with concealed handguns, while Senator Jay Rockefeller kept a military-style "assault weapon" in his home. They also surround themselves with armed, taxpayer-funded Capitol police. (The reader will note that this form of elitist hypocrisy is explored in some detail in Chapter Eight, Self-Defense & the Second Amendment in Soviet America!)

In their 1998 booklet, *Gun Control Is Racist,* Aaron Zelman and Richard Stevens[35] expose the racist roots of gun control in America. The total gun bans liberal Democrats, such as Senator Diane Feinstein, are calling for today are reminiscent of the total gun bans which white slave owners in Virginia and South Carolina placed on their slaves to keep them from rebelling. Today, liberals call for bans on so-called Saturday Night Specials, which are simply small, cheap, handguns. But, after the Civil War states such as Tennessee and Arkansas banned cheap handguns to keep former slaves defenseless.

Today, in the 21st century, liberal Democrats are calling for the licensing of all gun owners. Again, this is nothing new. According to Zelman and Stevens many states such as Delaware, Florida, Louisiana, Mississippi, and South Carolina required slaves to obtain a license from a police officer or a judge in order to possess a firearm. Today liberal Democrats, such as Barack Obama, are calling for extremely high taxes on guns and ammo so "ordinary" citizens will be unable to afford the tools they need to defend themselves, their families, and their freedom - as protected by the Second Amendment! Again, this is nothing new. This is precisely the tactic employed by white racists after the Civil War. For example, in Alabama and Texas extremely high taxes were placed on firearms so poor blacks could not afford to acquire them. As final thoughts, recall just a few quotes from Chapter Eight (underlines added):

1. "No free man shall ever be debarred the use of arms." - **Thomas Jefferson**

2. "[When] the resolution of enslaving America was formed in Great Britain, the British Parliament was advised by an artful man, who was governor of Pennsylvania, to disarm the people; that it was the best and most effectual way to enslave them; but that they should not do it openly, but weaken them, and let them sink gradually." - **George Mason**

3. "The most foolish mistake we could possibly make would be to permit the conquered Eastern peoples to have arms. History teaches that all conquerors who have allowed their subject races to carry arms have prepared their own downfall by doing so." - **Adolf Hitler**

Of course, liberal Democrats would agree with each of the above quotes, and that is precisely why they seek civilian disarmament through unconstitutional gun control laws. As predators they do not view their prey ("ordinary" Americans) as free men and women. Instead, they have been advised by artful tacticians to disarm the people because that is the best and most effectual way to enslave them; and they believe the most foolish mistake they could make would be to permit the conquered American people - their subject races - to carry arms.

Liberal Democrats: Still Fighting For Slavery & Racial Discrimination!

"If you criticize a minority group or a woman in America, you'll likely be labeled a bigot. But if you hammer white men, you could wind up with a great media job!" - Bill O'Reilly[36]

Throughout American history there has always been a group of predators who consistently sided with tyranny. During the American Revolution loyalists (liberals) sided with the tyrannical British Government headed by King George III, a madman who sought to disarm, subjugate, and overtax American patriots. During the American Civil War liberal Democrats fought for slavery, and after losing the war they fought for racial discrimination against blacks. They also fought to prevent blacks from owning firearms, and subjected blacks to a poll tax to keep them from voting. Today liberal Democrats continue to fight for racial discrimination. But now they discriminate against whites through biased legislation, biased court decisions, biased reporting, biased education, and biased entertainment. Moreover, they now seek to disarm, subjugate, and overtax all Americans, regardless of skin color!

In addition, with the help of Menshevik Republicans, Bolshevik Democrats have been working for decades to place their newly created Soviet America under the direct control of yet another foreign power - the United Nations. And, as discussed elsewhere in this book, the United Nations was enthusiastically endorsed by Joseph Stalin, Nikita Khrushchev, and other leaders of the Soviet Union because both the USSR and the UN were working toward the same goal. Moreover, the UN has always been run by a bunch of Marxists, socialists, fascists, and a wide variety of psychopathic tinhorn dictators - all of whom are hell bent on disarming, subjugating, and over-taxing the American people!

From British America, to Sovereign America, to Soviet America, liberals have never endorsed American-style liberty, and they have never changed their ultimate goal. Welcome to Soviet America!

Black Proletarians
Are Also Burying Black Progeny!

Ruth Bader Ginsburg,[37] Associate Justice on the U.S. Supreme Court, made a stunning statement consistent with her William Z. Foster-supported, ACLU roots. When discussing the issue of abortion, Justice Ginsburg stated that she believed the legalization of abortion via the 1973 *Roe v. Wade* decision was desired in order to reduce the number of people within undesirable populations. Her exact words were: "Frankly I had thought that at the time Roe was decided, there was concern about population growth and particu-larly growth in populations that we don't want to have too many of." This attitude, of course, is consistent with that of the Nazis, as discussed in Chapter Nine, who were prosecuted for crimes against humanity and war crimes which included performing abortions on Russian, Polish, and other non-Aryan women who belonged to populations that the Nazis did not "want to have too many of."

Recall that Ruth Bader Ginsburg was nominated to the U.S. Supreme Court by President Bill Clinton, a Bolshevik Democrat that had the enthusiastic support of the black community and was even hailed as "the first black president!" Keep in mind that Planned Parenthood - which is joined at the hip to the Democrat Party - has placed most of its abortion clinics in minority neighborhoods, with 60 percent located within the black community. Dr. Alveda King,[38] the niece of the late Reverend Martin Luther King, Jr., has called for an end to the federal funding of Planned Parenthood. According to Dr. Alveda King, "Planned Parenthood is definitely a racist organization - they have a racist agenda." She also noted that, "Since 1970, there has been something like 50 million abortions. About 17 million of those have been blacks. It's black genocide. They are killing our people and fooling us."

Day Gardner,[39] President of the National Black Pro-Life Union, stated that, "Abortion has become the #1 killer of black people in this country - killing more African Americans than accidents, heart disease, strokes, crimes, HIV/AIDS and all other deaths… COMBINED! If we stand up to this horrific practice…we shall overcome this, too." About 400,000 blacks are exterminated each year through abortion. While blacks make up roughly 13 percent of the population, about one-third of all abortions are performed on blacks. Dr. Alveda King[40] was quoted as saying, "The great irony is that abortion has done what the Klan only dreamed of."

Both the Ku Klux Klan and Planned Parenthood are Democrat operations!

Day Gardner[41] has been critical of Barack Obama and other black leaders for supporting Planned Parenthood - the nation's leading abortion provider. Gardner noted that Margaret Sanger laid the foundation for the creation of Planned Parenthood. In 1939 Margaret Sanger, a staunch eugenicist, wrote a letter to Dr. Clarence Gamble wherein she stated that, "We should hire three or four colored ministers, preferably with social-service backgrounds and with engaging personalities. The most successful educational approach to the Negro is through the religious appeal. We don't want the word to go out that we want to exterminate the Negro population." How does the Reverend Jesse Jackson, the Reverend Al Sharpton, and the Reverend Jeremiah Wright fit into this picture?

Again, we find another truly Orwellian situation in Soviet America. The liberal Democrats who support the extermination of the black population through abortion are portrayed as their saviors, and the conservative Republicans who oppose the extermination of the black population through abortion are portrayed as racists. Yes, in Soviet America that master dialectician - Bolshevik Big Brother - has manipulated the minds of tens of millions of Americans of all colors into believing the unbelievable: "Genocide is Freedom!"

Dictatorship Of The Black Proletariat: Soviet America's Most Reliable Proletariat

"It's very difficult for them to understand that we are part of one race - the human race - and racism is just fighting among ourselves." - Dr. Alveda King[42]

The black proletariat has been given special attention in this book for several reasons. Firstly, in his book *Toward Soviet America*, Communist boss William Z. Foster focused much attention on the role "Negros" would play in helping

Communists build their Soviet America. And Foster's book and its title served as a major inspiration for the writing and titling of the book you are now reading. Secondly, as stated earlier, J. Edgar Hoover, the Director of the FBI, wrote that a major goal of Communists "is to hoodwink the Negro, to exploit him and use him as a tool to build a Communist America." Thirdly, in terms of voting record, blacks are the most reliable voting block for the Democrat Party. Blacks consistently vote Democrat at a rate of roughly 85 to 95 percent. No other voting block is more reliable. While women, Hispanics, homosexuals, seniors, and others who have been fashioned into prole-tarians tend to vote Democrat, none approach the consistent average of 85 to 95 percent as found among blacks.

The fact that blacks vote Democrat in such high numbers is significant given what has been written about the Democrat Party in Chapter Four. Recall the following quotes from that chapter: Cleveland radio talk show host Mike Trivisonno said, "Sometimes I think this is Russia, and the Democrats are bringing back Communism." And, "They [the Democrats] now want to turn the United States of America into Russia." A caller into Michael Medved's radio talk show opined that the Democrat Party is "the new American Communist Party in a lot of ways." Pastor Ernie Sanders told his radio listeners that "I refer to the Democratic Party as the Communist Party."

Alan Caruba titled one of his articles as follows: "Democrat Party: The CPUSA in Disguise?" Aaron Klein placed the following title on one of his articles: "Communist Party strategists map out Obama's agenda." Tammy Bruce told a national radio audience that "The Democratic Party, with this shift, is the Marxist Party." In the chapter on health care we find the following quote from J. R. Dieckmann: "Communists weren't defeated with the fall of the USSR, they simply went underground then popped up here in America and hijacked the Democrat Party."

Given FBI Director J. Edgar Hoover's warning that a major objective of Communists is to deceive blacks into helping them build a Communist America, the unwavering allegiance of blacks to the Democrat Party leads one to conclude that Communists were remarkably successful in accom-plishing that objective - in spite of J. Edgar Hoover's warning!

If members of the black proletariat want to know what life will be like for them when the construction of Soviet America has been completed and the "dictatorship of the black proletariat" is no longer useful to the Bolshevik elite, they simply need to read the very next chapter and examine the plight of black proletarians in Soviet Cuba.

Welcome to Soviet America!

Good-bye to the Sovereign America that once aspired to be "One Nation Under God!"

------†††------

The Communist Party "will direct its attention to the great problems of the struggle of the proletariat. It will establish the real connections between the party and the masses and their struggle." - R. M. Whitney, *Reds in America*, 1924[43]

"Communism with its deceitful double talk exploits these basic human yearnings for better social conditions, racial equality, justice, and peace, and places them in the service of tyranny. In this way, strange as it may sound, Communists are able to entice free men to fight for slavery in the name of freedom." - J. Edgar Hoover, Director of the FBI, 1958[44]

"Socialists cry 'Power to the people,' and raise the clenched fist as they say it. We all know what they really mean - power over people, power to the State." - Margaret Thatcher, Prime Minister of the United Kingdom, 1979 - 1990[45]

"None are more hopelessly enslaved than those who falsely believe they are free." - Johann Wolfgang Von Goethe

Chapter Thirteen

Soviet Americans Love Soviet Cubans!

Fidel Castro:
Liberals Favorite Cuban Psychopath!

After mounting a successful revolution against Cuban dictator Fulgencio Batista, Fidel Castro established the first Communist dictatorship in the Western Hemisphere in 1959. While urban terrorists inflicted most of the damage on Batista forces, Fidel Castro and Ernesto "Che" Guevara led their revolutionaries into the Cuban capital and seized power. As one of his first duties, Castro began summarily executing Batista supporters, and about 600 people faced firing squads over a five-month period.[1] In the 1960s between 7,000 to 10,000 people were executed, and 30,000 Cubans who preferred freedom over Communism became political prisoners.[2]

In the same year Castro directed hardcore Marxists, backed by the army, to do what sociopaths with "a lust for power over others" love to do: they confiscated property, seized control of newspapers, forbade unions to strike, infiltrated churches, closed religious colleges and seized their property, removed honest people from government positions, created a secret police (known as the Red Gestapo, modeled after the Soviet Secret Police), established slave labor camps, suppressed rebellions, and they continued to incarcerate, torture, and execute "counter-revolutionaries." Homosexuals were singled out for special treatment. Many were publicly judged at their place of employment. Those who refused to give up their homosexual life-style faced loss of employment, imprisonment, and "re-education."

Nearly 50,000 members of the middle class were exiled soon after Castro seized power.[3] This is not surprising given that Marxism calls for the destruction of the middle class, or bourgeoisie, as a main goal of all Communist movements. However, like the bourgeois useful idiots of other fallen nations, many of the middle class exiles had initially supported the Sovietization of Cuba. Castro also suspended the Cuban Constitution, thus stripping Cubans of their fundamental rights. It was not until 1976 (the bicentennial of the USA) that a new Constitution was adopted.

Unfortunately for the Cuban people, Castro's Constitution, like the UN Charter, looked more like the Soviet Constitution than the U.S. Constitution.

In Castro's "workers' paradise" it was made illegal to be absent from work. Government agents determined where people worked and how they spent their money. Neighborhood committees were formed to keep everyone under constant surveillance. This would ensure no one engaged in "counter-revolutionary" activities. Cubans were now subject to arrest simply for expressing ideas that were deemed a threat to the revolution, thereby establishing what may be called "thought crimes." As in Soviet America, in Soviet Cuba diversity of thought is not tolerated!

In the prisons and slave labor camps of Castro's "workers' paradise" political prisoners and common criminals were subjected to various forms of torture. Many were forced to work nearly naked. Some were subjected to electric shock treatment, solitary confinement, and others were forced to cut grass - not with a lawn mower, but with their teeth! Some prisoners were drugged, sleep deprived (a technique borrowed from the Soviet Union), physically beaten, starved, placed in iron cages, and psychologically tormented. To add insult to injury, the family members of prisoners were stripped of employment and children were denied higher educational opportunities. Both men and women were subjected to imprisonment, and children and adolescents were placed in special prisons.[4]

It is, of course, against the law to leave Soviet Cuba without government permission. However, thousands of Cubans have died trying to escape from what JFK referred to as Fidel Castro's "imprisoned island." Most drowned attempting to escape to the USA on shabbily constructed rafts. Since 1959 about 2,000,000 people escaped from Castro's Cuba, a nation of 11,000,000 people.[5] Based on information available from the Cuba Archive, Castro's regime exterminated more than 112,000 people.[6] According to *The Black Book of Communism*, between 15,000 and 17,000 people were shot to death by government executioners.[7] Information available from Freedom House indicates that 500,000 Cubans have been thrown into prisons and slave labor camps.[8] Welcome to Soviet Cuba!

Raul Castro:
Liberals Second Favorite Cuban Psychopath!

Due to Fidel's declining health, his younger brother, Raul Castro, assumed the presidency of Cuba in February of 2006. In July of 2008, Steve Harrigan[9] of FOX News checked to see if Cuba had improved under Raul's leadership. Harrigan reported that 3,000 Cubans had been issued microwave ovens imported from Communist China - compliments of the Cuban government. A Cuban woman said she could never afford to buy a microwave oven on her own, adding that it would take her 20 years to do so. The microwave ovens were issued as part of a pilot project to determine if the Cuban electrical grid could handle the load.

Other improvements were also reported. For example, under their new president Cubans could now own cell phones and computers - if they could afford them. They were also permitted to enter Cuban hotels, behavior that was forbidden under Fidel. Steve Harrigan further noted that, given Raul's generosity, some Cubans hoped that perhaps someday they would be able to buy and sell cars, or even buy and sell houses - legally! Others hoped they could leave Cuba without asking permission from government authorities. Well, perhaps someday! (Are you beginning to understand why liberals love Castro - but hate the FOX News Network?)

In discussing Humberto Fontova's book, *Fidel - Hollywood's Favorite Tyrant*, Phil Brennan[10] of NewsMax.com points out that the people (proletariat) living in Castro's Cuba are worse off than the slaves who lived in 19th century Cuba. For example, in 1842 Cuban slaves ate more nutritious meals than contemporary Cuban proletarians. In Castro's Cuba the government issues 2 ounces of meat, chicken, and fish per person, but in 1842 Cuban slaves received 8 ounces of the same food. Today the people receive 3 ounces of rice while Cuban slaves received 4 ounces. Today Cubans are rationed 6.5 ounces of starches and one ounce of beans; however, 19th century Cuban slaves received 16 ounces of starches and 4 ounces of beans.

Before Castro seized power in 1959, Cuba had the second highest per capita income among all Latin American nations. It was also noted by Fontova that, in 1958, the year before Castro seized power, the average agricultural worker in Cuba received an hourly wage that exceeded the wages of workers in France, Belgium, and West Germany. A woman living in Cuba 50 years later, in 2008, stated that it would take her 20 years to save enough money to buy a microwave oven. Keep in mind that, from the liberal perspective, all of the above are reassuring signs of "progress." After all, thanks to Castro, Cubans are no longer exploited by evil corporate executives - as they are in America.

Soviet-Style Health Care In Soviet Cuba: A Reality Check!

"We are proud that in our institution [Havana General Psychiatric Hospital], we have a larger proportion of hospital inmates who have been lobotomized than any other mental hospital in the world." - Cuban physician[11]

As in the Soviet Union, health care in Soviet Cuba is a government-run, two-tiered system. Firstly, there is free, first-rate medical care available to the Communist elite. High ranking government officials, including upper echelon military personnel, and cash-paying foreigners have access to well-staffed, well-stocked medical facilities. It is this first-tier health care system that Fidel and Raul Castro put on display for useful idiots, such as leftist film-maker Michael Moore. Armed with disinformation they acquired with their own eyes, they serve as propagandists who lavish praise upon a stunningly inferior health care system.

However, the hidden, second-tier system is precisely what one would expect from a government-run, Soviet-style health care system. Under the second-tier system workers, farmers, peasants, and others members of the Cuban proletariat must bring their own food, blankets, sheets, fans, and aspirin - if they can find any - when seeking admission to a Cuban medical facility for treatment. There are long waiting lines, and some second-tier Cuban medical facilities have nurses but no doctors. Life-saving medicines, such as antibiotics, are almost non-existent in the facilities available to the lowly proletariat. Aspirin, when available, can only be purchased at government-run stores. Unfortunately, the price is marked up so high few Cubans can afford aspirin, and antibiotics are available to the proletariat only through the black market - if they can afford it.[12] Welcome to Soviet Cuba! Yes, that's the same Soviet Cuba held in such high esteem by the liberals who are building their Soviet America - complete with a two-tiered Soviet-style health care system.

Now, after that very brief summary of life in Communist Cuba, let's take a look at the issue of race and explore what liberal Americans have said about Fidel Castro, Raul Castro, and their beloved, Soviet-style, "worker's para-dise."

No Racism In Soviet Cuba! Just Ask Any Soviet American!

In what country are blacks stopped and questioned by the police far more often than whites? In what country do you find blacks under-represented in high government positions? In what country are blacks less likely than whites to be employed in more desirable jobs? In what country are 5 percent of the vehicles driven by blacks, when blacks make up at least 11 percent of the population according to one study? In what country are blacks more likely to live in less expensive homes than whites? In what country are black faces under-represented on television screens? No, that country is not the USA, it is Soviet Cuba, the "workers' paradise" created by the beloved Fidel Castro, liberals favorite Cuban psychopath.

But what you will never hear from Castro-loving liberal celebrities, journalists, educators, or government officials is that in America blacks who raise the issue of race are portrayed as civil rights workers and may find themselves exalted on television, radio, and in the print media; however, blacks who raise the issue of race in Cuba are labeled counter-revolutionaries and are thrown in jail. Carlos Moore, a Brazilian expert on race relations who was born in Cuba, flatly states that, "Blacks in Cuba know that whenever you raise race in Cuba, you go to jail. Therefore the struggle in Cuba is different. There cannot be a civil rights movement. You will have instantly 10,000 black people dead."[13]

Just one example, provided by Freedom House,[14] demonstrates how blacks are currently treated in Soviet Cuba: "Dr. Biscet, an Afro-Cuban medical doctor and founder of the Lawton Foundation for Human Rights, is currently in prison. He was sentenced to 25 years in jail for 'disorderly conduct' and 'counter-revolutionary activities' during the March 2003 crackdown on independent journalists, librarians and civil society actors across Cuba. Before his imprisonment, Dr. Biscet was a leading proponent of human rights advocacy through non-violence."

How do black American liberals react to Fidel Castro, a Communist thug who has been enslaving black Cubans for 50 years? While conservatives and libertarians have been highly critical of Fidel's regime, liberals have been praising this Communist dictator since he seized power in 1959. Let's check the statements of just a few prominent black liberals:

"Castro is the most honest and courageous politician I have ever met." - Jesse Jackson, political activist

Fidel Castro is "a source of inspiration to the world." - Naomi Campbell, model

"If you believe in freedom, if you believe in justice, if you believe in democracy, you have no choice but to support Fidel Castro." - Harry Belafonte, singer and actor

To his credit, Al Sharpton[15] is on record criticizing the Castro regime for human rights abuses. Focusing attention on black Cubans who have received lengthy prison sentences simply for criticizing Castro's "workers' paradise," Sharpton has invited Raul Castro to discuss the issue. Because Sharpton was lodging accurate claims of racism against a Communist dictator, and not lodging false claims of racism against innocent white "bourgeoisie" Americans, he was essentially ignored by the Soviet American media.

Congressional Black Caucus:
We Love Cuban Psychopaths, Too!

In April of 2009 members of the Congressional Black Caucus (CBC) were sharply criticized by some Republican lawmakers. What was their complaint? Members of the CBC visited Soviet Cuba, spent considerable time with Fidel and Raul Castro, but never criticized these Communist dictators for their 50-year long train of human rights abuses. For example, Josiah Ryan[16] of CNSNews.com reported that the U.S. State Department's *2008 Country Report on Human Rights Practices* was highly critical of the Castro regime. According to this report, at the end of 2007 there were 205 political prisoners and detainees in Cuba. In addition, as many as 5,000 Cuban citizens were imprisoned for "dangerousness." Unfortunately, the Cuban proletarians imprisoned for "dangerousness" were never charged with the commission of a crime. In Soviet Cuba, simply being viewed as a danger to the state justifies incarceration.

In addition, the U.S. State Department report noted that "The following human rights problems were reported: Beatings and abuse of detainees and prisoners, including human rights activists, carried out with impunity; harsh and life-threatening prison conditions, including denial of medical care; harassment, beatings, and threats against political opponents by government-recruited mobs, police and State Security officials; arbitrary arrest and detention of human rights activists."[17]

As Michelle Malkin[18] noted: "The U.S. Commission on International Religious Freedom reported last year that '(r)eligious belief and practice remain under tight governmental control in Cuba.... Both registered and unregistered religious groups continue to suffer official interference, harassment and repression. Political prisoners and human rights and pro-democracy activists continue to be denied the right to worship.' The panel compiled reports of religious leaders 'being attacked, beaten or detained for opposing govern-ment actions.'" As in the Soviet Union, in Soviet Cuba religious schools are forbidden. And, as in the Soviet Union and in Soviet America, in Soviet Cuba pre-born children do not have a right to life!

However, despite past and current monumental human rights abuses, Republican Representative Chris Smith noted that members of the Congres-sional Black Caucus "left Cuba gushing with praise of the Castros and their regime." Bolshevik Democrat Barbara Lee of California, who serves as the Chairman of the CBC, said "Former President Fidel Castro is very engaging, very energetic." Lee also stated that, "Our conclusion is, given the new direction in our foreign policy, it's time to look at a new direction in our policy toward Cuba."

In other words, Barbara Lee and other members of the CBC believe the U.S. Government should normalize trade and diplomatic relations with these homicidal Communist dictators - without demanding that they cease and desist in their outlandish predatory behavior. Michelle Malkin also noted that Lee, apparently star-struck by Fidel Castro, stated that he "looked directly into our eyes." In response to Representative Lee's teenage-like fascination with this Communist dictator, Michelle Malkin said, "Where was he supposed to look? Into their ears?"

Bolshevik Democrat Barbara Lee was not alone in her adulation of the Castro brothers. CBC member Representative Emanuel Cleaver, a Bolshevik Democrat from Missouri, stated that, "If there is repression in Cuba we didn't see it." Cleaver also reported that, "We've been led to believe that the Cuban people are not free, and they are repressed by a vicious dictator, and I saw nothing to match what we've been told." Cleaver further stated that Communist dictator Raul Castro is "one of the most amazing human beings I've ever met."

White Liberals:
We Love Cuban Psychopaths More Than You Do!

In view of the statements of Jesse Jackson, Barbara Lee, and other high profile black leftists, what do high profile white liberals have to say about Cuba's racist, homophobic, homicidal, sadistic, Communist slave master?

Let's review the statements of just a few:

"For me, he [Fidel Castro] is God. I love him very much." - Peter Jennings, former ABC news anchor

"To be a poor child in Cuba may in many instances be better than being a poor child in Miami…" - Eleanor Clift of *Newsweek* Magazine

"He [Fidel Castro] said he wanted to make a better life for Cuba's poor. Many who lived through the revolution say he succeeded.…Today even the poorest Cubans have food to eat, their children are educated and even critics of the regime say Cubans have better health care than most Latin Americans." - Paula Zahn, former CNN newscaster

"They are the healthiest and most educated young people in Cuba's history. For that, many of them say they have Castro and his socialist revolution to thank.…" - Ed Rabel, former NBC reporter

"Considered one of the most charismatic leaders of the 20th century… [Fidel] Castro traveled the country cultivating his image, and his revolution delivered. Campaigns stamped out illiteracy and even today, Cuba has one of the lowest infant mortality rates in the world." - Katie Couric, CBS news anchor

"He is a towering historic figure, and meeting and interviewing him was one of the most memorable experiences of a young reporter's life." - Geraldo Rivera, host of "Geraldo at Large," the FOX News Network

"Like these young dancers, Carlos [Acosta] benefited from Cuba's Communist system because it not only recognizes physical talent, it nurtures it, whether it's baseball, boxing, or ballet." - Christiane Amanpour, chief international correspondent with CNN

Fidel Castro is "Cuba's Elvis." - Dan Rather, former CBS news anchor

If you want more quotes, check out the Media Research Center (MRC) web site.[19] If you are tired of quotes from east coast liberals, how about a few from west coast Hollywood liberals?

"Meeting Fidel Castro" was "the eight most important hours of my life." - Steven Spielberg, filmmaker

Fidel Castro is "Very selfless and moral. One of the world's wisest men." - Oliver Stone, filmmaker

Fidel Castro "has brought a greater equality in terms of wealth distribution than I guess any country in the world today." - Saul Landau, filmmaker

"Fidel, I love you. We both have the same initials. We both have beards. We both have power and want to use it for good purposes." - Francis Ford Coppola, filmmaker

"He [Fidel Castro] is a genius. We spoke about everything." - Jack Nicholson, actor

"Socialism works...I think Cuba can prove that...I think it's conclusive that there have been areas where socialism has helped to keep people at least stabilized at a certain level." - Chevy Chase, actor and comedian

By praising the leadership of Soviet Cuba, liberals tell us precisely the kind of leaders they envision for Soviet America! God help us all!

Think about what these and other liberals have said about Ronald Reagan, George W. Bush, Dan Quayle, Newt Gingrich, Sarah Palin, and other Republicans - while fawning over Fidel Castro! We know, for example, that Dan Rather, who referred to Fidel as "Cuba's Elvis," tried to smear George W. Bush with false documents regarding his Air National Guard service. Rather also smeared Ronald Reagan, stating, for example, that Reagan was "neglecting his constitutional responsibilities," and "Children are already suffering from cutbacks during the Reagan Administration." An entire volume could be written to show how liberals offer praise to homicidal Communist dictators such as Fidel Castro while smearing Republicans or anyone else who appears to threaten the Democrat/Communist machine.

Liberals love Castro's Cuba, where people are arrested and jailed for what they think and for what they say. They love a leader who created a nation where people are undernourished, beaten, caged, tortured, and murdered to suppress intellectual and political diversity. They hold in high esteem an unelected leader who runs a nation where homosexuals and blacks are treated as substandard citizens. They love a system where children who are not imprisoned or murdered are indoctrinated into Communist ideology via "free" education, and also receive "free," second-tier, Soviet-style health care. What does this say about the moral IQ of liberals?

While leftists are severely punishing blacks in Cuba for emphasizing racial differences, they are rewarding blacks in America for emphasizing racial differences in order to propagandize black Americans into helping them build their Soviet America. If American blacks and homosexuals want to know what kind of treatment they can expect when the masks come off and liberals have finished manipulating them into building a Soviet America, they need to take a close, sober look at the treatment of blacks and homosexuals in Soviet Cuba. Obviously, liberals do not care about blacks, whites, homosexuals, or anyone else, in Cuba or in America. For both black and white liberal elites, blacks, homosexuals, and others are just proletarian pawns to be exploited in their quest to acquire and maintain political power. It really is as simple as that!

Liberals admire Fidel and Raul Castro because of the bone crushing power they exercise over others. Like them, the Castro brothers are predators who are to be admired for vanquishing their prey. The power the Castro brothers display over their Cuban prey is the power liberals desperately seek over their American prey. They admire, respect, and envy Fidel and Raul Castro because they have accomplished in Cuba what liberals have not yet accomplished in America - the complete subordination of a nation under a Soviet-style government! Only when that goal has been finally accomplished will American liberals win the respect of European socialists, Russian fascists, Cuban Communists, and other fellow travelers. Therefore, failure is not an option. Sovereign America must be conquered at any cost and replaced with a Soviet America!

Welcome to Soviet America, where liberal elites shower praise upon homicidal, racist, homophobic, Communist dictators!

Good-bye to the Sovereign America that once defended freedom, dignity, prosperity, and basic human rights!

------†††------

"The godless, truthless way of life that American Communists would force on America can mean only tyranny and oppression if they succeed. They are against the liberty which is America - they are for the license of their own. When they raise their false cry of unity, remember there can be no unity with the enemies of our way of life who are attempting to undermine our democratic institutions. The fascist-minded tyrant [Nazi dictator Adolf Hitler] whom we conquered on the battlefields is no different from the American Communistic corruptionist who now uses the tricks of the confidence man until his forces are sufficiently strong to rise with arms in revolt." - J. Edgar Hoover, Director of the FBI, 1970[20]

Chapter Fourteen

The Global Warming Hoax:
A UN Steppingstone Toward Soviet America
& Soviet-Style Global Government!

"Believe it or not, Global Warming is not due to human contribution of Carbon Dioxide (CO2). This in fact is the greatest deception in the history of science. We are wasting time, energy and trillions of dollars while creating unnecessary fear and consternation over an issue with no scientific justification." - Tim Ball, Ph.D., Canadian Climatologist[1]

"The 'global warming scare' is being used as a political tool to increase government control over American lives, incomes and decision making. It has no place in the Society's activities." - Harrison "Jack" Schmitt, Apollo astronaut, moonwalker, geologist, professor, and U.S. Senator[2]

Although the Soviet-bloc media tried to suppress the scandal, in late 2009 millions of Americans became aware of numerous emails revealing the shenanigans of global warming supporters at the University of East Anglia's Climate Research Unit in the United Kingdom. Containing words such as "trick" and "hide the decline" in global temperatures, the emails exposed the fact that data have been manipulated or suppressed to support a global warming hoax that has become increasingly difficult to defend. The emails further exposed long-term collusion among global warming advocates to defraud the public.

There may be a multitude of reasons why human-caused global warming and the purported climate change crisis may be discredited as a hoax. However, in addition to the above emails, only a dozen more reasons will be presented here, but considerable space will be devoted to those dozen reasons. Why? Firstly, the topic of global warming offers an excellent opportunity to demonstrate how liberals and other socialists employ deceitful, Soviet-style tactics to achieve goals that are remarkably consistent with Marxist ideology. Secondly, an examination of global warming in particular and environmentalism in general (as provided in this chapter and the following chapter) serves to expose the UN as a cloaked version of the USSR. Exposing the global warming hoax exposes the UN as an international den of thieves that should never be trusted. Lastly, if the perpetrators of the global warming hoax are successful, America will take another giant leap "Toward Soviet America!" Consider the following:

One: Temperature measuring devices used to monitor global warming have been placed in areas that record artificially high temperatures.

Meteorologist Anthony Watts reported in 2007 that the U.S. National Climate Data Center placed some of its temperature measuring devices on hot black asphalt. Others were located close to barrels used to burn trash, and some were placed next to heat exhaust vents. Some temperature measuring instruments were strapped to hot chimneys, and others were even located above outdoor grills.[3] The Earth doesn't have a fever, as Al Gore claims; instead, many of the temperature measuring devices used to monitor global warming have been given a fever.

Two: The United Nations Intergovernmental Panel on Climate Change, or UN-IPCC, has hidden critical documents from the public and has also falsified reports to deceive the gullible into endorsing human-made global warming.

For example, according to Andrei Kapitsa,[4] a Russian geographer and Antarctic ice core researcher, "A large number of critical documents submitted at the 1995 UN conference in Madrid vanished without a trace. As a result, the discussion was one-sided and heavily biased, and the UN declared global warming to be a scientific fact." Dr. Philip Lloyd,[5] a South African Nuclear Physicist and Chemical Engineer, said he is preparing "a detailed assessment of the UN IPCC reports and the Summaries for Policy Makers, identifying the way in which the Summaries have distorted the science...I have found examples of a Summary saying precisely the opposite of what the scientists said."

Indian geologist Dr. Arun D. Ahluwalia[6] reported that, "The IPCC has actually become a closed circuit; it doesn't listen to others. It doesn't have open minds... I am really amazed that the Nobel Peace Prize has been given on scientifically incorrect conclusions by people who are not geologists." To no one's surprise, Stanley B. Goldenberg,[7] a U.S. Government Atmospheric Scientist at the Hurricane Research Division of the National Oceanic and Atmospheric Administration (NOAA), noted that the media have spread the false notion of consensus among scientists who endorse the man-made global warming hoax: "It is a blatant lie put forth in the media that makes it seem there is only a fringe of scientists who don't buy into anthropogenic [man-made] global warming."

Three: Al Gore's so-called documentary, *An Inconvenient Truth*, is loaded with inexcusable, misleading errors.

"Do you know that while he preaches to us, Al Gore selfishly uses as much energy each year as 25 million Ugandans?" - Center for the Defense of Free Enterprise[8]

For example, on their web site the Science and Public Policy Institute (SPPI) has posted an article by Christopher Monckton of Brenchley that lists 35 factual errors in *An Inconvenient Truth*.[9] In addition, Stewart Dimmock filed a lawsuit in Britain claiming that Al Gore's film contained "serious scientific inaccuracies, political propaganda and sentimental mush." Judge Michael Burton of the British High Court concluded that, in order to prevent political indoctrination, guidance notes must be given to British students whenever *An Inconvenient Truth* is shown in British schools. The Court concluded that the film contained 11 inaccuracies which must be presented to students via the guidance notes. In addition, the guidance notes to teachers must state that Al Gore's film is a political work that promotes only one side of the argument. Teachers who fail to point out these problems when showing the film may be found guilty of political indoctrination, which is a violation of section 406 of the Education Act 1996.[10]

In discussing global warming Mona Charen made reference to the book, *Cool It: A Skeptical Environmentalist's Guide to Global Warming,* written by Bjorn Lomborg. Charen points out that the author debunks some popular myths of the environmentalists. For example, Al Gore and other environmentalists frighten school children by presenting stories of polar bears floating aimlessly on melting ice and facing inevitable drowning - all caused by human-generated global warming. However, the number of polar bears appears to be declining in only one or two of the 20 polar bear sub-populations. More than half of the subpopulations have remained stable, and two are actually increasing in number.[11]

Surprisingly, the number of polar bears worldwide has not been declining, but has actually ballooned from 5,000 in the 1960s to an astounding 25,000 today. And, even more surprisingly, the polar bear subpopulations that are declining in number inhabit areas that are cooling, and the subpopulations that are increasing in number live in areas that are warming. This is precisely the opposite of what Al Gore and other global warming alarmists have told us and our children to expect. Why does anyone listen to these hucksters?

Four: The science of global warming and climate change is incomplete, theoretical, and extremely complex.

Canadian climatologist Tim Patterson,[12] who initially supported global warming but later became a skeptic, said the study of climate change is very complex. Due to the complexity of the field, of 530 scientists surveyed from 27 countries, two out of three said the state of scientific knowledge (in 2003) was not sufficient enough "to allow for a reasonable assessment of the effects of greenhouse gases." However, eight years earlier in 1995 the United Nations Intergovernmental Panel on Climate Change had already concluded that global warming caused by human-generated carbon dioxide was an established fact.

In addition, according to scientist Bob Carter, various special interest groups, including political groups and an alarmist media, have frightened the public with global warming reports based on trends of the last 150 years which lack a geological context. Also, there is excessive reliance on predictions generated by invalidated computer model scenarios. These computer models, which give life to a virtual reality, are employed to predict future climate change based on poorly understood parameters. Unfortunately, the flawed virtual reality of climate change is given preference over the scientific reality which is extremely complex, but rooted in empirical testing.[13]

Five: Global warming on planet Earth is caused by changes in the sun and changes in the Earth's relationship to the sun. It is not caused by human-made carbon dioxide (CO2).

"The world has spent $50 billion on global warming since 1990, and we have not found any actual evidence that carbon emissions cause global warming."
- Dr. David Evans, Australian computer and electrical engineer[14]

When the radiant energy from the sun strikes the Earth, some of that energy is radiated back into the Earth's atmosphere. Natural greenhouse gases in the Earth's atmosphere trap the Earth's radiant energy and therefore increase the surface temperature of the planet. The most abundant natural greenhouse gas is water vapor, along with small amounts of naturally occurring carbon dioxide and methane. The burning of so-called fossil fuels such as coal, petroleum, and natural gas, releases human-generated carbon dioxide into the atmosphere. Consequently, we are told, human-generated carbon dioxide is added to the naturally occurring carbon dioxide and this additive factor enhances the greenhouse effect and facilitates global warming. And as global warming increases polar ice caps melt, polar bears drown for lack of floating ice rafts, and coastlines around the world may soon be submerged below ever increasing water levels. A whole host of other catastrophic events may also occur around the globe if carbon dioxide levels are not significantly reduced in short order - according to global warming alarmists!

Because of the alleged human-generated global warming threat the Industrialized nations, such as the USA, must reduce their "carbon footprint." That is, they must cut back on carbon producing behaviors such as driving cars, trucks, buses, construction equipment, watercraft, and aircraft. They must cut back on the operation of factories that generate excessive carbon dioxide and other greenhouse gases. Because oil and products made from oil, such as gasoline and diesel, are used to operate all the above vehicles as well as factory equipment and machinery, they must be modified to be more efficient in the use of such fuels. Moreover, alternative forms of energy such as bio-fuels that produce little or no carbon footprint must be developed to supplement and eventually replace all the carbon producing vehicles, equipment, and machinery.

In addition, until the carbon footprint generated by the inhabitants of the USA and other productive nations is dramatically reduced, they must be punished through a system of carefully crafted fines euphemistically called "carbon credits." That is, in addition to the hundreds of millions of dollars the American people are now giving annually to the America-hating United Nations, we must also fork over millions more, and perhaps billions more, to purchase "carbon credits" from the underdeveloped nations (that is, the nations that have been economically retarded by socialism) that generate little or no carbon dioxide. Keep in mind the confiscated wealth of Americans is not transferred directly to the backward, socialist nations from which the carbon credits are purchased, but instead the money is collected and managed by the United Nations or UN affiliates.

Of course, the carbon dioxide tsunami generated by Communist China and India may be overlooked given that they are still "developing" nations. In other words, the carbon credit scam is a new, creative, selective form of foreign aid. It is yet another scheme to cripple American manufacturing and transfer millions of hard-earned American tax dollars into the hands of UN bureaucrats. But unlike traditional foreign aid, now the transfer of wealth must be mandatory because, we are told, the Earth itself "hangs in the balance!"

But not everyone is falling for this Marxist-style, wealth transferring scheme!

As Canadian climatologist Professor Tim Patterson[15] has reported, planet Earth is heated and cooled as a function of solar cycles. The sun exhibits many cycles, one of which is about 1,500 years in length. As the sun heats and cools during various cycles, Earth heats and cools accordingly. Many climate scientists have concurred with this conclusion, including David Douglas of the University of Rochester, John Christy of the University of Alabama, and Benjamin Pearson and S. Fred Singer of the University of Virginia.[16] According to these climate scientists, the pattern of warming predicted by greenhouse models does not match observed warming trends. They have concluded that changes in the climate are due to changes in the sun. However, the greenhouse effect, which does exist, is not a significant factor in climate change.

Professor Tim Patterson also reported that over the time period which he studied he found that, "There is no meaningful correlation between CO2 levels and Earth's temperature..." He stated further that, "In fact, when CO2 levels were over ten times higher than they are now, about 450 million years ago, the planet was in the depths of the absolute coldest period in the last half billion years." Professor Patterson posed the following question: "On the basis of this evidence, how could anyone still believe that the recent relatively small increase in CO2 levels would be the major cause of the past century's modest warming?"[17]

Professor Bob Carter, an Adjunct Research Professor at James Cook University in Australia, has 35 years training and experience as a paleontologist, stratigrapher, marine geologist, and environmental scientist. According to Professor Carter, "It is concluded that natural climate change is a hazard that - like other similar natural hazards - should be dealt with by adaptation. Attempting to mitigate human-caused climate change is an expensive exercise in futility."[18]

While global warming supporters claim that increases in CO2 leads to increases in the Earth's surface temperature, Professor Carter wrote in 2007 that from 1979 the amount of carbon dioxide in the Earth's atmosphere increased by 17 percent. However, there has been little or no detectable global warming during this time period.[19] When testifying before the U.S. Senate in 2006 Professor Carter stated that increases in CO2 tend to occur hundreds of years after, not before, increases in global warming. So, if there is a relationship between CO2 and global warming, it appears to be precisely the opposite of what the global warming alarmists want us to believe. Professor Carter further noted that the temperature of the surface of the Earth has remained stable since 1998, and the temperature of the troposphere (the lowest region of the atmosphere) has not changed significantly since 1979 when El Nino and volcanic eruptions are incorporated into the analysis.[20]

Six: Carbon dioxide is essential to life on planet Earth, and moderate increases may be beneficial, not harmful, to plant and animal life. Moreover, current efforts to reduce CO2 may threaten the world food supply.

Nitrogen makes up about 78 percent of the Earth's atmosphere. While oxygen makes up slightly less than 21 percent, argon slightly less than 1 percent, carbon dioxide makes up only about 0.038 percent. As retired geologist Dudley J. Hughes[21] has noted, the 0.038 percent tells us that, for every 10,000 elemental particles in the Earth's atmosphere, only 4 are composed of carbon dioxide. So, why are environmentalists in a state of alarm? Why are governments around the world demanding a Soviet-style clampdown on "fossil fuel" production and usage? Why is the United Nations demanding a Marxist-style transfer of wealth from highly industrialized nations to a centralized authority which supposedly acts on behalf of the backward socialist nations of the world?

The answer: Because over the last 150 years the amount of carbon dioxide in the Earth's atmosphere has increased from 3 parts per 10,000 to 4 parts per 10,000. Add to this the fact that about 30 times more carbon dioxide is produced by nature than by humans, and the Earth's oceans produce about 80 percent of all greenhouse gases, we must conclude that the "global warming crisis" will never be solved by UN Bolsheviks and bureaucrats, but it may be solved by a team of psychiatrists and criminologists who have extensive experience dealing with the criminally insane!

It is important to note that carbon dioxide (CO2) is not an environmental contaminant. It is not a pollutant. We humans, along with other animals, release carbon dioxide into the atmosphere every time we exhale. More significantly, carbon dioxide is to plants what oxygen is to us. We inhale oxygen and exhale carbon dioxide. At the same time plants absorb our exhaled carbon dioxide and release oxygen in return. It's a natural, symbiotic, plant/animal relationship. The plants that produce the fruits {apples, pears, peaches, etc.} and vegetables {carrots, potatoes, and cucumbers, etc.} require carbon dioxide to blossom into nutritious food to be eaten by animals and humans - including liberal vegetarians who hate carbon dioxide!

Eliminate carbon dioxide and you will eliminate all the plant life that requires carbon dioxide to live. Eliminate all such plant life and you will soon eliminate all animal life, including human life. Do you see where this is going? Carbon dioxide is essential for life as we know it on planet Earth. Carbon dioxide is not only good, it is essential. We cannot live without it. As Dudley J. Hughes[22] has noted, scientific experiments have shown that, as the amount of carbon dioxide is increased in the atmosphere, the rate of plant growth also increases. Conversely, as the amount of carbon dioxide decreases in the atmosphere, plant growth tends to decrease as well.

Today, the amount of carbon dioxide in the Earth's atmosphere is extremely low by historical standards; therefore, lowering it further could lead to a decrease in the world food supply. Consequently we must ask, are global warming alarmists trying to rescue plants, animals, and humans from environmental destruction, or are they inadvertently or deliberately leading us down a road toward global famine? Perhaps we should pose that question to environmentalists who share the late Jacques Cousteau's penchant for systematically depopulating the planet well beyond the numbers envisioned by Hitler, Stalin, or Mao![23]

While decreases in atmospheric carbon dioxide may possibly threaten world food supplies, some scientists further point out that humans are at greater risk of starvation during times of global cooling than during periods of global warming. Scientists tell us the Earth passes through natural cycles of warming and cooling. The cooling periods result in ice ages and mini ice ages. During these cooling periods agriculture declines significantly and food becomes scarce, causing widespread starvation. However, as we pass out of an ice age, as we have recently done, the Earth warms and agriculture increases, often abundantly. Many living species, including threatened and endangered species, tend to die off during periods of global cooling and scarcity, but tend to thrive during periods of global warming and abundance. Yes, as common sense would tell us, global warming is preferable to global cooling, and global stagnation is impossible due to cyclical variations in the sun's intensity.

In 2008 extraordinary increases in food prices caused rioting in Burkina Faso, Cameroon, Cote d'Ivoire (aka the Ivory Coast), Egypt, Ethiopia, Indonesia, Madagascar, the Philippine Islands, and Senegal. Rioting also occurred in Haiti which caused the deaths of at least four people, and many more were injured.[24] But what has driven the cost of food so high that people in poorer nations could no longer afford to put food in their mouths? Certainly rising fuel costs have driven up the price of food production and transportation. Volatile weather has reduced food production in India, Canada, Argentina, Australia, the United States, and Africa. Speculators have driven up food prices by investing heavily in food staples such as wheat.

Also, because China has been dumping socialism and replacing it with capitalism, millions of Chinese are experiencing a new level of prosperity. And they are using their new found wealth to purchase food of much greater quality and quantity. Lastly, however, environmentalists have mandated increasing levels of bio-fuel production across the globe to reduce the usage of carbon producing fuels such as gasoline. So, to fight global warming we have been burning food in our vehicles instead of using it to feed the poor - who are rioting because they cannot afford to buy food - thanks to liberals.

Iain Murray, a senior fellow at the Competitive Enterprise Institute, has authored a book with the enlightening title, *The Really Inconvenient Truths: Seven Environmental Catastrophes Liberals Don't Want You to Know About - Because They Helped Cause Them.* In discussing the use of food as fuel Murray blames Al Gore and other environmentalists for the global food crisis. For example, Murray points out that about 450 pounds of corn are needed to produce enough ethanol to fill a 25 gallon fuel tank. However, those 450 pounds of corn could have fed one person for an entire year. Also, the corn used in 2007 to produce 6.5 billion gallons of ethanol could have fed 216 million people for an entire year. In a world where millions of people go to bed hungry every night, Bolshevik Democrats and Menshevik Republicans recently passed an energy bill that will convert even greater amounts of food into fuel.[25]

But converting corn into ethanol is not the only threat to the world food supply. As Bethany Stotts[26] has reported, if environmentalists succeed in eliminating nitrogen fertilizer from farming in order to reduce greenhouse gases, the world's crop fields would be cut in half, thus leaving half the world hungry. When millions of people around the world are already underfed, are Marxist environmentalists demanding that we implement unconscionable food reducing measures in order to decrease the amount of CO_2 in the atmosphere, or are they following the example of Lenin, Stalin, Khrushchev, and other Marxists who systematically starved to death millions of people? Morally mature Americans cannot allow morally insane liberals to implement such dastardly solutions to solve a problem that exists only in their heads!

The next time you see an advertisement or an infomercial by a charitable organization such as Feed The Children wherein malnourished, underfed, or starving children are shown, ask yourself, why are liberals burning food for fuel when they should be donating it to organizations such as Feed The Children?

Seven: Global warming has been recorded throughout our solar system, not just on planet Earth.[27]

As reported by writer Lorne Gunter[28] of the *National Post*, many prominent scientists have noted that global warming is occurring throughout our solar system, and these changes correspond to changes in solar activity. Mars, Jupiter, and Pluto have all exhibited signs of global warming. In addition, Triton, which is a moon of Neptune, is also experiencing global warming. When Pluto revolves around the sun it is 2.75 billion miles away at its closest point, and 4.53 billion miles at its farthest point. Thus, the average distance of Pluto from the sun, and from Earth, is about 3.6 billion miles. Are we to conclude that Americans driving SUVs on planet Earth are causing global warming on a dwarf planet such as Pluto, which is billions of miles from Earth?

We are forced to ask, if global warming on planet Earth is due to human-generated carbon dioxide, what is causing global warming on Mars, Jupiter, Pluto, and Triton? Changes in CO_2 levels on planet Earth could not cause these solar system-wide temperature changes, but variations in the intensity of the sun certainly could - and does!

Eight: Global warming appears to have stopped, and planet Earth may be cooling, not warming.

"Earth has cooled since 1998 in defiance of the predictions by the UN-IPCC....The global temperature for 2007 was the coldest in a decade and the coldest of the millennium...which is why 'global warming' is now called 'climate change.'" - Dr. Richard Keen, climatologist, Department of Atmospheric and Oceanic Sciences, University of Colorado[29]

Planet Earth has been warming naturally since 1850 when a mini ice age ended. Ice ages have come and gone many times over a period of several billion years. So what caused global warming during the previous cycles that occurred before productive, carbon-generating humans walked this Earth?

Because a mini ice age has recently ended, the average surface temperature of planet Earth around the year 2000 was roughly 0.8 degrees Celsius warmer than it was in 1900. However, this warming trend appears to have ended as we entered the 21st century. According to Australian scientist David Evans,[30] satellites that measure the temperature of planet Earth indicate that global warming ended in 2001. Others have reported that global warming ceased in 1998, while others believe it stopped way back in 1979. Other scientists have reported that the temperature of Earth has actually dropped roughly 0.6 degrees Celsius during the last year, thus cancelling out most of the 0.8 degrees Celsius gained since 1900. Instead of developing a "fever" as Al Gore has claimed, the temperature of planet Earth has actually dropped to the same level as recorded back in 1980.

Global cooling seems to be a trend developing in many areas, and some scientists report that planet Earth is, indeed, entering a period of global cooling, not global warming. For example, early in 2008 Alan Caruba[31] reported that China experienced its heaviest snowfall in thirty years. A cooling trend was noted across the Southern Hemisphere, with South America experiencing one of its coldest winters in decades. Snow fell in Buenos Aires, for example, for the first time since 1918. In Johannesburg, South Africa, residents experienced their first significant snowfall in 26 years. And in Sun parched Australia the month of June was the coldest in recorded history!

Steve McIntyre[32] of climateaudit.org has reported that, on a global basis, world sea ice reached "unprecedented" levels in April, 2008. Moreover, while April levels were the third highest since records began in 1979, March was also the third highest for that month, and January world sea ice levels were the second highest on record. Also, the CBC reported record snowfall in Ottawa, Canada, in the winter of 2008. Newsmax.com[33] reported that two explorers recently planned to cross the frozen Arctic Ocean on foot to demonstrate the extent to which global warming was heating the Arctic. However, the expedition had to be cancelled as one of the explorers suffered frostbite on her toes due to frigid temperatures that dropped 100 degrees below zero.

On December 10, 2008, eleven days before the official start of the winter season, residents of Houston, Texas, New Orleans, Louisiana, and parts of Mississippi were shocked by unexpected snowfall and freezing temperatures. According to records, since 1895 snow has fallen this early in Houston just once, and that was back in 1944. One Houston resident complained saying, "This is crazy. It's Houston - we shouldn't need to keep ice scrapers in our cars."[34] Schools, government offices, and bridges were closed due to heavy snow and freezing temperatures in southern Louisiana and Mississippi.[35] In Lafayette, Louisiana a judge ended testimony in a murder trial because witnesses were unable to travel to New Orleans. Due to unexpected snowfall the Louis Armstrong International Airport in New Orleans had been closed. Even helicopter transportation had been discontinued.[36]

Science writer Robert W. Felix authored the book, *Not by Fire, But by Ice*.[37] At his web site (http://www.iceagenow.com/) the visitor finds links to numerous articles supporting the premise that the Earth is cooling, not warming. From among those articles we learn that on December 15, 2008 Northeast Siberia experienced extreme cold temperatures down to -60 degrees Celsius; Antarctica snowfall has doubled since 1850 when the mini ice age ended; Alaskan glaciers are now growing for the first time in 250 years; all seven glaciers on California's Mount Shasta are growing; from 2005 to 2007 the volume of ice on Mount Blanc in France has nearly doubled; and on December 12, 2008 - nine days before the start of winter - 6 ½ feet of snow fell in 48 hours in Austria. That's the heaviest snowfall in Austria in 80 years!

Frustrated by claims of an impending global warming crisis amidst the obvious, abundant, empirical signs of global cooling, Dr. David Gee,[38] a geologist and chairman of the science committee of the 2008 International Geological Congress, has presented the following question: "For how many years must the planet cool before we begin to understand that the planet is not warming?"

Nine: If a consensus is building among scientists, the consensus may be expressed as follows: There is no verifiable scientific evidence to support the UN-IPCC conclusion that human-generated carbon dioxide is a significant contributor to global warming and climate change; however, there is a growing body of verifiable scientific evidence to refute this conclusion.

In 2007 the United Nations Intergovernmental Panel on Climate Change released a Summary for Policymakers. Building upon previous UN-IPCC work, the Summary for Policymakers reinforced previous conclusions that atmospheric carbon dioxide was increasing, much of it was man-made, and it was harmful to the environment. The Summary concludes that from 1850 to 2000 the global average temperature has risen; this temperature increase has caused the melting of glaciers, which in turn caused a global rise in sea level from the years 1870 to 2000; and Northern Hemispheric snow cover has declined from the years 1910 to 2000. The cause: human-generated increases in carbon dioxide, methane, nitrous oxide, and other greenhouse gases. In summary the UN-IPCC concluded that, "Most of the observed increase in global average temperatures since the mid-20th century is *very likely* due to the observed increase in anthropogenic [human-generated] greenhouse gas concentrations."[39]

While 52 scientists and climate change researchers have contributed to the UN-IPCC Summary, more than 650 scientists and climate change researchers from around the world have formally challenged their conclusions in a report submitted to the U.S. Senate in December of 2008.[40] The list of challengers includes some current and former members of the UN-IPCC. They have challenged the notion of consensus, the notion that human-generated carbon dioxide is causing global warming, and they have challenged the honesty and motivation of the UN-IPCC.

Also, 24 scientists from 15 nations refuted the UN-IPCC with a report titled, *Nature, Not Human Activity, Rules Climate Change*."[41] This report was assembled by the Nongovernmental International Panel on Climate Change, or NIPCC. According to the NIPCC report the UN-IPCC Summary for 1990 ignored satellite data because no global warming was noted through this temperature measuring method - even though this is the most accurate way to measure the surface temperature of the Earth! The UN-IPCC report for 1995 contained "significant alterations" after it was endorsed by scientists. These modifications slanted the report in favor of human-caused global warming.

The UN-IPCC report for 2001 employed the infamous hockey-stick graph to support the claim of global warming. However, independent researchers later discredited the hockey-stick graph. And, in the 2007 climate change report the UN-IPCC diminished the enormous contribution made by the sun. These independent scientists concluded that, "The IPCC is pre-programmed to produce reports to support the hypotheses of anthropogenic warming and the control of greenhouse gases, as envisioned in the Global Climate Treaty."

Furthermore, 31,072 scientists have signed a petition rejecting the notion of human-caused global warming, rejecting Al Gore's notion of scientific consensus, and rejecting the notion of impending climatic disaster due to global warming. Among the list of scientists we find 9,021 who possess Ph.D.s, 6,961 holding master's degrees, 2,240 with doctoral level medical degrees, and 12,850 with baccalaureate degrees or equivalent academic degrees.

According to the petition, "There is no convincing scientific evidence that human release of carbon dioxide, methane, or other greenhouse gases is causing or will, in the foreseeable future, cause catastrophic heating of the Earth's atmosphere and disruption of the Earth's climate." The petition further states that, "Moreover, there is substantial scientific evidence that increases in atmospheric carbon dioxide produce many beneficial effects upon the natural plant and animal environments of the Earth."[42]

News Editor Bob Unruh of WorldNetDaily.com interviewed Art Robinson, the originator and director of the Petition Project which gathered the 31,072 signatures challenging the human-generated global warming hypothesis. According to Robinson, "...many scientifically invalid claims about impending climate emergencies are being made. Simultaneously, proposed political actions to severely reduce hydrocarbon use now threaten the prosperity of Americans and the very existence of hundreds of millions of people in poorer countries." In referring to the Kyoto Protocol and other plans, Robinson said they "would harm the environment, hinder the advance of science and technology, and damage the health and welfare of mankind."

At his web site (http://www.newswithviews.com) Art Robinson provides articles that are extremely critical of Al Gore and the United Nations. According to Robinson, the ban on the use of DDT and the restrictions on energy use, both of which are supported by Al Gore, are blatant acts of genocide. Environmentalists banned the use of the insecticide DDT because it caused the thinning of the egg shells of some predatory birds. However, DDT is extremely effective in killing malaria-carrying mosquitoes. According to Robinson, after the ban on DDT some 30 million children in Africa and Asia died unnecessarily from malaria, and another 500 million adults have been stricken with preventable chronic illness. He writes further that, "Al Gore and his United Nations retainers have received the Nobel Prize for Peace. The only peace that they are offering to the world's people, however, is the peace of the grave."[43]

Ten: Environmentalists complain when humans add carbon dioxide to the atmosphere, and environmentalists complain when humans remove carbon dioxide from the atmosphere. (Yes, you read that correctly!) Klaus Lackner, who holds a Ph.D. in theoretical particle physics, is a professor at Columbia University. Professor Lackner has been working with Global Research Technologies, LLC (GRT), based in Tucson, Arizona to develop what has been dubbed a "CO2 Scrubber." With his team of researchers professor Lackner has built and successfully demonstrated a prototype "air extraction" device that captures carbon dioxide from the atmosphere. This technology holds the promise of producing numerous commercially viable devices that collectively could capture tons of carbon dioxide from the atmosphere on a daily basis.[44]

Other carbon capture and storage (CCS) devices have been proposed, but they require expensive retrofitting of existing power plants. Disposal of captured carbon dioxide has also presented problems, and plans have been proposed to funnel the captured CO_2 into depleted gas wells, oil wells, and various natural underground caverns. However, professor Lackner's CO_2 scrubber may be located anywhere, may be produced economically, and the captured CO_2 may be funneled into greenhouses to accelerate the growth of fruits and vegetables - especially in sections of the planet where food production is inadequate.

Sounds great, right? Well, some environmentalists have actually led protests against devices that capture CO_2 from the atmosphere and sequester it in underground locations. Why? A Greenpeace report has described carbon capture and storage as a "false promise." According to Greenpeace, CCS is unproven, too expensive, requires too much energy to operate, prolongs dependence on fuels that pollute the air with carbon dioxide, rewards polluters, will be available too late to prevent catastrophic damage to the environment, and underground storage is too risky. These are just some of the reasons Greenpeace opposes CCS and favors improving energy efficiency and reliance on renewable energy such as wind and solar. Greenpeace also boasts support from more than 85 non-governmental organizations "in demanding that CCS not be used as an excuse for building new coal-fired power plants."[45]

Armed with a Greenpeace report, Students Promoting Environmental Action and Save Our Cumberland Mountains held a demonstration in Knoxville, Tennessee to protest against the sequestering of carbon dioxide. According to the protesters, we should not focus on removing carbon dioxide from the atmosphere; instead, we should work on phasing out coal as soon as possible.[46]

Eleven: Climate change and global warming are not driven by hard science, as explained above. Instead, they are driven by politically motivated thought control measures reminiscent of the Soviet Union. Consider the following line of reasoning:

I arrived for basic training at Great Lakes Naval Training Center in the summer of 1965. One of the first instructions given to the new recruits was similar to the following: "In the past you had two ways of doing things: the right way and the wrong way. Now there are three ways of doing things: the right way, the wrong way, and the Navy way. From now on you will do everything the Navy way." So, when given an order the recruit is not to think, for example, about right or wrong, but to act according to instructions. The recruit is to do everything "the Navy way." This facilitates learning within a tight training schedule, ensures everyone follows procedure, reduces the probability of error, and programs the recruits to follow orders without hesitation or question.

A few years later when aboard ship, a subordinate sailor was explaining his errant behavior to a senior enlisted man. When the sailor began explaining his behavior with the words, "I thought…" the senior enlisted man interrupted and said, "You're not paid to think, you're paid to follow orders." Again, lowly sailors aren't supposed to think about right or wrong or anything else when performing their duties; they are to follow orders, follow procedure, and do everything "the Navy way." Period!

This seems harsh, but the Navy wants everyone trained to perform in a specific manner so that when under pressure, such as the pressure of combat, they fall into their routine and perform precisely as they were trained to perform. When sailors start freelancing with untested techniques they produce outcomes the leadership cannot anticipate or control, and the command and control structure breaks down. For this reason the military operates as a benign dictatorship.

However, this militaristic, dictatorial attitude is reminiscent of the attitude of Communists and their nihilistic, humanistic approach to the issue of right and wrong, as well as every other important issue. Although nihilists and humanists tend to look down upon the U.S. military, the Navy's attitude toward right and wrong was morally superior to that of the nihilists and humanists, given that the Navy at least admitted that there was a right and wrong way of doing things; they just didn't apply to naval personnel when on duty. For those who believed in right and wrong when off duty, that was their own business. Not so with nihilists and humanists. For them there is no right and no wrong - period! Consequently, in Soviet America there is no right way or wrong way of doing things, there is only the Soviet way of doing things, and from now on you will do everything, think everything, and say everything, the politically correct, Soviet way!

This "Soviet way or no way" mentality is often manifested where freedom of thought was once traditionally encouraged. For example, when Sovereign

Americans attempt to speak at Soviet-bloc colleges or universities, they must make special security arrangements so they are protected from violent student body Bolsheviks and proletarians. Ann Coulter, David Horowitz, Chris Simcox, and other Sovereign Americans have all been physically attacked for not thinking, speaking, and acting the Soviet way while on campus. When wandering outside the politically correct "neighborhood of ideas" on Soviet-bloc campuses, Sovereign American speakers must take precautionary measures. They must behave as American cold warriors operating behind enemy lines.

Sovereign American speakers must keep in mind that discussing Intelligent Design, exploring biological evidence supporting the reality of human life within the womb, criticizing the federal illegal alien crime syndicate, pointing out that "separation of church and state" is found in the Soviet Constitution but not in the U.S. Constitution, or denouncing planks of *The Communist Manifesto* - such as their beloved "Heavy progressive or graduated income tax" - are all viewed as intolerable intrusions of a foreign ideology into Soviet American territory.

Soviet-style intolerance is apparent on nearly every important issue, including climate change. For example, at Al Gore's Live Earth gathering on July 7, 2007, Robert F. Kennedy, Jr., a leftist Democrat from Massachusetts, responded to challengers of human-generated global warming by stating that, "This is treason, and we should start treating them now as traitors."[47] But Kennedy failed to recognize that most of those who challenge the dogma of human-caused global warming could not be traitors because most of them are Sovereign Americans. Only a Soviet American can commit treason against Soviet America. Only if Kennedy's comrades and other members of the environmental proletariat challenge Soviet American dogma can he label them traitors. Sovereign Americans who challenge dogma of any sort are simply behaving like free-thinking Americans, and freedom of thought was once a cherished tradition in the former land of the free and home of the brave!

In another example of Soviet-style thinking regarding climate change, Doctor Heidi Cullen, a climate expert with The Weather Channel, had noted that the American Meteorological Society's (AMS) official position is that human activity is a major contributor to climate change.[48] For this reason, Cullen contends the AMS should take an additional step and deny the AMS Seal of Approval to any meteorologist who questions the human factor in global warming. According to Cullen, to make such a challenge is to create "junk controversy." So, like the lowly deck sailor, the independent thinking meteorologist should be told by the AMS that, "You're not paid to think, you're paid to follow orders," and, "In Soviet America there's only one way of doing things, and that's the Soviet American way."

From this perspective the meteorologist is no longer viewed as an open-minded, American-style scientist who is expected to explore relevant, controversial data. Instead, the meteorologist is reduced to a Soviet-style propagandist whose goal is not scientific exploration but rather the main-tenance of political dogma which is immune to scientific examination. Like Robert F. Kennedy Jr., Dr. Heidi Cullen seems to view an inquisitive mind as a treasonous mind when discussing the topic of climate change.

Cullen, like other global warming dogmatists, wants us to accept without question that, while meteorologists are sometimes wrong when predicting weather change for the next few days, they are never wrong when predict-ing climate change for the next few decades! Unfortunately, millions have accepted this illogical line of reasoning. We can only hope the AMS doesn't buy this militaristic, Soviet-style method of thought control - on this or any other controversy. To his credit, John Coleman, the founder of The Weather Channel, has unequivocally proclaimed that global warming is "the greatest scam in history!" Coleman noted that, "In time, a decade or two, the outrageous scam will be obvious."[49]

Dr. David Deming, a professor of geology at the University of Oklahoma, has been a vocal critic of global warming who has paid a high price for his criticism. For example, when he testified before the U.S. Senate in 2006 he characterized media coverage of global warming as "irrational hysteria." In October of 2008 his "general education" certification was revoked for the class he taught at the University. This revocation is somewhat mysterious given that Dr. Deming has taught at the University for more than ten years and has consistently received "outstanding student evaluations." Dr. Deming has stated he is not aware of a previous revocation of this type in the history of the University of Oklahoma.[50]

Marlo Lewis, a senior fellow at the Competitive Enterprise Institute (CEI), had written editorials critical of the human-caused global warming hoax. Angered by the audacity of Marlo Lewis to question global warming dogma, Michael T. Eckhart, President of the American Council on Renewable Energy (ACORE), fired off a threatening email wherein he wrote the following: "It is my intention to destroy your career as a liar. If you produce one more editorial against climate change, I will launch a campaign against your professional integrity. I will call you a liar and charlatan to the Harvard community of which you and I are members. I will call you out as a man who has been bought by Corporate America. Go ahead, guy. Take me on."[51] So much for liberal tolerance and open-mindedness. Apparently Marlo Lewis was unaware that in Soviet America there is only one way of doing things, and that's the Soviet American way!

Scientists have reported unethical behavior by journal editors who refuse to publish articles authored by skeptics of global warming. Some scientists avoid conferences wherein data are presented that refute global warming dogma because they fear their attendance may threaten their careers.[52] David Suzuki, a Canadian scientist and former board member of the Canadian Civil Liberties Association, has challenged fellow global warming alarmists to seek ways of taking legal action against politicians who oppose the global warming hoax. Suzuki wants such politicians jailed because, according to him, questioning human-generated global warming (like all counter-revolutionary activities) constitutes "a criminal act."[53]

John Stossel, a former co-anchor of "20/20," has exposed many scams in his career, and the global warming hoax is no exception. He reported that Al Gore and other global warming advocates are attempting to silence critics through intimidation. Moreover, according to Stossel one scientist continues to denounce the global warming hoax in spite of the fact that he has had his life threatened for doing so. How could it be possible for a scientist to have his life threatened for challenging what is supposed to be a scientific theory? One would not expect that kind of intimidation in 21st century America, but, unfortunately, one would certainly expect threats of that nature in Soviet America.[54]

We may ask, in what scientific endeavor do we find no hypotheses to be tested, only theorems to be assumed? In what scientific field do we find no facts to be challenged, only mandates to be followed? When we find ourselves asking such questions we know we have exited the world of objective, American-style science, and we have entered the world of repressive, Soviet-style pseudo-science. Whether the topic is global warming, evolution, abortion, illegal immigration, or whatever, in Soviet America there really is only one way of doing things and only one way of thinking about things - and that one way is the Soviet American way; otherwise, you may place your career, or even your life, in jeopardy! Welcome to liberal America! Welcome to progressive America! Welcome to Soviet America!

Twelve: The global warming hoax provides Marxist environmentalists with the counterfeit "moral authority" to confiscate and redistribute tens of billions of dollars annually on a global scale. This will provide the UN with the funds needed to continue its transformation into a global, Soviet-style government.

"But it is the awareness itself that will drive the change, and one of the ways it [the "cap and trade" climate change bill] will drive the change is through global governance and global agreements." - Al Gore[5]

"More and more scientists are coming forth to say this [climate change] is a hoax, a scam, which is designed to transfer wealth and power from the private sector to the government sector, and from the government of the United States to a world government, which is what we are going to have in Copenhagen when we get the Kyoto II agreement." - Patrick J. Buchanan[56]

For the criminal masterminds behind the global warming swindle, there are very important reasons why they: 1) plant temperature measuring devices in areas that record artificially high temperatures; 2) hide documents critical of global warming; 3) falsify reports by scientists; 4) employ flawed theoretical computer models; 5) ignore hard data that suggest the Earth may be cooling, not warming; 6) ignore the fact that global warming has been occurring on other heavenly bodies in our solar system; 7) ignore the fact that there is no evidence to support the hypothesis that increases in CO_2 contributes significantly to global warming; 8) ignore ice core samples that show increases in CO_2 follow, rather than precede, global warming; 9) ignore research that shows increases in CO_2 are beneficial rather than detrimental to the environment; 10) punish critics of global warming; 11) reward advocates of global warming; and, 12) do not want to remove carbon dioxide from the atmosphere while they complain about it presence.

Under the rubric of environmentalism, the need to solve a "global warming crisis" provides the United Nations with the "moral authority" needed to confiscate the hard-earned income of productive people on a global basis. Armed with feigned moral authority, the prospect of controlling billions in confiscated wealth, and a Soviet-style game plan, the United Nations is building another global mechanism to micromanage all the people and all the nations of the world. This explains why Communists, flying Soviet-style flags complete with hammers and sickles, were crying for "Climate Justice" as they marched in the streets of Copenhagen, Denmark, during the United Nations Climate Change Conference in December of 2009.

No doubt there are many sincere environmentalists who want to save the planet from evil corporations that pollute our land, sea, and air. However, behind those sincere environmentalists are predators who, like Bolshevik Democrat Rahm Emanuel, view every crisis - whether genuine or manufactured - as an opportunity that must be exploited. As recorded by *The Wall Street Journal* Digital Network, Barack Obama's White House Chief of Staff, Rahm Emanuel, has boldly stated that, "You never want a serious crisis to go to waste. And what I mean by that is an opportunity to do things you think you could not do before."[57] In light of this statement, it should come as no surprise that the Obama Administration embraces, rather than debunks, the global warming hoax and the cap and trade (cap and tax) scam it produces.

About six months after Barack Hussein Obama became president, Walter E. Williams[58] wrote the following regarding the efforts of the Obama Administration to push "cap and trade" upon the American people: "'Cap and trade' is first a massive indirect tax on the American people and hence another source of revenue for Congress. More importantly 'cap and trade' is just about the most effective tool for controlling most economic activity short of openly declaring ourselves a Communist nation and it's a radical environmentalist's dream come true."

And what can socialists do with a manufactured climate change crisis that they would have greater difficulty doing without such a crisis? They can do what socialists always do whenever they create or exacerbate a crisis - they raise taxes, confiscate property, and enact programs to expand their political empires. They can institute a system of global wealth confiscation and global wealth redistribution that Lenin, Stalin, and Khrushchev achieved only in their dreams. As proclaimed by Emma Brindal, a "Climate Justice Coordinator" with an organization called Friends of the Earth, "A climate change response must have at its heart a redistribution of wealth and resources."[59] If alive today, Karl Marx would certainly agree with that statement!

Clearly, Dr. Eduardo Tonni, head of the Paleontology Department at the University of La Plata, Buenos Aires, was correct when he said, "The [global warming] scaremongering has its justification in the fact that it is something that generates funds."[60] Martin Durkin, producer of the 2007 documentary, *The Great Global Warming Swindle,* acknowledged the fund-raising potential of global warming when he said, "There's more money going into global warming research than there is chasing a cure for cancer."[61]

While enormous sums of money are going into global warming research by public and private organizations, the UN will be a major beneficiary of government confiscated funds. And how much money does the UN expect to generate from this scam? At the 2007 United Nations climate conference in Bali, Indonesia, Othmar Schwank, an advocate of global taxation, said they could confiscate at least "$10-$40 billion dollars per year." And of course Schwank noted that wealthy industrialized nations - such as the USA - must pay more than other nations given that they generate greater amounts of carbon dioxide.[62] And as Alan Caruba has noted, Japan, Spain, and Italy agreed to reduce carbon dioxide production but failed to do so. Consequently, in 2007 they faced fines up to $33 billion.[63] Welcome to Soviet America! Welcome to the new, global, Soviet Union!

Keep in mind that, since 1917, the builders of the old Soviet Union, Soviet China, Soviet Cambodia, and elsewhere, exterminated hundreds of millions of men, women, and children through abortion, slave labor camps, mass executions, starvation, and any other method that would feed their insatiable, predatory appetite to inflict death upon their innocent, defenseless prey. From 1973 the builders of Soviet America have exterminated tens of millions of innocent, defenseless pre-born American children through abortion alone - a practice first legalized in Soviet Russia after the establishment of Communism - using techniques employed in Nazi concentration camps. Worldwide, the builders of the New Soviet Union have exterminated hundreds of millions of innocent, defenseless children through abortion alone.

Environmentalist and liberal icon Jacques Cousteau advocated the systematic extermination of people in order to protect mother Earth. But unlike Lenin, Stalin, Khrushchev, Mao, Pol Pot, Castro (and William Ayers), environmentalists such as Jacque Cousteau envision the extermination, not of tens of millions nor even hundreds of millions of people, but rather the extermination of billions of people. Given that he is held in high esteem by environmentalists today, it is clear that the builders of the New Soviet Union share his vision.

Today, the builders of the New Soviet Union want to burn food for fuel when tens of millions of people around the world are underfed, malnourished, or starving to death. Today, the builders of the New Soviet Union want to decrease the concentration of atmospheric carbon dioxide when research shows decreases in the amount of carbon dioxide decreases food production. Today, the builders of the New Soviet Union are working to remove restrictions on abortion to increase the body count. Today, the builders of the New Soviet Union are working relentlessly to disarm law-abiding people worldwide to leave us as defenseless as the tens of millions of men, women, and children who were disarmed and exterminated in the old Soviet Union.

Clearly, the threat we face is not global warming - it is global government - as envisioned by Communist William Z. Foster, Joseph Stalin, Al Gore, and a massive army of deceitful and determined accomplices!

Many underestimated the homicidal and genocidal tendencies of the socio-paths who built the old USSR. Consequently, tens of millions of innocent, defenseless men, women, and children were worked, beaten, tortured, starved, stabbed, hung, and shot to death. We must not make the same deadly mistake and underestimate the homicidal and genocidal instincts of the sociopaths who are now building the new USSR. Following in the footsteps of their forefathers, they are currently exterminating tens of millions of pre-born children in abortion clinics across the globe. Given their history, and given the expressed desires of Jacques Cousteau and his fanatical, contemporary, environmentalist fellow travelers, there is no reason to expect the mass killings to remain exclusively inside the doors of the abortion clinics. Never underestimate the criminal mind!

1984 In The 21st Century!

"Al Gore doesn't want you to think about what he makes from a FALSE CRISIS!" - Center for the Defense of Free Enterprise[64]

In the "Afterword" of a 1984 commemorative edition of George Orwell's book, Nineteen Eighty-Four, social psychologist Erich Fromm wrote that the society depicted by Orwell resembled "the Stalinist and Nazi dictator-ships..."[65] According to Erich Fromm, in the "negative utopia" of Oceana depicted in Nineteen Eighty-Four the reader discovers a "completely bureaucratized society in which man is a number and loses all sense of individuality." This is achieved by "terror combined with ideological and psychological manipulation."[66] Fromm further noted that "The basic question that Orwell raises is whether there is any such thing as 'truth.' 'Reality,' so the ruling party holds, 'is not external. Reality exists in the human mind and nowhere else...whatever the Party holds to be truth is truth.' If this is so, then by controlling men's minds the Party controls truth."[67]

Therefore, in Nineteen Eighty-Four truth is determined by those in power, and not by any objective criteria. Most certainly the world described by

George Orwell and the world in which Americans now find themselves show frightening similarities. For example, Fromm wrote that in Orwell's *Nineteen Eighty-Four* "...in a successful manipulation of the mind the person is no longer saying the opposite of what he thinks, but he thinks the opposite of what is true." Moreover, "...he feels free because there is no longer any awareness of the discrepancy between truth and falsehood."[68]

This precisely describes the psychological state of tens of millions of citizens in 21st century Soviet America. Truth about global warming, climate change, and clean energy is not determined by objective data; not by external reality; but by psychopathic minds playing a game of global chess. Members of the United Nations panel on climate change hide, destroy, distort, and fabricate data to produce "truth" about climate change that everyone must agree upon. Officials at the highest levels of the U.S. Government, the media, and the education establishment all agree that truth about climate change - and all other important topics - will be determined by those in power, not by data obtained through rigorous scientific testing.

Moreover, everyone possessing lesser power or no power must pretend a phenomenon is true when in fact it has been demonstrated to be false. Hence, the First Amendment's protection of freedom of religion - clearly written in black and white - becomes freedom from religion. The individual right to keep and bear arms, as plainly protected by the Second Amendment, becomes a government right. The Ninth and Tenth Amendments and all other constitutional restrictions on the federal government cease to be restrictions. And of course, a baby's inalienable right to enjoy life is trumped by a woman's Soviet-style right to choose death.

Likewise, in Soviet America massive taxation is imposed through "cap and trade" to supposedly fight climate change and other schemes to solve a problem that does not exist outside Big Brother's criminal mind. And when the confiscated money is used to finance unconstitutional government expansion and control it is not called fraud; it is not called theft; it is not criminal; it is not tyrannical; instead, it is relabeled as "charity" or "fairness" or "social justice." The criminal nature of the activity is subordinated to a "greater good," such as "saving the environment," or "leveling the playing field" and "spreading the wealth" - all of which are contrived slogans.

Again, truth is no longer determined by objective data. Instead, lies masquerading as truth are imposed upon the people by predators occupying positions of enormous power in a public/private axis of evil. With "cap and trade" government will micromanage your use of electricity, natural gas, propane, gasoline, diesel, and all other fuels - as well as the buildings, vehicles, equipment, and tools that use those fuels. Through "universal" health care government will supervise what you eat, what you drink, what you smoke, and what type of recreation you choose. Virtually all lifestyle choices - except whether or not to have an abortion - will be subject to government oversight given that government, thanks to the taxpayer, now has a financial stake on nearly every decision you make. Given the government's track record of micro-mismanagement, deficit spending, and heavy handedness, your use of energy and health care will, of course, be rationed by government commissars.

Most appropriately Erich Fromm ended his analysis with this final warning: "Books like Orwell's are powerful warnings, and it would be most unfortunate if the reader smugly interpreted 1984 as another description of Stalinist barbarism, and he does not see that it means us, too."[69]

Welcome to George Orwell's Oceana in Nineteen Eighty-Four!

Welcome to William Z. Foster's Soviet America in the 21st century!

And of course, Good-bye Science-Based America!

------†††------

"Communism does not permit an objective search for truth. Communism tolerates only efforts to justify the validity of its allegedly 'scientific' principles... As developed by Lenin, the primary goal of this ideology is the seizure of total power by any and all means in all areas of society and on a worldwide scale by an elite minority group - the Communist Party." - J. Edgar Hoover, Director of the FBI, 1962[70]

Chapter Fifteen

More Socialism Disguised As Environmentalism: More UN Steppingstones Toward Soviet America & Soviet-Style Global Government!

"The American Communists worked energetically and tirelessly to lay the foundations for the United Nations which we were sure would come into existence...The United Nations is the instrument for victory...The Soviet Union is an essential part of the United Nations." - Earl Browder, General Secretary of the Communist Party, USA, from 1934 to 1945[1]

UN World Heritage Sites & Biosphere Reserves

"That we now live in a country where our private property is no longer safe and the very government that supposedly exists to protect it has become the thief we have to worry about." - Star Parker, We've legalized theft in America[2]

In 1992 the United Nations proposed Agenda 21, which was adopted by 178 nations, including the United States of America. Although it was not approved by Congress, George H. W. Bush (aka George "New World Order" Bush) signed onto Agenda 21 at the United Nations Conference on Environment and Development (UNCED) in Rio de Janerio, Brazil. According to the UN, "Agenda 21 is a comprehensive plan of action to be taken globally, nationally and locally by organizations of the United Nations System, Governments, and Major Groups in every area in which human impacts on the environment." Agenda 21 includes the "Rio Declaration on Environment and Development" and the "Statement of principles for the Sustainable Management of Forests."

Note that Agenda 21 involves the UN "in every area in which human impacts on the environment."[3] Thus, every human action that impacts the environment falls under Agenda 21. Not surprisingly, it may be difficult to identify a human activity that does not directly or indirectly impact the environment. Keep in mind that you, the reader, are a human who impacts the environment every time you breathe. Yes, every time you inhale you deplete the atmosphere of oxygen, and every time you exhale you release that dreaded greenhouse gas, carbon dioxide, into the Earth's atmosphere. Consequently, Agenda 21 theoretically places your life-sustaining behavior under the administration of the new USSR - the United Nations!

UNESCO, or the United Nations Educational, Scientific, and Cultural Organization, offers a map listing 851 World Heritage Sites located within numerous nations across the globe. Currently 22 of those sites are located in the United States, and many additional sites are planned for the USA. The UN World Heritage Sites include Monticello, which was the home of President Thomas Jefferson, as well as the Statue of Liberty, Independence Hall, and Yellowstone National Park.[4] Of the existing 22 UN World Heritage Sites located in the USA, nine of those sites are also listed as UN Biosphere Reserves, which is another designation of the United Nations. There are a total of 47 Biosphere Reserves in the United States.[5]

We must ask, why are important American sites being labeled UN World Heritage Sites and Biosphere Reserves? Why are foreign perpetrators of the global warming hoax involved in the internal affairs of America? How does this UN incursion violate U.S. sovereignty and private property rights? Why is the new USSR involved in USA property decision making - especially when the old USSR did not believe in private property and planned to confiscate and occupy all the private property and all the sovereign government property of every nation on planet Earth? Are Soviet American politicians, bureaucrats, environmentalists, journalists, reporters, educators, and professors, incrementally building a Soviet America and slowly submerging it under the control of a new USSR - the United Nations? The answer to this last question is, of course, a resounding "YES!"

After William Z. Foster released his 1932 book, *Toward Soviet America*, Communist bosses expressed concern because Foster had brazenly revealed their plans for the construction of a Soviet America. Distribution of the book was eventually halted, not by Conservatives, but by Communists who wanted to restrict knowledge of their plans to covert operatives. However, Foster's book was later republished by Sovereign Americans in order to warn other patriots.

The UN seems to have followed a similar pattern of behavior, and once again, so have Sovereign Americans. In 1995 the United Nations released a document titled *Our Global Neighborhood: Report of the Commission on Global Governance.* This UN document called for a 1998 meeting to discuss how to implement this plan, but the meeting never materialized. It appears such a meeting would have drawn too much attention to the UN plan for global government, just as Foster's book drew too much attention to the Communist plan for a Soviet America that would fall under the control of a global Soviet government. Fortunately, Henry Lamb, a Sovereign American, prepared an excellent summary of this UN plan and made it available at Sovereignty.net.[6]

When the builders of Soviet America, or their useful idiot followers, call UN critics conspiracy theorists, right-wing paranoids, or other derogatory names when reference is made to UN plans for global government, they should be referred to this UN document and Sovereignty.net. They should also be referred to W. Cleon Skousen's classic book, *The Naked Communist* (available at: http://www.skousen2000.com) where they will find this former FBI agent exposed Communist goal number 11 as follows: "Promote the UN as the only hope for mankind. If its charter is rewritten, demand that it be set up as a one-world government with its own independent armed forces. (Some Communist leaders believe the world can be taken over as easily by the UN as by Moscow. Sometimes these two centers compete with each other as they are now doing in the Congo.)"[7] As stated earlier, the entire 45 Communist goals were placed into the Congressional Record in 1963 by Representative Albert Herlong, Jr. - a Conservative Democrat from Florida.

What will visitors find at Sovereignty.net? Among a multitude of other global government steppingstones, they will find that the UN called for an International Criminal Court, a goal they succeeded in achieving three years later in 1998. They will also learn that, in 1995, the United Nations called for a system of global taxation, which is consistent with the UN-IPCC global warming and wealth transfer scheme debunked in the previous chapter. It is also consistent with the UN LOST initiative, which is discussed below.

While considering UN efforts to impose global taxation, keep in mind that taxation is a function of government, and not a function of an international deliberative body, which is the role initially claimed by the UN. Also at Sovereignty.net visitors will find that, consistent with Skousen's delineation of Communist goal number 11, which calls for the UN to "be set up as a one-world government with its own independent armed forces," the UN document titled, *Our Global Neighborhood: Report of the Commission on Global Governance,* calls for a standing UN Army.

Soviet America Will Be A LOST America!

"LOST also opens the door to a long-sought UN goal: the redistribution of wealth by taxing Americans." - Oliver North[8]

In light of the above quote, it can be discerned that the global warming scam is not the only Marxist-inspired wealth confiscation and redistribution scheme fabricated by the international criminal masterminds working deep within the bowels of the UN. The United Nations Convention on the Law of the Sea (UNCLOS) is also known as the Law of the Sea Treaty, which has been given the appropriate acronym of LOST. A product of the UN Law of the Sea Treaty is the International Seabed Authority, or ISA. Note that the title of this UN creation contains the words "International" and "Authority." Therefore, the UN has created, out of thin air, an organization that has been infused with "Authority" that is "International" in scope, with the power to regulate activities on the "Seabed." The oceans, along with the seabed below them, cover nearly 71 percent of the Earth's surface. That's almost three-quarters of the surface of the entire planet!

The UN-created ISA claims authority over all the oceans of the world, and authority over access to the untold wealth of gas, oil, and all other mineral resources within the seabed. It can also control any land-based activity that could pollute the waters resting upon the seabed, and it has assumed the authority to regulate the vessels of member nations that traverse the oceans of the world that rest upon the seabed. By charging fees and royalties from individuals, organizations, and nations that wish to have access to the world's seabed, the UN-created ISA has assumed the authority to collect taxes on a global basis - just as one would expect from a global government.

Although the USA has not signed onto LOST, 155 nations have done so. Why have so many nations signed onto the Law of the Sea Treaty? Because they expect wealthier nations, especially the USA, to seek access to the vast mineral resources within the seabed. In doing so, the USA will be required to pay various fees and royalties (taxes) to the ISA. In turn, the ISA will redistribute some of the confiscated American wealth to the member nations that have been economically retarded by socialism. Yes, it's just another Marxist-inspired, criminal master plan designed to confiscate the wealth of the productive "bourgeoisie" nations, skim large sums for UN "Bolsheviks," and transfer the remainder to the unproductive, "proletariat" nations.

For decades the USA has been under pressure to sign onto this wealth-robbing, sovereignty-destroying treaty. Fortunately, President Reagan wisely rejected this effort to place the USA under the thumb of a de facto global governmental entity. Unfortunately, however, presidents Clinton, Bush, and Obama are advocates of LOST, and Vice-President Joe Biden has been a staunch promoter for years. By determining their stance on UN schemes such as LOST, global warming, and "cap and trade," even a casual observer can separate the Soviet Americans from the Sovereign Americans!

But controlling access to nearly three-quarters of the Earth still leaves about one-quarter of the Earth free from UN regulators. So, as noted above, the ISA has also been infused with the authority to regulate various activities on land that may affect the seabed or the waters that rest upon the seabed - such as flushing one's toilet! (No, this is not a joke!) As reported by Cliff Kincaid,[9] UN inspectors have the authority regulate "Domestic Wastewater." Therefore, water discharged from your toilet, shower, bathtub, kitchen sink, or laundry would be subject to UN inspection and regulation - if America signs onto this Bolshevik Big Brother treaty!

Americans already endure excessive federal, state, county, and city taxation and regulation with representation. If the USA signs onto LOST, Americans will also be forced to endure additional, unnecessary ISA taxation and regulation without representation. For those who recall early American history, taxation without representation fueled the American Revolution against King George III of England. The American propensity to rebel against foreign tyrants helps to explain why the gang of foreign leftist tyrants running the UN seeks civilian disarmament through international gun control laws. As reported in The Washington Times,[10] "Whatever you think about guns, without them there would never have been any liberty in the United States." And without them, we will most certainly lose every last shred of remaining liberty. Just look at what they are doing to us while we are still armed!

When British troops marched toward Lexington and Concord, they had two main objectives. Firstly, they sought to arrest Samuel Adams and John Hancock at Lexington. Secondly, they wished to disarm American patriots by confiscating their store of weapons and munitions at Concord. Colonial Minutemen challenged the British troops as they approached Lexington, shots were fired, and the American Revolution turned bloody. If early American patriots had not been armed - and had not refused to be disarmed - America would have remained a subservient collection of British colonies.

With their knowledge of history, the UN gangsters know that, without guns, neither Americans nor any other freedom-loving people will possess the potential power to stop excessive national taxation and regulation with representation, nor will they be able to stop punitive international taxation and regulation without representation. Soviet Americans may argue that America has a UN ambassador, and thus we have representation at the international level. However, the USA has only one ambassador (who is often a Soviet American agent) among the nearly 200 foreign ambassadors to the UN. Moreover, many of those ambassadors represent nations such as Communist North Korea, Communist China, fascist Russia, and fascist Iran, among others, which have a deep-seated hatred of America. Why should Americans pay taxes to a deceitful, greedy, power hungry organization run by foreigners who hate America?

Gail Collins, the former editor of *The New York Times* editorial page, wrote that it is "crazy" for anyone to be opposed to the Law of the Sea Treaty.[11] However, as Phyllis Schlafly[12] has noted, if America were to join the other 155 nations which have signed onto LOST, whenever America had a dispute with another nation or nations, our chances of securing a UN-ISA ruling in America's favor "are about 1 in 155." If the USA signs onto LOST, Sovereign America will most certainly become LOST, perhaps forever! Furthermore, as Malcolm A. Kline[13] has reported, "The appropriately named LOST would cede American sea bed rights to the UN in the hope that it would give them back to us." And if the UN did decide to give our LOST seabed rights back to us, we would have to pay them to do so. Contrary to Gail Collin's position, it is not "crazy" to be opposed to LOST, instead, from an American perspective, it is crazy to support LOST! Signing onto LOST is an act of national suicide. Therefore, it is not just crazy, but pure moral insanity!

Believe it or not, it gets even worse!

As noted by Admiral James Lyons,[14] in 1962 Communist dictator Nikita Khrushchev sent Soviet vessels carrying nuclear-tipped missiles to Cuba - just 90 miles from Florida. In response to this threat to our national security President Kennedy ordered the U.S. Navy to set up a blockade around Cuba. When gathering intelligence during the Cold War, U.S. Navy submarines tapped into communications cables lying on the seabed. Moreover, when vessels are suspected of carrying biological, chemical, or nuclear weapons, they are stopped by U.S. Navy warships, boarded, and inspected.

But if America signs onto LOST, we will need to obtain what Oliver North[15] calls "permission slips" from the UN in order to engage in similar national security measures in the future. Asking hostile foreign dictators for permission to protect America from hostile foreign dictators is insane and clearly suicidal. Although signing onto the UN Law of the Sea Treaty would pose a serious threat to U.S. national security and sovereignty - it has been endorsed by the U.S. Navy! Why? Because the U.S. Navy lawyers who make recommendations regarding LOST are all liberal (Soviet American) lawyers. They are what Michael Savage would call "The enemy within."

Moreover, while the U.S. Navy has been downsized from 1,000 ships during the Vietnam War to less than 300 ships today, plans are being made to incorporate what is left of the U.S. Navy into a 1,000 ship global UN Navy.[16, 17, 18] If the new USSR is not evolving into a global government, why does it need a global navy and a global army? Currently, the U.S. Navy protects America from the fascist Russian and the Communist Chinese navies. However, with the U.S. Navy submerged into a UN Navy, the fascist Russian and Communist Chinese navies would share in the responsibility of protecting America from the fascist Russian and Communist Chinese navies. That kind of logic could only make sense to a Soviet American!

Cliff Kincaid of Aim.org has investigated the roots of the UN Law of the Sea Treaty and found it was the brainchild of World Federalists devoted to world government. Some members of the World Federalist Society founded other organizations with patriotic sounding names such as the "American Freedom Association." But why did world federalists feel the need to push the UN Law of the Sea Treaty through newly created organizations with patriotic sounding names? Cliff Kincaid answered this question when he stated that, "...some of the world federalists groups were accused of being infiltrated and manipulated by Communists sympathetic to the Soviet Union."[19]

Another Socialist Wealth Transferring Scheme

"A thief takes property by stealth; a robber uses force or the threat of force." However, "Fraud, in law," is defined as "intentional deception to cause a person to give up property or some lawful right." - *Webster's New Twentieth Century Dictionary*, Unabridged, Second Edition, 1971

The planned transfer of wealth from productive, carbon producing nations such as the USA to backward, unproductive, socialist nations via global warming carbon credits and LOST fees and fines, represent just two schemes in an endless parade of schemes generated behind closed doors at the United Nations. For example, for several decades another fabricated environmental concern has already facilitated a massive, ongoing transfer of wealth from "bourgeoisie" America to foreign "proletariat" nations.

As oil expert T. Boone Pickens[20] has reported, in 1970 the USA imported 24 percent of its oil. By 1990 oil imports rose to 42 percent, and in 2008 it was nearly 70 percent. Our massive increase in dependence on foreign oil is unrelated to the huge increase in demand in China, India, and other developing nations. Our massive increase in dependence on imported oil is a direct result of 30 plus years of sabotage by Bolshevik Democrats who have made it illegal for Americans to drill for oil on American soil or even near American soil. And what is their cover story? Environmentalism! They claim they must protect tiny segments of the environment from unsightly oil rigs that may disturb nearby animals or plants.

Keep in mind that, at the heart of nearly all criminal master plans - including the one laid out by Karl Marx in *The Communist Manifesto*, we find the eventual transfer of money and/or property from targeted victims to skillful thieves - and to those who aid and abet those thieves. As a result of Bolshevik Democrats making us more dependent on foreign imports, "over 700 billion dollars are leaving this country to foreign nations every year, and it's killing our economy," according to T. Boone Pickens. Most shockingly he concludes that, "It will be the largest transfer of wealth in the history of mankind." Consequently, by making it illegal for Americans to drill on American soil or even near American soil, Bolshevik Democrats are forcing Americans to purchase oil from foreigners - resulting is a massive transfer of wealth from "bourgeoisie" America to foreign "proletariat" nations.

To whom do we Americans give our 700 billion dollars to each year? The top ten nations that receive most of that money are, firstly, Canada, our socialist neighbor to the North; secondly, Saudi Arabia, the nation that supplied most of the 9/11 hijackers; followed by Mexico, the nation that is bankrupting our hospitals, schools, and social welfare agencies by flooding us with illegal aliens; Nigeria, a nation with an extensive history of military dictatorships; Venezuela, currently run by Communist dictator Hugo Chavez; Iraq, Saddam Hussein's former piggy bank; Angola, a nation run primarily by Marxists since 1975; Algeria, a military dictatorship impersonating a democracy; Brazil, our largest socialist-led neighbor to the South; and lastly Kuwait, a constitutional monarchy.

In addition to the massive, chronic transfer of wealth out of our economy, we the people must also be subjected to federal micro-mismanagement of our daily lives. As each year passes life in Soviet America is beginning to eerily resemble life in the Soviet Union. A centralized authority tells us how much water we must have in our toilets; what kind of lights bulbs we must have in our homes; how much mileage our vehicles must achieve; what kinds of vehicles we must drive; what we can and cannot do with our own private property so we do not disturb various rats, snakes, and bugs placed on the endangered and threatened species lists; and we are told how much of a fine we must pay, or how much prison time we must serve, if we fail to comply with environmental regulations. This is change only Soviet Americans can believe in.

Throughout human history people with criminal minds have been plotting and scheming with one main goal in mind: to transfer money and property from intended victims to criminals through the use of deceit and/or force. While street-level criminals create plans to rob liquor stores, car-jack motorists, or burglarize houses, international corporate and governmental criminals fabricate plans to rip off cities, states, and even entire nations. International criminals who operate through corporations and governments tend to do a lot of scheming, which they back with varying degrees of threat, as well as the actual use of force - especially the force of law.

The genius of Marx's master plan is that it allows international corporate and government criminals (Bolsheviks and Mensheviks) to confiscate the money and property of their middle class victims (bourgeoisie) with the enthusiastic help of street-level criminals (proletarians). Moreover, the proletarians are not called criminals, but are given the euphemism of "revolutionaries" who are not stealing from victims, but are overthrowing the bourgeoisie which Marxist dialecticians have relentlessly portrayed as selfish and greedy, and thus worthy of being deceived, robbed, or even killed. Corporate and government criminals can confiscate the money and property of their intended victims not with guilt but with false pride, given that they convince others that they are not stealing for themselves, but on behalf of the lowly, exploited "toiler" proletariat, or for the benefit of planet Earth - the new USSR's largest proletariat!

The UN: A Dr. Jekyll Persona For Vladimir Hyde!

"Socialists have always spent much of their time seeking new titles for their beliefs, because the old versions so quickly become outdated and discredited." - Margaret Thatcher, Prime Minister of the United Kingdom, 1979 - 1990[21]

"The dictatorship of the proletariat which has risen to power as the leader of the democratic revolution is inevitably and, very quickly confronted with tasks, the fulfillment of which is bound up with deep inroads into the rights of bourgeoisie property." - Leon Trotsky, Commissar of War for the Soviet Union[22]

Environmentalism, global warming, climate change, and cap and trade, are simply newfangled Cold War stratagems reminiscent of old-fashioned, Soviet-style Communism.

Vaclav Klaus,[23] the President of the Czech Republic, has authored a book titled, *Blue Planet in Green Shackles: What is Endangered: Climate or Freedom.* In this eye-opening book President Klaus describes how contemporary environmentalism is strangling freedom in a manner reminiscent of Soviet-style Communism. President Klaus is in a unique position to draw such a comparison given that he lived much of his life under the repressive hand of Soviet Communism. During his visit to the United States in the spring of 2008 he made several prominent appearances.

When speaking at the National Press Club he stated that, like Communists, contemporary environmentalists "will be certain that they have the right to sacrifice man and his freedom to make their idea reality." President Klaus added that, "In the past, it was in the name of the masses or of the proletariat; this time in the name of the planet. Structurally, it is very similar." When appearing at the Competitive Enterprise Institute he spoke of "The ambitious politicians who try to mastermind the world and their fellow citizens..." President Klaus noted that they "have been dreaming for decades" to find a doctrine like environmentalism because environmental issues, such as climate change, are difficult to prove or disprove, and thus they can be immunized from reality.[24]

Cliff Kincaid of Aim.org quotes from President Klaus' book as follows: "In the past 150 years (at least since Marx), the socialists have been very effectively destroying human freedom under humane and compassionate slogans, such as caring for man, ensuring social equality, and fostering social welfare. The environmentalists are doing the same under equally noble-minded slogans, expressing concern about nature more than about people (recall their radical motto 'Earth first'). In both cases, the slogans have been (and still are) just a smokescreen. In both cases, the movements were (and are) completely about power, about the hegemony of the 'chosen ones' (as they see themselves) over the rest of us, about the imposition of the only correct worldview (their own), about the remodeling of the world."[25]

The human-caused global warming hoax may be used as a good example of why Karl Marx called for Communist control of media and education along with control of government. Only by controlling news, information, and education can they ensure that generation after generation will fall for the same Marxist-style scams over and over again. Nowhere in the Soviet American media or the Soviet American education establishment will you find honest professionals alerting the citizenry to the repeated use of Soviet-style psychological manipulation to achieve Marxist-style goals. As noted by Bethany Stotts, "Major news coverage of Klaus' two speeches was limited to CSPAN and FOX News, given that the *Washington Post, Los Angeles Times,* and *New York Times* virtually ignored his visit."[26]

Perhaps it would be appropriate to provide a quote from an article posted on the web site of the Communist Party, USA. The reader will note that, like the Communist-sanctioned Obama Administration, the CPUSA fully endorses the position of the UN-IPCC that human-generated carbon dioxide, and not natural processes, is a root cause of global warming. A review of the entire article (available at CPUSA.org) reveals that, like the UN-IPCC, the CPUSA calls for immediate action to curb human-generated CO2 to prevent catastrophic climate change:

"Industrial, agricultural, and transportation systems created and used by humans are pushing nature's systems out of their normal ranges. This is not some unstoppable natural process beyond human control - it has been caused by human activity, can be slowed by changes in human activity, or can be made worse if we continue to accelerate the rate at which carbon dioxide is spewed into the atmosphere." - Marc Brodine, Communist Party, USA[27]

The UN, which is a prime mover behind environmentalism, global warming, and climate change hysteria, has morphed into an avant-garde version of the USSR, pursuing the power to confiscate money, confiscate and control property, and manipulate, control, and exploit people on a global scale. Clearly, the masterminds behind the UN have the same "lust for power over others" as the masterminds behind the USSR.

As noted in the previous chapter, there are financial and political reasons some militant environmentalists at the highest levels oppose efforts to clean the air of what they claim is excessive carbon dioxide. For these environmentalists the deployment of technology to reduce the concentration of atmospheric carbon dioxide would destroy the very opportunity they have worked so hard to manufacture. A global problem demands a global solution. And everyone knows a global solution requires a global mechanism to administer that solution. On that basis global government can be rationalized, and when there is global government there will be global taxation, global regulation, global manipulation, and other forms of global exploitation.

For those who study the criminal mind it becomes clear that UN environmental policies that encompass the global warming "crisis," UN World Heritage Sites, Biosphere Reserves, and the UN Law of the Sea Treaty, provide the near perfect opportunity for political predators to achieve what Lenin, Stalin, and Khrushchev aspired to achieve, but failed to achieve - a Soviet-style global government that has the "moral authority" to micromanage the internal affairs of every nation on Earth!

Placed in historical perspective, the position of secretary general of the United Nations is being molded into a position that is akin to, but far more powerful than, the position of general secretary of the Communist Party's Central Committee within the old USSR. Joseph Stalin held that position from 1922 until his death in 1953. Mikhail Gorbachev was general secretary from 1985 until 1991 when the USSR collapsed under the weight of its failed socialist policies. Viewed from an historical perspective, perhaps we could mark 1991 as the year the torch was officially passed from the USSR's general secretary to the UN's secretary general. The restructuring of the UN into a 21st century version of the USSR tells us that Mikhail Gorbachev's efforts to achieve perestroika were not limited to the internal affairs of the Soviet Union.

However, unlike the Bolsheviks of the USSR, the UN Bolsheviks plan to succeed in their efforts to operate on a truly global scale. They intend to succeed where the Soviet Union failed. Consequently, in this plan America, or more correctly, Soviet America, will finally fulfill its proper role as a subservient, Soviet-bloc, donor nation in the "global community" that comprises the constantly evolving New World Order. As stated in 2000 by Jacques Chirac, the President of France at that time, the United Nation's Kyoto Protocol represents "the first component of an authentic global governance."[28]

Just as the leaders of the Soviet Union looted the nations that it conquered and submerged into the USSR, environmentalism will be employed to accelerate the current looting of America and the West. Global warming will have global consequences, but they will be more political and economic than climatic. In summary, global warming will usher in something closely akin to global Communism - and you will not only be forced to live in it, you will be forced to finance it as well! Just as American taxpayers are being forced to finance the construction of Soviet America, through "Operation Global Warming" and other UN schemes, American taxpayers will be forced to finance the construction and maintenance of an ever-expanding, global, Soviet-style evil empire called the United Nations!

Given all that has been written about the United Nations, we should not be surprised to learn that a side by side comparison of the USSR emblem and the UN emblem shows they possess striking similarities. (Check it out for yourself online.) But such similarities should be expected given that G. Edward Griffin has reported that, "The man in charge of the U.S. Government department which designed the UN emblem was a secret member of the Communist Party."[29] It should also come as no surprise that, after investigating the UN, Pierre J. Huss and George Carpozi, Jr. uncovered a nest of Soviet agents operating within the United Nations. They documented the results of their investigation in their 1965 book, *Red Spies in the UN*.[30] And of course, with the help of our deaf, dumb, and blind "watchdogs" in the leftist media, Soviet agents and their fellow travelers have enjoyed free reign within the UN - and everywhere else - for many generations.

In his 1981 book titled *The United Nations Conspiracy*, author Robert W. Lee[31] provided abundant evidence to show that, while the Soviet Union publicly feigned opposition to the UN, the Soviets were truly staunch supporters. For example, when the establishment of the UN was under consideration an editorial in *The New York Times* noted that "Soviet Russia" was willing to compromise "on at least ten important issues in order to assure the prompt and successful establishment of the U.N."[32] In *Pravda* - the official newspaper of the Communist Party of the Soviet Union - the homicidal Soviet dictator Joseph Stalin was quoted saying, "I attribute great importance to the U.N.O. since it is a serious instrument for preservation of peace and international security."[33] Andrei Vishinsky, the Soviet Deputy Foreign Minister stated that, "The policy of the USSR with regard to the United Nations calls for strengthening that body..."[34]

Furthermore, in the *Daily Worker* - a now defunct daily newspaper of the Communist Party, USA - it was written that "...it's not the UN that merits your scorn and active opposition, but the policies that have undermined the UN."[35] Moreover, the Preamble to the Constitution adopted by the Communist Party, USA, in 1957 stated that, "the true national interest of our country and the cause of peace and progress require...the strengthening of the United Nations as a universal instrument of peace."[36] When Soviet dictator Nikita Khrushchev visited the United Nations and addressed the General Assembly in 1960 he stated that, "Experience of the work of the United Nations has shown that this body is useful and necessary..."[37]

Recall in Chapter Two, Understanding the Psychology of Soviets, Socialists & Other Sociopaths, it was noted that sociopaths wear social masks to hide their moral insanity, and sometimes they wear group masks. Those who have studied Communism know that they are notorious for constructing fronts, or front groups, which are in effect group masks worn to deceive the gullible. This was the purpose of the UN. With the USSR totally discredited, the UN was constructed as a new mask designed to mislead the public on the world stage.

Although the "liberal" media (Soviet-bloc media) did everything in their power to hide the thievery, slave labor camps, torture, and genocide conducted by the Soviet government, the truth still leaked out through legitimate sources of news and information. Given the inability of Soviet Communists to hide their crimes against humanity, they saw the establishment of the UN as an opportunity to construct a non-partisan appearing mask. From behind that UN mask they could hide their moral insanity and continue to pursue their goal of a global, Soviet-style government - and do so with impunity.

Operating within the UN they could dupe the nations of the world into financing the very mask they would use to help them conquer and loot those same charitable, gullible, nations. Hence, the need to maintain the dysfunctional, discredited, impoverished USSR became less imperative when the torch could easily be passed to an alter ego with a less threatening public face. After all, why try to subvert the USA from Moscow when it could be done far more conveniently from New York City? Why continue to run the USSR which is composed of 15 thoroughly plundered nations when you can run the UN and gain access to the resources of nearly 200 nations - including the wealthiest nations on Earth? Given that the stated goal of the Soviets was world domination, what difference does it make whether that goal is achieved through the USSR or the UN - as long as that goal is eventually achieved?

Ask yourself this question: How would the world have responded if the USSR had fabricated the same discredited global warming hoax and proposed the same "wealth redistribution" scheme as now fabricated and proposed by the UN? Obviously, Communism is not dead, nor is the USSR. Their operatives are simply wearing different masks!

The Soviet American media continue to provide cover for their fellow sociopaths operating behind various masks, including the UN mask. But, unfortunately for the criminal masterminds behind "Operation Global Warming," once again legitimate sources of news and information are leaking the truth to the public. Honest, courageous scientists, researchers, journalists, commentators, writers, and radio talk show hosts are blowing the cover on this latest UN scam. They are exposing global warming as a massive fraud designed to rob the people of the world of their health, wealth, and liberty. Like the proverbial "wolf in sheep's clothing," the creatures running the UN are nothing more than mask-wearing predators - and we are their prey!

No honest, rational person can dismiss the fact that numerous documented Soviet goals are being systematically pursued and achieved by the United Nations. Nor can anyone deny the enthusiastic support Soviet Communists had given to the UN. Therefore, every time George H. W. Bush, William Jefferson Clinton, George W. Bush, Barack Hussein Obama, or any other president endorsed a UN policy or program, they drove another nail into the coffin of the Sovereign America founded by Washington, Adams, Jefferson, and Madison. Every single day *The New York Times*, *Washington Post*, *Los Angeles Times*, ABC, CBS, NBC, CNN, MSNBC, PBS, *Newsweek*, and *Time* magazine choose not to warn us of the transfer of power from elected American political leaders to the unelected hostile foreign leaders running the new USSR, they push us another step closer toward the Soviet America envisioned by Foster, Khrushchev, and other America-hating Communists.

Welcome to Soviet America!

Good-bye Self-Governing America!

------†††------

"The American Soviet government will join with the other Soviet governments in a world Soviet Union." - William Z. Foster, National Chairman of the Communist Party, USA, *Toward Soviet America,* 1932[38]

"The time has come to recognize the United Nations for the anti-American, anti-freedom organization that it has become. The time has come for us to cut off all financial help, withdraw as a member, and ask the United Nations to find headquarters location outside the United States that is more in keeping with the philosophy of the majority of voting members, someplace like Moscow or Peking." - Senator Barry Goldwater, Conservative Republican from Arizona, Congressional Record, 1971

Chapter Sixteen

Barack Obama:
Change Soviet Americans Can Believe In!

"It's The Communism, Stupid!" – Cliff Kincaid

"When a Communist heads a government of the United States, and that day will come just as surely as the sun rises, that government will not be a capitalist government, but a Soviet government, and behind this government will stand the Red Army to enforce the dictatorship of the proletariat." - William Z. Foster, National Chairman of the Communist Party, USA, 1939[1]

"Obama is a radical Communist, and I think it is becoming clear. That is what I told people in Illinois and now everybody realizes it's true. He is going to destroy this country, and we are either going to stop him or the United States of America is going to cease to exist." - Alan Keyes, former U.S. Ambassador, 2009[2]

Barack Obama's 2008 presidential campaign touted several slogans, including, "Change We Can Believe In." Our TV screens were filled with numerous Obama supporters waving professionally crafted signs and posters displaying this message. But, in light of the below endorsements, it is obvious that liberals, progressives, and moderates were not the only people who saw Barack Obama as a man who would bring "Change We Can Believe In."

Change Communist Terrorists Can Believe In

"Obama is not running to change government he's running to overthrow government. Ayers wins." - Zombietime forum page blogger[3]

For more than 20 years Barack Obama has had the enthusiastic support of William Ayers, a former Communist terrorist. Like Timothy McVeigh, William Ayers is an unrepentant domestic terrorist who reportedly bombed buildings on American soil - knowing those buildings housed innocent people. He founded the Weather Underground terrorist organization, and is suspected of personally participating in the bombing of the U.S. Capitol, the Pentagon, and various other targets. William Ayers purportedly trained fellow domestic terrorists in bomb making techniques, instructed them to place metal objects and incendiaries in the bombs to ensure maximum carnage, and allegedly instructed fellow terrorists on strategic bomb placement in order to inflict maximum casualties among the Americans he targeted for destruction.

According to FBI reports, Ayers' wife, Bernardine Dohrn,[4] is also a former Communist terrorist who is suspected of murdering a police officer and critically wounding another. On February 16, 1970, a bomb was planted on a window ledge of a police station. The bomb contained "heavy metal staples and lead bullet projectiles." Clearly, this was an anti-personnel weapon designed to kill and maim. When it exploded, it did what it was designed to do. The bomb killed Sergeant Brian V. McDonnell and wounded and partially blinded Officer Robert Fogarty, both of the San Francisco Police Department.

Larry Grathwohl, an Army veteran and FBI informant who had infiltrated the Weather Underground, had gained the confidence of William Ayers at the time of the California police station bombing. When testifying before a U.S. Senate subcommittee, Grathwohl stated that William Ayers informed him that Bernardine Dohrn had built and planted the bomb that killed Sergeant McDonnell and seriously wounded Officer Fogarty.[5] Armed with this knowledge, William Ayers later married Bernardine Dohrn.

Dohrn is no stranger to jail. She was incarcerated for refusing to testify before a grand jury investigating a 1983 Brinks truck robbery. Who was she protecting? The robbers were fellow Weather Underground terrorists and members of the Black Liberation Army who had shot to death one guard and killed two New York State Troopers. In 1981 Dohrn was fined $1,500 and given three years probation for her participation in the Communist-inspired "Days of Rage" Chicago riots of 1969.[6, 7]

Just prior to the 2008 presidential election, Larry Grathwohl, now retired, was interviewed by investigative journalists who operate outside the Soviet-bloc media. (Predictably, those within the Soviet-bloc media showed no interest in providing American voters with "insider" information obtained by Grathwohl while he had operated deep within a notorious domestic, Communist, terrorist organization.) According to this FBI informant, in February of 1970, William Ayers was planning to explode two bombs containing 44 sticks of dynamite. The targets were the Detroit Police Officers' Association building and the 13th Precinct. According to Grathwohl, Ayers said the bombs must contain fence staples to create shrapnel, and propane bottles to create fire. After learning where the bombs would be planted, Grathwohl warned Ayers that one of the bombs could also damage a nearby Red Barn Restaurant frequented by blacks. Ayers' response: "Innocent people have to die in a revolution."[8] Spoken like a true 19th century nihilistic Russian Narodnik! Fortunately, Grathwohl forewarned law enforcement.

This same William Ayers used his home to launch the political career of Barack Obama; served on several boards with Obama; and is suspected of ghostwriting Obama's book, *Dreams from My Father*. Ayers also received from Obama an endorsement for his book titled, *A Kind and Just Parent: Children of the Juvenile Court*; and an organization run by Ayers received $800,000 from an organization chaired by Obama. Moreover, Michelle Obama worked at the same law firm as Bernardine Dohrn, and both William Ayers and Bernardine Dohrn made financial contributions to Barack Obama's initial political campaign. Lastly, in 1997 Michelle Obama invited both Barack Obama and William Ayers to serve on a panel at a university event she had organized.[9]

In spite of the above, Obama described Ayers as a guy who lives in his neighborhood; a guy he did not exchange ideas with "on a regular basis;" and a guy who engaged in some "detestable acts" when Obama was just 8 years old. But as investigator Bob Owens has noted, when the Weathermen participated in the 1983 Brinks truck robbery and murders, Barack Obama was not 8 years old; he was in his early 20s. Given the long history of numerous past entanglements, few people outside the Soviet American community are willing to pretend that Barack Obama's description of his relationship to William Ayers is credible.

In his article titled "It's The Communism, Stupid," Cliff Kincaid[10] wrote the following: "For his part, Ayers wasn't just a terrorist; he was a Communist terrorist aligned with and manipulated by Moscow's Communist apparatus, operating through Cuba, against the United States." According to Conserva-pedia.com,[11] "He [William Ayers] is best known as a founder of the Soviet sponsored Weather Underground (WUO) terrorist organization and friend of U.S. President Barack Obama." In light of all the information presented above, it is clear that Obama supporters William Ayers and Bernardine Dohrn are not your everyday, run-of-the-mill, non-incarcerated, homicidal liberals.

Due to reported FBI mishandling of the case, Ayers, Dohrn, and several other Weathermen were never prosecuted for their terrorist activities. Ayers is on record stating that he is "Guilty as hell," and "Free as a bird." Both William Ayers and Bernardine Dohrn remain unrepentant to this day.

Although the Weathermen may have bombed 25 domestic targets, Ayers recently said, "I don't regret setting bombs. I feel we didn't do enough." Unlike Timothy McVeigh, the domestic terrorist who was executed for his crimes, today William Ayers is a professor in the College of Education at the University of Illinois at Chicago. Bernardine Dohrn, who was once on the FBI's Top 10 Most Wanted List and described by FBI Director J. Edgar Hoover as the "most dangerous woman in America," is now a Clinical Associate Professor of Law and the Director of the Children and Family Justice Center at Northwestern University School of Law in Chicago, Illinois.[12, 13, 14] Yes, Welcome to Barack Obama's America! Welcome to Soviet America!

Change Advocates Of World Communism Can Believe In

Howard Machtinger, Jeff Jones, Steve Tappis, and Mark Rudd endorsed Barack Obama for the presidency of the United States. Like William Ayers, all four are former leaders of the domestic terrorist organization known as the Weather Underground, or Weathermen. While Jeff Jones co-authored a book with William Ayers and Bernardine Dohrn, Howard Machtinger was one of the founders of the Weathermen and co-author of its original mission statement. Consistent with the tenets found in William Z. Foster's book, *Toward Soviet America*, that mission statement called for the destruction of the United States *from within* and the establishment of "World Communism." Perhaps this explains their desire to have Barack Obama operating *from within* the highest office of the United States Government.

These four revolutionaries provided their endorsement of Barack Obama via an online petition created by *Progressives for Obama*, an organization teeming with radicals. Among their members are found radicals who belong to, or have belonged to, the Communist Party, USA, and the Black Radical Congress. We also find former members of Students for a Democratic Society, or SDS, a radical 1960s organization from which the Weathermen splintered. SDS was founded by Tom Hayden, a former California state senator who "traveled many times to North Vietnam, Czechoslovakia and Paris to strategize with Communist North Vietnamese and Viet Cong leaders on how to defeat America's anti-Communist efforts."[15] Hayden is also a former husband of actress Jane Fonda, better known to Vietnam veterans as "Hanoi Jane" as a consequence of her treasonous behavior during the Vietnam War.

Change A Communist-Tinged
Preacher Can Believe In

The Reverend Jeremiah Wright was Barack Obama's pastor for nearly 20 years. He married Barack Obama and his wife Michelle, and baptized their two daughters. He also provided Obama with the title of his book, *The Audacity of Hope*. For decades Barack Obama has had the support of the Reverend Jeremiah Wright, who screams from the pulpit "God damn America," and who preaches black liberation theology - a form of Christianity corrupted by Marxist principles.[16] As discussed in Chapter Six, those who preach liberation theology and social gospel are championing Communist principles and mislabeling them as Christian principles. So, for nearly two decades Barack Obama chose to attend a church where the congregation received a steady diet of Marxism masquerading as Christianity! Why?

Change A Communist-Tainted
Preacher Can Believe In

Barack Obama has the support of the Reverend Jim Wallis, a former Chicago community organizer (proletariat organizer) who is steeped in the social gospel movement and liberation theology in order to pursue Marxist-style "social justice." The Reverend Jim Wallis, along with the Reverend Jeremiah Wright, supported the Communist Sandinistas of Nicaragua in the 1980s. Wallis actually traveled to Nicaragua to support the Communist regime. In 1979 the Reverend Jim Wallis was quoted expressing his desire that someday "more Christians will come to view the world through Marxist eyes." (Keep in mind Karl Marx was an anti-religion atheist.) Barack Obama has referred to the Reverend Jim Wallis as a "good friend."[17]

Change A Connecticut Communist Can Believe In

Joelle Fishman, the chair of the Connecticut Communist Party and the chair of the Communist Party, USA, Political Action Commission, was excited about the prospects of an Obama presidency.[18] This Obama supporter was asking her readers to go to the Communist Party, USA, web site (www.-cpusa.org) to learn about the Party's "emergency program to repair, renew and rebuild America." After defeating Hillary Clinton in the Democrat primary, Fishman wrote that Obama's "unity appeal and outreach to Clinton supporters deeply touched the country and was greeted around the world."

Fishman wrote that Obama could bring the "unity" needed to defeat "Bush-McCain" and the "Republican ultra-right."

According to Fishman,[19] John McCain "speaks of never-ending war and shrinking government, privatizing services and cutting funds for human needs." However, Barack Obama "speaks of strengthening government to provide health care and jobs, address global warming and end the war in Iraq." Note that she rejects the Sovereign American notion of limited government, and advocates the Soviet American notion of massive, expansive government. This Obama supporter calls for "strengthening government" to provide services such as health care and jobs, neither of which are authorized by the U.S. Constitution - but are clearly enumerated in the Soviet Constitution!

Change An Hawaiian Communist Can Believe In

In his 1995 book, *Dreams from My Father*, Obama (or ghostwriter William Ayers) refers to a man named Frank who served as a mentor during Obama's youth. Strangely, Obama never provides Frank's last name. But this omission is understandable given that Frank has been identified as Frank Marshall Davis, a man who was investigated by the FBI and Congress and determined to be a member of the Communist Party, USA. In his book Obama acknowledges that Frank advised him on issues of race, values, and higher education. When Obama attended high school in Hawaii, Frank entertained Obama with some poems he had written.[20]

One of Frank's poems "was a tribute to the Soviet Red Army." Keep in mind that soldiers in the Soviet Red Army behaved as one would expect from soldiers in a Communist-controlled military. For example, after the Soviets invaded Afghanistan in 1980, soldiers of the Soviet Red Army bayoneted pregnant women; they slit the throats of children in the presence of their parents; and they stacked men like firewood, poured gasoline on them and lit them on fire.[21] A poem written as a tribute to such an army[22] provides significant insight into the moral IQ of the author - as well as the moral IQ of his protégé.

Change A Communist Newspaper Can Believe In

When it was founded in 1924, the official newspaper of the Communist Party, USA, was called the *Daily Worker*. Today it is called the *People's Weekly World*. On their official web site the CPUSA states that their Party does not endorse political candidates. However, the July 2008 editorial of the *People's Weekly World* was quite critical of McCain but unabashedly complimentary of Obama. For example, in the editorial the reader found the following: "One thing is clear. None of the people's struggles - from peace to universal health care to an economy that puts Main Street before Wall Street - will advance if McCain wins in November."

When writing of Obama, however, the reader found the following: "A broad multiclass, multiracial movement is converging around Obama's 'Hope, change and unity' campaign because they see in it the thrilling opportunity to end 30 years of ultra-right rule and move our nation forward with a broadly progressive agenda."[23] There's that word "progressive" again. It may be the most popular euphemism employed by the Communist Party and the Democrat Party. It is their favorite substitute for the word they are still strategically avoiding - Marxism!

Recall that during the 2008 Democrat presidential primary, Hillary Clinton referred to herself as a "progressive." Dick Morris, a former adviser to President Bill Clinton, stated that "Hillary is not a Communist by any stretch, but she thinks like one." Given that Barack Obama's Senate voting record is to the left of Hillary Clinton's Senate voting record, we may conclude that Barack Obama thinks more like a Communist than does Hillary Clinton!

Change A Communist Web Site Can Believe In

Of course, inanimate objects such as Communist newspapers and Communist web sites cannot "believe in change," but their writers and editors surely can - and do! As stated in a previous paragraph, at the CPUSA web site it is stated that the Party does not endorse political candidates. However, like their official newspaper, their web site contained glowing reports regarding Barack Obama, such as "Barack Obama's campaign has so far generated the most excitement, attracted the most votes, most volunteers and the most money. We think the basic reason for this is that his campaign has the clearest message of unity and progressive change..."

In addition to offering praise for the Obama campaign we find the CPUSA "views the 2008 elections as a tremendous opportunity to defeat the policies of the right-wing Republicans and to move our country in a new progressive direction." And, "We will work with others to defeat the Republican nominee and to end right-wing control of the new Congress."[24]

So, CPUSA web site readers may not find an official endorsement of Barack Obama by the Communist Party, USA, but they will find the CPUSA in favor of the Democrat presidential candidate and in strong opposition to the Republican presidential candidate. Given their deep dissatisfaction with a Republican Party that has not just drifted, but has actually leaped to the left during George W. Bush's second term as president, one can only imagine their dissatisfaction with members of the Constitution Party, the Libertarian Party, and others who manifest a burning desire to re-institute constitutional government at the federal level.

Change Sovereign Americans Cannot Believe In

"Writing in the *Dallas Morning News* (reprinted in *Human Events*, November 8, 1969) veteran correspondent Dick West relates an incident that happened two years after the close of World War II. Andrei Gromyko, at that time the head of the Russian delegation to the United Nations, was attending a party on top of the Waldorf in New York. From a corner of the ballroom he looked out over the imposing scene, the symbol of business, finance, industry, the arts, education and religion. Millions of lights twinkling before him. [Unlike the ubiquitous darkness and poverty of Soviet Russia] Turning, perhaps in an unguarded moment, he remarked to West: 'You over here would be fools ever to change.'" - Howard E. Kershner, *Dividing The Wealth*, 1971[2]

Keep in mind that the deadliest psychopaths of the 20th century were Communists. As stated elsewhere in this book, the list includes Vladimir Lenin, Joseph Stalin, Nikita Khrushchev, Mao Zedong, Pol Pot, and Fidel Castro, all of who committed mass murder. While Nazis disarmed and exterminated about 21 million people during the 20th century, Soviet Communists disarmed and liquidated 61,911,000 men, women, and children, and the Maoist Chinese Communists disarmed and murdered about 76,702,000 men, women, and children.[26] Again, these figures do not include battlefield casualties or victims of the abortion holocaust.

Like Nazis, all Communist mass murderers were gun control fanatics. All disarmed the populations under their control to pave the way for government confiscation of money, property, businesses, banks, homes, schools, churches, hospitals, and the establishment of slave labor camps and mass graves. And yes, Barack Obama is a gun control fanatic.

Obama voted to prosecute American citizens who use firearms to defend themselves and their families against criminal attack in their own homes.[27]

Obama has supported a ban on all handguns; a ban on the sale or transfer of all semi-automatic handguns, rifles, and shotguns; a ban on concealed carry permits; and a ban on private firearms kept in the home for personal and familial defense.[28] Obama has supported banning hundreds of rifles and shotguns and nearly all rifle ammunition frequently used by hunters and sport shooters; voted to permit lawsuits against the firearms industry; supported a 500 percent increase on firearms and ammunition taxes; and he supports a mandated national registry of all firearms owners.[29]

As discussed earlier in this book, in 1920, shortly after the Communist takeover, Russia became the first nation to legalize abortion in the modern era. In 1973 the practice of abortion was decriminalized across the USA. Like his Soviet brethren, Barack Obama supports all forms of abortion, including surgical abortion, saline solution abortion, and partial birth abortion. He also supports infanticide. Obama voted several times to deny life-saving medical treatment to babies born alive after botched abortions.[30] He is also committed to the so-called Freedom of Choice Act. This Act would eliminate state laws, such as those requiring parental involvement in abortion decision-making for under-aged girls; it would compel taxpayer funding of abortions, and it would force faith-based health care facilities to perform abortions.[31]

About a week or so before the 2008 presidential election Rush Limbaugh spoke extensively on his radio talk show about Barack Obama. Most strikingly he said that Obama is not "cool" as many perceive him to be, but instead he is "cold." Given his views on abortion, infanticide, and his desire to disarm law-abiding, crime-fighting Americans and render them defense-less against violent criminal attack by predators in both the public and private sectors, it appears Rush is right! Like all cold-blooded predators, Obama seeks to disarm his prey - under the guise of "protecting them against gun violence," of course!

Instead of choosing to protect the lives of the most innocent and defense-less among us, he supports their extermination. Like nearly everyone in a leadership position within the Democrat Party, Obama is as cold as Vladimir Lenin, Nikita Khrushchev, Fidel Castro, Adolf Hitler, and every other abortion holocaust perpetrator! (May God have mercy on Barack Obama's soul! If you voted for him, may God have mercy on your soul!)

Change Genocidal Communists Can Believe In

"...the cleverly tricky Communists, whose method of procedure is to advance any kind of theory to effect change, in the belief that the more changes made, the easier it will be to bring about the great change, the establishment of the Dictatorship of the Proletariat." - R. M. Whitney, *Reds in America*, 1924[32]

Returning to FBI informant Larry Grathwohl and the Weather Underground, we find that the leaders of the Communist terrorist organization founded by Barack Obama's friend, William Ayers, were not satisfied with attempting to kill innocent Americans by the dozens or by the hundreds. Instead, they were preparing their own Nazi-style "final solution" to the problem of counter-revolutionaries in Soviet America. They were actually discussing contingency plans to kill Sovereign Americans on a scale that exceeded Hitler's genocidal rampage and rivaled that of Lenin, Stalin, Khrushchev, and Chairman Mao. According to Grathwohl, the Weathermen estimated that they may need to exterminate 25 million Americans in order to establish their version of a Soviet America. Yes, this is what can happen in this nation when mask-wearing predators with "a lust for power over others" end up in government, instead of prison! Given that they also envisioned a USSA occupied by Communist North Koreans, Cubans, Chinese, and Russians, perhaps they believed they could delegate that detail to fellow "progressives" who were experienced in the art of genocide.[33, 34]

Barack Obama is on record stating that, "We cannot continue to rely on our military in order to achieve the national security objectives that we've set. We've got to have a civilian national security force that's just as powerful, just as strong, just as well-funded." Keep in mind that the U.S. military receives about half a trillion dollars each year in federal funding. What would Obama do with a "civilian national security force" of that magnitude? What have Marxists in the USSR and other Communist nations done with similar internal national security forces?

According to Lee Cary[35] of the AmericanThinker.com, Obama plans to increase the Peace Corps, Americorps, USA Freedom Corps, Senior Corps, as well as VISTA and the Youthbuild Program. Obama also plans to "form a Classroom Corps, Health Corps, Clean Energy Corps, Veterans Corps, Homeland Security Corps, Global Energy Corps, and a Green Jobs Corps."

But none of these unconstitutional federal programs could fall under the heading of a "civilian national security force" comparable to the U.S. military. And if such a force is created, who would be in charge? We know that Obama had given Van Jones, an avowed Communist, the position of Special Adviser for Green Jobs, Enterprise and Innovation at the White House Council on Environmental Quality. Therefore, we can be sure it would be someone of his moral stature. And of course, the Commissar in charge of the "civilian national security force" would certainly share Obama's affinity for partial birth abortion, infanticide, euthanasia, wealth confiscation and redistribution, and the pre-totalitarian, pre-genocidal act of civilian disarmament through gun control. Given that William Ayers did not get the job of Secretary of Homeland Security, perhaps he, or one of his fellow domestic Communist terrorists who planned to exterminate 25 million Americans, will become "Secretary of Civilian National Security Enforcement!"

We must ask the following questions: Why would Barack Obama be friends with someone like William Ayers who created a Communist terrorist organization that planned to exterminate 25 million Americans? Why would President Obama appoint Anita Dunn to the position of White House Communications Director, given that she has praised Mao Zedong - who may be the deadliest genocidal maniac in human history with a body count exceeding 76 disarmed million men, women, and children - not including government-forced abortions? Why would Barack Obama support the killing of babies who survive botched abortions?

Why would Barack Obama have an ornament hanging on the White House Christmas tree that contained an image of Mao Zedong? Why would Obama appoint Ron Bloom as "Car Czar," given that Ron Bloom said, "We know this is largely about power, that it's an adults-only, no-limit game. We kind of agree with Mao that political power comes largely from the barrel of a gun?" Why would Barack Obama want to ban firearms and ammunition, and seek to prosecute law-abiding citizens who use a firearm to defend themselves and their families against violent criminal attack in their own homes?

Why would Barack Obama say we need "a civilian national security force that's just as powerful, just as strong, just as well-funded" as the U.S. military? What happened in the Soviet Union, Communist China, Communist Cuba, Communist Cambodia, and Nazi Germany when these pro-abortion governments developed and maintained similarly powerful internal national security forces and enacted similarly restrictive gun laws?

Why would Barack Obama make Van Jones a "Green Jobs Czar" in the White House Council on Environmental Quality, given that Van Jones is a self-proclaimed Communist? Why would Barack Obama appoint Mark Lloyd "Chief Diversity Officer" at the Federal Communications Commission, given that Mark Lloyd has praised Communist dictator Hugo Chavez?

What does all this say about the moral IQ of Barack Obama? Furthermore, what is the moral IQ of so-called journalists, reporters, and other self-proclaimed "watchdogs" in the media who refuse to report the above ominous signs to the American people, and viciously attack patriots like Glenn Beck who strive to keep the American people fully informed?

When Democrats Win, Communists Win!

Voters of my generation can remember a time when the electorate could choose from among presidential candidates from the Democrat Party, the Republican Party, and the Communist Party. But the Democrat Party leaped so far to the left that Communists stopped fielding their own candidates and began to support Democrat presidential candidates instead. Of course, as shrewd psychological warriors, they are careful to not provide the American electorate with clues that could hurt their Democrat comrades. Consequently, Communist leaders declare Communist Party neutrality in presidential elections - while cheering for the Democrat presidential candidate and degrading the Republican presidential candidate. The election of Democrat Barack Obama, a true Marxist who enjoys widespread support among members of the Communist Party, USA, serves to demonstrate that the two parties truly share the same goal - the construction of William Z. Foster's Soviet America!

Liberal Democrats Help
Nikita Khrushchev Become A Prophet!

Having been elected president, Barack Obama serves as living proof that the Cold War is not over on the American front - and Sovereign America is losing. The American electorate chose Barack Obama, a candidate who has widespread support among Communists, and they rejected John McCain, a man who fought against Communism in the Vietnam War. This is just one more bit of datum to support the conclusion that Soviet dictator Nikita Khrushchev (a Marxist) was correct when he told President Kennedy (who was assassinated by a Marxist) in the early 1960s that his grandchildren would live in a Socialist America.

However, JFK could never have imagined that his only daughter, Caroline, would someday campaign for Barack Obama (a Marxist) and help make Khrushchev's prediction unfold in a timely manner. JFK could never have imagined that one day his daughter would endorse a politician who would befriend a man like William Ayers (a Marxist) - who dedicated a book to the man who murdered JFK's brother and Caroline's uncle. Yes, William Ayers, along with Bernardine Dohrn, Jeff Jones, and Celia Sojourn (all of whom are Marxists) co-authored the book, *Prairie Fire: The Politics of Revolutionary Anti-Imperialism.* Described as "William Ayers' forgotten Communist Manifesto," the book was dedicated to a list of radicals, including Sirhan Sirhan.[36] As Caroline Kennedy most certainly knows, Sirhan Sirhan is the man convicted of assassinating Robert F. Kennedy, JFK's younger brother and Caroline's own uncle. Clearly, truth is sometimes stranger than fiction! (Yes, Michael Savage, "Liberalism is a mental disorder." It is a mental disorder rooted in a moral disorder!)

In this book William Ayers and his co-authors stated that "We are Communist women and men..." and "We need a revolutionary Communist Party in order to lead the struggle, give coherence and direction to the fight, seize power and build the new society." The "new society" of William Ayers is, of course, the same new society envisioned by William Z. Foster. Both of these Communists worked diligently to build a Soviet America!

Given what we know about race, politics, and economics, clear-thinking Americans would rather have a black capitalist president than a white socialist president - or a Communist president of any color or sex. Cliff Kincaid is correct. It's not Obama's skin color that fills town hall meetings and inspires 21st century Tea Parties. But rather, "It's the Communism, Stupid!"

Welcome to Barack Obama's America!

Welcome to Soviet America!

Good-bye government of the people, by the people, and for the people!

------†††------

"The trained member is one on whom the [Communist] Party depends to commit espionage, derail a speeding train, and organize riots. If asked, gun in hand, to assault the <u>Capitol</u> of the United States, he will be expected to obey. These members are today working to promote a Soviet America." - J. Edgar Hoover, Director of the FBI, 1958[37] (Underline added.)

"TV ad asks: Why would Barack Obama be friends with someone [like former Communist terrorist William Ayers] who bombed the <u>Capitol</u>?" - Jim Kouri[38] (Underline added.)

"Actually, the Communists are desperately seeking to change their public image - to be accepted as legitimate elements of our society. Let's be careful. Remember that Communists are not loyal to our democratic traditions. They come as wolves garbed in sheep's clothing. Despite what they say, in beguiling language, they hate and detest the United States. Their chief interest is not to build, but to wreck and destroy." - J. Edgar Hoover, Director of the FBI, 1967[39]

"Another champion of socialism [Communist dictator Fidel Castro] endorsed Barack Obama... People will endorse those that they admire for their stand. This shows these people agree with Barack Obama's political stand. That means that Barack Obama's political goals parallel the views of such as Castro, Ahmadinejad, Chavez, Bin Laden, and other totalitarian monsters. This gives us all an idea of what Barack Obama has in mind for the United States. Scary, isn't it?" - Vladimir Val Cymbal[40]

"Quick question: how many Marxists, Communists, Domestic Terrorists and raving racialists does the President [Obama] get to associate with before reasonable people can assume that the President on some level shares their particular vision of America?" - Joseph C. Phillips[41]

"Through the Communist Party, the mentality of the Russian Bolsheviks is being transmitted to America, together with the belief that man can be completely redesigned from a child of God into a soulless social cog...This is the 'man' the Kremlin hopes will place the hammer and sickle above the White House and establish a Soviet America as part of a world empire, with Soviet Russia as the master of all." - J. Edgar Hoover, Director of the FBI, 1958[42]

Chapter Seventeen

Socialism: Change
Communists & Nazis Can Believe In!

"...but now we face a new 'Evil Empire.'
It's called Socialism..." - Michael Reagan[1]

"...socialism is evil. It employs evil means."[2] And, "Government income redistribution programs produce the same result as theft. In fact, that's what a thief does; he redistributes income."[3] And, "There is neither moral justification nor constitutional authority for what amounts to legalized theft."[4] - Walter E. Williams, Professor of Economics, George Mason University

Keep in mind that socialism has been embraced by both Communists and Nazis - the two deadliest psychopathic groups of the 20th century. USSR is an abbreviation for the Union of Soviet Socialist Republics. It should also be noted that Nazi stands for National Socialist German Workers' Party. (Underlines added.) The inclusion of the word "Socialist" places Nazis on the same side of the political spectrum as Communists, liberals, progressives, and others who embrace socialism. Yes, socialism has been embraced by evil.

Walter E. Williams has stated unequivocally that socialism is "evil." Socialism is evil because it involves the forced confiscation and redistribution of other people's money and property, which is theft masquerading as fairness and compassion. Williams points out that, of the three trillion dollars confiscated from taxpayers each year by federal agents, more than two trillion dollars are redistributed to others. According to Walter E. Williams this constitutes "legalized theft."

Although slavery was declared legal in the past, it has always been a crime from a moral perspective. Similarly, when people with criminal minds insinuate themselves into the highest levels of government and write laws to make it legal for them to confiscate money and property from some people and redistribute it to others in exchange for votes and political power, such behavior will always be a crime in the moral sense - regardless of what is said or done to justify this behavior. Like slavery, stealing is always evil, even when done under the color of law. Stealing is stealing, even when the thief is a politician and the victim is a taxpayer.

292   Welcome to Soviet America: Special Edition

The Ninth and Tenth Amendments to the U.S. Constitution place severe restrictions on the scope of federal authority. Combined with the fact that only eighteen powers have been delegated to the U.S. Government through the U.S. Constitution, the bulk of the money confiscated and redistributed at the federal level is done in a manner which is clearly unconstitutional - and therefore illegal. Whether in the public sector or the private sector, those who illegally take money or property from others are engaging in theft.

Socialists: Deceitful, Selfish & Hypocritical!

"From capitalism to Communism, through the intermediary stage of Socialism; that is the way American society, like society in general, is headed." - William Z. Foster, National Chairman of the Communist Party, USA, *Toward Soviet America*, 1932[5]

"The American people will never knowingly adopt Socialism. But under the name of 'liberalism' they will adopt every fragment of the Socialist program, until one day America will be a Socialist nation, without knowing how it happened." - Norman Thomas, presidential candidate, Socialist Party of America, 1948

"We Are All Socialists Now." - *Newsweek* magazine, February 16, 2009

While campaigning for the presidency Barack Obama found himself under criticism because he told "Joe the plumber" that he wanted to tax working people in order to spread the wealth - a clear reference to a Marxian principle. To mitigate this justifiable criticism Obama later said that people may call him a Communist because, when he was a child, he shared his toys with other children. But his self-portrayal as a generous child fails to justify his desire to confiscate and redistribute other people's money and property. When a child freely shares his own toys with others - that is charity! But when a child uses force to take toys that do not belong to him, and he gives those toys to his friends in exchange for favors, that is not charity. That is called bullying. That is called stealing. Obama knows this, and every American knows this as well!

Clearly, charity occurs when someone freely redistributes his own money or property. But when politicians use government force to confiscate and redistribute the assets of others against their will - to finance blatantly unconstitutional (unlawful) programs and activities - that's stealing, not charity. That's tyranny, not compassion! That's socialism, not capitalism. And falsely portraying "legalized theft" as charity is nothing short of devious.

Consequently, it should come as no surprise that research by Arthur C. Brooks[6] has shown that, while conservatives tend to be stingy with other people's money, they are quite generous with their own money. Conversely, while liberals are very generous with other people's money, they are stingy with their own money. This liberal behavior is consistent with the observation of Dennis Prager,[7] who wrote that, "Not only does bigger government teach people not to take care of themselves, it teaches them not to take care of others. Smaller government is the primary reason Americans give more charity and volunteer more time per capita than do Europeans living in welfare states. Why take care of your fellow citizen, or even your family, when the government will do it for you?" Stingy liberals, who are notorious for cheating on their taxes (like Democrats Charlie Rangle, Tim Geithner, Tom Daschle, and Nancy Killefer), demand higher taxes on others so they can excuse themselves from taking care of the needy. They want government, via the taxpayer, to do the "charity" work for them.

Sadly, as Walter E. Williams[8] has stated, through taxation and redistribution "...we've become a nation of thieves..." But that's just another way of saying we've become a nation of socialists, or we've become a nation of Marxists. Yes, Walter E. Williams is correct: "Socialism is evil!" As noted in Chapter Four, Michael Reagan[9] stated that, "My father wasn't afraid to call evil what it was - and neither am I. He defeated the 'Evil Empire' called the Soviet Union - but now we face a new 'Evil Empire.' It's called Socialism, and it's taken over our once-free nation through the victories of Obama, Pelosi and Reid." Yes, "our once-free nation" has been taken over by socialism through the victories of Bolshevik Democrats such as Obama, Pelosi, and Reid, but also through the victories of Menshevik Republicans such as Bush, McCain, and Graham.

Toward Socialist America

"Bush in 2008 spent 21 percent of GDP. States, counties and cities spent another 12 percent. Thus, one third of GDP is spent by government at all levels. Obama and Co. propose to raise that by another 10 percent of GDP. We may soon be north of 40 percent of gross domestic product controlled and spent by government. That is Eurosocialism." - Patrick J. Buchanan[10]

As Dick Morris and Eileen McGann[11, 12] have noted, during the 2008 G-20 economic summit, George W. Bush agreed to integrate the United States into the European economy. This sovereignty-diminishing act subjects American businesses to the strangulating, prosperity-stunting regulations of the European Union, or EU - an entity that represents an evolving, European version of the Soviet Union. The characterization of the EU as a European version of the USSR is not an exaggeration; it was provided by Mikhail Gorbachev, the Communist leader who presided over the Soviet Union during its inevitable collapse.

Keep in mind that our Founders fought a long and bloody war to remove America from under the stifling control of Europe. But at the G-20 summit Bush took steps to restore European control over America, thus dishonoring the sacrifices of thousands of American soldiers and militiamen who fought, suffered, and died in the Revolutionary War. During that war Americans were split between "rebels" (conservatives) who wanted a free and inde- pendent America and "loyalists" (liberals) who remained loyal to the British Crown. Clearly, at the G-20 summit George W. Bush followed in the foot- steps of Benedict Arnold, not George Washington.

In addition, tens of thousands of Americans died fighting in Korea, Vietnam, and in other foreign lands to prevent the spread of Soviet-style socialism throughout the so-called "free world." But at the G-20 summit Bush facilitated the spread of European-style socialism across the globe by reinserting America under Europe's administrative thumb. Hence, Morris and McGann have concluded that Bush's legacy will be "European Socialism" - the same conclusion reached by Patrick J. Buchanan! From this perspective we may observe the seamless transition from liberalism to European socialism to Soviet-style Communism. This transition was acknowledged by Soviet Americans as well. For example, eleven days after the election of Barack Obama to the presidency, Sam Webb,[13] the National Chairman of the CPUSA, said in a speech to the National Committee of the Communist Party, USA, that America was now "on the road to socialism." As noted above, his fellow travelers at *Newsweek* magazine agreed, adorning a February 16, 2009 magazine cover with, "We Are All Socialists Now!"

In addition to selling us out to international socialists via the 2008 G-20 economic summit and his sovereignty-blurring North American Union, in his eight years in office George W. Bush increased federal spending by over $1 trillion.[14] This figure does not include massive increases in federal spending to finance his Medicare Prescription Drug Program - which increased centralized, governmental control over health care. Nor does it include the $787 billion taxpayer dollars Bush used to bail out (nationalize/Sovietize) banks and auto manufacturers - a bailout opposed by 75 percent of the American people! Bush also increased spending for the Soviet-inspired U.S. Department of Education through his "No Child Left Behind Act," thereby increasing centralized, governmental control over our children's education. And, as discussed in Chapter Four, Menshevik Republican George W. Bush signed the "Real ID Act" in 2005, thus requiring Americans to possess the equivalent of a nationalized ID card - as carried by Soviet citizens beginning in 1932.

You can be sure that if it were not for extreme pressure from Christian conservatives, we would have Alberto Gonzales and Harriet Miers sitting on the U.S. Supreme Court instead of John Roberts and Samuel Alito. And, while Bush approved the huge, Soviet-style bureaucracy called the U.S. Department of Homeland Security and he nationalized (Sovietized) airport security to more closely monitor U.S. citizens, he failed to monitor foreigners crossing our borders and illegal immigration increased under his watch. He also signed the unconstitutional "Patriot Act." Bush kept us safe from foreign terrorists after 9/11, but he worked cooperatively with the domestic powers that are building a Soviet America and he worked cooperatively with foreign powers that seek to submerge America under a Soviet-style global government. Hence, like his father, George W. Bush is a Menshevik Republican, not a Conservative Republican! Recall in Chapter Three that Pastor Ernie Sanders said "Communism is socialism with a police state." Unfortunately, George W. Bush contributed significantly to both!

Socialism Doesn't Work – And Socialists Know It!

Socialism doesn't work. That's why Lenin adopted the New Economic Policy, or NEP, whereby many confiscated, government-run businesses were trans-formed into privately operated businesses. That's why the Soviet Union collapsed after it abandoned Lenin's NEP. That's why Cuba and North Korea are economic basket cases. That's why the Communist Chinese abandoned socialism in favor of fascist-style capitalism. The builders of Soviet America know socialism doesn't work; that's why they exempt themselves from the government-run systems they force everyone else to endure. That's why they set up two-tiered systems - one for themselves and one for everyone else. The top tier is for them - the predators. The bottom tier is for everyone else - their prey.

That's why there was a two-tiered health care system in the Soviet Union. The Soviets did have well-run, well-financed, well-staffed, well-supplied medical facilities for the elite and nightmarish medical facilities for the lowly proletariat. We find the same two-tiered medical systems in nations such as Communist Cuba, France, Germany, Britain, Canada, and others that have adopted "free" and "universal" Soviet-style health care systems. That's why U.S. Senators, Representatives, and the President exempted themselves and all federal employees from the government-run health care system they have fabricated for the rest of us. That's why we find two-tiered educational systems wherein the elite send their children to private schools while entrapping the children of the proletariat in inferior, government-run schools. This is why most public school teachers send their children to private schools. Money is not the problem. For example, District of Columbia public schools, which are among the worst in the nation, receive around $24,600 per pupil in total funding, according to Andrew J. Coulson[15] of the Cato Institute. That's $10,000 more than elite D.C. private schools receive.

As Jonah Goldberg[16] has noted, the government ran the food services for both the U.S. House of Representatives and the U.S. Senate. However, food services were both inferior and expensive, so they both privatized their food services. The switch was necessary because the federal government micro-mismanaged their food service operations the same way they run our schools, guard our borders, and control federal spending. As Goldberg noted, after eating in the government-run Senate cafeteria he concluded that, "the Senate cafeteria has a decidedly Soviet attitude toward variety." Goldberg further noted that the House restaurant switched to private contractors before the Senate did. While the House restaurant made $1.2 million in commissions since 2003 with private contractors, the government-run Senate food service had lost $18 million from 1993. Yes! Socialism doesn't work - and socialists know it!

Sabotaging The Mortgage & Banking System
So Socialist Saboteurs Can Seize Control!

The establishment of Communism in a nation calls for "Centralization of credit in the hands of the State, by means of a national bank with State capital and exclusive monopoly." - Karl Marx, *The Communist Manifesto,* 1848 (Underline added.)

To build a Soviet America, "In finance it will mean the nationalization of the banking system and its concentration around a central State bank." - William Z. Foster, National Chairman of the Communist Party, USA, *Toward Soviet America,* 1932[17] (Underline added.)

"U.S. Treasury Secretary Henry Paulson Jr., armed with a $700 billion authorization from Congress, <u>ordered</u> the chief executives of the nation's nine largest banks to agree to a government purchase of shares in a <u>nationalization</u> even he opposed just days earlier." - WorldNetDaily.com, 2008[18] (Underlines added.)

The builders of Soviet America want you to believe that the mortgage and banking meltdown of 2008 occurred because federal politicians and their political operatives did not have sufficient regulatory control over the financial systems they were sabotaging and pilfering. Surprisingly, millions have been duped by the Marxist media into giving these saboteurs greater control over the very financial systems they have skillfully impaired. Soviet Americans created a perfect financial storm, then, as always, they blamed it on the "capitalists" who tried to stop them.

At the root of the 2008 financial downturn we find the mortgage and banking fiasco. But at the core of the mortgage and banking fiasco we find federal politicians and their political operatives insinuating themselves into the financial affairs of privately owned businesses - with no constitutional authority to do so! Let's examine in some detail how this slow-motion hostile takeover by federal operatives unfolded.

Laying The Foundation For Nationalized Banks: Who Done It?

It all began in 1938 under Democrat President Franklin D. Roosevelt, who involved the federal government, and thus the taxpayer, into the housing business through the creation of Fannie Mae, the Federal National Mortgage Association. In 1968 Democrat President Lyndon B. Johnson took Fannie Mae off budget, and he restructured it into a federally chartered mortgage company. So, President Johnson converted Fannie Mae from a government organization into a government sponsored enterprise, or GSE, owned by shareholders. Fannie Mae's role was to purchase mortgages from banks, thus freeing up banking capital for additional mortgages.

In 1970 the U.S. Congress, under Republican President Richard M. Nixon, created Freddie Mac, the Federal Home Loan Mortgage Corporation to supposedly compete with Fannie Mae. As private businesses, investors reap the profits from these mortgage companies; however, as federally insured businesses, American taxpayers get stuck with the losses. As noted in a Congressional Report,[19] politicians privatized the profits but socialized the losses. The best of both worlds - for the political elite at the expense of the taxpayer! Together, Fannie Mae and Freddie Mac controlled about $5 trillion in mortgages, which is almost half of a $12 trillion total.

In 1977 the U.S. Congress, under Democrat President Jimmy Carter, enacted the Community Reinvestment Act, or CRA. It was strengthened in 1995 under Democrat President Bill Clinton, and it was amended in 2005 under Republican President George W. Bush. According to the Federal Reserve web site, "The Community Reinvestment Act is intended to encourage depository institutions to help meet the credit needs of the communities in which they operate, including low- and moderate-income neighborhoods, consistent with safe and sound operations."

In practice, however, mortgage companies and banks were compelled to extend mortgages to people who could not afford them. In their September 30, 1999 issue, *The New York Times* wrote that "Fannie Mae, the nation's biggest underwriter of home mortgages, has been under increasing pressure from the Clinton Administration to expand mortgage loans among low and moderate income people and felt pressure from stock holders to maintain its phenomenal growth." During the Clinton Administration Democrat political operatives quietly took managerial control over Fannie Mae.

Enter The Saboteurs

In 1992 the Boston Federal Reserve reported evidence of discrimination against racial minorities in granting home mortgages. However, when all the serious mistakes and typographical errors were removed from their study, no evidence of discrimination was found. However, the Fed used the seriously flawed study to intimidate banks into extending mortgages to minorities who could not afford them. The Fed chastised banks for using "outdated" (bourgeois) criteria for making home mortgages, such as credit history, down payment, closing costs, and sources of income.[20]

In addition, banks that were not willing to commit financial suicide by abandoning sound financial practices faced a terrible dilemma: the Boston Federal Reserve reminded banks that discrimination could result in individual actions of $10,000 and class actions of $500,000 or more.[21] So, banks could either commit financial suicide by extending extremely high risk subprime mortgages or they could be fined and sued to death for not doing so! Faced with a "Chicago-style" offer they couldn't refuse, they choose the former. Keep in mind the Federal Reserve (aka "The Creature from Jekyll Island") also kept interest rates low to entice speculators and unqualified wannabe home owners to seek out subprime mortgages. Therefore, acting in a manner consistent with Karl Marx's "national bank" and Marx's Hegelian-inspired dialectic materialism, the Federal Reserve motivated both ends of the Marxian dialectic - the bourgeoisie bankers and the minority proletariat!

Janet Reno, as Attorney General under President Bill Clinton, threaten legal action against lending institutions that failed to extend a sufficient number of mortgages to black, Hispanic, and other proletarian groups. According to Neal Boortz,[22] "Congress set up processes...whereby community activist groups and organizers could effectively stop a bank's efforts to grow if that bank didn't make loans to unqualified borrowers." These Marxist-inspired activities empowered the proletariat (antithesis) to intimidate banks (thesis) into engaging in unsound business practices - which led to financial instability and Soviet-style nationalization (synthesis)!

Democrat community organizer (proletariat organizer) Barack Obama provided legal advice to ACORN (Association of Community Organizations for Reform Now), one of many leftist organizations that pressured banks to extend mortgages to people who could not afford to make their mortgage payments. So, when President Barack Obama said he "inherited" the mortgage and banking mess, he was actually one of many leftist "organizers" who applied "Chicago-style" pressure to the very financial institutions he would later blame for the mess.

The government-designed mortgage lending strategy was summarized by Franklin D. Raines, a Democrat political operative and CEO of Fannie Mae: "The mortgage finance system needs to bend to consumers' needs, not vice versa."[23] In 2002 Raines reported that he had altered the policies of Fannie Mae to "deal with people who have less than perfect credit."[24] Therefore, in order to achieve "social justice" in the realm of home ownership, Fannie Mae would back large numbers of very risky, subprime mortgages. The mortgages would eventually be bundled and sold as mortgage-backed securities to mutual funds, investment houses, and banks. Predictably, the subprime mortgages would slowly morph into "toxic assets" as millions of income-challenged home owning proletarians failed to pay their adjustable rate mortgages.

In 2002 Congress passed the American Dream Down Payment Assistance Act. Encouraged by Republican President George W. Bush, this federal Act subsidized the down payments of low income proletarians. Bush also encouraged Congress to enact legislation so the FHA, or Federal Housing

Administration, could make "zero-down-payment loans at low-interest rates to low income Americans," according to Walter E. Williams.[25] Bush did make multiple attempts to bring some level of oversight to Fannie and Freddie.[26] However, with the exception of *The Wall Street Journal*, the media ignored or downplayed the risks. After all, this multi-trillion dollar scam was orchestrated primarily by Democrats - who denied Bush's claims of excessive risk.

In response to Bush's 2003 attempt to bring oversight to the management of Fannie and Freddie, Democrat Barney Frank, the chairman of the House Financial Services Committee, said "These two entities - Fannie Mae and Freddie Mac - are not facing any kind of financial crisis." Congressman Frank also stated that, "The more people exaggerate these problems, the more pressure there is on these companies, the less we will see in terms of affordable housing." Greg Mankiw, chairman of the Council of Economic Advisers under President Bush, warned about lax mortgage lending practices. In response Barney Frank stated that, "he is worried about the tiny little matter of safety and soundness rather than 'concern about housing.'"[27]

Sabotaging For Dollars

Under this scam Democrat political operatives such as Franklin D. Raines, as CEO of Fannie Mae, pocketed between $90 million to $100 million. He retired under a cloud when "the Securities & Exchange Commission's top accountant declared that mortgage giant Fannie misstated earnings for 3 ½ years, leading to an estimated $9 billion restatement that will wipe out 40% of profits from 2001 to mid-2004."[28] Democrat Jim Johnson, Barack Obama's campaign manager, preceded Franklin Raines as CEO of Fannie Mae. In just one year Johnson's personal bank account swelled by $21 million. Democrat political operative Jamie Gorelick, who held the position of Vice-Chairman of Fannie Mae, reportedly stuffed her bank account with about $26 million.

(Democrat Jamie Gorelick, as Deputy Attorney General under Janet Reno and Bill Clinton, may have helped pave the way for the second World Trade Center terrorist attack on 9/11 2001. In 1995, two years after the first terrorist attack against the World Trade Center in 1993, Gorelick made it impossible for America's intelligence agencies to exchange intelligence information with law enforcement. As "punishment" for sabotaging our intelligence capabilities in this manner, Gorelick was appointed to the 9/11 Commission. Now she could "investigate" the cause of the 9/11 terrorist attacks - the very attacks she may have facilitated![29, 30]) Welcome to Soviet America!

According to OpenSecrets.org,[31] the top five recipients of campaign contributions from Fannie, Freddie, and their employees are all Democrats. From 1989 to 2008, Democrat Senator Chris Dodd, the chairman of the Senate Banking Committee, received $133,900; Democrat Senator John Kerry received $111,000; Democrat Senator Barack Obama pulled in $105,849; Democrat Senator Hillary Clinton was given $75,550; and Democrat Representative Paul Kanjorshi received $65,500. It appears there was a symbiotic relationship between Fannie, Freddie, and federal politicians - especially the Democrats. Fannie and Freddie provided generous campaign contributions. In return Democrat politicians provided "Chicago-style" political protection by discouraging oversight activities that could expose Fannie and Freddie's creative bookkeeping and personal pocket stuffing! By overstating earnings, the Democrat operatives running Fannie and Freddie could justify, on paper, their multi-million dollar incomes and bonuses.

Sabotaging For Control

So, Democrat political operatives were stuffing their bank accounts with hundreds of millions of dollars while sabotaging the mortgage and banking sectors of the economy, thereby paving the way for taxpayers to get stuck with a $787 billion government bailout, devastating personal investment losses, and a Soviet-style takeover of numerous private enterprises! As government sponsored enterprises, Fannie Mae and Freddie Mac were not required to pay income taxes. Doing so, of course, would ease the financial burden on hard working taxpayers. However, the builders of Soviet America had no problem with Fannie and Freddie receiving billions in taxpayer dollars to pay for the federally-inflicted damage. Again, privatized profits for Democrat political operatives and socialized losses for the beleaguered American taxpayer. What a scam!

The "bourgeois" middle class mortgage criteria are essentially elitist and racist - according to Marxist class warfare rules of engagement. So, instead of raising the ability of the proletarian to secure a home mortgage in a manner consistent with the bourgeois value system, the Marxist dialecticians lowered the bourgeois standard to secure a home mortgage down to the level of the proletarian. And when millions of proletarians were predictably unable to make mortgage payments, the entire home mortgage and banking system was placed in jeopardy.

This, of course, destabilized America's entire capitalist economy. The stock market plummeted, and so did most everyone's retirement account. But with a Rahm Emanuel-style financial crisis of this magnitude, the builders of Soviet America were provided with a skillfully manufactured "opportunity to do things you think you could not do before" - like nationalizing mortgage companies, banks, auto manufactures, and other privately owned industries - in a manner that would have made Karl Marx, Vladimir Lenin, Joseph Stalin, and William Z. Foster proud!

Together Fannie and Freddie lost over 90 percent of their stock value since the beginning of 2008. In addition, of the $5 trillion in mortgages, they held at least $1 trillion in bad mortgages that federal politicians and their political operatives cleverly crafted. Fannie Mae and Freddie Mac were included in the federal seizures, and both were nationalized in September of 2008,[32] giving the builders of Soviet America control over nearly half the mortgages in the USA. A dream come true for political predators who posses "a lust for power over others."

The end product of the mortgage and banking fiasco: The politicians and political operatives who sabotaged and pilfered the mortgage and banking system seized Soviet-style control over the very system they sabotaged and pilfered. As Sher Zieve[33] of RenewAmerica.com stated, "The very people who created this problem will now be in charge of 'correcting' it!" Yes, in Soviet America, crime really does pay! Jeff Poor[34] of the Business & Media Institute wrote an article titled, "Nationalization: It's Not Just for Communists Anymore." That's correct. Nationalization is not just for Communists anymore, it's also for people who think and act like Communists.

Republican Senator Jim Bunning[35] correctly labeled the $787 billion federal bailout "financial socialism" and "un-American." Moreover, Senator Bunning compared the federal bailout to actions one would expect in Communist China. According to Senator Bunning, "No company fails in Communist China, because they're all partly owned by the government." Senator Bunning could have said, "Sabotaged companies are 'too big to fail' in Soviet America, because Marxist saboteurs have prepared them to be partly, or entirely, owned by government."

According to Republican Senator Tom Coburn,[36] "This [bailout] bill does not represent a new and sudden departure from free market principles as much as it represents an emergency response to congressional actions that have ignored free market principles, and our Constitution, for decades. If anyone in Washington should offer their resignation it should be the members of Congress who peddled the fantasy of free home ownership without risk. No institution in our country is more responsible for the myth of borrowing without consequences than the United States Congress." And, "As much as members of Congress want to find scapegoats, the root of this [mortgage and banking] problem is political greed in Congress." Translation: The root of the problem is "a lust for power over others" by predators in Congress.

Welcome to Soviet America!

Good-bye Prosperous, Free Enterprise America!

------†††------

"...Socialist governments traditionally do make a financial mess. They always run out of other people's money." - Margaret Thatcher, Prime Minister of the United Kingdom, 1979 - 1990[37]

Chapter Eighteen

Losing The Cold War On American Soil!

Ugly Americans, The Proletariat & Psychological Warfare!

The Communist Party "will direct its attention to the great problems of the struggle of the proletariat. It will establish the real connections between the party and the masses and their struggle." - R. M. Whitney, *Reds in America*, 1924[1]

In 1958, in the midst of the Cold War between the Soviet Union and the United States, authors Eugene Burdick and William Lederer[2] published their political novel, *The Ugly American*. This work of fiction, reportedly based on actual characters and events, conveyed to the reader the alarming notion that America was losing the Cold War not long after it began. (In 1963 *The Ugly American* was made into a movie starring Marlon Brando) America's loss seemed inevitable because Americans operating in foreign lands made little or no effort to learn the language or understand the culture of the indigenous people. Although Americans attempted to help the native people and win them over to our way of thinking, Americans distanced themselves from the natives socially - and thus psychologically. Consequently, Americans were perceived as loud, arrogant, superficial, and aloof. In a word, foreigners viewed Americans as "Ugly."

Communists, however, immersed themselves into the targeted culture. They learned the language and understood the wants and needs of the indigenous people at a personal level. Clearly, Americans were untrained and Communists were well trained in the art and science of psychological warfare. Communists were, and remain, seasoned culture warriors. As a consequence, the Soviets were achieving one decisive victory after another in what was considered "the battle for the hearts and minds" of people in a Cold War waged on a global scale.

Today when we think of Europe we think of "European socialism." When people spoke of Europe in earlier centuries they referred to it as "Christendom." So, it is obvious who won the Cold War in Europe, and it wasn't the Americans. It certainly wasn't the "Christian Right." Europe's trek toward socialism is interesting in light of a statement made by Communist William Z. Foster[3] in his 1932 book, *Toward Soviet America*. According to Foster the Soviet Union was formed after World War I; therefore, a World War II may very well produce a "Soviet Europe." His statement was truly prophetic. Approximately seventy years later British author Peter Hitchens[4] would refer to the newly created European Union as "The New Soviet Union of Europe." Observing the current state of China, Africa, South America, and even our neighbor to the north, Canada, it is clear that Communist culture warriors have been winning the Cold War on every front - not just the American front.

Throughout the Cold War against the Soviet Union most Americans remained "Ugly Americans." Given the continuous criticism of the USA by France, England, Germany, Sweden, Canada, and other conquered nations, it is painfully clear that Americans continue to be viewed as "Ugly" on foreign soil. Perhaps even more disturbing, one may also argue that today Sovereign Americans appear as "Ugly Americans" even on American soil. In terms of winning the hearts and minds of the American people, Soviet Americans, like their Soviet Russian counterparts, have been far more effective culture warriors than Sovereign Americans.

Communists and people who think like Communists have convincingly won the hearts and minds of far too many special interest groups. They have done so through the strategic use of the news media, the entertainment media, the education establishment at every level, the legal system, the churches, synagogues, and mosques, and through every other institution that could be used as a weapon to win "the battle for the hearts and minds" of the American people across generations. But how did they do it?

Yes, Bolshevik Big Brother Is Watching You!

When I was a kid, "People were free to speak their minds, even if what they had to say was contemptible; people who didn't like it were free to say so in no uncertain terms - anywhere, particularly in that bastion of ideas, the university." - G. Gordon Liddy, *When I Was A Kid, This Was A Free Country*, 2002[5]

Yakov Smirnoff often appeared on national television years ago. This Russian comedian, who immigrated to America many years before the collapse of the USSR, would humorously compare life in the Soviet Union to life in the United States. He said, for example, people would ask him, "Name one thing we have in America that they do not have in the Soviet Union?" Smirnoff's answer: "Warning shots!" But what is relevant today is the joke Smirnoff told regarding the privacy we Americans enjoyed that was sorely lacking in the KGB-laden Soviet Union. Perhaps one of his best one-liners regarding privacy was the following: "In America people watch TV; in the Soviet Union the TV watches you!"

During one of his sermons in the spring of 2009, Pastor John Hagee of San Antonio, Texas mentioned that he visited East Berlin before the collapse of the Soviet Union. While walking down an East Berlin street one of the locals commented, "You're not from around here, are you?" When Pastor Hagee asked how he came to that conclusion, the East Berliner replied with, "Because you never turn around to see if anyone is following you!" Those words of Pastor Hagee, although paraphrased, demonstrate the quintessential difference between living in a Soviet-style society and a free society. In a free, American-style society, the people watch the government; however, in a Soviet-style society the government, or its proxies, watch the people!

When living in Moscow, East Berlin, or some other Soviet-dominated city or town, a "Bolshevik Big Brother" monitored your behavior. Therefore, the extent to which Americans find themselves monitored by government agents - or their non-governmental foot soldiers - serves as a useful gauge to help determine the extent to which Soviet America has become a reality. When strangers monitor your speech, electronic communications, interpersonal behavior, medical records, health care choices, retail purchases, education, religious beliefs and practices, income, financial transactions, transportation, private property usage, energy usage, etc., you can be certain that you no longer live in a free society. You can be confident you no longer live in the Sovereign America founded by George Washington, Thomas Jefferson, and James Madison, but are now living in the Soviet America envisioned by William Z. Foster, Joseph Stalin, and Nikita Khrushchev.

As noted earlier, in his 1932 book *Toward Soviet America,* William Z. Foster[6] quoted Vladimir Lenin as follows: "...the dictatorship of the proletariat will produce a whole series of restrictions of liberty in the case of the oppressors, exploiters and capitalists." But how could Communists accomplish this goal in the "land of the free and the home of the brave?" How could agents of the U.S. Government become like agents of the Soviet Government? How could they monitor and intervene in nearly every basic, personal, familial, and social relationship in a manner that restricts the liberty of the American "bourgeoisie?"

Karl Marx's formula of dividing people into proletariat victim groups who reportedly suffer at the hands of an oppressive bourgeoisie provided the answer. Victims need a champion, someone to closely monitor victim interactions with the perpetrators, and Bolshevik Democrats and Menshevik Republicans have eagerly assumed that role. Of course, the plight of the victims must be portrayed as so urgent that presidents, legislators, and judges must push aside the U.S. Constitution to deal with an endless series of pressing proletarian emergencies. Eventually, the people become desensitized to an ever-growing, unconstitutional, Big Brother government.

As pseudo champions of the downtrodden, Soviet-style federal bureaucracies must be created by Soviet Americans to monitor the interpersonal relations between men and women to "protect the rights" of the feminist proletariat from sexist bourgeois males; monitor the interpersonal relations between whites and blacks to protect the black proletariat from white bourgeois racists; and monitor the interpersonal relations of parents and children so parents do not indoctrinate their proletarian children with traditional bourgeois values, thus violating the "rights of the child."

It soon becomes obvious why the builders of Soviet America adopted the motto, "Diversity is our strength." In transforming America from a melting pot into a multicultural tempest pot, the builders of Soviet America can create a large army of diverse proletariat groups. The greater the number of proletariat groups the more proletariat/bourgeoisie conflicts can be incited requiring greater government monitoring, intervention, and control.

It is clear that the current culture war, which escalated in the mid 1960s, is a manifestation of the Cold War being fought on American soil. Therefore, the Cold War is not over. It may never be over. Just as Communists won the hearts and minds of foreigners on foreign soil, they are also winning the hearts and minds of Americans on American soil. The Marxian formula of pitting the proletariat (the lower class) against the bourgeoisie (the middle class) to overthrow the "establishment" has been employed globally throughout the Cold War. Members of every conceivable special interest group have been surreptitiously recruited as soldiers and deputized as speech police in a masterfully executed battle plan to win the hearts and minds of Americans - one proletariat group after another.

In addition to the manufactured need to protect the feminist proletariat, the black proletariat, and the child proletariat, Soviet-style bureaucracies must be erected to "protect" the Hispanic proletariat, the Native American proletariat, the illegal alien proletariat, the senior proletariat, the disabled proletariat, the atheist proletariat, the homosexual proletariat, the youth proletariat, the student proletariat, the union proletariat, the sick proletariat, the poor proletariat, the uninsured proletariat, the substance abusing proletariat, the criminal proletariat, and the unemployed proletariat. Soviet Americans have even created a terrorist proletariat! Clearly, the hearts and minds of the classical proletarians have been won over to Soviet-style thinking through very careful, longstanding, psychological manipulation, control, and exploitation.

Let's not forget the manufactured need for Soviet-style agencies to protect the endangered and threatened species proletariat as well as the environment proletariat. The latter may be subdivided into the land proletariat, the sea proletariat, the air proletariat. Whether male or female, animal or plant, citizen or non-citizen, healthy or unhealthy, animate or inanimate, rich or poor, gay or straight, of color or not of color, employed or unemployed, young, old, or somewhere in between, through massive psychological manipulation Marxist dialecticians have created and empowered massive, expensive, heavy-handed, unconstitutional, Soviet-style bureaucracies to extract trillions upon trillions of dollars from the "offending" bourgeoisie to redistribute to the "offended" proletariat. The ongoing process of wealth confiscation and redistribution serves to finance the establishment of massive Soviet-style bureaucracies that exercise unconstitutional, dictatorial control over everyone and everything - just as we saw in the Soviet Union - and just as William Z. Foster predicted for his Soviet America!

In fighting the Cold War against Communism on American soil, too many Americans have been either "sleeping with the enemy," declared themselves "conscientious objectors," "non-combatants," or they have simply stuck their heads in the sand and said "what culture war?" Too many are simply "Ugly Americans" who cannot produce solutions that compete with those offered by the builders of Soviet America. Given the large number of Americans who simply sit on the side lines in this Marxist-inspired culture war, we may ask, are we a "Nation of Cowards," too fearful to defend ourselves, our families, and our posterity, as suggested by Jeff Snyder?[7] Or, are we "A Nation of Sheep" and thus easy prey for the predators among us, as feared by Judge Andrew P. Napolitano?[8]

One thing is certain: we are no longer "the land of the free and the home of the brave." When we make such a statement today, we fool only ourselves. The reality of Soviet America has become an open secret. We now find ourselves psychological prisoners of war in our own homeland, restrained by speech codes and other examples of political correctness, all enforced by hostile proletarians waiting, even hoping, to be offended by a slip of the tongue, a public religious display, an insensitive joke, a disturbed Spotted Owl, or any one of a thousand honest, but personally disconcerting, statements of fact.

Perhaps we are not yet watched by our TVs, but we are certainly monitored closely by tens of millions covert and overt agents. They are the proletarian field agents who report every politically incorrect offense - whether real or fabricated - to the ACLU and numerous other Soviet-style social monitors that dutifully report offenses to the Soviet-bloc media and a Soviet-style governmental agency that takes a keen interest in just about everything we say or do. Welcome to Soviet America!

Building A Soviet America – With A Feminist Proletariat!

"The free Russian woman is a trail blazer for the toiling woman of the world. She is beating out a path which, ere long, her American sister will begin to follow." - William Z. Foster, National Chairman of the Communist Party, USA, *Toward Soviet America*, 1932[9]

Easy (no fault) divorce, child care centers that "free the women from the enslavement of the perpetual care of her children" so she can work side by side with men, Communist-inspired, mafia-managed trade union protection for women, equal pay as men (whether or not there is an equal commitment to work), sexual promiscuity among women, social acceptance of women crafting fatherless, crime-creating families, women serving as generals in the army, women serving as ambassadors, and women freed of "housework slavery" are all benefits that Soviet American women will share with their Soviet Russian sisters, according to William Z. Foster. He made those predictions in 1932.

In the 21st century we may take the preceding "accomplishments" of the women's movement for granted. But in 1932, thirty-plus years before the Soviet American Cultural Revolution of the 1960s, many doubted Foster's predictions would become a reality. Given the compromised state of the media both then and now, Americans were not informed of the Communist roots of these goals, but instead, they were encouraged to pursue them with revolutionary vigor. The extent to which these objectives have been accomplished is a measure of the extent to which Communists trained in the art and science of psychological warfare have achieved their objective of creating the feminist proletarian, or the Soviet American woman!

But Foster failed to tell his readers that the purpose of "emancipating" or "liberating" the American woman by removing her from the home and placing her into the workforce was twofold: Firstly, it separated her from her children during early childhood when children are most susceptible to parental guidance. Well-trained in psychological warfare, Communists are aware of the age-old belief that men build houses, but women turn them into homes. As Marx had written, parents and children must be separated because parents tend to pass along their "bourgeois" values to their children. In Communist nations children are to be raised by the state, not by their parents. Children are to be indoctrinated by atheistic Communists, and not by religious leaders or Bible-believing parents.

This explains why Karl Marx called for free (taxpayer-funded), mandatory education in government-controlled schools, as we now have in Soviet America. It further explains why the Soviet constitutional principle of "separation of church and state" is so rigidly enforced by the Roger Baldwin-created ACLU and other subversive organizations. While women are away at work, the schools are to serve as transmission belts for Communist ideology. As detailed in Chapter Five, Re-Education in Soviet America, American public schools have been transformed into Soviet American indoctrination centers. After assessing the extent to which Marxist ideology has been introduced into colleges and universities in the USA, David Horowitz titled one of his books, "Indoctrination U." American schools, colleges, and universities are, in fact, re-education camps that teach children and young adults an ideology that was foreign to their patriotic, self-sufficient, hard-working grandparents and great-grandparents.

Secondly, taken out of the home and placed into the workforce, like men, women become susceptible to Karl Marx's heavy progressive income tax. A woman with children who works only in the home works at cross-purposes with the state. She is working for the family, not for the state. And, under Communism, everyone must serve the state, not the family. The more success she has in the workforce, the more she pays to the government under Marx's heavy progressive system of taxation. With two wage earners in the family, it becomes easier for the state to continue to raise taxes. As every good Soviet American culture warrior knows, a family with two wage earners will complain less about continuous tax increases than a family that is dependent solely upon one wage earner! (Isn't psychological warfare fun?)

The Founding Mother Of
The Soviet American Feminist Proletariat

"The USSR shows the general lines along which the emancipation of woman will also proceed in a Soviet America." - William Z. Foster, National Chairman of the Communist Party, USA, *Toward Soviet America*, 1932[10]

Keep in mind that the Soviet American Cultural Revolution began in the mid 1960s, and that the modern women's liberation movement began in 1963 with the publication of Betty Friedan's book, *The Feminist Mystique.* David Horowitz,[11] who abandoned his Marxist roots and switched sides to become a courageous Sovereign American culture warrior, has investigated Betty Friedan and her politics. Horowitz points out that while she presented herself to the public as a middle class (bourgeois) woman who felt trapped in her role as a traditional American housewife, Betty Friedan was actually a closet Communist. She was striving to liberate women, but she did not seek an American form of liberation. Instead, as a Communist, her job was to create a feminist proletariat. Her job was to liberate women from their roles as transmitters of traditional Sovereign American values and transform them into transmitters of Moscow-directed, Soviet American values. As David Horowitz wrote, Betty Friedan's "interest in women's liberation was just a subtext of her real desire to create a Soviet America."

In the 1960s and 1970s Betty Freidan was a frequent guest on all the Soviet American television talk shows. Of course, she was not presented as a closet Communist, but was held up as a role model for all American women to emulate. Today, in the 21st century, she remains a liberal icon, especially on Soviet American college and university campuses. When she is criticized by contemporary liberal feminists, it is not for being a closet Communist. Instead, she is criticized for presenting the complaints of the middle class bourgeois woman while ignoring the concerns of the poor, the minority, and the lesbian woman. From a Soviet American perspective, she unnecessarily limited the size and scope of the feminist proletariat. Of course, her contemporary fellow travelers have corrected that mistake!

For those who lived through the onset of the Soviet American Cultural Revolution of the 1960s and 1970s, they may recall that feminists lamented that women were the victims of oppressive men in a male dominated society. Americans were told that marriage was created by men to enslave women. Men wanted women to be pregnant and barefoot so they could be dependent and easily dominated. Men were economically free, but women were economically dependent upon their sexist husbands.

There certainly were legitimate complaints, but what Soviet American operatives conveniently failed to convey is that both men and women are being cunningly maneuvered into a position where both eventually become totally dependent upon a centralized, Soviet-style, Big Brother government. When all is said and done, neither men nor women will enjoy the economic liberty that can only be enjoyed in a capitalistic system which is free of intrusive, strangulating, oppressive, confiscatory government. The evil geniuses behind Communism have tricked tens of millions women (and men) into believing that they are fighting for "women's liberation" when in fact they are fighting for women's and men's subordination under a totalitarian Soviet-style government that does not tolerate freedom of thought, freedom of word, nor freedom of action. It may be appropriate here to repeat a few quotes presented in Chapter Twelve:

"Communism with its deceitful double talk exploits these basic human yearnings for better social conditions, racial equality, justice, and peace, and places them in the service of tyranny. In this way, strange as it may sound, Communists are able to entice free men to fight for slavery in the name of freedom." - J. Edgar Hoover, Director of the FBI, 1958[12]

This diabolical form of psychological trickery was also exposed by Margaret Thatcher,[13] the Prime Minister of the United Kingdom from 1979 to 1990, when she said: "Socialists cry 'Power to the people,' and raise the clenched fist as they say it. We all know what they really mean - power over people, power to the State." A third quote will be added here given that Margaret Thatcher[14] also recognized the destruction of liberty that occurs, for example, when both husband and wife work and government confiscates what is earned: "There can be no liberty unless there is economic liberty!"

Ugly Americans
Need Training In Psychological Warfare!

Carrie Lukas[15] has described how conservative American men (Sovereign American cultural warriors) such as Rush Limbaugh, may be very effective in discussing issues in ways that appeal to other men, but are far less effective than liberal Democrats (Soviet American culture warriors) in discussing issues in ways that appeal to women. Lukas notes, for example, that women are far more safety and security conscious than men. So, while conservatives try to appeal to voters by talking about how big, Soviet-style government stifles opportunities for people to excel, women are more concerned about hanging on to what they already have. For this reason women are more susceptible to manipulation, control, and exploitation by well-trained culture warriors who offer a Bolshevik Big Brother government to protect them.

Liberal Democrats, like their Soviet Russian counterparts, have mastered the art of exploiting women's fears of loss. They convince women that a big, Soviet-style government is needed because, like a Bolshevik Big Brother (who will displace that sexist good-for-nothing husband) it can provide the safety and security women seek. What conservatives need to do is point out how women are actually less safe and secure because government programs reportedly enacted to protect women have actually made them far less safe. Conservatives must emphasize, for example, how Democrat-sponsored government programs have replaced crime-preventing two parent families with crime-creating one parent families. Conservatives must remind women that the most dangerous place in America today is a Democrat-controlled city! Conservatives must inform women that the most impoverished, the most miserable, the most self-destructive, and the most unsafe people in America today are those who have been brainwashed into depending upon government for their safety, security, and prosperity!

To win the Cold War on American soil, conservative American men must win the battle for the hearts and minds of American women. They must close the gender gap. Conservative American men must not allow themselves to be perceived as "Ugly Americans" who are out of touch with the basic needs and concerns of American women. The stakes are too high. Given the fate of the "bourgeoisie" who lost the war on Soviet Russian soil, failure is not an option for the American bourgeois male now fighting on Soviet American soil!

In addition to discussing the role of women in Soviet America, William Z. Foster[16] made reference to the criminal proletariat, stating that, "Capitalism blames crime on the individual, instead of upon the bad social conditions which produce it." This is in sharp contrast to the position of President Ronald Reagan, a conservative Republican who said, "We must reject the idea that every time a law's broken, society is guilty rather than the law-breaker. It is time to restore the American precept that each individual is accountable for his actions."

Comrade Foster also mentioned the illegal alien proletariat: In Soviet America, "foreign-born workers, now denied the right to vote and ruthlessly deported, will enjoy the fullest rights of citizenship."[17] And, "The wholesale deportation of radical workers and leaders is an attempt to illegalize the Communist Party..."[18] Now we know why Bolshevik Democrats and Menshevik Republicans seek amnesty for the illegal alien proletariat! Foster further made reference to an environmental proletariat: "Socialism will also conserve the natural resources of the country..."[19] Now we know one of the reasons the "No Drill" Democrats will not allow Americans to drill for oil on American soil. It appears William Z. Foster's book, *Toward Soviet America,* is a Democrat playbook. But the proletariat given special attention by the National Chairman of the Communist Party, USA, in building his Soviet America was the African American, which he referred to as the Negro. For this and other reasons an entire chapter, Chapter Twelve, has been dedicated to the "Dictatorship of the Black Proletariat."

Psychological Warfare & Mental Iron Curtain On American Soil!

"The Communist world is a world of walls, searchlights, and guards - a prison for the heart, mind and soul." - J. Edgar Hoover, Director of the FBI, 1970[20]

Several versions of a book titled *Brain-Washing: A Synthesis of the Russian Textbook of Psychopolitics,* have been circulated. The book was allegedly written by Laventi Pavlovich Beria, a former head of the Soviet Secret Police. According to Kenneth Goff, who also claimed authorship, psychopolitics is defined as "the art and science of asserting and maintaining dominion over the thoughts and loyalties of the individuals, officers, bureaus, and masses, and the effecting of the conquest of the enemy nations through 'mental healing.'" However, many have concluded the true author of this book was not Beria or Goff, but rather it was written by L. Ron Hubbard, the founder of Dianetics and Scientology.

Regardless of the authorship and authenticity of the book, psycho-political techniques that may be characterized as psychopolitics have clearly been operational not just in America, but across the globe. Today, anyone who closely observes politicians, government bureaucrats, reporters, journalists, educators, and community organizers will conclude that psychology is routinely employed to deceive the American people into accepting political goals and objectives that are consistent with the construction of a Soviet America.

Clearly, one may dismiss the term psychopolitics as a fabrication, but one would have great difficulty refuting the fact that the American people in general, and selective individuals in particular, have been the target of psychological warfare. The relentless Communist-style smear campaign waged against a wholesome woman such as Sarah Palin serves as a prime example of psychological warfare waged against a politically incorrect individual whose very existence threatens the builders of Soviet America.

Psychological warfare may, of course, be employed to deceptively rid individuals or entire nations of politically incorrect thinking while replacing it with government-approved thinking that is conducive to the establishment and maintenance of socialism with a police state, which is Soviet-style Communism. Works such as *Rules for Radicals: A Practical Primer for Realistic Radicals*, authored by community organizer (proletariat organizer) Saul D. Alinsky, and *The Art of War*, written by military strategist Sun Tzu 500 years before Christ walked the Earth, may be practical guides employed by those who are engaging in psychological warfare against the American people. (They may also be employed defensively by American patriots.)

Political correctness, hate crime laws, sensitivity training, multicultural-ism/diversity training, values clarification, campaign finance reform, and the so-called Fairness Doctrine, are all examples of the application of un-American psycho-political methods designed specifically to squelch govern-ment-disapproved thinking and encourage government-approved thinking that is conducive to the establishment and maintenance of socialism with a police state. Each of these methods places government enforced legal limitations, or academic and media enforced cultural limitations, on thought and behavior that may threaten the builders of Soviet America.

In earlier stages of the Cold War the Soviets built a series of walls and fences to keep people from physically escaping from the Soviet-controlled sectors into the freer sectors. Collectively, these walls and fences were referred to as the "Iron Curtain." Following the successful conquest of Europe, Asia, Africa, and the Americas through the widespread embedding of Communist principles and practices within targeted governments and cultures, the physical Iron Curtain was no longer needed. It was no longer needed because it had been replaced with a pervasive psychological Iron Curtain that punishes people for escaping, for example, from a Soviet German mindset to a Sovereign German mindset, just as someone like Associate Justice Clarence Thomas may be punished for escaping from the Soviet American "neighborhood of ideas" into the Sovereign American "neighbor-hood of ideas!"

Hence, tactics of psychological warfare may be employed to erect a "psychological Iron Curtain" around people to keep them from escaping into freedom of thought, word, and action. In addition, an army of street-level culture warriors would be needed to ensure no one escapes from the government-erected "psychological Iron Curtain" and into American-style freedom of thought, word, or action. Using Marxian terminology, those street-level culture warriors would be called the proletariat, more specifically, the "dictatorship of the proletariat." You may say, "Welcome to Soviet America," but if you are not a hard-line Bolshevik or an obedient proletarian dedicated to an omnipotent state, Soviet America will not welcome you in return!

Welcome to Soviet America!

Good-bye Independent-Thinking America!

------†††-- ---

Under Communism "Intellectuals are encouraged to think, if they think the 'right way;' but any independent thinking is not allowed... It [the Communist Party] fears that they might start thinking for themselves." - J. Edgar Hoover, Director of the FBI, 1958[21]

"Communism (Marxism-Leninism) is the revolutionary, materialistic ideology used by its adherents to justify their efforts to seize power by any and all means for the forcible establishment of a worldwide totalitarian social order." - J. Edgar Hoover, Director of the FBI, 1962[22]

Chapter Nineteen

The U.S. Government
Versus The U.S. Constitution!

We Have A Constitution,
And We Have A Government; Unfortunately,
We Do Not Have A Constitutional Government.

"With him [the Communist] the end justifies the means. Whether his tactics be 'legal' and 'moral,' or not, does not concern him, so long as they are effective. He knows that the laws as well as the current code of morals, are made by his mortal enemies...Consequently, he ignores them in so far as he is able and it suits his purposes. He proposes to develop, regardless of capitalist conceptions of 'legality,' 'fairness,' 'right,' etc., a greater power than his capitalist enemies have." - William Z. Foster, National Chairman of the Communist Party, USA[1]

Foster's description of the Communist may also be used to describe the sociopath. He is describing a lawless, power-hungry individual who believes that laws do not apply to him or her. Publicly the sociopath would produce rationalizations and state, for example, that a law is "flexible" when applied to him or her (situational ethics). Or, in a thinly veiled ploy to expand governmental power clearly beyond constitutional limits we may be told that the U.S. Constitution is a "living" document. In nihilistic fashion, there is no "right or wrong" way (there is only the "Soviet" way) to interpret the supreme law of the land when the interpreter is a lawless sociopath. These are the kinds of preposterous rationalizations we receive from law making and law enforcing dictators who consider themselves to be "above the law."

Consider the following: Before a new house is built, architects invest a lot of time and effort to assemble a building plan. No intelligent person would attempt to build a house without first putting together a building plan. And, the closer the builders stick to the plan, the less likely they are to create structural or foundational problems for the future residents of that house. These principles also apply when people build a new government. Before our Founding Fathers could create a new government for a new nation, they had to assemble a blueprint, or a building plan. The plan they put together is the U.S. Constitution. It is the blueprint for the U.S. Government.

As discussed below, the Soviet Constitution empowers government to bestow rights upon the people. However, consistent with the Declaration of Independence, the U.S. Constitution acknowledges the pre-existing, inalienable, God-given rights of the people - which are to be secured by government. The Declaration of Independence clearly states that we Americans are endowed by our Creator with certain unalienable rights, and to secure these rights governments are instituted among men, and that the powers of the government are derived from the people who are to be governed. Because we are Americans, and not Soviet Americans, our rights truly come from God and not from government, and it is the role of government to secure our God-given rights. This premise is clearly reflected in the wording of the Bill of Rights - the first ten Amendments to the U.S. Constitution.

For example, the First Amendment states that "the right of the people peaceably to assemble" shall not be abridged by the federal government. The Second Amendment states that "the right of the people to keep and bear arms shall not be infringed" by government. The Fourth Amendment states that "The right of the people to be secure in their persons, houses, papers, and effects, against unreasonable searches and seizures, shall not be violated..." In each of these Amendments it is clearly implied that we the people have rights that are natural and pre-existing, and therefore government does not bestow rights and government shall not violate rights. Instead, it is the role of government to secure human rights that we possess independent of any document or any government; rights we possessed before the Constitution and the federal government were created.

In Article 44 of the 1977 Soviet Constitution[2] it is stated that, "Citizens of the USSR have the right to housing." Article 45 states that, "Citizens of the USSR have the right to education." In Article 46 it is written that, "Citizens of the USSR have the right to enjoy cultural benefits." However, in Article 39 we find that, "Citizens of the USSR enjoy in full the social, economic, political and personal rights and freedoms proclaimed and guaranteed by the Constitution of the USSR and by Soviet laws." So, in the Soviet Union the people have rights and freedoms that are "proclaimed and guaranteed" by the Soviet Constitution. What about rights and freedoms not "proclaimed and guaranteed" by the Soviet Constitution, such as the right to keep and bear arms? In the Soviet Union rights and freedoms that were not "proclaimed and guaranteed" by the Soviet Constitution simply did not exist in that "joyless land where there was always winter, but never Christmas."

So, while the role of the U.S. Government is to protect the pre-existing rights of the people, the role of the Soviet Government was to grant or bestow rights by proclaiming them into existence, then guaranteeing only those rights that were proclaimed. However, those who have negotiated with the Soviet Government know how much trust one could place in a Soviet guarantee. Just ask anyone who managed to survived the Soviet Gulag!

Also, the Soviet Constitution was created by individuals to construct an all powerful central government to rule over all other individuals. Contrastingly, the U.S. Constitution was created by the states to construct a limited central government to perform specific duties for the states and for the people. Therefore, the states created the federal government to be a servant to the states and to the people, although the builders of Soviet America in government, the media, and the education establishment act as if the reverse was true.

The 18 powers granted under Article I, Section 8 of the U.S. Constitution strictly limit the role of the federal government. As clearly stated in the Ninth Amendment, "The enumeration in the Constitution of certain rights shall not be construed to deny or disparage others retained by the people." So, the specific rights protected by the Bill of Rights are not the only rights retained by the people. But perhaps the Amendment most loathed and ignored by those who possess "a lust for power over others" is the Tenth Amendment which states that, "The powers not delegated to the United States by the Constitution, nor prohibited by it to the states, are reserved to the states respectively, or to the people." Therefore, the federal government has no powers other than those 18 powers listed under Article I, Section 8 of the Constitution. All other powers belong to the states or to the people, and the Commerce Clause cannot cancel out the Tenth Amendment!

The U.S. Constitution
Is The Supreme Law Of The Land

"Dictatorship is power based on force and unrestricted by any laws. The revolutionary dictatorship of the proletariat is power won and maintained by the violence of the proletariat against the bourgeoisie - power that is unrestricted by any laws." - Vladimir Lenin, first Communist dictator of the Soviet Union[3]

Moreover, the U.S. Constitution is a legal document, but it is not an ordinary legal document; instead, it is the "supreme law of the land," as stated in

Article VI, paragraph 2 of the U.S. Constitution. It does not say that senators, representatives, presidents, or judges are the supreme law of the land; it says the U.S. Constitution is the supreme law of the land. To say that legislators, the president, or judges are the supreme law of the land is to follow the principles found within the Soviet Constitution, not the U.S. Constitution. As stated in Article 30 of the 1936 Soviet Constitution,[4] "The highest organ of state authority of the USSR is the Supreme Soviet of the USSR." So, in the USSR the Soviet Constitution was not the supreme law of the land, instead, the "Supreme Soviet," which was the highest council of Soviet leaders, was the supreme law of the land. Therefore, the Soviet people were governed by men, not by laws.

We must keep this in mind at all times because increasingly the American people are subjected to legislation that is blatantly unconstitutional. The federal government has not just slipped, but has been pushed off its constitutional foundation. Today we have a Constitution and we have a government, but we no longer have anything that closely resembles a constitutional government. As in the Soviet Union, we are now governed by men, not by laws. We are governed by government officials - who refuse to be restricted by the supreme law of the land.

Because the U.S. Constitution is a legal blueprint as well as a legal contract, it tells us what kind of government we have, and what government agents can and cannot do for us - or to us. When legislators create a federal law that violates the U.S. Constitution; when a president signs it into law; and when the U.S. Supreme Court deems as "constitutional" any law that is clearly unconstitutional, every one of those federal officials has violated the supreme law of the land. In addition, each and every one has violated his or her solemn oath to uphold the Constitution of the United States. Because such violations of our rights occur with predictable regularity, and such violations are often requested by or even demanded by the media and education establishment, we the people have grown accustomed to having our rights violated by an increasingly lawless government.

In America, Your Rights Come From God! In Soviet America, Your Rights Come From Government!

"Law, morality, religion, are...so many bourgeoisie prejudices, behind which lurk in ambush just as many bourgeoisie interests." - Karl Marx, *The Communist Manifesto*, 1848

Even if the U.S. Constitution and the Bill of Rights did not exist, we Americans would still have those codified rights and many others - because all our rights come from God, not from government. As Americans, our rights certainly do not come from socialists who think like Karl Marx, Vladimir Lenin, or Joseph Stalin. Again, these principles are available for all to read in our Declaration of Independence: "We hold these truths to be self-evident, that all men are created equal, that they are endowed by their Creator with certain unalienable Rights that among these are Life, Liberty, and the pursuit of Happiness. That to secure these rights, Governments are instituted among Men, deriving their just powers from the consent of the governed."

The principle of God-given rights was reiterated by our second president, John Adams: "You have rights antecedent to all earthly governments; rights that cannot be repealed or restrained by human laws; rights derived from the Great Legislator of the Universe." Thus, the builders of Soviet America cannot take from us rights granted to us by God, including the right to pray or read the Bible, the right to keep and bear arms, the right to control our own health care, the right to control the education our children, the right to keep the fruits of our own labor, and the right to constitutional government - to name just a few.

Consistent with our pre-existing, inalienable right to keep and bear arms Sir William Blackstone, the master authority in English law, has stated that self-defense is "justly called the primary law of nature, so it is not, neither can it be in fact, taken away by the laws of society." We must all keep in mind what Chief Justice Warren wrote in *Miranda v. Arizona*: "Where rights secured by the Constitution are involved, there can be no rule making or legislation which would abrogate them." In addition, Chief Justice John Marshall in *Marbury v. Madison,* stated that "Anything repugnant to the Constitution is null and void." Therefore, any federal law, judicial ruling, police or military order, that is "repugnant to the Constitution," must be viewed as "null and void."

The U.S. Constitution is a restriction on the federal government; it is not a restriction upon "We the People," as leftists try to mislead us to believe. Thomas Jefferson, the primary author of the Declaration of Independence, said the U.S. Constitution restricts the federal government. Because it limits the federal government, it frees the American people. The history of freedom is the history of limited government. This principle was acknowledged by Democrat Woodrow Wilson, who was a staunch progressive and our 28th president: "Government, in its last analysis, is organized force." And, "The history of liberty is a history of resistance. The history of liberty is a history of the limitation of governmental power, not the increase of it."

In the Declaration of Independence and the U.S. Constitution we find the principles upon which Sovereign America was built and made operative. However, in the pamphlet *The Communist Manifesto,* in the Soviet Constitution, and in the books *Toward Soviet America* and *The Naked Communist* we find the principles upon which Soviet America was built and made operative.

Reigning In Lawless Lawmakers With The Enumerated Powers Act!

"The Federal Government has ignored the Constitution and expanded its authority into every aspect of human conduct, and quite sadly, it is not doing many of those things very well." - Congressman John Shadegg[5]

As noted in Chapter Four, the title of Judge Andrew P. Napolitano's book, *The Constitution in Exile,* tells us the U.S. Constitution has been discarded by those who have sworn to preserve, protect, and defend it. The book titled *Who killed the Constitution?* by Thomas E. Woods, Jr. and Kevin R. C. Gutzman tells us the U.S. Constitution is not only dead, but it did not die from natural causes. If the U.S. Constitution is dead, then the Sovereign America founded by Washington, Jefferson, and Madison is also dead. And, many of the builders of Soviet America who are guilty of killing the U.S. Constitution remain in power today.

In an effort to resuscitate the U.S. Constitution and restore constitutional government, Representative John Shadegg, a conservative Republican from Arizona, has introduced and reintroduced the Enumerated Powers Act (EPA) each year since 1995. The Enumerated Powers Act would force federal representatives to identify where in the U.S. Constitution they find the authority to enact each and every piece of legislation. EPA simply states that, "Each Act of Congress shall contain a concise and definite statement of the constitutional authority relied upon for the enactment of each portion of that Act. The failure to comply with this section shall give rise to a point of order in either House of Congress..."

Unfortunately, while there are 435 representatives in Congress, each year between 20 and 52 representatives have supported EPA. That means roughly 85 to 95 percent of our elected federal representatives have actively refused to obey the supreme law of the land. Year after year since 1995 they have refused to honor the oath they took to support the Constitution when challenged to do so. In 2008 a similar bill was introduced in the Senate by Senator Tom Coburn, a conservative Republican from Oklahoma. From among 100 senators, Coburn found only 22 were interested in lawful government.

(We should never forget the one word that most accurately describes a person who refuses to be bound by legitimate law, and that word is "lawless" - a word often used to describe the sociopath. It is also a word found throughout the *Holy Bible*; for example, in 2 Thessalonians 2:9 we find the following: "The coming of the lawless one is according to the working of Satan, with all power, signs, and lying wonders,...")

Reigning In Lawless Lawmakers With State Sovereignty & The Tenth Amendment!

"Why did the Founders of our nation give us the Bill of Rights? The answer is easy. They knew Congress could not be trusted with our God-given rights. Think about it...They knew that some government was necessary but they rightfully saw government as the enemy of the people and they sought to limit government and provide us with protections." - Walter E. Williams[6]

As noted above, the Tenth Amendment states that, "The powers not delegated to the United States by the Constitution, nor prohibited by it to the states, are reserved to the states respectively, or to the people." Consequently, the federal government has no powers other than those 18 powers listed in Article I, Section 8 of the Constitution; all other powers belong to the states or to the people. Therefore, the federal government has no constitutional authority to interfere with education, health care, religious expression, workplace safety, social welfare, environmental issues, marriage and family issues, and nearly all law enforcement issues - to mention just a few.

With the massive, unconstitutional, Soviet-style expansion of the federal government many state governments and individual citizens have begun to remind federal politicians of the restriction placed upon them by the Tenth Amendment. Out of shear exasperation, a lot of freedom-loving Americans are beginning to ask federal officials to start obeying the law. Unfortunately, lawless politicians and bureaucrats who possess "a lust for power over others" find that obeying the law stifles their predatory instincts. Predators are always on the prowl looking for ways to manipulate, control, and exploit their prey. This predatory tendency was understood by Wendell Phillips who said "Eternal vigilance is the price of liberty." Because we the people have not been eternally vigilant, predators have used the government, media, education establishment, and even our churches and synagogues to ensnare us and prey upon us!

As noted elsewhere in this book, Rahm Emanuel, the White House Chief of Staff in the Obama Administration has stated, "You never want a serious crisis to go to waste. And what I mean by that is an opportunity to do things you think you could not do before." Spoken like a true predator who keeps a watchful eye on his prey - always looking for an opportunity to take advantage of weaknesses! For example, the crisis of 9/11 supposedly justified Bush's federal takeover of airport security, not to mention the creation of the Soviet-style bureaucratic monster known as the U.S. Department of Homeland Security. The federally-created home mortgage crisis conveniently led to the federal takeover of General Motors, AIG, numerous banks, and other private companies - reminiscent of Vladimir Lenin's business seizures when he assumed power in Russia and began building his Soviet Union!

According to Representative Ron Paul,[7] a Libertarian Republican from Texas, when it comes to the U.S. Constitution, "…too many people in Washington - Republicans and Democrats - don't understand it and don't really believe in it, so they can hardly sell it." Representative Ron Paul therefore encourages politicians to "read the Constitution and follow it."

He also reminds them that "freedom is popular. The people still believe it." Wow! What further evidence do we need to conclude that, we have a Constitution, and we have a government, but we do not have a constitutional government! Ron Paul is also a physician, and he has earned the nickname "Dr. No" because he routinely says "No" to proposed legislation which he deems unconstitutional.

If members of Congress do not read, do not understand, and do not believe in the Constitution, then what guides their legislative agenda? Could it be that they are driven by a desire for economic, political, and personal power - precisely as one would expect from those who possess "a lust for power over others?"

Adding clarity to the State Sovereignty and Tenth Amendment movement, State Representative Charles Key introduced Joint Resolution 1089 in the Oklahoma State Legislature. Join Resolution 1089 (available at:

webserver1.lsb.state.ok.us/2007-08HB/HJR1089_int.rtf) states: "WHEREAS, the Tenth Amendment to the Constitution of the United States reads as follows: "The powers not delegated to the United States by the Constitution, nor prohibited by it to the States, are reserved to the States respectively, or to the people."; and WHEREAS, the Tenth Amendment defines the total scope of federal power as being that specifically granted by the Constitution of the United States and no more; and WHEREAS, the scope of power defined by the Tenth Amendment means that the federal government was created by the states specifically to be an agent of the states; and WHEREAS, today, in 2008, the states are demonstrably treated as agents of the federal government; and WHEREAS, many federal mandates are directly in violation of the Tenth Amendment to the Constitution of the United States; and WHEREAS, the United States Supreme Court has ruled in <u>New York v. United States,</u> 112 S. Ct. 2408 (1992), that Congress may not simply commandeer the legislative and regulatory processes of the states; and WHEREAS, a number of proposals from previous administrations and some now pending from the present administration and from Congress may further violate the Constitution of the United States.

"NOW, THEREFORE, BE IT RESOLVED BY THE HOUSE OF REPRESENTATIVES AND THE SENATE OF THE 2ND SESSION OF THE 51ST OKLAHOMA LEGISLA-TURE: THAT the State of Oklahoma hereby claims sovereignty under the Tenth Amendment to the Constitution of the United States over all powers not otherwise enumerated and granted to the federal government by the Constitution of the United States. THAT this serve as Notice and Demand to the federal government, as our agent, to cease and desist, effective immediately, mandates that are beyond the scope of these constitutionally delegated powers. THAT a copy of this resolution be distributed to the President of the United States, the President of the United States Senate, the Speaker of the United States House of Representatives, the Speaker of the House and the President of the Senate of each state's legislature of the United States of America, and each member of the Oklahoma Congressional Delegation."

Walter E. Williams[8] placed the State Sovereignty movement in perspective when he quoted James Madison, the fourth President of the United States and "the father of the U.S. Constitution" who wrote the following in Federalist Paper 45: "The powers delegated...to the federal government are few and defined. Those which are to remain in the State governments are numerous and indefinite. The former will be exercised principally on external objects, [such] as war, peace, negotiation, and foreign commerce... The powers reserved to the several States will extend to all the objects which, in the ordinary course of affairs, concern the lives, liberties, and properties of the people." In addition, Thomas Jefferson, America's third president, said the states were not "subordinate" to the federal government, and that the state governments were to be concerned with domestic affairs while the federal government was to be concerned with foreign affairs. Why is this not taught in our schools, colleges, and universities?

In a later article Walter E. Williams[9] noted that the Tenth Amendment resolution of New Hampshire stated that, "and that whensoever the General Government assumes undelegated powers, its acts are unauthoritative, void, and of no force." This, of course, is consistent with Chief Justice Warren's statement that, "Where rights secured by the Constitution are involved, there can be no rule making or legislation which would abrogate them," and Chief Justice John Marshall's statement that, "Anything repugnant to the Constitution is null and void." Approximately 36 states are considering or assembling State Sovereignty resolutions under the Tenth Amendment, and all are on solid constitutional ground. Will the states be able to stand up to a federal government that has become far more intrusive, far more confiscatory, and far more tyrannical than the government of King George III that our Founding Fathers had to face? If push comes to shove, state governments have the option to consider **nullification** or even **secession**. Nullification is explored at the TenthAmendmentCenter.com and elsewhere online.

Recall from Chapter Eight the quote from Congressman Earl Landgrebe who said, "The liberal position on privately owned guns is entirely consistent with the liberal position on all private property; there shouldn't be any; all private property should be controlled, regulated or confiscated by the omnipotent state. The liberals have no objections to guns - only guns they do not control." And "the purpose of the gun control lobby" is "the elimination of citizen opposition to their socialist plans."

Given what has been presented in this book, we may conclude that liberals, progressives, Communists, Nazis, and all other predators and parasites, have no objections to capital - only capital they do not control. They have no objections to health care - only health care they do not control. They have no objections to property - only property they do not control. They have no objections to education - only education they do not control. They have no objections to religion - only religions they do not control. They have no objections to business - only businesses they do not control. They have no objections to media - only media they do not control. And, they have no objections to people - only people they do not control.

Welcome to Soviet America!

Good-bye Constitutional America!

------†††------

"The only law the Left obeyed was Don't Look Back - for if it did, the only accomplishments it would see were famine, gulags and mass death." - Ronald Radosh, former American Communist[10]

"Constitutions have to be written on hearts, not just paper." - Margaret Thatcher, Prime Minister of the United Kingdom, 1979 - 1990[11]

"Why have we fought for 230 years to keep foreign governments from eviscerating our freedoms if we will voluntarily let our own government do so?" - Judge Andrew P. Napolitano[12]

"The two enemies of the people are criminals and government, so let us tie the second down with the chains of the Constitution so the second will not become the legalized version of the first." - Thomas Jefferson[13]

"There is no safety for honest men except by believing all possible evil of evil men." - Edmund Burke[14]

------†††------

www.WelcomeToSovietAmerica.com

Notes

Chapter 1: Soviet Russia: How It Got That Way & Who Done It!

1. Gary Selikow, Amazon.com customer reviewer of *The Rise and Fall of the Soviet Empire*, Second Edition, by Raymond Pearson, Melbourne, Australia: Palgrave Macmillan, 2002. http://www.amazon.com/Rise-Fall-Soviet-EmpireSecond/dp/0333948076/ref=sr_1_2?ie=UTF8&s=books&qid=1246537073&sr=1-

2. Robert V. Daniels, *Red October: The Bolshevik Revolution of 1917*, NY: Charles Scribner's Sons, 1967, p. 20.

3. J. Edgar Hoover, *Masters of Deceit*, NY: Pocket Books, 1968, pp. 30-31. (Henry Holt Edition published in 1958)

4. J. Edgar Hoover, *Masters of Deceit*, p. 30.

5. Brian Clowes, *Pro-life Activists Encyclopedia*, Stafford, VA: American Life League, 1994, Chapter 94: Communist Leaders Speak Their Minds. Reprint of Chapter 94 available at: http://www.ewtn.com/library/PROLENC/ENCYC094.HTM.

6. Nicolas Werth, Chapter 10, "The Great Terror (1936 - 1938)," Part I. A State Against Its People: Violence, Repression, and Terror in the Soviet Union. In Stephane Courtois et al., *The Black Book of Communism: Crimes, Terror, Repression,* Cambridge, MA: Harvard University Press, 1999, picture caption between pp. 202-203.

7. Nicolas Werth, Chapter 8, "The Great Famine," citing A. Blum, *Naitre, vivre, et mourir en URSS 1917-1991*, Paris: Plon, 1994, p. 99; Part I. A State Against Its People: Violence, Repression, and Terror in the Soviet Union. In Stephane Courtois et al., *The Black Book of Communism: Crimes, Terror, Repression,* p. 159.

8. R. J. Rummel, *Death By Government*, New Brunswick, NJ: Transaction Publishers, 1994. Data available at: http://www.hawaii.edu/powerkills/NOTE1.HTM.

9. W. Cleon Skousen, *The Naked Communist*, Eleventh Edition, Salt Lake City, UT: The Reviewer, 1962, p. 210. (First Edition published in 1958. New Edition available at: http://www.skousen2000.com/political%20products/communist.htm)

10. W. Cleon Skousen, *The Naked Communist*, p. 211.

11. W. Cleon Skousen, *The Naked Communist*, p. 221.

12. W. Cleon Skousen, *The Naked Communist*, p. 212.

13. Nicolas Werth, Chapter 10, "The Great Terror (1936 - 1938)," picture caption between pp. 202-203.

14. Nicolas Werth, Chapter 8, "The Great Famine," p. 159.
15. David Horowitz on *Glenn Beck*, FOX News Network, 4 September 2009.
16. J. Edgar Hoover, *A Study of Communism*, NY: Holt, Rinehart & Winston, 1962, p. 75.
17. J. Edgar Hoover, *A Study of Communism*, p. 73.
18. G. Gordon Liddy, *When I Was A Kid, This Was A Free Country,* Washington, D.C.: Regnery Publishing, 2002, p. 6.

Chapter 2: Understanding The Psychology Of Soviets, Socialists & Other Sociopaths!

1. Nicholas Stix, "Red America," The Conservative Voice, 2 December 2007. http://www.theconservativevoice.com/articles/article.html?id=29369.
2. Michael Stone, M.D., *Most Evil*, Investigation Discovery, the Discovery Channel, 28 February 2009.
3. Vonda Pelto, Ph.D., guest on *Coast to Coast AM* with George Noory, Premiere Radio Networks, 23-24 March 2009. http://www.vondapelto.com/.
4. Katherine Ramsland, *Inside the Minds of Health Care Serial Killers,* NY: Praeger, 2009. http://www.katherineramsland.com/main.html.
5. Michael Savage, *The Savage Nation,* Talk Radio Network, 7 April 2007.
6. J. C. Prichard, *Treatise on Insanity*, Philadelphia, PA: Haswell, Barrington, and Haswell, 1837.In James D. Page, *Psychopathology: The Science of Understanding Deviance,* Chicago, IL: Aldine Publishing Company, 1975, p. 302.
7. James A. Brussel, M.D., *The Layman's Guide to Psychiatry*, Second Edition, NY: Barnes & Noble, 1967, p. 114.
8. J. Edgar Hoover, *Master's of Deceit*, NY: Henry Holt & Company, 1958.
9. James A. Brussel, M.D., *The Layman's Guide to Psychiatry*, p. 115.
10. James D. Page, *Psychopathology: The Science of Understanding Deviance*, Chicago, IL: Aldine Publishing Company, 1975, p. 301.
11. Walter J. Coville, Timothy W. Costello, and Fabian L. Rouke, *Abnormal Psychology*, New York: Barnes & Noble, 1960, p. 125.
12. H. Cleckley, *The Mask of Sanity*, Fourth Edition, St. Louis, MO: Mosby, 1964. In *Abnormal Psychology: Current Perspectives*, Del Mar, CA: CRM Books, 1972, p. 194.
13. H. R. Schaffer and P. Emerson, "The development of social attachments in infancy," *Monographs of the Society for Research in Child Development*, 1964, 29, Number 3. In L. Joseph Stone and Joseph Church, *Childhood & Adolescence: A Psychology of the Growing Person*, NY: Random House, 1973, pp. 66-69, 107.

14. Evan Esar, *Esar's Comic Dictionary*, Fourth Edition, Garden City, NY: Doubleday & Company, 1983, p. 440.

Chapter 3: Understanding The Philosophy Of Soviets, Socialists & Other Sociopaths!

1. Edmund Fuller, Editor, *4800 Wisecracks, Witty Remarks, and Epigrams for all Occasions,* NY: Avenel Books, 1980, p. 297.
2. Joseph Laffan Morse, Editor in Chief, *Universal Standard Encyclopedia*, NY: Standard Reference Works Publishing Company, 1956, Volume 17, p. 6163.
3. Pastor Ernie Sanders, *WRWL (What's Right, What's Left) Radio Ministries,* 8400 Mayfield Road, Chesterland, OH 44026.
4. Karl Marx, *The Communist Manifesto*, 1848.
5. Nicolas Werth, Chapter 11, "The Empire of the Camps," Part I. A State Against Its People: Violence, Repression, and Terror in the Soviet Union. In Stephane Courtois et al., *The Black Book of Communism: Crimes, Terror, Repression,* Cambridge, MA: Harvard University Press, 1999, pp. 206-207.
6. Karel Bartosek, Chapter 20, "Central and Southeast Europe," Part III. The Other Europe: Victim of Communism. In Stephane Courtois et al., *The Black Book of Communism: Crimes, Terror, Repression,* pp. 421-422.
7. Eugene Rose (the future Fr. Seraphim), "Nihilism: The Root of the Revolution of the Modern Age." http://www.columbia.edu/cu/augustine/arch/nihilism.html.
8. Karel Bartosek, Chapter 20, "Central and Southeast Europe," p. 407.
9. Michael Suozzi, "Comrades on Campus," *The New American*, 6 November 1989.

Chapter 4: Sovereign Americans Are Beginning To Wake Up In Soviet America!

1. William Z. Foster, *Toward Soviet America,* Balboa Island, CA: Elgin Publications, 1961. (Originally published in 1932)
2. Gerald Celente, Founder and Director of The Trends Research Institute, on *Coast to Coast AM* radio program with George Noory, Premiere Radio Networks, 28-29 April 2008.
3. Gerald Celente, 18-19 September 2008. Gerald Celente was referring to the government takeover of businesses, such as Fannie Mae, Freddie Mac, and AIG. He said we used to call such takeovers "Communism."

4. Michael Savage, *The Savage Nation*, Talk Radio Network, 8 September 2006.
5. Drew Zahn, "Alan Keyes Launches 'Liberty' blog, Warns of 'Obama's push to make U.S. Soviet-style state,'" WorldNetDaily.com, 7 March 2009.
6. Michael Reagan, Conservative News Alerts, 20 November 2008.
7. Pat Robertson, *The 700 Club*, CBN News Channel, 22 August 2006.
8. Mark Levin, *The Mark Levin Show*, ABC Radio Networks, 16 February 2009.
9. Mark Levin, *The Mark Levin Show*, 13 August 2008.
10. Conservative News Alerts, 19 February 2009.
11. Dan Caplis, *The O'Reilly Factor*, FOX News Network, 8 November 2007. Dan Caplis is a radio talk show host at 630 KNOW in Denver, CO. Rebecca Boyle, Fort Collins NOW reporter, also appeared on *The O'Reilly Factor*.
12. Floyd and Mary Beth Brown, "MSNBC is in Big Trouble Without Bush to Bash," Townhall.com, 15 February 2009.
13. http://www.thomasbrewton.com/index.php/truth/.
14. Ann Coulter, "The Elephant in the Room," WorldNetDaily.com, 16 January 2008.
15. Ann Coulter made this statement on the Matt Drudge radio program, 22 October 2006.
16. William Z. Foster, *Toward Soviet America,* p. 67.
17. *Hannity*, FOX News Network, 22 January 2009.
18. John Cox, Republican presidential candidate speaking on C-SPAN, *American Perspectives*, 3 March 2007. (On Videotape and DVD, C-SPAN.org/shop)
19. Laura Ingraham, *Laura Ingraham Show*, Talk Radio Network, 16 January 2007.
20. Laura Ingraham, *Laura Ingraham Show*, Talk Radio Network, 27 February 2008. (See Alliance Defense Fund)
21. Billy James Hargis, *Communist America...Must It Be?* Butler, IN: Printed by Higley-Huffman Press, 1960. Distributed by Christian Crusade, Box 977, Tulsa, OK.
22. Glenn Beck, the *Glenn Beck Show*, CNN Headline News, 9 September 2008.
23. Glenn Beck, the *Glenn Beck Show*, interviewing Mike Huckabee, former Arkansas Governor and GOP presidential candidate, CNN Headline News, 19 October 2007.
24. Irvin Baxter of End Times Ministries, on *Coast to Coast AM* talk radio with George Noory, 2 June 2006.
25. Billy James Hargis, *Communist America...Must It Be?* p. 23.

26. Michael Savage, *The Savage Nation*, Talk Radio Network, 21 May 2006.

27. Michael Savage, *The Savage Nation*, Talk Radio Network, 7 April 2007.

28. Rush Limbaugh, "Transcript: Stalinists Have Taken Over the Left," *The Rush Limbaugh Show,* Premiere Radio Networks, 3 October 2007. Transcript available at: http://www.rushlimbaugh.com/home/daily/ Site_100307/content/01125108.guest.html

29. *Hannity & Colmes*, FOX News Network, 9 January 2009.

30. W. Cleon Skousen, *The Naked Communist,* Eleventh Edition, Salt Lake City, UT: The Reviewer, 1962. (First Edition published in 1958. New Edition available at: http://www.skousen2000.com/political%20 products/communist.htm)

31. Mike Trivisonno, WTAM 1100, News Radio in Cleveland, OH, 3 October 2007. Mike Trivisonno was talking about attempts by Democrats to silence Rush Limbaugh by attacking him rather than debating him.

32. Michael Medved, *The Michael Medved Show*, Salem Communications, 19 November 2007.

33. Pastor Ernie Sanders, *WRWL (What's Right, What's Left) Radio Ministries*, 8400 Mayfield Road, Chesterland, OH 44026, 26 June 2006.

34. Alan Caruba, "Democrat Party: The CPUSA in Disguise?" *Canada Free Press*, 22 June 2008. http://canadafreepress.com/index.php/ article/3562.

35. Aaron Klein, "Communist Party strategists map out Obama's agenda," WorldNetDaily.com, 16 November 2008.

36. Tammy Bruce, filling in for Laura Ingraham, *The Laura Ingraham Show*, Talk Radio Network, 9 August 2006.

37. Kevin Trudeau, *More Natural "Cures" Revealed,* Elk Grove Village, IL: Alliance Publishing Group, 2006, p. 58.

38. Mitt Romney, *Kudlow & Company,* Videotape on CNBC, 30 August 2007.

39. David Horowitz, discussing his book, *The Professors*, at Duke University, in Duran, NC.

40. J. Neil Schulman, *Stopping Power: Why 70 Million Americans Own Guns*, Pulpless.com, 1994.

41. Ryan Byrnes, "Forbes Says Card Check Bill Means 'Soviet-Style' Union Elections," CNSNews.com, 8 April 2009.

42. Roger Hedgecock, substitute host on *The Rush Limbaugh Show*, Premiere Radio Networks, 23 June 2005.

43. Devvy Kidd, "Congress' response to Kelo decision: Same old cowardice," WorldNetDaily.com, 8 July 2005.

44. Karl Marx, *The Communist Manifesto*, 1848.

45. William Z. Foster, *Toward Soviet America,* p. 321.

46. William Z. Foster, *Toward Soviet America,* p. 321.

47. Mike Gallagher, radio promotional sound bite for *The Mike Gallagher Show*, Salem Communications, 5 May 2006.

48. Thomas Sowell, *Hannity & Colmes*, FOX News Network, 28 May 2007.

49. Admiral Mike Mullen, in his first public address as Chairman of the Joint Chiefs of Staff, said, "We are part of a New World Order." He was discussing "National Security Challenges" at the Center for a New American Security on C-SPAN, 25 October 2007.

50. Bill Cunningham, *Live On Sunday Night, It's Bill Cunningham*, Premiere Radio Networks, 5 April 2009.

51. In an email exchange Professor Chomsky stated the quote appears to have been generated in a talk or discussion, and therefore he could not be certain it was generated by him. However, he added that it is the type of statement he would make.

52. Judge Andrew P. Napolitano, *The Constitution In Exile: How the Federal Government Has Seized Power by Rewriting the Supreme Law of The Land,* Nashville, TN: Thomas Nelson, 2006, p. 233.

53. Thomas E. Woods, Jr. and Kevin R. C. Gutzman, *Who Killed the Constitution?: The Federal Government vs. American Liberty from World War I to Barack Obama,* NY: Three Rivers Press, 2009.

54. William Z. Foster, *Toward Soviet America*, pp. 135-136.

55. Linda Kimball, "The New Soviet Union: America and the West." 6 March 2007. http://www.alainsnewsletter.com/s/spip.php?article333.

56. Doug Giles, "Note to Church: Pray Dirty Harry Prayers for Our Nation," Townhall.com, 19 July 2009.

Chapter 5: Re-Education In Soviet America!

1. Vladimir Lenin, http://www.brainyquote.com/quotes/authors/v/vladimir_lenin_2.html.

2. William Z. Foster, *Toward Soviet America*, Balboa Island, CA: Elgin Publications, 1961, p. 316. (Originally published in 1932)

3. Thomas Sowell, *Inside American Education: The Decline, The Deception, The Dogmas,* New York: The Free Press, 1993, pp. 42-43.

4. Thomas Sowell, *Inside American Education: The Decline, The Deception, The Dogmas,* p. 367.

5. Thomas Sowell, *Inside American Education: The Decline, The Deception, The Dogmas,* p. 36.

6. *Child Abuse in the Classroom*, Phyllis Schlafly, Editor, Westchester, IL: Crossway Books, 1988, p. 53.

7. William J. Bennett, excerpts from *What Really Ails America*, condensed from a December 7, 1993 speech he delivered at the Heritage Foundation, Washington, D.C., and reprinted in *Reader's Digest*, April, 1994.
8. William Z. Foster, *Toward Soviet America*, p. 317.
9. William Kilpatrick, *Why Johnny Can't Tell Right From Wrong: Moral Illiteracy and the Case for Character Education,* NY: Simon & Schuster, 1992.
10. Jonathan Kozol, *Illiterate America*, NY: Anchor Books, 1985.
11. Testimony before the U.S. Department of Education, cited in *Child Abuse in the Classroom*, Phyllis Schlafly, Editor, Westchester, IL: Crossway Books, 1988, p. 57.
12. Testimony before the U.S. Department of Education, cited in *Child Abuse in the Classroom*, p. 244.
13. *Child Abuse in the Classroom*, p. 99.
14. Linus Wright, "Sex Education: How to Respond," *The World & I*, September 1989, p. 515.
15. W. Cleon Skousen, *The Naked Communist,* Eleventh Edition, Salt Lake City, UT: The Reviewer, 1962, p. 261.
16. Rob Hood, "When Schools Stray from Real Education," The Conservative Voice, 30 August 2007.
17. W. Cleon Skousen, *The Naked Communist*, p. 261.
18. William F. Jasper, "The State of Our Decline: A Postmortem on Public Education," *The New American,* 8 August 1994.
19. William Z. Foster, *Toward Soviet America*, p. 316.
20. William Z. Foster, *Toward Soviet America*, p. 316.
21. The Right Stuff, *The New American*, 8 August 1994.
22. Peter Schweizer, *Do As I Say (Not As I Do): Profiles in Liberal Hypocrisy,* NY: Doubleday, 2005.
23. Ashley Herzog, "Ignorance is no excuse," Townhall.com, 30 March 2009.
24. Michael Suozzi, "Comrades on Campus," *The New American*, 6 November 1989.
25. Lev Navrosov, "Chapter 94 - Communist Leaders Speak Their Minds," American Life League, Ewtn.com. http://www.ewtn.com/library/PROLENC/ENCYC094.HTM.
26. Kevin Mooney, "New Film Exposes Apparent Lack of Academic Freedom in U.S.,"CNSNews.com, 8 October 2007.
27. David Horowitz, *Indoctrination U.: The Left's War Against Academic Freedom,* encounterbooks.com. http://www.encounterbooks.com/books/indoctrinationu/.
28. Glenn Beck, *Glenn Beck,* FOX News Network, 10 March 2009. (An open letter by David Horowitz posted on Townhall Spotlight was also used as an information source.)

29. William Z. Foster, *Toward Soviet America*, pp. 135-136.
30. *A Nation At Risk - April 1983*, Archived Information, http://www.ed.gov/pubs/NatAtRisk/risk.html.
31. W. Cleon Skousen, *The Naked Communist,* 1962, p. 260.
32. Jeff Jacoby, "Big Brother at School," *The Boston Globe,* 17 October 2007. http://www.jeffjacoby.com/348/big-brother-at-school.
33. http://www.brainyquote.com/quotes/authors/a/alexis_de_tocqueville.html.

Chapter 6: The Gospel
According To Mao, Marx, Lenin & Stalin!

1. Anatoly V. Lunarcharsky, Russian Commissar of Education, *U.S. Congressional Record*, Vol. 77, pp. 1539-1540, cited in *The Naked Communist*, Eleventh Edition, by W. Cleon Skousen, Salt Lake City, UT: The Reviewer, 1962, p. 308.
2. Vladimir Lenin, quoted in *Lenin: Selected Works*, cited at: http://www.ewtn.com/library/PROLENC/ENCYC094.HTM.
3. Vladimir Lenin, "Young Communist Truth," October 18, 1947, cited in *The Naked Communist,* p. 307.
4. The Harvard Guide: History, Lore, and More, "The Early History of Harvard University." http://www.hno.harvard.edu/guide/intro/index.html.
5. Yale University, About Yale/History. http://www.yale.edu/about/history.html.
6. The View From 1776, *Truth*. http://www.thomasbrewton.com/index.php/truth/.
7. The View From 1776, *Truth*.
8. Official statement, Radio Leningrad, 27 August 1950, cited in *The Naked Communist*, p. 310.
9. Sol Stern, "ACORN's Nutty Regime for Cities," *City Journal*, Spring 2003. http://www.city-journal.org/html/13_2_acorns_nutty_regime.html.
10. Official Statement, "Young Bolshevik," Number 5-6, 1946, p. 58, cited in *The Naked Communist,* p. 307.
11. Joseph Cardinal Ratzinger, *Liberation Theology*, Christendom-awake.Org. http://www.christendom-awake.org/pages/ratzinger/liberationtheol.html.
12. Vladimir Lenin, *Religion*, p. 14, cited in *The Naked Communist*, p. 310.
13. Stanislav Mishin, "American capitalism gone with a whimper," *Pravda*, 27 April 2009. http://english.pravda.ru/opinion/columnists/107459-0/.
14. Jonah Goldberg, "Don't Call It 'Socialism'!" Townhall.com, 4 June 2009.

15. Joseph Stalin, "The Great Patriotic War of the Soviet Union," Moscow, 1946, p. 55, cited in *The Naked Communist*, p. 308.
16. WorldNetDaily.com, "Obama pastor's theology: Destroy 'the white enemy,'" 17 March 2008.
17. WorldNetDaily.com, "Obama pastor's theology: Destroy 'the white enemy.'"
18. http://www.cincinnatiskeptics.org/blurbs/lincoln-cannots.html.

Chapter 7: Church, State & Religious Liberty In Soviet America!

1. Constitution (Fundamental Law) of the Union of Soviet Socialist Republics. http://www.departments.bucknell.edu/russian/const/77cons02.html#chap07.
2. John W. Whitehead, *The Second American Revolution*, Elgin, IL: David C. Cook Publishing Company, 1982, pp. 99 & 100.
3. John W. Whitehead, *The Second American Revolution*, p. 100.
4. Gaillard Hunt, Editor, *Writings of James Madison*, 9 volumes, NY: G. P. Putnam's Sons, 1900-1910, 5: pp. 176 & 132.
5. Vladimir Lenin, in *Lenin: Selected Works*, cited at: http://www.ewtn.com/library/PROLENC/ENCYC094.HTM.
6. DiscoverTheNetworks.org: A Guide to the Political Left. http://www.discoverthenetworks.org/individualProfile.asp?indid=1579.
7. Devvy Kidd, "ACLU fulfilling Communist agenda," WorldNetDaily.com, 3 December 2004.
8. W. Cleon Skousen, *The Naked Communist,* Eleventh Edition, Salt Lake City, UT: The Reviewer, 1962, p. 261.
9. William Z. Foster, *Toward Soviet America*, Balboa Islands, CA: Elgin Publications, 1961, p. 134. (Originally published in 1932)
10. Anatoly V. Lunarcharsky, Russian Commissar of Education, *U.S. Congressional Record*, Volume 77, pp. 1539-1540, cited in *The Naked Communist*, p. 308.
11. Bob Unruh, "'Hate crimes!' They're ba-ack!" Plan to federalize penalties for 'perceptions' reappears in Congress, WorldNetDaily.com, 15 January 2009. http://www.wnd.com/index.php?fa=PAGE.view&pageId=86215.
12. Robert H. Knight, "'Hate Crime' Laws: An Assault on Freedom," Concerned Women For America, 27 September 2005. http://www.cultureandfamily.org/articledisplay.asp?id=2575&department=CFI&categoryid=papers.

13. J. Edgar Hoover, *J. Edgar Hoover On Communism,* NY: Random House, 1970, p. 106.
14. Robert H. Knight, "'Hate Crime' Laws: An Assault on Freedom."
15. Bob Unruh, "'Hate crimes!' They're ba-ack!"
16. Robert H. Knight, "'Hate Crime' Laws: An Assault on Freedom."
17. Bob Unruh, "'Hate crimes!' They're ba-ack!"
18. Bob Unruh, "'Jail grandma' hate speech debate begins," WorldNetDaily.com, 17 April 2007.
19. Bob Unruh, "'Jail grandma' hate speech debate begins."

Chapter 8: Self-Defense & The Second Amendment In Soviet America!

1. Nicolas Werth, Chapter 4, "The Dirty War," Part I. A State Against Its People: Violence, Repression, and Terror in the Soviet Union. In Stephane Courtois et al., *The Black Book of Communism: Crimes, Terror, Repression,* Cambridge, MA: Harvard University Press, 1999, p. 99.
2. Nicolas Werth, Chapter 4, "The Dirty War," p. 99, citing *Izvestiya TsKPSS*, Number 6 (1989), pp. 177-178.
3. Wayne LaPierre, *Guns, Crime, & Freedom,* Washington, D.C.: Regnery Publishing, 1994.
4. Quote of U.S. Representative Henry A. Waxman from Citizens Committee for the Right to Keep and Bear Arms, email from "Right Versus Left," 12 June 2007.
5. Quotes from Constitutional Commentators, excerpted from *The Right to Arms: Does the Constitution or the Predilection of Judges Reign?* By Robert Dowlut (Copyright © 1983 *Oklahoma Law Review*). http://www.guncite.com/gc2ndcom.html.
6. William Z. Foster, *Toward Soviet America,* Balboa Islands, CA: Elgin Publications, 1961. (Originally published in 1932)
7. Congressmen Earl Landgrebe, *The New American*, Fall/Winter, 1994.
8. Accuracy In Media, *What Liberals Say*. http://www.aim.org/wls/category/gun-control. (Aim.org cites two sources: "Views on One World Government by Leading World Figures," *The Oil Patch,* May 2001, pp. 2-3, and *The American Sentinel,* March 1998, p. 11.)
9. Aaron Zelman, *American Survival Guide*, November 1990.
10. William Z. Foster, *Toward Soviet America.*
11. Edmund Fuller, Editor, *4800 Wisecracks, Witty Remarks, And Epigrams For All Occasions,* NY: Avenel Books, 1980, p. 179.

12. James Bovard, "The Assault-Weapons Scam, Part 2," The Future of Freedom Foundation, April 1996. http://www.fff.org/freedom/0496d.asp.
13. John Gizzi, "Races of the week: Wolfe vs. Rockefeller," *Human Events,* 19 August 2002. http://findarticles.com/p/articles/mi_qa3827/ is_200208/ai_n9096972/.
14. Citizens Committee for the Right to Keep and Bear Arms, email from "Right Versus Left," 12 June 2007.
15. Citizens Committee for the Right to Keep and Bear Arms.
16. Citizens Committee for the Right to Keep and Bear Arms.
17. Jim Kouri, "Gun Control Hypocrites: Senators Schumer and Feinstein Pack Heat," *The National Ledger,* 24 September 2005. http://www.nationalledger.com.
18. "Gun Report," *The New American,* 21 March 1994.
19. "The Sullivan Act," Gun Law News. http://www.gunlawnews.org/sullivan.html.
20. Charley Reese, "The problems with gun control," *Conservative Chronicle,* 13 April 1994.
21. William F. Jasper, "The Rise of Citizen Militias," *The New American,* 6 February 1995.
22. Stephen P. Holbrook, *That Every Man Be Armed: The Evolution of a Constitutional Right,* Washington, D.C.: The Independent Institute, 1984.
23. Joyce Lee Malcolm, *To Keep and Bear Arms: The Origins of an Anglo-American Right,* Cambridge, MA: Harvard University Press, 1994.
24. J. Neil Schulman, *Stopping Power: Why 70 Million Americans Own Guns,* Pulpless.com, 1994.
25. Robert W. Lee, "Gun Control Would Not Reduce Crime," In *Gun Control (Current Controversies),* Charles P. Cozic, Editor, San Diego, CA: Greenhaven Press, 1992.
26. Wayne LaPierre, *Guns, Crime, & Freedom.*
27. William Z. Foster, *Toward Soviet America.*
28. Thomas Sowell, *Inside American Education: The Decline, The Deception, The Dogmas,* New York: The Free Press, 1993.
29. *Child Abuse in the Classroom*, Phyllis Schlafly, Editor, Westchester, IL: Crossway Books, 1988, p. 351.
30. *Child Abuse in the Classroom*, p. 44.
31. Thomas Sowell, *The Gun Owners* [of America] newsletter, 29 October 1999.
32. John R. Lott, Jr., *More Guns, Less Crime: Understanding Crime and Gun Control Laws,* Chicago, IL: The University of Chicago Press, 1998.

33. John R. Lott, Jr. and William Landes, *Multiple Victim Public Shootings, Bombings and Right-to-Carry Concealed Handgun Laws,* working paper, April 1999.
34. Alec Wilkinson, *The New Yorker,* January 1994.
35. R. J. Rummel, *Death By Government,* New Brunswick, NJ: Transaction Publishers, 1994.
36. Howard Zinn, *A People's History of the United States,* NY: HarperCollins Publishers, 1980.
37. Most figures obtained from R. J. Rummel, Professor Emeritus of Political Science, University of Hawaii, "20th Century Democide." http://www.hawaii.edu/powerkills/20TH.HTM.
38. Jeff Snyder, *Nation of Cowards: Essays on the Ethics of Gun Control,* St. Louis, MO: Accurate Press, 2001.

Chapter 9: The Abortion Holocaust: From Russia – Without Love!

1. Morris Faulkner, "Mother Teresa's Speech on Abortion 'Blacked Out,'" *The Prescott Daily Courier*, 12 July 1995.
2. David C. Reardon, "Legal Abortion Has Not Improved Women's Health," In *Abortion: Opposing Viewpoints*, by David L. Bender, San Diego, CA: Greenhaven Press, 1991.
3. Frederic V. Grunfeld, *The Hitler File: A Social History of Germany and the Nazis - 1918 - 45,* NY: Random House, 1980.
4. Pastor Ernie Sanders, *WRWL (What's Right, What's Left) Radio Ministries*, 8400 Mayfield Road, Chesterland, OH 44026, 26 June 2006.
5. La Verne Tolbert, "Inside the Soul of Planned Parenthood," *Destiny Magazine*, August 1994.
6. *Nuremberg Military Tribunals*, IV: 1081-84. Nuremberg: NO-3512. http://cpforlife.org/abortion_map_of_us.htm.
7. John Hunt, Ph.D., "Abortion and Eugenics Policies In Nazi Germany," *Association for Interdisciplinary Research in Values and Social Change*, Volume 16, Number 1, 2001. Reprinted by LifeIssues.Net. http://www.lifeissues.net/writers/air/air_vol16no1_2001.html.
8. John Hunt, "Abortion and the Nuremberg Prosecutors: A Deeper Analysis," University Faculty for Life. http://www.uffl.org/vol%207/hunt7.pdf.
9. U.S. Representative Mike Pence, "Deny federal funding to Planned Parenthood," The Hill's Congress Blog, 22 July 2009. http://blog.thehill.com/2009/07/22/deny-federal-funding-to-planned-parenthood-rep-mike-pence/.

10. Karl Marx, *The Communist Manifesto*, 1848.
11. Bumper sticker observed by a representative of Arizona Right to Life. Reported on the TV program *On Target* with Thom Strawn, on KUSK TV, Prescott, AZ. 1 January 1995.
12. U.S. Representative Mike Pence, "Deny federal funding to Planned Parenthood," The Hill's Congress Blog, 22 July 2009.
13. Roger Highfield, "Babies may feel pain of abortion," *The Electronic Telegraph,* 29 August 2000.
    http://www.sweetliberty.org/issues/hate/babies.htm.
14. Jennifer A. Dlouh, "High court to revisit capital punishment," *The Washington Times*, 6 January 2008. Hearst Newspapers.
    http://www.washingtontimes.com/article/20080106/NATION/191486418.
15. "Pain of the Unborn: What does an unborn child feel during an abortion?" National Right to Life Educational Trust Fund, Washington, D.C., 20004.
    http://www.nrlc.org/abortion/Fetal_Pain/FetalPain091604.pdf.
16. Paul Ranalli, M.D., "Abortion and the Unborn Baby: The Painful Truth," California Pro-Life Council, 2306 J Street, Ste 200, Sacramento, CA 95816. http://www.californiaprolife.org/resources/abortion_information/abortion_and_the_unborn_baby.
17. A Woman's Right to Know, Addendum.
    http://www.awomansrighttoknowok.org/addendum_pain.html.
18. Unborn Child Pain Awareness Act of 2006, introduced in House as H.R. 6099.
    http://www.congress.gov/cgi-bin/query/z?c109:H.R.6099.
19. Amelia Wigton, "Sam Brownback Reintroduces the Unborn Child Pain Awareness Act," 31 January 2007, Concerned Women for America.
    http://www.cwalac.org/article_456.shtml.
20. Ronald Reagan, *Abortion and the Conscience of the Nation*, Nashville, TN: Thomas Nelson, 1984.
21. Roger Highfield, "Babies may feel pain of abortion," *The Electronic Telegraph,* 29 August 2000.
    http://www.sweetliberty.org/issues/hate/babies.htm.
22. National Right to Life Educational Trust Fund. Washington, D.C.
    http://www.nrlc.org/abortion/Fetal_Pain/FetalPain091604.pdf.
23. Vonda Pelto, Ph.D., guest on *Coast to Coast AM* with George Noory, Premiere Radio Networks, 23-24 March 2009.
    http://www.vondapelto.com/.

24. Nancyjo Mann, Founder of Women Exploited By Abortion (WEBA), In *Aborted Women: Silent No More*, by David C. Reardon, Westchester, IL: Crossway Books, 1987. Additional testimony by Nancyjo Mann reprinted and available at: http://www.physiciansforlife.org/content/view/1139/26/.

25. Andrea Lafferty, "Kansas Planned Parenthood Clinic Charged Over Illegal Late-Term Abortions," Traditional Values Coalition, 29 October 2007. http://traditionalvalues.org/.

26. Andrea Lafferty.

27. Andrea Lafferty.

28. Katie Short, *Games Abortionists Play*, News Letter, Life Legal Defense Foundation, Dana Cody, Editor, Spring 2007. Available at: http://www.lldf.org/.

29. Katie Short, *Games Abortionists Play.*

30. John-Henry Westen, "Former Soviet Union Countries Commemorate Fifty Years of Abortion." http://www.lifesite.net/ldn/2005/nov/05112407.html.

31. Susan Walk, *The 700 Club,* CBN News Channel, 29 August 1995.

32. Ronald Reagan, *Abortion and the Conscience of the Nation*, Nashville, TN: Thomas Nelson, 1984.

33. Morris Faulkner, "Mother Teresa's Speech on Abortion 'Blacked Out,'" *The Prescott Daily Courier*, 12 July 1995.

34. David C, Reardon, "The Abortion/Suicide Connection," *Elliot Institute*. http://www.abortionfacts.com/reardon/abortion_and_suicide.asp. (Originally published in *The Post-Abortion Review*, 1 (2) Summer, 1993.)

35. "Women's Suicide Rates Highest After Abortion, New Study." http://www.abortionrecoverycounseling.com/Page8.html.

36. "Women's Suicide Rates Highest After Abortion, New Study."

37. *Fact Sheet,* Courtesy of the Elliot Institute, PO Box 73478 Springfield, IL 62791-7348. http://www.abortionfacts.com/reardon/post_Abortion_syndrome_character.asp.

38. Penny Starr, "Pro-Life Students Videotape Abortion Provider Boasting of Lies," CNSNews.com, 21 January 2008. (Joanie Barrett is a founding member of Students for Life of America at Wayne State University in Detroit, MI)

39. Michael Stone, M.D., *Most Evil*, Investigation Discovery, the Discovery Channel, 28 February 2009.

40. "Russian Abortion Killing and Sterilizing Millions: Demographic Collapse Likely to be Worse than Previously Predicted," LifeSiteNews.com, 12 April 2005. http://www.lifesite.net/ldn/2005/apr/05041209.html.

41. C. Everett Koop, M.D., and Francis A. Schaeffer, *Whatever Happened to the Human Race,* Revised Edition, Westchester, IL: Crossway Books, 1983.
42. David Gersten, M.D., "The Modern Oath of Hippocrates." http://www.imagerynet.com/hippo.ama.html.
43. Nancyjo Mann, Founder of Women Exploited By Abortion (WEBA), In *Aborted Women: Silent No More.*
44. L. Brent Bozell III and Brent H. Baker, Editors, *And That's The Way It Isn't: A Reference Guide to Media Bias.* Alexandria, VA: Media Research Center, 1990.
45. *Genocide Awareness Project.* http://www.abortionno.org/Resources/abortion.html.
46. Michael Savage, *The Savage Nation*, Talk Radio Network, 5 June 2007.
47. Robert H. Bork, *Slouching Towards Gomorrah: Modern Liberalism And American Decline,* NY: Reganbooks/HarperCollins Publishers, 1997.
48. Joseph A. D'Agostino, "The Conscience Protection Amendment and NARAL's "D" Rating of the U.S.," *PRI Weekly Briefing*, LifeSite Special Report, 24 November 2004. http://www.lifesite.net/1dn/2004/nov/041124a.html.

Chapter 10: Health Care Perestroika In Soviet America!

1. William Z. Foster, *Toward Soviet America,* Balboa Island, CA: Elgin Publications, 1961, p. 318. (Originally published in 1932)
2. John Gizzi, "Races of the week: Wolfe vs. Rockefeller," *Human Events,* 19 August 2002. http://findarticles.com/p/articles/mi_qa3827/is_200208/ai_9096972/.
3. Mark G. Field, *Russian History Encyclopedia: Soviet Health Care Services,* Answers.com. http://www.answers.com/topic/soviet-health-care-services.
4. Diane Rowland and Alexandre V. Telyukov, "Soviet Health Care from Two Perspectives,"HealthAffairs.com, Fall 1991. http://content.healthaffairs.org/cgi/reprint/10/3/71.pdf.
5. Oliver North, "Return of the Bear," Townhall.com, 17 August 2007.
6. Daniel S. Schultz, M.D., and Michael P. Rafferty, M.D., "Soviet Health Care and Perestroika," *American Journal of Public Health*, February 1990; Volume 80 (2), pp. 193-197. http://www.pubmedcentral.nih.gov/pagerrender.fcgi?artid=1404625&pageindex=1.
7. Matt Cover, "Congressmen Who Vote for Government-Run Health Care Agency Should Be Its First Customers, Legislation Says," CNSNews.com, 9 July 2009.

8. Thomas Sowell, "Care Versus Control," Townhall.com, 4 August 2009.

9. John Stossel, "Sick Sob Stories," *The Wall Street Journal*, 13 September 2007, p. A16.

10. Walter E. Williams, "Sweden's Government Health Care," TownHall.com, 4 March 2009.

11. Senator Tom Coburn, *Sequoyah County Times, 23 August 2007.*

12. Glenn Beck, "The One Thing: America's health care is better than Europe's," *Glenn Beck,* FOX News Network, 16 July 2009. http://www.foxnews.com/glennbeck/.

13. John Stossel, "Sick Sob Stories," *The Wall Street Journal*, 13 September 2007, p. A16.

14. http://www.breitbart.tv/obama-its-the-post-office-thats-always Having-problems/.

15. Phyllis Schlafly, "A New Argument Against Immigration," WorldNetDaily.com, 23 May 2008.

16. Rush Limbaugh, "The Real Reason Hospitals Close," *The Rush Limbaugh Show,* Premier Radio Networks, 24 September 2007. http://www.rushlimbaugh.com/home/today.guest.html.

17. Daniel Costello and Susannah Rosenblatt, "Financial Woes Jeopardize Area Hospitals," *Los Angeles Times*, 23 September 2007.

18. Sean Hannity, "The Price We Pay," Parts 3 and 6, *Hannity,* FOX News Network, http://www.foxnews.com/hannityandcolmes/. (Videos were available at the FOX News website on 24 March 2008)

19. Pamela Hughes/KTAR, "Money for Illegals' Care Runs Out" 17 March 2008. http://www.ktar.com/?nid=6&sid=765971.

20. President Ronald Reagan, The President's Inaugural Address, 20 January 1981.

21. William Campbell Douglass II, M.D., "8 ways illegal immigrants are making you sick." http://www.douglassreport.com/reports/immigration.html.

22. Joseph Farah, "Time for Debate on Health Care," WorldNetDaily.com, Exclusive Commentary, 1 March 2008.

23. J. R. Dieckmann, "Fixing the Healthcare Problem," *Great American Journal,* 14 October 2007. http://www.greatamericanjournal.com/editor/archives/FoxingtheHealthcareproblem.html.

24. Carol Plato, Representing Martin Memorial Medical Center, speaking before the Florida House Committee on State Affairs, April 2007. http://www.youtube.com/watch?v=bLJxmJZXgNI.

25. Kaitlynn Riely, "Medicaid, Medicare Made $23 Billion in Improper Payments," CNSNews.com, 30 June 2008.

26. David Limbaugh, "More Health Care Lies," TownHall.com, 21 July 2009.

27. Greta Van Susteren, *On The Record*, FOX News Network, 21 July 2009.

28. David Limbaugh, "More Health Care Lies."

29. Sean Hannity, *Hannity,* FOX News Network, 28 July 2009.

30. Brent Baker, "Nets Advance Taxing Big Soda to Pay for ObamaCare," Media Research   Center, 27 July 2009. http://www.mrc.org/biasalert/2009/20090728125511.aspx.

31. Christopher Neefus, "New York Times Poll Showing 72% Support for Obama's Health Care Plan Was Stacked With Obama Supporters," CNSNews.com, 24 June 2009.

32. Dr. David Gratzer, "The Ugly Truth About Canadian Health Care," City-Journal.org.

33. Dr. Len Horowitz, http://www.drlenhorowitz.com/.

34. George Noory, *Coast to Coast AM,* Past Shows, 11 March 2008.

35. Autistic Society, http://www.autisticsociety.org/News/article/sid=437.html.

36. John Hanchette, "Precipitous Increase in Autism Cases May be Tied To Childhood Vaccines," *Niagara Falls Reporter*, 24 February 2004. http://www.niagarafallsreporter.com/hanchette103.html.

37. Dr. David Gratzer, "The Ugly Truth About Canadian Health Care."

38. Robert F. Kennedy, Jr., "Deadly Immunity," RollingStone.com, 20 June 2005.

39. Dr. Joseph Mercola, "Dr. Mercola's Comments," Mercola.com. http://articles.mercola.com/sites/articles/archive/2009/07/18/Robert-F-Kennedy-Jr-Explains-the-Autism-Coverup.aspx. (At this web site the reader will find a link to the YouTube.com video titled by Dr. Mercola as, "Robert F. Kennedy Explains the Autism Cover-up.")

40. Conservative News Alerts, 19 June 2009. (According to Conservative News Alerts this statement was made by a French journalist at the Heritage Foundation, and was forwarded to Conservative News Alerts by GrassTopsUSA.)

41. John Velleco, "GOA backs Burr Bill to Protect Veterans," *The Gun Owners* [of America] newsletter, Volume XXVIX, Number 3, 27 July 2009.

42. Bob Unruh, "Life With Big Brother: Economic stimulus? Feds want your medical records," WorldNetDaily.com, 27 January 2009.

43. Austin Hill, "Democrats, Health Care 'Reform,' And Your 'Duty To Die,'" Townhall.com, 15 February 2009.

44. J. R. Dieckmann, "Fixing the Healthcare Problem."

45. Charles Krauthammer, "Health Care Reform: A Better Plan," Townhall.com, 7 August 2009.

46. Ann Coulter, "Liberal Lies About National Health Care: First in a Series," Townhall.com, 19 August 2009.

47. Penny Starr, "Physician Disputes Obama's Claim of 46 Million Uninsured Americans," CNSNews.com, 24 June 2009.

48. J. R. Dieckmann, "Fixing the Healthcare Problem."

Chapter 11: The Soviet-Bloc Media!

1. Joseph Stalin, *"Leninism,"* Volume I, p. 404. In W. Cleon Skousen, *The Naked Communist,* Eleventh Edition, Salt Lake City, UT: The Reviewer, 1962, p. 313.
2. Mark Lloyd, *Prologue to a Farce: Communication and Democracy in America (History of Communication)*, Champaign, IL: University of Illinois Press, 2006. Cited by Seton Motley, Newsbuster.org/blogs, 28 August 2009.
3. W. Cleon Skousen, *The Naked Communist*, Eleventh Edition, Salt Lake City, UT: The Reviewer, 1962, p. 210.
4. Newt Gingrich interviewed by Greta Van Susteren, *On The Record,* FOX News Network, 22 October 2008. http://gretawire.foxnews.com.
5. Glenn Beck, *The Glenn Beck Program,* Premiere Radio Networks, 24 February 2009. Glenn Beck was discussing the unfair treatment Alaskan Governor Sarah n received from the news media during the 2008 presidential campaign. His guest was John Ziegler, the producer of the documentary "Media Malpractice." The subtitle is: "How Obama Got Elected and Palin Was Targeted." Numerous video clips from the documentary are available for viewing at http://www.HowObamaGotElected.com.
6. Ronald Radosh, *Commies: A Journey Through the Old Left, the New Left and the Leftover Left,* San Francisco, CA: Encounter Books, 2001, p. 170.
7. Greta Van Susteren, *On the Record*, FOX News Network, 10 November 2008.
8. Augusta Chronicle Staff, "Presence of malice: Media poison our politics," AugustaChronicle.com, 26 October 2008.
9. Media Research Center, "Scant Media Attention for a Litany of Gaffes by Barack Obama," CyberAlerts, 28 May 2008. http://www.mrc.org/cyberalerts/2008/cyb20080528.asp#3.
10. Patrick J. Buchanan was interviewed by Raymond Arroyo, host of *The World Over*, EWTNews, 9 November 2008.
11. "Study shows McCain media coverage negative," FOX News Network, 22 October 2008. http://elections.foxnews.com/2008/10/22/Study-shows-mccain-media-coverage-negative/.

12. Barbara West (WFTV, Orlando, FL) Joe Biden Interview, 23 October 2008. "Real Reporter Asks Real Questions - Obama Campaign Angry." http://video.google.com/videosearch?hl=en&q=Barbara+West&um =1&ie=UTF-8&sa=X&oi=video_result_group&resnum=7&ct=title#.
13. Andrey Vyshinsky, *Law of the Soviet State,* NY: MacMillan Company, 1948, p. 617. Cited in *The Naked Communist*, p. 312.
14. L. Brent Bozell III and Brent H. Baker, Editors, *And That's The Way It Isn't: A Reference Guide To Media Bias*, Alexandria, VA: Media Research Center, 1990. Contact information: http://www.mediaresearch.org/, Media Research Center, 325 S. Patrick Street, Alexandria, VA 22314.
15. Billy James Hargis, *Communist America...Must It Be?* Butler, IN: Printed by Higley-Huffman Press, 1960, p. 25. Distributed by Christian Crusade, Box 977, Tulsa, OK.

Chapter 12: Marxist Class Warfare & The Black Proletariat!

1. J. Edgar Hoover, *Masters of Deceit,* NY: Pocket Books, 1968, p. 229.
2. Media Research Center, *The Best Notable Quotables for 1991: The Linda Ellerbee Awards for Distinguished Reporting,* Borking Award (For Character Assassination), Quoting Carl Rowan, on *Inside Washington*, 7 July 1991. http://www.mediaresearch.org/ notablequotables/bestof/1991/best1012.asp.
3. Richard Wright, *The God That Failed,* Richard Crossman, Editor, NY: Bantam Books, 1952, p. 135.
4. William Z. Foster, *Toward Soviet America*, Balboa Island, CA: Elgin Publications, 1961, p. 225. (Originally published in 1932)
5. Erich Fromm, *Escape from Freedom,* NY: Farrar & Rinehart, 1941.
6. Karl Marx, *The Communist Manifesto*, 1848.
7. The Reverend Jesse Jackson, guest on *FOX & Friends Weekend,* FOX News Network, 6 July 2008.
8. William Z. Foster, *Toward Soviet America*, p. 134.
9. *The View*, ABC, 17 July 2008.
10. Peter Schweizer, *Do As I Say (Not As I DO): Profiles in Liberal Hypocrisy.* NY: Doubleday, 2005.
11. *Time* magazine, "Foreign News: We Will Bury You," 26 November 1956.
12. Nikita Khrushchev, Speech in Yugoslavia, 24 August 1963. Available at: http://www.quotationspage.com/quote/33389.html.
13. William Z. Foster, *Toward Soviet America*, p. 70.

14. "NAACP buries the N-word in Detroit, Michigan."
    http://www.foxnews.com/story/0,2933,288649,00.html.

15. David Edwards & Josh Catone, "CNN: Texans have funeral to 'bury the N-word' in graveyard," 8 July 2007. http://rawstory/com/news/2007/ CNN_Texans_gather_to_buty_Nwoed_0708.html.

16. Jeremy P. Meyer, "Students bury N-word in Denver, Colorado," *The Denver Post*, 11 October 2007.
    http://www.denverpost.com/news/ci_7142407.

17. Nicholas Stix, " Keepin' It Red," NicholasStixUncensored.Blogspot.com, 16 November 2007.

18. Walter E. Williams, "Media conceal black interracial crimes," WorldNetDaily.com, 26 December 2007.

19. William Z. Foster, *Toward Soviet America*, p. 225.

20. William Z. Foster, *Toward Soviet America*, p. 70.

21. William Z. Foster, *Toward Soviet America*, p. 130.

22. William Z. Foster, *Toward Soviet America*, pp. 92 & 137.

23. William Z. Foster, *Toward Soviet America*, pp. 92 & 225.

24. Reverend Jesse Lee Peterson speaking to Bill Cunningham on, *Live On Sunday Night, It's Bill Cunningham*, Premiere Radio Networks, 26 July 2009.

25. Kevin Roeten, "Media Stoking the Fires of Racism - Part I," TheConservativeVoice.com, 18 November 2007.

26. Patrick J. Buchanan, "The Color of Crime," TheConservativeVoice.com, 21 August 2007.

27. *The Color of Crime: Race, Crime and Justice in America,* (Second, Expanded Edition), Oakton, VA: New Century Foundation, 2005.
    http://www.colorofcrime.com/.
    (*The Color of Crime* is available online as a free PDF download at:
    http://www.colorofcrime.com/colorofcrime2005.pdf).

28. Larry Elder, *The Ten Things You Can't Say In America*, NY: St. Martin's Press, 2000. Larry Elder's web site:
    http://www.larryelder.com/home.html.

29. YouTube conversation between Larry Elder and Travis Smiley available at: http://www.youtube.com/watch?v=QVLjIJUCiAs.
    Larry Elder also authored the book, *What's Race Got To Do With It?* The book is subtitled: Why race-baiters and hacks who call themselves "black leaders" - and their white allies - are the worst enemies of black Americans.

30. Morris Faulkner, "Mother Teresa's Speech on Abortion 'Blacked Out.'" *The Prescott Daily Courier*, 12 July 1995.

31. Vladimir Lenin, What Is To Be Done? "The Plan For an All-Russia Political Newspaper," 1901.
http://www.mrxists.org/archive/lenin/quotes.htm.
32. Patrick J. Buchanan, "The Jena Six - And Other Scams,"
33. Roger Hedgecock, "Drenched in blood of slavery," WorldNetDaily.com Exclusive Commentary, 21 June 2009.
34. George Orwell, *Nineteen Eighty-Four,* Commemorative Edition, NY: The New American Library, 1984. (Authorized reprint of 1949 hardcover edition published by Harcourt Brace Jovanovich).
35. Aaron Zelman and Richard Stevens, *Gun Control Is Racist!* Second Edition, Hartford, WI: Jews For The Preservation of Firearms Ownership (JPFO), 1998.
36. Bill O'Reilly, Talking Points titled "Evil White Men," *The O'Reilly Factor*, FOX News Network, 15 July 2009.
37. WorldNetDaily.com, "Ginsburg: I thought Roe was to rid undesirables," 8 July 2009.
38. Josiah Ryan, "Planned Parenthood Has 'Racist Agenda,' MLK's Niece Says," CNSNews.com, 17 April 2008.
39. Kevin Roeten, "The Race Card in an Unexpected Place," The Conservative Voice, 9 September 2007. (Kevin Roeten stated the King quote came from Steven Ertelt of *LifeNews.*)
40. Kevin Roeten, "The Race Card in an Unexpected Place."
41. Randy Hall, "NAACP Urged to help De-Fund Planned Parenthood," CNSNews.com, 17 July 2008.
http://www.cnsnews.com/public/content/article.aspx?RsrcID=32513.
42. Josiah Ryan, "Planned Parenthood Has 'Racist Agenda,' MLK's Niece Says."
43. R. M. Whitney, *Reds in America*, Boston, MA: Western Islands Publishers, 1970, p. 21. (Originally published in 1924; Copyright 1924 by Beckwith Press).
44. J. Edgar Hoover, *Masters of Deceit*, NY: Pocket Books, 1968, p. 99. (Henry Holt Edition published in 1958)
45. Margaret Thatcher quote available at:
http://www.quotesby.net/Margaret-Thatcher.

Chapter 13: Soviet Americans Love Soviet Cubans!

1. Pascal Fontaine, Chapter 25, "Communism in Latin America," Part V. The Third World. In Stephane Courtois et al., *The Black Book of Communism: Crimes, Terror, Repression*, Cambridge, MA: Harvard University Press, 1999, p. 648.

2. Pascal Fontaine, p. 656.

3. Pascal Fontaine, p. 650.

4. Pascal Fontaine, p. 659.

5. Pascal Fontaine, p. 663.

6. Humberto Fontova, "Castro, Not Pinochet, Is the Real Villain," HumanEvents.com, 21 December 2006.

7. Pascal Fontaine, p. 664.

8. Humberto Fontova.

9. *Special Report with Brit Hume,* Steve Harrigan reporting, FOX News Network, 28 July 2008.

10. Phil Brennan, "Fidel Castro: Hollywood's Favorite Tyrant," NewsMax.com, 29 March 2005.

11. Ronald Radosh, *Commies: A Journey Through the Old Left, the New Left and the Leftover Left,* San Francisco, CA: Encounter Books, 2001, p. 127.

12. Ryan Balis, "'Sicko' Presents False View of Cuba's Health System," The National Center for Public Policy Research, National Policy Analysis, #557, Nationalcenter.org, July 2007.

13. Miami Herald Staff Report, "A Barrier for Cuba's blacks: New attitudes on once-taboo race questions emerge with a fledgling black movement," MiamiHerald.com, 20 June 2007.

14. Freedom House Press Release, "Jailed Cuban Dissident Receives Highest Civil Award," 5 November 2007. http://www.freedomhouse. org/template.cfm?page=70&release=581.

15. Mimi Li, "Al Sharpton to Cuba: Free Afro-Cuban Prisoners," *The Epoch Times,* 22 July 2008. http://en.epochtimes.com/n2/united-states/al-sharpton-to-cuba-free-afro-cuban-prisoners-1540.html.

16. Josiah Ryan, "GOP Lawmakers Criticize Black Caucus Members' Praise of Cuba's Communist Regime," CNSNews.com, 10 April 2009.

17. Josiah Ryan.

18. Michelle Malkin, "CBC: Congressional Bootlickers for Castro," Townhall.com, 10 April 2009.

19. Media Research Center (MRC). http://www.mrc.org/SpecialReports/2007/castro/welcome.asp.

20. J. Edgar Hoover, *J. Edgar Hoover On Communism*, NY: Random House, 1970, pp. 67-68.

Chapter 14: The Global Warming Hoax: A UN Steppingstone Toward Soviet America & Soviet-Style Global Government!

1. Tim Ball, "Global Warming: The Cold, Hard Facts? CanadaFreePress.com, 5 February 2007.
2. U.S. Senate Minority Report: More Than 650 International Scientists Dissent Over Man-Made Global Warming Claims. Scientists Continue to Debunk "Consensus" in 2008. U.S. Senate, 11 December 2008. http://www.heartland.org/policybot/results.html?articleid=24313. http://epw.senate.gov/public/index.cfm?FuseAction=Minority. Blogs&ContentRecord=id2674e64f-802a-23ad-490b-bd9faf4dcdb7.
3. Alan Caruba, "The Demise of the Global Warming Hoax," TheConservativeVoice.com, 2 September 2007.
4. U.S. Senate Minority Report:
5. U.S. Senate Minority Report:
6. U.S. Senate Minority Report:
7. U.S. Senate Minority Report:
8. Center for the Defense of Free Enterprise, online advertisement for the book, *Energy Keepers Energy Killers: The New Civil Rights Battle*, by Roy Innis, Alan Gottlieb, Sean Hannity, and Paul Driessen, Conservative Action Alerts, 23 January 2009.
9. Christopher Monckton of Brenchley, "35 Inconvenient Truths: The Errors in Al Gore's Movie," ScienceAndPublicPolicy.org, 18 October 2007.
10. Bob Unruh, "Heat of the moment: Hundreds of scientists reject global warming," WorldNetDaily.com, 21 December 2007.
11. Mona Charen, "Of Polar Bears and Consensus," TheConservativeVoice.com, 12 October 2007.
12. Dennis T. Avery, "Canadian Climatologist Says Sun Causing Global Warming," Hudson Institute, 7 July 2007. http://www.canadafreepress.com/2007/avery070707.htm.
13. Dr. Robert M. Carter, "Public Misperceptions of Human-Caused Climate Change: The Role of the Media," Committee on Environment and Public Works, United States Senate, 6 December 2006. http://epw.senate.gov/109th/Carter_Testimnoy.pdf.
14. David Evans, "No smoking hot spot," *The Australian*, 18 July 2008. http://www.theaustralian.news.com.au/story/0,,24036736-17803,00.html.
15. Dennis T. Avery, "Canadian Climatologist Says Sun Causing Global Warming," Hudson Institute, 7 July 2007. http://www.canadafreepress.com/2007/avery070707.htm.

16. Monisha Bansal, "Sun, Not Man, Main Cause of Climate Change, New Study Says," CNSNews.com, 11 December 2007.
17. Tom Harris, "Scientists respond to Gore's warnings of climate catastrophe: 'The Inconvenient Truth' is indeed inconvenient to alarmists," CanadaFreePress.com, 12 June 2006.
18. Dr. Robert M. Carter, "Public Misperceptions of Human-Caused Climate Change: The Role of the Media."
19. Alan Caruba, "The Demise of the Global Warming Hoax."
20. Dr. Robert M. Carter, "Public Misperceptions of Human-Caused Climate Change: The Role of the Media."
21. Dudley J. Hughes, "Carbon Dioxide Levels Are a Blessing, Not a Problem," *Environment & Climate News,* The Heartland Institute, May 2007.
    http://www.heartland.org/policybot/results.html?articleid=20952.
22. Dudley J. Hughes, "Carbon Dioxide Levels Are a Blessing, Not a Problem."
23. "What Liberals Say," Aim.org.
    http://www.aim.org/wls/author/jaques-cousteau/.
24. James Bone, "UN peacekeeper killed in Haiti riots over food prices," *The Times*, 14 April 2008. http://www.timesonline.co.uk/tol/news/world/us_and_americas/article3740174.ece.
25. Bethany Stotts, "Inconvenient Truths and Global Crisis," CampusReportOnLine.com, 5 May 2008.
26. Bethany Stotts, "Warm and Fuzzy Global Regulation," Aim.org, 4 June 2008.
27. Lorne Gunter, "Bright sun, warm Earth. Coincidence?" Breaking: Warming On Jupiter, Mars, Pluto, Neptune's Moon & Earth Linked to Increased Solar Activity, Scientists Say. *National Post*, 13 March 2007. http://www.canadafreepress.com/2007/global-warming031307.htm.
28. Lorne Gunter, "Bright sun, warm Earth. Coincidence?"
29. U.S. Senate Minority Report:
30. David Evans, "No smoking hot spot," *The Australian*, 18 July 2008. http://www.theaustralian.news.com.au/story/0,,24036736-17803,00.html.
31. Alan Caruba, "Calm Sun, Cold Earth," TheConservativeVoice.com, 20 February 2008.
32. Steve McIntyre, "Southern Hemisphere Sea Ice Reaches 'Unprecedented' Levels," 4 May 2008. http://www.climateaudit.org/?p=3066.
33. "Cold Chills Global Warming Expedition," Newsmax.com, 12 March 2007.
34. Eric Berger, Jennifer Latson, and Jennifer Leahy, "Surprise flurries warm Houston Hearts," *Houston Chronicle*, 10 December 2008. http://www.chron.com/disp/story.mpl/metropolitan/6156862.html.

35. "Rare snow hits New Orleans," *Associated Press*, 11 December 2008. http://www.rockymountainnews.com/news/2008/dec/11/rare-snow-hits-new-orleans/?partner=RSS.

36. Paul Purpura, "Marinello murder trial stalled because snow affects witnesses travel," *The Times-Picayune*, 11 December 2008. http://www.nola.com/news/index.ssf/2008/12/marinello_murder_trial_stalled.

37. Robert W. Felix, *Not By Fire But By Ice: Discover What Killed The Dinosaurs...and Why It Could Kill Us,* Bellevue, WA: Sugarhouse Publishing, 1999.

38. U.S. Senate Minority Report:

39. IPCC, 2007: Summary for Policymakers, In *Climate Change 2007: The Physical Science Basis.* Contribution of Working Group 1 to the Fourth Assessment Report of the Intergovernmental Panel on Climate Change [Solomon, S., D. Qin, M. Manning, Z. Chen, M. Marquis, K. B. Averyt, M. Tignor and H. L. Miller (Editors.)]. Cambridge University Press, Cambridge, United Kingdom and New York, NY, USA.

40. U.S. Senate Minority Report:

41. S. Fred Singer, Editor, "Nature, Not Human Activity, Rules the Climate: Summary for Policymakers of the Report of the Nongovernmental International Panel on Climate Change," Chicago, IL: The Heartland Institute, 2008. http://www.heartland.org/custom/semod_policybot/pdf/22835.pdf.

42. Bob Unruh, "Heat of the moment: 31,000 scientists reject global warming agenda," WorldNetDaily.com, 19 May 2008.

43. Art Robinson, "Nobel Prize for Death," NewsWithViews.com, 9 May 2008.

44. "'CO2 scrubber' could help slow global warming," LondonDailyTelegraph.com, 3 September 2008.

45. Greenpeace USA, "Carbon Capture and Storage: A Corporate Boondoggle That Shortchanges Environment, Consumers, Says New Greenpeace Report," 5 May 2008. http://us.greenpeace.org/site/PageNavigator/PR_Carbon_Capture_Boondoggle.

46. Krystle Russin, "Environmentalists Oppose New CO2 Scrubber Idea," *Environment & Climate* News, The Heartland Institute, 1 August, 2008. http://www.heartland.org/Article.cfm?artId=23547.

47. Marlo Lewis, "Ignorance Is Strength, Dissent Is Treason," National Review Online, 16 July 2007.

48. Melanie Morgan, "Con Job at The Weather Channel," WorldNetDaily.com, 5 January 2007.

49. Noel Sheppard, "Weather Channel Founder: Global Warming 'Greatest Scam in History,'" Newsbusters.org, 7 November 2007.

50. Warner Todd Huston, "U. of OK Decertifies Teacher Over His Global Warming Skepticism?" Conservablogs.com, 29 October 2008.

51. "EPA Chief Vows to Probe E-mail Threatening to 'Destroy' Career of Climate Skeptic," U.S. Senate Committee on Environment and Public Works, The Inhofe EPW Press Blog, 26 July 2007. http://epw.senate.gov.

52. Marc Morano, "Climate Skeptics Reveal 'Horror Stories' of Scientific Suppression," The Inhofe EPW Press Blog, 6 March 2008. http://epw.senate.gov.

53. "How to Silence Global Warming Skeptics," http://nospeedbumps.com/?p=1465.

54. "John Stossel Exposes Global Warming Myths," NewsMax.com, 17 October 2007.

55. Bob Unruh, "Gore boasts: 'Global governance' coming with carbon tax," WorldNetDaily.com, 10 July 2009.

56. Patrick J. Buchanan, discussing on MSNBC, the cap and trade climate bill being pushed by President Obama in the summer of 2009. http://www.youtube.com/watch?v=zRs-n37UNYE&NR=1.

57. Seton Motley, "Media MIA on Emanuel's Crisis Comment," NewsBusters.org, 21 November 2008. http://newsbusters.org/blogs/seton-motley/2008/11/21/media-mia-emanuels-crisis-comment.

58. Walter E. Williams, "EPA Cover-Up," Townhall.com, 15 July 2009.

59. Marc Morano, "Global Carbon Tax Urged at UN Climate Conference," The Inhofe EPW Press Blog, 13 December 2007. http://epw.senate.gov.

60. U.S. Senate Minority Report:

61. Martin Durkin, "Up against the warming zealots," *The Australian*, 21 July 2007. http://www.theaustralian.news.com.au/story/0,25197,22105154-30417,00.html.

62. Marc Morano, "Global Carbon Tax Urged at UN Climate Conference."

63. Alan Caruba, "Global Warming's Climate of Crisis," TheConservativeVoice.com, 9 December 2007.

64. Center for the Defense of Free Enterprise, online advertisement for the book, *Energy Keepers Energy Killers: The New Civil Rights Battle*, by Roy Innis, Alan Gottlieb, Sean Hannity, and Paul Driessen, Conservative Action Alerts, 23 January 2009.

65. George Orwell, *Nineteen Eighty-Four,* Commemorative Edition, NY: The New American Library, 1984, p. 260. (This is an authorized reprint of the 1949 hardcover edition published by Harcourt Brace Jovanovich).

66. George Orwell, *Nineteen Eighty-Four,* p. 260.

67. George Orwell, *Nineteen Eighty-Four,* p. 263.

68. George Orwell, *Nineteen Eighty-Four,* p. 265.

69. George Orwell, *Nineteen Eighty-Four,* p. 267.
70. J. Edgar Hoover, *A Study of Communism*, NY: Holt, Rinehart & Winston, 1962, p. 90.

Chapter 15: More Socialism Disguised As Environmentalism: More UN Steppingstones Toward Soviet America & Soviet-Style Global Government!

1. Earl Browder, *Victory – And After,* Paperback Edition, NY: International Publishing, 1942. http://quotes.liberty-tree.ca/quote/earl_browder_quote_e409.
2. Star Parker, "We've legalized theft in America," Townhall.com, 23 March 2009.
3. UN Department of Economics and Social Affairs, Division for Sustainable Development, Documents, Agenda 21, 15 December 2004. http://www.un.org/esa/sustdev/documents/agenda21/.
4. "Seventy One More United Nations Heritage Sites Planned," American Policy Center. http://www.americanpolicy.org/un/seventyonemore.htm.
5. "U.S. - UN Man and Biosphere & World Heritage Sites," Sovereignty International, Inc. http://www.sovereignty.net/p/land/mapmabwh.htm.
6. "Our Global Neighborhood: Report of the Commission on Global Governance," Oxford, England: Oxford University Press, 1995. A Summary Analysis by Henry Lamb, first published in *eco-logic*, January/February, 1996. Available at: http://www.sovereignty.net/p/gov/gganalysis.htm.
7. W. Cleon Skousen, *The Naked Communist*, Eleventh Edition, Salt Lake City, UT: The Reviewer, 1962, p. 260.
8. Oliver North, "Permission Slip for the Sea," TheConservativeVoice.com, 12 October 2007. http://www.theconservativevoice.com/articles/article.html?id=28582.
9. Cliff Kincaid, "Bush's Toilet Bowel Treaty," Aim.org, 29 October 2007.
10. *The Washington Times*, 11 May 1993.
11. "AIM Report: Sinister Secrets of the UN," Aim.org, 15 November 2007.
12. Phyllis Schlafly, "Sink the Law of the Sea Again," TheConservativeVoice.com, 28 September 2007.
13. Malcolm A. Kline, "Paradise LOST," Aim.org, 31 August 2007.
14. Patrick J. Buchanan, "George W. Bush, Globalist," TheConcervativeVoice.com, 12 October 2007. http://www.theconservativevoice.com/articles/article.html?id=28584.

15. Oliver North, "Permission Slip for the Sea," TheConservativeVoice.com, 12 October 2007.

16. Malcolm A. Kline, "Paradise LOST," Aim.org, 31 August 2007.

17. Gidget Fuentes, "Thoughts on the global 1,000-ship Navy," navytimes.com, 5 February 2007.

18. Playbook, June 2007. http://www.cnrc.navy.mil/PAO/Playbook2007.pdf.

19. "AIM Report: Sinister Secrets of the UN."

20. http://www.pickensplan.com/.

21. Margaret Thatcher, *Statecraft: Strategies for a Changing World*, Norwalk, CT: Easton Press, 2002, p. 427. http://www.rightwingnews.com/quotes/thatcher.php.

22. Marxist Internet Archive Library, "The Bolsheviks." http://www.marxists.org/archive/.

23. Vaclav Klaus, *Blue Planet in Green Shackles*: *What Is Endangered: Climate Or Freedom*? Second Edition, Mass Market Paperback, Washington, D.C.: Competitive Enterprise Institute, 2008.

24. Bethany Stotts, "Warm and Fuzzy Global Regulation," Aim.org, 4 June 2008.

25. Cliff Kincaid, "The New Communism," Aim.org, 9 June 2008.

26. Bethany Stotts, "Warm and Fuzzy Global Regulation."

27. Marc Brodine, "Global Warming Report to March 2008 NC," CPUSA.org, 17 April 2008.

28. Marc Morano, "Global Carbon Tax Urged at UN Climate Conference," The Inhofe EPW Press Blog, December 13, 2007. http://epw.senate.gov.

29. G. Edward Griffin, *The Fearful Master: A Second Look At The United Nations,* Belmont, MA: Western Islands, 1964.

30. Pierre J. Huss and George Carpozi, Jr., *Red Spies in the UN*, NY: Coward-McCann, 1965.

31. Robert W. Lee, *The United Nations Conspiracy,* Belmont, MA: Western Islands, 1981, p. 73.

32. Robert W. Lee, *The United Nations Conspiracy,* p. 73, citing Corliss Lamont, *Soviet Foreign Policy,* Second Edition, NY: Philosophical Library, Inc., 1955, pp. 300-301.

33. Robert W. Lee, *The United Nations Conspiracy,* p. 73, citing Department of State, *The Kremlin Speaks,* Publication Number 4264, released October, 1951, p. 35.

34. Robert W. Lee, *The United Nations Conspiracy,* p. 73, citing Richard N. Gardner, *In Pursuit of World Order,* NY: Frederick A. Praeger, 1964, p. 47.

35. Robert W. Lee, *The United Nations Conspiracy,* p. 73, citing *Daily Worker,* December 21, 1954, p. 5.

36. Robert W. Lee, *The United Nations Conspiracy,* p. 73, citing Constitution of the Communist Party, USA., NY: Century Publishers, April, 1957, pp. 4-5.
37. Robert W. Lee, *The United Nations Conspiracy,* p. 73, citing Richard N. Gardner, *In Pursuit of World Order,* NY: Frederick A. Praeger, 1964, p. 60.
38. William Z. Foster, *Toward Soviet America,* Balboa Island, CA: Elgin Publications, 1961, p. 272. (Originally published in 1932)

Chapter 16: Barack Obama:
Change Soviet Americans Can Believe In!

1. William Z. Foster, National Chairman of the Communist Party, USA, testifying before a Congressional Committee. In *The Naked Communist,* p. 175. Citing the Report of the Special Committee on Un-American Activities, 3 January 1939, pp. 18-21.
2. Drew Zahn, "Alan Keyes: Stop Obama or U.S. will cease to exist," WorldNetDaily.com, 21 February 2009.
3. Zombietime.com forum page. http://www.zombietime.com/zomblog/?p=64.
4. Cliff Kincaid, "FBI Informant Implicates Obama Associate in Murder," Aim.org, 2 November 2008.
5. "Did Ayers' wife kill policeman? FBI report said Dohrn named as bomb builder, planter," WorldNetDaily.com, 16 October 2008.
6. Ben Smith, "Obama once visited '60s radicals," Politico.com, 22 February 2008.
7. Bob Owens, "Twisting History to Protect Bill Ayers," (George Wallis may have encouraged violent attacks, but Obama's political mentor carried them out himself). Pajamasmedia.com, 23 October 2008. http://pajamasmedia.com/blog/congressman-twists-history-to-protect-ayers/
8. Bob Owens, "Eyewitness to the Ayers Revolution," Pajamasmedia.com, 28 October 2008. http://pajamasmedia.com/blog/eyewitness-to-the-ayers-revolution./
9. Aaron Klein, "Michelle Obama organized event with Ayers, husband: Invited domestic terrorist to discuss treatment of child murderers as adults," WorldNetDaily.com, 16 October 2008.
10. Cliff Kincaid, "It's The Communism, Stupid," Aim.org, 28 May 2008.
11. http://www.conservapedia.com/William_Ayers.
12. Wes Vernon and Cliff Kincaid, "Blood on the Hands of Obama Terror Associate," Aim.org, 23 July 2008.

13. WorldNetDaily.com, "See it with your own eyes: Obama's book blurb for Ayers." As state senator, presidential candidate praised work of former leader of Weather Underground, 20 October 2008. http://wnd.com/index.php?fa=PAGE.view&pageId=78640.
14. Fred Lucas, "Obama-Run Foundation Gave Millions to Liberal Groups, Including One Run by Bill Ayers," CNSNews.com, 13 October 2008.
15. Aaron Klein, "4 Weathermen terrorists declare support for Obama," WorldNetDaily.com, 2 October 2008.
16. WorldNetDaily.com, "Obama pastor: Not God bless, but God d--- America!" 13 March 2008.
17. *Investor's Business Daily,* "Sojourning Socialists," 9 September 2008. http://www.ibdeditorials.com/IBDArticles.aspx?id= 305851942725035.
18. Cliff Kincaid, "Communist Party Backs Obama," Aim.org, 3 July 2008.
19. Joelle Fishman, "Big political shifts are under way," *People's Weekly World Newspaper,* 23 June 2008. http://www.pww.org/article/articleview/13259/1/443/.
20. Jerome R. Corsi, "Report: Obama mentored by Communist Party figure," WorldNetDaily.com, 22 May 2008.
21. Description of the Soviet Red Army given in the documentary *The True Story of Charlie Wilson's War*, by The History Channel. Aaron Sorkin, screenwriter for the 2007 movie *Charlie Wilson's War*, provided the description.
22. Cliff Kincaid, "Special Report: Red Faces Over Obama's Red Mentor," Aim.org, 27 July 2008.
23. PWW/NM Editorial Board, "Editorial: Eye on the Prize," CPUSA.org, 15 July 2008.
24. "CPUSA 2008 Electoral Policy," CPUSA.org, 21 March 2008.
25. Howard E. Kershner, *Dividing The Wealth: Are You Getting Your Share?* Old Greenwich, CT: Devin-Adair Company, 1971, p. 129.
26. R. J. Rummel, *Death By Government,* New Brunswick, NJ: Transaction Publishers, 1994. http://www.hawaii.edu/powerkills/NOTE1.HTM.
27. Texas Law Enforcement Officer video was available at: http://www.NRAPVF.org/.
28. http://www.GunBanObama.com.
29. NRA Political Victory Fund advertisement, *Guns and Ammo Magazine*, November, 2008.
30. David Brody, "Abortion Vote Returns to Haunt Obama," CBN News Channel, 22 August 2008. http://www.cbn.com/cbnnews/430978.aspx.
31. Americans United for Life. http://www.fightfoca.com/.

32. R. M. Whitney, *Reds in America*, Boston, MA: Western Islands Publishers, 1970, pp. 48-49. (Originally published in 1924; Copyright 1924 by Beckwith Press)

33. WorldNetdaily.com, "Ayers' group foresaw genocide of capitalists: informer says Communist U.S. envisioned, re-education centers, 25 million 'eliminated,'" 23 October 2008.

34. Bob Owens, "Eyewitness to the Ayers Revolution," 28 October 2008. http://pajamasmedia.com/blog/eyewitness-to-the-ayers-revolution/.

35. Lee Cary, "Obama's Civilian National Security Force," AmericanThinker.com, 20 July 2008.

36. Zombietime.com, "William Ayers' forgotten Communist Manifesto: Prairie Fire," 22 October 2008. http://www.zombietime.com/prairie_fire/.

37. J. Edgar Hoover, *Masters of Deceit*, NY: Pocket Books, 1968, p. 77. (Henry Holt Edition published in 1958)

38. Jim Kouri, "TV ad asks: Why Would Barack Obama Be Friends With Someone Who Bombed The Capitol?" TheConservativeVoice.com, 21 August 2008.

39. J. Edgar Hoover, FBI Director, "A Statement on Communism," 27 March 1967. (Pamphlet)

40. Vladimir Val Cymbal, "Cuba's Fidel Backs Obama," TheConservativeVoice.com, 21 June 2008.

41. Joseph C. Phillips, "Revolution Anyone?" Townhall.com, 8 September 2009.

42. J. Edgar Hoover, *Masters of Deceit*, p. 71.

Chapter 17: Socialism: Change Communists & Nazis Can Believe In!

1. Michael Reagan, Conservative News Alert, 20 November 2008.

2. Walter E. Williams, "Evil Concealed by Money," 19 November 2008. http://economics.gmu.edu/wew.

3. Walter E. Williams, "A Nation of Thieves," Townhall.com, 6 August 2008.

4. Walter E. Williams, "Our Problem is Immorality," Townhall.com, 1 April 2009.

5. William Z. Foster, *Toward Soviet America,* Balboa Island, CA: Elgin Publications, 1961, p. 269. (Originally published in 1932)

6. Arthur C. Brooks, *Who Really Cares: The Surprising Truth About Compassionate Conservatism,* NY: Basic Books, 2006.

7. Dennis Prager, "The Bigger the Government, the Smaller the Citizen," Townhall.com, 1 September 2009.

8. Walter E. Williams, "A Nation of Thieves."

9. Michael Reagan, Conservative News Alert, 20 November 2008.

10. Patrick J. Buchanan, "Socialist Republic," 29 November 2008. http://buchanan.org/blog/2008/11/pjb-socialist-republic/.

11. Dick Morris and Eileen McGann, "Bush's Legacy: European Socialism," Townhall.com, 19 November 2008.

12. Dick Morris, "Bush Hands Over Reins of U.S. Economy to EU," NewsMax.com, 19 November 2008.

13. Sam Webb, "A Springtime of Possibility." Speech to the November 15, 2008 National Committee, CPUSA.org.

14. Matt Hadro, "Economists Say Bush 'Chucked' Free Market Principles Long Before Financial Crisis," CNSNews.com, 13 January 2009.

15. Andrew J. Coulson, "The Real Cost of Public Schools," Cato Institute for Educational Freedom. http://www.cato-at-liberty.org/2008/04/07/the-real-cost-of-public-schools/

16. Jonah Goldberg, "Dining-Room Dollars," National Review Online Archive, 11 June 2008. http://author.nationalreview.com.

17. William Z. Foster, *Toward Soviet America,* p. 278.

18. WorldNetDaily.com, "How Paulson nationalized biggest banks in the U.S.," 15 October 2008.

19. Fred Lucas, "Federal Government Was Culprit in Housing and Economic Crisis, Says Congressional Report," CNSNews.com, 8 July 2009.

20. John R. Lott, Jr., "Analysis: Reckless Mortgages Brought Financial Market to Its Knees," FOXNews.com, 18 September 2008.

21. John R. Lott, Jr.

22. Neal Boortz, "The Rest of the Meltdown Story," Townhall.com, 19 September 2008.

23. Matt Cover & Matt Hadro, "Carter, Clinton Era Budget Official Ran Institution at Center of Financial Crisis," CNSNews.com, 22 September 2008.

24. Matt Cover & Matt Hadro.

25. Walter E. Williams, "The Housing Boom and Bust," Townhall.com, 27 May 2009.

26. GatewayPundit.Blogspot.com, "Bush Called For Reform of Fannie Mae & Freddie Mac 17 Times in 2008 Alone...Dems Ignored Warnings," 21 September 2008.

27. Drew Zahn, "Guess again who's to blame for U.S. mortgage meltdown: Analysts point not to greed, but to social activist politics," WorldNetDaily.com, 19 September 2008.

28. Businessweek.com, "The Best & Worst Managers of 2004 - The Worst Managers: Franklin Raines/Fannie Mae" 10 January 2005.

29. C. Edmund Wright, "Mistress of Disaster: Jamie Gorelick," AmericanThinker.com, 19 September 2008.

30. OpinionJournal.com, "Gorelick's Wall: The Commissioner belongs in the witness chair," 15 April 2004. http://www.opinionjournal.com/editorial/feature.html?id=110004956.

31. Lindsay Renick Mayer, "Fannie Mae and Freddie Mac Invest in Democrats," 16 July 2008. http://www.opensecrets.org/news/2008/07/top-senate-recipients-of-fanni.html.

32. Matt Cover & Matt Hadro.

33. Sher Zieve, "Democrats caused current financial crisis," RenewAmerica.com, 20 September 2008. http://www.renewamerica.com/columns/zieve/080920.

34. Jeff Poor, "Nationalization: It's Not Just for Communists Anymore," Business & Media   Institute, 25 February 2009. http://www.businessandmedia.org.

35. Cliff Kincaid, "Senator Blasts 'Financial Socialism,'" Aim.org, 24 September 2008. http://www.aim.org/aim-column/senator-bunning-blasts-financial-socialism/.

36. Press Release: "Dr. Coburn Says a Financial Stabilization Plan is Necessary: Says political greed in Congress is root of the problem," 29 September 2008. http://coburn.senate.gov/public/index.cfm?FuseAction=LatestNews.PressRelease&ContentRecord_id=af06a07f-802a-23ad-4568-72d6b136c139.

37. Margaret Thatcher quote available at: http://www.snopes.com/politics/quotes/thatcher.asp.

Chapter 18: Losing The Cold War On America Soil!

1. R. M. Whitney, *Reds in America*, Boston, MA: Western Islands Publishers, 1970, p. 21. (Originally published in 1924; Copyright 1924 by Beckwith Press.)

2. Eugene Burdick and William Lederer, *The Ugly American*, NY: W. W. Norton, 1958.

3. William Z. Foster, *Toward Soviet America*, Balboa Island, CA: Elgin Publications, 1961, pp. 64-65. (Originally published in 1932)

4. Peter Hitchens, "The New Soviet Union of Europe is upon us," DailyMail.com, 19 May 2003.

5. G. Gordon Liddy, *When I Was A Kid, This Was A Free Country,* Washington, D.C.: Regnery Publishing, 2002, back cover.

6. William Z. Foster, *Toward Soviet America*, p. 134.

7. Jeff Snyder, *Nation of Cowards: Essays on the Ethics of Gun Control*, St. Louis, MO: Accurate Press, 2001.

8. Judge Andrew P. Napolitano, *A Nation of Sheep*, Nashville, TN: Thomas Nelson, 2007.
9. William Z. Foster, *Toward Soviet America*, p. 309.
10. William Z. Foster, *Toward Soviet America*, p. 307.
11. David Horowitz, "Betty Friedan's Secret Communist Past," Salon, 18 January 1999.
12. J. Edgar Hoover, *Masters of Deceit*, NY: Pocket Books, 1968, p. 99. (Henry Holt Edition published in 1958)
13. Margaret Thatcher quote available at: http://www.quotesby.net/Margaret-Thatcher.
14. Margaret Thatcher quote available at: http://www.brainyquote.com/quotes/authors/m/margaret_thatcher_3.html.
15. Carrie Lukas, "Rush Doesn't Need to Win Women, but Conservatives Do," Townhall.com, 3 March 2009.
16. William Z. Foster, *Toward Soviet America*, p. 321.
17. William Z. Foster, *Toward Soviet America*, p. 304.
18. William Z. Foster, *Toward Soviet America*, p. 305.
19. William Z. Foster, *Toward Soviet America*, p. 268.
20. J. Edgar Hoover, *J. Edgar Hoover On Communism,* NY: Random House, 1970, p. 152.
21. J. Edgar Hoover, *Masters of Deceit*, NY: Pocket Books, 1968, p. 114. (Henry Holt Edition published in 1958)
22. J. Edgar Hoover, *A Study of Communism*, NY: Holt, Rinehart & Winston, 1962, p. 90.

Chapter 19: The U.S. Government Versus The U.S. Constitution!

1. William Z. Foster, "Syndicalism," p. 9. In W. Cleon Skousen, *The Naked Communist,* Eleventh Edition, Salt Lake City, UT: The Reviewer, 1962, p. 305.
2. Constitution (Fundamental Law) of the Union of Soviet Socialist Republics, Bucknell University, Lewisburg, PA. Translation by Novosti Press Agency Publishing House, Moscow, 1985.
3. Vladimir Lenin, *Lenin: Selected Works,* Vol. VII, p. 123. In *The Naked Communist,* p. 313.
4. 1936 Constitution of the USSR, Adopted December 1936. Chapter III, Article 30, Bucknell University, Lewisburg, PA.
5. Chelsea Schilling, "Act forces Congress' return to limited government," WorldNetDaily.com, 9 April 2009.
6. Walter E. Williams, "Why a Bill of Rights?" Townhall.com, 1 July 2009.

7. Nicholas Ballasy, "Ron Paul: GOP Leaders Need to Read Constitution," CNSNews.com, 11 March 2009.
8. Walter E. Williams, "Oklahoma Rebellion," CNSNews.com, 17 July 2008.
9. Walter E. Williams, "States Rebellion Pending," 24 March 2009. http://economics.gmu.edu/wew.
10. Ronald Radosh, *Commies: A Journey Through the Old Left, the New Left and the Leftover Left,* San Francisco, CA: Encounter Books, 2001, p. 195.
11. http://www.quotesby.net/Margaret-Thatcher.
12. Judge Andrew P. Napolitano, *The Constitution In Exile: How the Federal Government Has Seized Power by Rewriting the Supreme Law of The Land,* Nashville, TN: Thomas Nelson, 2006, p. 233.
13. http://freedomkeys.com/vigil.htm.
14. http://freedomkeys.com/vigil.htm.

Special Message:

We Must Stop The Slaughter - Not Expand It!

Nothing in this book is to be considered anti-government. The author is, of course, highly critical of the current state of government. The author is a strong supporter of government, and has written this book in an effort to help restore honest, lawful, constitutional, fiscally-responsible, sovereignty-respecting, liberty-defending, and life-preserving government.

As stated elsewhere in this book, Pastor Ernie Sanders has described Soviet-style Communism as socialism with a police state. As we have seen, the 9/11 Islamo-fascist terrorist attacks set the stage for the builders of Soviet America to federalize (Sovietize) airport security and to create the so-called U.S. Department of Homeland Security. These acts, of course, significantly expanded the power of the police state, thus driving us closer to fulfilling William Z. Foster's dream of building a Soviet America. (This may help explain liberal/progressive public sympathy for Islamo-fascist terrorists!)

In light of the above expansion of the police state, it must be concluded that violence benefits the builders of Soviet America and works against the re-builders of Sovereign America. Therefore, Sovereign Americans must not follow in the footsteps of Barack Obama's friends and supporters, such as William Ayers, Bernardine Dohrn, and other unrepentant, former domestic Communist terrorists who bombed buildings, purportedly killed and maimed innocent people and advocated genocide for the 25 million Americans who could not be "re-educated" to live as docile sheep under a full-blown Soviet American dictatorship!

We must not emulate Anita Dunn, Barack Obama's former White House Communications Director, who praised Mao Zedong - a Communist who may be the deadliest genocidal maniac in human history with a body count exceeding 76 million disarmed men, women, and children - not including government-forced abortions. We must not follow people like Barack Obama who honor Mao Zedong by hanging on the White House Christmas tree an ornament containing an image of this deadly sociopath!

We must not imitate Barack Obama and others who support the killing of babies through abortion, and the extermination of babies who survive botched abortions? We must not mimic Obama's political allies who deny anesthesia to babies as they are shredded or chemically burned and poisoned to death in the wombs of their mothers - when research shows that many of these tiny victims experience extreme levels of pain as their lives are terminated in such a cold-blooded manner.

We must stop the slaughter - not expand it!

Sovereign Americans must do nothing to aid and abet the builders of Soviet America by inadvertently manufacturing what may be labeled a crisis. In doing so, Rahm Emanuel-type predators are handed "an opportunity to do things they thought they could not do before," such as advancing socialism or expanding the police state to supposedly deal with the crisis. For this and other reasons the author believes information, education, litigation, political participation, and nullification (under state sovereignty and the Tenth Amendment) are the only logical tools to be used in dismantling William Z. Foster's Soviet America and effecting restoration of George Washington's Constitutional Republic.

About the Author

Michael T. Petro, Jr. is a veteran of the U.S. Navy. Initially he worked in naval security, and later served in the gunnery division aboard the USS Kennebec during the Vietnam War. After returning to his native state of Ohio, he earned a Bachelor of Arts degree (Magna Cum Laude) from Cleveland State University.

When relocating to California he earned a Master of Science degree in Psychology and a Master of Arts degree in Education from California State University at Los Angeles. Michael initially worked as an aide and counselor in psychiatric hospitals in the greater Los Angeles area. Later he worked extensively as a researcher, training coordinator, and manager at an alcohol and drug recovery program located on skid row in Los Angeles.

Before leaving California, Michael received a National Leadership Award from the National Headquarters of the Volunteers of America. The award was presented for his success in restoring operational integrity to a dysfunctional alcohol and drug recovery program and for his efforts to create drug-free zones within the skid row community. Today, Michael works as a writer and self-publisher in Cleveland, Ohio.

7226930R0

Made in the USA
Charleston, SC
07 February 2011